WILLIAM GOLDMAN

FIVE SCREENPLAYS

WILLIAM GOLDMAN

FIVE SCREENPLAYS
WITH ESSAYS

ALL THE PRESIDENT'S MEN
MAGIC • HARPER • MAVERICK
THE GREAT WALDO PEPPER

APPLAUSE
NEW YORK • LONDON

An Applause Original

WILLIAM GOLDMAN: FIVE SCREENPLAYS

New Material Copyright © 1997 by William Goldman

Harper — Copyright © 1966 by Warner Bros. Based on the novel *The Moving Target* by Jo
    Macdonald. Copyright © 1949 by Alfred A. Knopf Inc.; renewal © 1976 by John R
    Macdonald (pseudonym of Kenneth Millar). Assigned to The Margaret Millar Charita'
    Remainder Unitrust u/a 4/12/82. Published by Alfred A. Knopf Inc. and Warner Bo‹
    Inc. Used by permission.

The Great Waldo Pepper — Screenplay by William Goldman (story by George Roy Hill) co¡
    right © 1975 by MCA, Inc. Used with permission of Dell Books, a division of Bant
    Doubleday Dell Publishing Group, Inc.

All the President's Men — Copyright © 1976 by Warner Bros. Based on the book by B
    Woodward and Carl Bernstein. Copyright © 1974 by Carl Bernstein and Bob Woodwa
    Published by Simon & Schuster, Inc. All rights reserved.

Magic — Copyright © 1980 by Joseph E. Levine Presents, Inc., released by Twentieth Century F
    Film Corporation. Based on the novel copyright © 1976 by William Goldman. Used w
    permission of Dell Books, a division of Bantam Doubleday Dell Publishing Group, Inc.

Maverick — Copyright © 1994 by Warner Bros. and Icon Distribution, Inc. Used by permissi‹

The author gratefully acknowledges the permission granted by Stephen Sondheim for the use
    lyrics from *Follies* in the general introduction.

Library of Congress Cataloging-in-Publication Data

Library of Congress Catalog Card Number: 96-78575

ISBN: 1-55783-266-8

British Library Cataloging-in-Publication Data

A catalog record of this book is available from the British Library.

APPLAUSE BOOKS   A&C BLACK
211 West 71st Street   Howard Road, Eaton Socon
New York, NY 10023   Huntington, Cambs PE19 3EZ
Phone (212) 496-7511   Phone 0171-242 0946
Fax: (212) 721-2856   Fax 0171-831 8478

Distributed in the U.K. and European Union by A&C Black

CONTENTS

INTRODUCTION

Here is how I work: I write the bastard.

I don't talk about it. I never show anything to anybody until I've finished. And most of all, I never look, while I'm writing, at what I wrote yesterday. Or any yesterday before that.

In other words, I never read anything I've written.

Until Armageddon.

For a book, that's that day before I meet with my editor. A movie, before I meet with my Producer or Director or Star. I only read it then because I would seem such a prancing idiot if I wasn't remotely knowledgeable about my own work.

Putting this collection together then forced me to read, for the first time in up to thirty years (*Harper*), what I've put down. I was, please believe this, terrified at what I might find. But, as I am still alive, clearly it wasn't as bad as I'd feared. I'm not saying any of it's good, and there was hardly a sequence when I didn't shake my head at the silly mistakes in structure, the smart-ass dialogue, the endless moments when I wish I'd been, well, just better. Still, I suppose that what makes these pieces, in various degrees, hold is their sense of story.

Movies are finally, centrally, crucially, primarily *only* about story.

I don't like my writing, and I am not shit-kicking when I say that. Some of the moments in these movies were so golden in my head. But what came out on paper was only black and white. Can't help that. I constantly remind myself of my two salvations. First: I really did do the best I knew at the time. Second: I have only written stuff I wanted to write.

These are the anchors that have kept me able to face tomorrow.

I suppose what pleases me most is that these range from the sixties to the nineties. I have been flavor of the month Out There for twenty-five years and a leper for five. Thirty years may not seem such an achievement for a professor or a businessman, but for a screenwriter, oh yes. As Mr. Sondheim so gloriously wrote in *Follies*:

> Good times and bum times,
> I seem 'em all
> and my dear.
> I'm still here.
> Plush velvet sometimes,
> Sometimes just pretzels and beer,

But I'm here.
I've run the gamut,
A to Z.
Three cheers and dammit,
C'est la vie.
I got through all of last year,
And I'm here.
Lord knows at least I've been there.
And I'm here!
Look who's here!
I'm still here!

Can't ask for more.

HARPER

DIRECTOR	JACK SMIGHT
PRODUCERS	ELLIOTT KASTNER
	JERRY GERSHWIN
CINEMATOGRAPHER	CONRAD HALL
EDITOR	STEFAN ARNSTEN
ART DIRECTOR	ALFRED SWEENEY
MUSIC	JOHNNY MANDEL
SCREENPLAY	WILLIAM GOLDMAN
	(FROM THE NOVEL
	THE MOVING TARGET
	BY ROSS MACDONALD)

In 1993, I was working with Shane Black, both of us trying to doctor *The Last Action Hero*. (A wonderful idea for a movie totally wasted by the insane needs of studios today, where films come out not when they are ready, but when there is a holiday date to fill.) My memory is that Shane was specializing in the action scenes whereas I was primarily working on the characters. (Do you know how *crazy* that is? What a nutty way to run a railroad? And do you know when I was involved in the madness it seemed totally logical?)

Anyway.

We are sitting in my living room and he looks at me and says these words: "Do you know why I envy you?"

Since he was barely thirty and already the most commercially successful young screenwriter in history, I replied thusly: "Shane, I cannot think of a single reason in this world."

"Well," he explained, "you got to write movies in the sixties."

I understood.

And he was right.

In thirty years, the landscape has significantly altered.

It wasn't that the stars were so different. Here is the Quigley list of the top ten box office stars of 1966, the year *Harper* was released.

1) Julie Andrews
2) Sean Connery
3) Elizabeth Taylor
4) Jack Lemmon
5) Richard Burton
6) Cary Grant
7) John Wayne
8) Doris Day
9) Paul Newman
10) Elvis Presley

We could mix and match these performers with the stars of today. Sharon Stone would have been fine in *Who's Afraid of Virginia Woolf*. Just as Jack Lemmon would have been swell in *Mr Holland's Opus*. Of course, only Cary Grant was ever close to being Cary Grant, but Matthew McConaughey is Paul Newman and Harrison Ford is John Wayne. You get the idea.

And it wasn't that the Oscar pictures were so different from today. Here is a list of the five Best Picture Nominations.

Alfie
A Man For All Seasons
The Russians Are Coming, The Russians Are Coming
The Sand Pebbles
Who's Afraid of Virginia Woolf

Not a great year, but not so terrible. *The Sand Pebbles* is not a dissimilar genre from *Apollo 13* nor *Braveheart* from *A Man For All Seasons*. Clearly, Broadway is no longer the breeding ground for movies that it once was, but I would think any of the '66 crop could have been made, with appropriate changes, today.

Well, if the performers aren't that radically different and the kinds of quality films weren't that radically different, what happened? Two things, really.

1) *Jaws*
2) Creative Accounting

JAWS

For me, one of the masterpieces of commercial filmmaking. I have seen it within the last months, and it is still great. But the quality of the film is not what made it important. It was the money. *Jaws* grossed more than any executive dreamed possible. And it did that in a blink. It literally leaped onto the top of the all time lists. The studios never knew, 'til then, that such a vein of gold existed.

Well, they are not dumb Out There. If one special effects bloodbath struck it rich, guess what? They knew it could happen again. And they were right. I don't think *Twister* would have happened if *Jaws* had not shown the way. And if you are sick of the mindless screaming stuff that has come out in the summer of '96, well, too bad. Two summers from now there will be shitloads more. (Next summer's movies are already shooting.) Studios stopped looking for middle of the road stuff that might profit a million or two. The blockbuster era had been launched.

What *Jaws* did, then, was totally alter *what got made*.

CREATIVE ACCOUNTING

The studios do not steal. But if you are going to make very expensive movies — and special effects are not now and never will be an exact science — there are going to be consequences.

When I got into the business, my agent, the late and very great Evarts Ziegler, explained to me the great value of being a profit participant. "Two and a half times the negative, you're in profit." I asked for an explanation and this is what he said: if a movie, say, had an actual negative cost of two million dollars, when that movie had box office rentals (not gross) of five million, it was in profit.

Box office rentals are rule of thumb, half of theater gross.

In other words, once our two million dollar baby took in approximately ten million at the box office, everything was shared. (I think, don't hold me to this but I think, *Harper* cost a little over three and went into profit at eight in rentals. Well, it did more than that and for thirty years now, I have been receiving annual checks, small, sure, but found money is the best thing in the world after true love and cough drops.)

I got my small percentage of every piece of revenue that Warner Brothers received on *Harper*. If it was shown on a cable station in Nome, I got something. If it was sold for theaters in China, I got my percentage. That was how it worked in the sixties.

I had another hit in the seventies with another studio. And it was a waaaaay bigger hit. (I think it cost eight and did thirty. Thereabouts, anyway. And using the old formula, it would have broken even at twenty million in rentals and the next ten million would have been shared between the studio (which took all the financial gambles), and the profit participants.

OK, I get my first statement on the seventies' flick and was the least bit taken aback in that it was not just in the red, it was *trillions* in the red. But it obviously could not stay that way. The next year, the number had been reduced into the billions. And as the decades went on, the number actually got pronounceable. Finally, one year, I actually got a profit check. It was three figures (I swear) but still, as has been noted, better than a sharp stick in the eye.

The next year's statement came with a note saying that owing to some silly bookkeeping errors and oversights, we were back where we started, trillions from breaking even and will stay there 'til the world looks level.

Now, this excursion is not about robbing Billy. I was properly recompensed for my efforts. But something took place in that decade that has accelerated today. Two great stars, Mr. Eastwood and Mr. Heston, were famous for taking far less than their going rates in exchange for a large percentage of the profits. Heston, a gent, felt that if a movie was a flop, he wanted it to be as inexpensive a flop as possible. If a success, he wanted a share of it.

Not today, folks.

Oh, agents and studios will scream at each other over this profit percentage definition or that, but it is mostly masturbatory. They both know there ain't going to be any.

So?

So today, major stars could care less about profits. They want gross. They want gross and they get it, and and and, they also want up front salary. And they get that too.

And so do top directors. And so would writers if we could.

What this does is escalate the already terrifying cost of filmmaking. And since the only kinds of movies that feel to the studios that they might justify these costs are special effects flicks, the desire to gamble on them is higher than ever.

And since in this world you get what you pay for, the kind of movie that used to get made doesn't get made.

Which is why we are now living in a world of lowest common denominator movies that are essentially made for mouth breathing young men in Southeast Asia.

Following is the first draft of the first Hollywood film that I ever had made. *Archer* obviously changed my life in that from this time on, at least in part of my head, I was suddenly a screenwriter.

It was called *Archer* then, because that is the name of the Ross MacDonald series character, Lew Archer. But as I remember, the producers had not bought the rights to the series, just to the one book on which the movie is based, *The Moving Target*. So we needed a different name and Harper seemed OK, the guy harps on things, it's essentially what he does for a living. This stupendously uninteresting paragraph is important to me only in that it was the only time I ever got to talk to Ken Millar, MacDonald's real name. He was and is, for me, a major novelist and the best ever at writing a detective series. (Try *The Chill*.)

Harper is about a private detective who's hired by an unloving wife to find her rich drunk husband. That's it. Things happen, people live and die, but essentially it's not a story with a great deal of phony size in the sense that studios demand today. Today, if you told this story, Lew Harper would not have been just an honest detective who liked his job when he could get work. He would also have some terrible back story of operatic pain that would get exorcised as he solved the case. And the rich guy would have to be a special rich guy, not just your ordinary West Coast millionaire. Bill Gates, maybe. And probably there would have been some kind of connection between the two men back when they were both young. *Yeesh*, as Calvin would say.

Anyway, here's a screenplay from the sixties. Over to you.

CAST LIST

PAUL NEWMAN	HARPER
LAUREN BACALL	MRS. SAMPSON
JULIE HARRIS	BETTY FRALEY
ARTHUR HILL	ALBERT GRAVES
JANET LEIGH	SUSAN HARPER
PAMELA TIFFIN	MIRANDA SAMPSON
ROBERT WAGNER	ALAN TAGGERT
ROBERT WEBBER	DWIGHT TROY
SHELLEY WINTERS	FAY ESTABROOK
HAROLD GOULD	SHERIFF SPANNER
STROTHER MARTIN	CLAUDE
ROY JENSON	PUDDLER
MARTIN WEST	DEPUTY
JACQUELINE DE WIT	MRS. KRONBERG
EUGENE IGLESIAS	FELIX
RICHARD CARLYLE	FRED PLATT

FADE IN ON

LEW HARPER'S FACE

in CLOSE UP. *This is someone who is tough, bright and poor. A good man in a bad world.*

PULL BACK TO REVEAL

HARPER, standing in front of what might very well be (and are) the impressive closed gates to an impressive estate. Behind HARPER is his car with the motor running; like its owner, the car has been around. HARPER speaks into a microphone set in the gate.

HARPER
My name is Lew Harper. To see Mrs. Sampson.

After a pause, there is a click. After the click, the door swings open. HARPER gets back in his car and starts to drive forward.

CUT TO

First view of the Sampson house. It is enormous, surrounded by a great expanse of lawn. Beyond the house lies the ocean. Among other things visible are a tennis court, a swimming pool with patio and pool house, a large garden filled with flowers.

CUT TO

HARPER, driving, taking it all in. He is watching the house itself now.

CUT TO

Inside the house. A woman stands by the shut front door, staring out a window at the approaching car. The woman is MRS. KRONBERG. Large and powerful, she is head housekeeper for the Sampson's and is dressed in a maid's uniform. As she stares out, it is clear she is not smiling.

CUT TO

HARPER, driving up to the house.

CUT TO

The garden. Midst the flowers, staring at the car, stands FELIX, a small Mexican butler. He holds a flower basket in one hand and has been cutting flowers with the other. His eyes are very cold; he is not smiling either.

CUT TO

HARPER, braking the car, opening the door, getting out, slamming the door shut.

CUT TO

MIRANDA SAMPSON. She is standing by the edge of the pool. At the sound of the slam-

ming car door, she glances out toward the car. She has been swimming, and her body glistens in the sun. It is a glorious body, young and supple and strong. Her long hair is wet and hangs down below her shoulders. Her face is everything a 20-year-old heiress' should be. In short: a hunk, but well bred. She glances up toward

ALAN TAGGERT standing on the high diving board. TAGGERT is in his late twenties, blonde and well built. A beautiful young man. He glances back toward HARPER, shrugs, then moves forward onto the board, executing a high, arching swan dive. As he hits the water, MIRANDA dives in after him.

CUT TO

HARPER, moving up toward the front door. Before he reaches it, it is opened by MRS. KRONBERG who gestures for him to enter.

CUT TO

In the foyer. There is a small elevator. MRS. KRONBERG gestures toward it.

DISSOLVE TO

The elevator opening on the second floor. MRS. KRONBERG gets out, gestures for HARPER to follow. She moves to a door, knocks, enters. HARPER moves to the doorway and stops, looking around the walls of the room.

CUT TO

A PAN SHOT of the walls. They are filled with pictures of a woman in various athletic poses: skiing, golfing, etc. The preponderance of pictures, however, show the woman riding horses.

CUT TO

MRS. KRONBERG. She is standing in front of some large open French doors. She gestures for HARPER to go through them, then leaves.

HARPER
(As she goes, he watches. To himself)

Gossip. *(to someone we cannot see)* Mrs. Sampson?

MRS. SAMPSON'S VOICE (off-screen)

Come out. Please.

CUT TO

ELAINE SAMPSON. The woman in the pictures, she is lying on a chaise in the bright sunshine. Her skin is so tanned she might be made of wood. She is holding a large reflector and it flashes even more sun onto her face. Beside the chaise is a wheelchair. She is probably fifty, certainly attractive. Throughout the following, she keeps her eyes tightly closed most of the time. At other moments, when she suspects he might not be looking, she glances up at HARPER. Now, as he looks around the sun deck, she stares at him briefly.

MRS. SAMPSON

A drink?

HARPER

Not before lunch, thanks. I'm the new type detective.

MRS. SAMPSON

I wired you on the recommendation of my husband's lawyer, Albert Graves.

CUT TO

HARPER. At the mention of Albert's name, he smiles.

HARPER

I've known Albert since he was the D.A. up here. It's about time he threw some business my way.

CUT TO

The two of them, the wheelchair between them.

MRS. SAMPSON

He said you were good at finding people. My husband Ralph has disappeared.

HARPER

Tried missing persons?

MRS. SAMPSON

That might mean publicity. Ralph loathes publicity. I simply want you to find him and tell me who he's with, female or male.

HARPER

Which particular female?

MRS. SAMPSON

I haven't the least notion. And Ralph needn't ever know about this. He'd undoubtedly think I was gathering material for divorce proceedings. I have no intention of divorcing Ralph. I only want to outlive him; I only want to see him in his grave. *(And she suddenly smiles.)* What a terrible thing to say.

HARPER
(deadpan)
People in love will say anything. *(softly; businesslike)* When did your husband disappear, Mrs. Sampson?

CUT TO

The two of them.

MRS. SAMPSON

Yesterday, Alan — he's our pilot — had just flown Ralph up from Las Vegas. When they reached the Burbank airport, Alan went to put the plane away. When he came back, Ralph was gone.

HARPER

For any reason?

MRS. SAMPSON
(vehement)

He was drunk! I don't like him drunk on the loose. He gets sloppy senti-mental. He gives away things. The last time it happened he gave away a mountain. Complete with hunting lodge. To some half-clad religious nut from Los Angeles.

HARPER

L.A. is the big leagues for religious nuts.

MRS. SAMPSON

So if you could find him quickly, I'd be grateful. (staring at HARPER now) And if he's with a woman, well . . . I'd be more than interested — (loud) — come out of there!

CUT TO

FELIX, standing half hidden in the doorway; he holds a vase filled with freshly cut flow-ers. He hurries out.

FELIX

I did not want to interrupt.

MRS. SAMPSON

Nonsense, Felix; you're always lurking in doorways and you know it.
(FELIX puts the flowers down near her)
You can go. I'll lunch up here as usual. (closing out the interview) Any more particulars you can get from Alan. The matter of fee I'll leave with Albert Graves. He's in Santa Barbara; Felix can drive you in after lunch. You can leave your car here. Good-bye, Mr. Harper.

HARPER

It might help if I knew what your husband looked like.

MRS. SAMPSON

Silly of me. (She reaches to a table by the chaise, gives HARPER a snap shot.)

INSERT: Photo of RALPH SAMPSON. The face is that of a man who might once have been handsome but who is now fat, puffy and old.

CUT TO

HARPER, looking at her for a moment. Then he turns sharply, puts the picture of SAMPSON in his coat pocket, and starts to exit.

CUT TO

HARPER, coming down the stairs of the Sampson house. He looks at his watch, turns, starts off toward the kitchen.

CUT TO

MRS. KRONBERG busy with lunch in the kitchen.

> **HARPER**
> Where's a phone? I have to call Los Angeles.
> *(she gestures — HARPER follows gesture)*

CUT TO

BUTLER'S PANTRY. There is a phone on a wall; a swinging door cuts it off from the kitchen. HARPER stands in the doorway.

> **HARPER**
> *(to MRS. KRONBERG)*
> Anything with a little more privacy?

> **MRS. KRONBERG**
> That's the phone the help is supposed to use.

CUT TO

HARPER. He gives her a look, dials, shuts the swinging door. He wipes his forehead now, something he did not do during the scene with MRS. SAMPSON in the sun. He is, for the first time, nervous; nervous and upset. As soon as there is a sound from the receiver, he starts to talk, softly.

> **HARPER**
> Fred, it's me. Susan there yet?

> **FRED PLATT'S VOICE** (off-screen)
> Just. She's in the outer office —

> **HARPER**
> — listen, I'm not going to be able to make it today. I got called on a case and —

> **FRED PLATT'S VOICE** (off-screen)
> — she's coming in now, Lew.

CUT TO

A LAWYER'S OFFICE.

A secretary is ushering in SUSAN. FRED PLATT *looks like a lawyer, stuffy and slim.*

Throughout the following scene, the CAMERA *stays fixed at a spot behind the desk where the lawyer is talking on the phone.* SUSAN *moves in and out of range; sometimes* FRED *blocks her off entirely.*

> SECRETARY
> *(announcing)*

Mrs. Harper. *(she goes, closing door)*

> SUSAN
> *(enters room at farthest point from* CAMERA,
> *crosses toward* FRED, *standing at his desk)*

Hello, lawyer.

> FRED

Hello, Susan.

> SUSAN

Where's Lew?

> FRED
> *(indicating phone)*

Right here. He can't make it.

> SUSAN
> *(Nods, not surprised. Then she sits slowly
> down into a chair across from the desk.)*

And we were going to get everything settled today. *(quietly; controlled)* Where is he?

> HARPER'S VOICE (off-screen)

I'm up in Santa Barbara. Tell her Albert Graves needed me. She'll understand.

> FRED
> *(sits in his desk chair)*

Something about Albert Graves. And you'll understand.

> SUSAN
> *(almost a sigh)*

No; no I don't. We've been trying to get this divorce thing settled for too long now and I have lately been running low on understanding.

> HARPER'S VOICE (off-screen)

I heard. Fred, you tell her —

SUSAN
(up out of the chair, she begins
pacing quickly around the office)
—we're supposed to be handling this like adults. I don't want a screaming
match, but the last time we were going to meet something came up too.

HARPER'S VOICE (off-screen)
That wasn't my fault.
(Everyone is talking faster now.
The dialogue begins overlapping, faster
and faster until the scene is done.)

FRED
Lew says—

SUSAN
—I don't care what he says. He's just trying to stall because he thinks I'm
gonna change my mind about this and I may change a lot of things from
now on but my mind isn't about to be one of them—

HARPER'S VOICE (off-screen)
—lemme talk to her—

FRED
(rising, extending phone)
—here—

SUSAN
(shaking her head)
—no—

HARPER'S VOICE (off-screen)
—*put her on.*

FRED
(reaching out with phone)
Take it. Talk to him.

SUSAN
I have taken it. Every year we were married I took it. And I've talked to
him too. He holds no more surprises. Tell him that. You hear me, Lew?
No more surprises. No more nothing. *(louder now; she is upset)* Let's just
do it and quick. You hear me, Lew? I don't love you and you can get shot
in some alley and I'll be a little sorry, sure, but that's all, just a little sorry.
Tell him that, lawyer. Tell the man he is not loved!
(There is a loud click as the
phone is slammed down.)

FADE OUT

FADE IN ON

A TABLE SET FOR THREE BESIDE THE SWIMMING POOL.

FELIX is finishing putting food out. ALAN TAGGERT stands by, a towel slung around his neck. MIRANDA stands very close beside him. HARPER walks into the picture.

> TAGGERT

Top of the morning. *(moving to him, smiling)* I'm Alan Taggert, Sampson's pilot. This is his daughter, Miranda.

> HARPER

Lew Harper.
> *(They shake hands.)*

> TAGGERT
> *(MIRANDA nods briefly, moves to table*
> *and sits. TAGGERT and HARPER also sit.*
> *As they do, pointing to HARPER's glass —)*

What're you drinking?

> HARPER

Milk.

> TAGGERT

I thought you were a detective.

> HARPER

It's fermented mare's milk.
> *(TAGGERT laughs; not so MIRANDA)*

> MIRANDA

My stepmother — *(she gestures with her thumb toward the house)* — Lady Macbeth — is always going to extremes. Hiring detectives —

> HARPER

— do you mean me? I'm a very moderate type, Miss Sampson.

> MIRANDA

Not you especially.
> *(She reaches out for TAGGERT's hand.*
> *He ignores the gesture. She pulls*
> *her hand back. During this —)*

Other women fall off horses without getting paralyzed. Not Elaine. I think it's psychological. She's not a raving beauty anymore so she decided to retire from competition. For all I know, she fell off intentionally.

> TAGGERT

Come on, Miranda; you've been reading a book.

> MIRANDA

That's something you'll never be accused of. *(She throws her napkin onto the table. To* HARPER*)* And you've got to admit it's pretty extreme, hiring a detective when your husband's gone just one night.

CUT TO

HARPER'S FACE. He is watching her.

> HARPER

If you say so, Miss Sampson. *(He turns to* TAGGERT.*)* Tell me about Sampson's disappearance.

CUT TO

The three of them as TAGGERT *starts talking.* TAGGERT *looks at* HARPER. MIRANDA *looks at* TAGGERT.

> TAGGERT

About three thirty yesterday afternoon, we landed at Burbank airport...

CAMERA PANS TO

MIRANDA. She is watching TAGGERT *still. One has the feeling she could watch him for hours on end; she adores him.*

> TAGGERT'S VOICE (off-screen)

They had to move another crate before I could park the plane. Mr. Sampson went to call the Valerio to send a limousine.

> MIRANDA

Ralph keeps a bungalow there.

> TAGGERT'S VOICE (off-screen)

When I got to the airport entrance, Mr. Sampson wasn't there. I waited. Then I went to the Valerio and waited some more. Then I flew back here.

CUT TO

HARPER watching MIRANDA *watch* TAGGERT.

> HARPER

What about luggage? Was he planning to spend the night?

> TAGGERT'S VOICE (off-screen)

He told me he was; he didn't have any luggage but that doesn't mean anything.

CUT TO

MIRANDA. Aware of HARPER *now, she turns and faces him.*

MIRANDA

Ralph keeps a lot of clothes at the bungalow. He likes to be able to pick up fast.

HARPER

How long did it take to park the plane?

TAGGERT

Fifteen minutes. Twenty at the outside.

HARPER

That's pretty good time for a limousine from the Valerio. He may never have called there at all; someone may have met him at the airport.

MIRANDA

Will you be going back to Los Angeles?

HARPER
(nods)

After I see Albert Graves.

MIRANDA
(to TAGGERT)

You can fly Mr. Harper down, if you want to. Or unless you'd rather stay here . . . *(the "here with me" is implicit)*

TAGGERT

I'll fly. *(he gives her a big smile)* It'll keep me from getting bored.
*(Without a moment's hesitation, MIRANDA
stands up, turns and walks off, a pretty piece
angry. TAGGERT glances at her, then turns to
HARPER. The following lines go very quickly.)*
You in a hurry?

HARPER

Sort of.

TAGGERT

You like salmon? *(They have been eating salmon.)*

HARPER

No.

TAGGERT

Me too. Let's blow.

HARPER

Sold.
(They start to rise.)

DISSOLVE TO

A ROLLS-ROYCE ROARING DOWN A ROAD.

CUT TO

Inside the Rolls. FELIX is driving. There is a closed glass partition between him and the back seat. In the back seat, HARPER sits and TAGGERT sprawls, his feet up on the jump seat. He has changed to a khaki suit and tie and loafers.

> TAGGERT
>
> How long you going to be with Graves?

> HARPER
>
> Not very.

> TAGGERT
>
> Then I'll wait outside with my friend Felix. *(he presses a button, the glass partition slides down)* Are we friends, Felix?

> FELIX
>
> Yes, Mr. Taggert.
>
> > *(TAGGERT presses the button
> > again, closing the partition.)*

> TAGGERT
>
> He's as big a liar as I am.

INSERT: The rear view mirror. FELIX's eyes are clearly reflected. During this:

> TAGGERT'S VOICE (off-screen)
>
> He's always watching people. I get the feeling he could see my heart on a clear day.

CUT TO

A shot from above of the two men. HARPER sits as before; TAGGERT is really sprawled out now, miming playing a ukulele.

> HARPER
>
> Why so hard on Miranda?

> TAGGERT
>
> Everybody jumps to conclusions about me and Miranda. She's an adolescent; I can't help the way she feels. Anyway, I got me a woman.

> HARPER
>
> How does Miranda get on with Sampson?

> TAGGERT
>
> OK until a little while ago, when he started trying to make her get married.

                              HARPER
To anyone in particular?

                              TAGGERT
                        *(He is still strumming
                        his imaginary ukulele)*
Your buddy Albert Graves.

CUT TO

HARPER. The news takes him by surprise.

CUT TO

TAGGERT. He is looking up at HARPER, wildly strumming his ukulele, smiling.

FADE OUT

FADE IN ON

HARPER

going through a door on which is printed the name ALBERT GRAVES.

CUT TO

A lawyer's reception room, tastefully done. A secretary sits at a desk.

                              HARPER
Lew Harper.

                             SECRETARY
You're expected.
                        *(She gestures toward inner door.
                        HARPER opens it, sticks head in)*

                  ALBERT GRAVES' VOICE (off-screen)
Lew!

CUT TO

Inside the office. ALBERT GRAVES hurries to the door, right hand out.

ALBERT GRAVES is over forty. He has a pleasant face, thinning hair and brisk, forthright manner of speaking. He is, legitimately, one of the decent people. He and HARPER have known each other for a long time and regard each other with obvious great good will.

                              ALBERT
                        (as they shake)
You look like death warmed over.

                              HARPER
Always nice to hear from my fans.

                              ALBERT
How's Susan?

                              HARPER
Fine, fine.

                              ALBERT
Wonderful. *(He is in his shirt sleeves. During the above they have been moving toward an open door across the room.)*

CUT TO

Inside a small room as they enter. An exercycle machine is visible.

                              ALBERT
I was just staying in shape. It's important. I do the Royal Canadians every morning and yogurt for lunch, then this — it's all paying off, don't you think?

                              HARPER
I've never seen you more ravishing than you are at this moment.

                              ALBERT
                    (gives him a look, then starts to pedal)
Listen, I heard about you and Susan.

                              HARPER
                        (very casually)
Oh?

                              ALBERT
Yes. Naturally, I'm sorry, and —

CUT TO

HARPER. CLOSE UP. He is angry.

                              HARPER
If you knew, then what the hell'd you ask about her for?

CUT TO

The two of them.

                              ALBERT
                        (stops pedaling)
Don't get sore. If I *hadn't* asked about her, you'd have gotten sore, right?

HARPER
(after a beat; softer)

Right, right, right.

ALBERT
(he starts to pedal again)

You talk to Mrs. Sampson?

HARPER

Nice warm lady —

ALBERT
(nodding)

— a love.

HARPER

Albert, I don't know why she hired me, do you?

ALBERT

I should — because I talked her into it.

HARPER

Why?

ALBERT
(pedaling away)

Because I think Sampson needs protection. On the hoof he's worth ten million and he's an alcoholic. That's just for openers. I also think he's losing his mind — did she mention Claude the holy man he gave the mountain to?
(HARPER nods)

HARPER

Mrs. Sampson thinks he's with a woman.

ALBERT

That's because I encouraged her to think that. She'd never spend a penny on him if she only thought he was in danger for his life.

HARPER

What about going to the cops?

ALBERT

I can't. If they found him, he'd fire me. He's got an abnormal fear of police — and last year when he disappeared, I found him in a whorehouse in San Francisco.

HARPER

What kind of a guy is Sampson?

CUT TO

ALBERT, *stopping pedaling.*

> **ALBERT**
> I'll tell you everything in one word:

CUT TO

ALBERT, CLOSE UP.

> **ALBERT**
> Moneymaker. That's all he was, is, cares about. It's the only way he can prove to himself he's breathing. He had a son, you know. Robert. A pilot. Killed a few years back. That's when his mind started going. He's got this fellow now, Alan Taggert.

CUT TO

HARPER, CLOSE UP.

> **HARPER**
> We met; nice looking boy.

CUT TO

ALBERT, *suddenly pedaling again, faster than before.*

> **ALBERT**
> Looks, looks, who cares about looks? The point is we're not two hours drive from Los Angeles, so what does he need a pilot for? It's an obvious son substitute. Of course, personally I like Alan, but from a business point of view, I do feel he's an unnecessary expense.

CUT TO

HARPER.

> **HARPER**
> Except it isn't your money.

CUT TO

ALBERT. *He turns his head sharply, looks at* HARPER.

> **ALBERT**
> Of course it isn't. But I'm paid to advise. *(stops pedaling)* That's enough. *(dismounts)* I don't want to get too strong.
> > (*They start into* ALBERT's *office.*)

CUT TO

ALBERT'S OFFICE. *The two men entering.*

ALBERT
(*trying to be as casual as possible*)
You didn't happen to run into Miranda?

HARPER
The ugly skinny kid? We passed in the night.

ALBERT
(*he slips into his suitcoat before it bursts
out of him — throughout the following, his emotions are almost adolescent*)
Oh Lew, isn't she incredible?

CUT TO

HARPER. *Deadpan. He says nothing.*

CUT TO

ALBERT. *He is crestfallen.*

ALBERT
Go on — you think I'm too old for her.

CUT TO

The two of them.

HARPER
No, no; when she's 100, you'll only be 124.

ALBERT
You think I'm old enough to be her father?

HARPER
You are old enough to be her father.

ALBERT
Go to hell.

HARPER
Some of the best marriages I know are based on neurotic foundations.

ALBERT
(*up again, childlike*)
Lew, Lew, I'm in love. Isn't that ridiculous? I'm 45 years old and I love her.

CUT TO

ALBERT. *He begins to do a clumsy dance step, concentrating very hard.*

ALBERT

I'm tone deaf but I sing songs all day long. *(whispering)* Don't tell but I'm taking dancing lessons. *(loud suddenly)* Stuffy old Albert Graves is in love. *(abruptly stops dancing and—)* Did she say anything about me?

CUT TO

HARPER.

HARPER

No.

CUT TO

ALBERT. Crestfallen again.

ALBERT

She didn't even mention my name?

CUT TO

The two of them.

HARPER

I only met her for a second.

ALBERT
(bright again)

That explains it.

HARPER

She loves you?

ALBERT

She's young; you remember how that was. They're very cautious people. But I have great expectations. *(starting toward reception room door)*

HARPER
(moving with ALBERT)

So do I; my going rate is 100 a day and expenses.

ALBERT
(at the door)

It's fifty a day and expenses but you're a friend of mine. *(opening door)* I'll give you fifty-five.

HARPER
(exiting)

With friends like you—

> ALBERT
> *(exiting too)*
> —yeah, yeah, yeah, who needs enemies?
> *(And they are gone.)*

DISSOLVE TO

THE SIDEWALK.

HARPER AND ALBERT are walking toward the Rolls. FELIX scurries out to open the door.

CUT TO

ALBERT stopping dead.

CUT TO

Inside the Rolls. MIRANDA SAMPSON sits close beside TAGGERT.

> MIRANDA
> I decided to fly down to L.A. with you; all right?

CUT TO

ALBERT AND HARPER. HARPER shrugs, gets into car without looking at ALBERT. FELIX closes the door.

CUT TO

Inside the car. ALBERT is looking plaintively through the window. He knocks on the glass. The glass is lowered.

> ALBERT
> *(trying to smile, embarrassed;*
> *it is almost painful)*
> Hello, Miranda.

> MIRANDA
> *(barely recognizing his existence)*
> Oh; hello Albert.

FELIX is in the front seat now. The great car starts to move.

CUT TO

ALBERT, waving good-bye. He just stands there, trying very hard to smile. Sometimes he makes it, sometimes he doesn't. CAMERA HOLDS ON ALBERT.

FADE OUT

FADE IN ON

A TWO MOTOR AIRPLANE ABOVE BURBANK AIRPORT.

DISSOLVE TO

THE PLANE ON THE GROUND, COMING TO A STOP.

HARPER is making ready to get out.

HARPER

Wait for me at the main entrance.

TAGGERT
(MIRANDA is sitting beside him)

Solid.

(HARPER starts to leave)

DISSOLVE TO

HARPER, WALKING TO FRONT OF AIRPORT.

He approaches a taxi starter, who is helping a lady into a cab. This done, he turns and faces HARPER, who has taken the photo of SAMPSON from his pocket.

HARPER

Familiar?

THE TAXI STARTER is a little old man with an ENORMOUSLY LOUD VOICE. Everything he says BOOMS INCONGRUOUSLY.

TAXI STARTER

Mister, I got the most fantastic memory you ever seen — *(he sticks out his hand, palm up, for money)* — but don't try and bribe me. Don't put five dollars in my hand. We're both gentlemen — let's keep it that way.

(HARPER gives him some money)

Yesterday. Yesterday afternoon. He was what I would call semi-blotto.

HARPER

Was he alone?

TAXI STARTER

He was.

HARPER

How did he leave here?

TAXI STARTER

I'll tell you how he left here — *(the right hand is out again)* — you asked me as a gentleman so as a gentleman, I'll answer — but don't try and gimme no money — I don't want your money — I'm here just to give service and that's all —

> *(HARPER gives him some more money.)*

A black limousine. It didn't carry no sign is why I noticed it. Maybe from one of the hotels.

HARPER

You recognize the driver?

TAXI STARTER

Naw; they're always changing. This was a skinny guy, I think. Skinny face; pale. Pale like he was dying.

> *(Behind him, an elderly woman has*
> *started for a cab. He catches a glimpse,*
> *whirls, holds door open for her.)*

Let me help you; it's my job and I love it so whatever you do, don't tip me. I beg you whatever you do don't tip me, I might get spoiled . . .

> *(He helps the fat lady into the cab.)*

DISSOLVE TO

A SIGN ON A BUILDING THAT SAYS VALERIO HOTEL.

HARPER is paying a taxi driver. TAGGERT AND MIRANDA stand near.

DISSOLVE TO

The lobby of the Valerio. HARPER, TAGGERT, AND MIRANDA walk through. Then HARPER gestures with an arm and TAGGERT AND MIRANDA move off.

CUT TO

A lady at the telephone switchboard. She is very fat and round and sweet. She looks up as HARPER approaches.

HARPER

Were you working yesterday at about this time?

> *(she nods)*

Did you get a call from the airport from Ralph Sampson?

TELEPHONE OPERATOR

I would love to help you except if I did it would cost me my job.

HARPER

(sighs, produces a bill from his pocket)

This is my day for sad stories. *(hands it over)*

TELEPHONE OPERATOR

Yes.

HARPER

Did you send a limousine out there?

TELEPHONE OPERATOR
No.

HARPER
Why didn't you? — wait — don't tell me — you would love to help me ex-
cept if you did it would cost you your job.
(She nods — he hands over another bill.)

TELEPHONE OPERATOR
He canceled it. He called up and then he called back and said not to send it.

HARPER
You're sure it was Sampson both times?

TELEPHONE OPERATOR
Oh yes; he's been coming here for years.
(HARPER nods, turns away)

CUT TO

THE VALERIO LOBBY.

MIRANDA stands alone. HARPER moves up to her.

MIRANDA
Father hasn't been here for a month. I asked the manager.

HARPER
He give you the key?

MIRANDA
Of course. Alan's gone on ahead to open the bungalow.
(She starts to move, HARPER follows.)

DISSOLVE TO

HARPER AND MIRANDA COMING TO A WROUGHT IRON DOOR.

He holds it open.

CUT TO

*The view when you come through the door: a series of spiffy bungalows set in rows. The
whole area is surrounded by a high wall. There are tennis courts, a pool, etc.*

CUT TO

*MIRANDA entering the front room of a large bungalow, HARPER a step behind. TAGGERT
is lying stretched out on the couch.*

CUT TO

A PAN SHOT OF THE ROOM, FROM HARPER'S POINT OF VIEW. It is plainly furnished, impersonally. During this —

> **TAGGERT'S VOICE** (off-screen)
> I'm beat. I think maybe I'll sack out awhile, then buzz some buddies of mine.

> **MIRANDA'S VOICE** (off-screen)
> *(this is half whispered)*
> I thought we might do something together.

> **TAGGERT'S VOICE** (off-screen)
> The thing about you, Miranda, is you're such a drag.

CUT TO

HARPER. He moves toward an arch and the bedroom beyond.

> **HARPER**
> *(steps into the archway, turns
> on the light, stops cold)*
> Wow. Your father wouldn't by any chance be interested in astrology?

CUT TO

The bedroom. It is an astrologer's dream of heaven. Twelve-sided and windowless, it is lit red, with red walls, and on each of the twelve wall panels is embroidered in gold one of the signs of the zodiac — the bull, the archer, the twins, etc.

CUT TO

HARPER moving into the room, MIRANDA behind him. There is a large bed. HARPER moves to it, looks around, then goes to the closet. MIRANDA hesitates, then walks to the bed and lies down. During this —

CUT TO

> **MIRANDA**
> *(nods)*
> Ever since my brother died. I've tried to argue him out of it but — *(and
> she gestures to the walls)* — not too successfully, obviously.

> **HARPER'S VOICE** (off-screen)
> No wonder he took to the sauce. I would too if I had to sleep here.

CUT TO

HARPER at the closet, beginning to go through SAMPSON's suits.

> **HARPER**
> Any particular astrologist?

> MIRANDA'S VOICE (off-screen)

Not that I know of. Harper?

> HARPER

What?

> MIRANDA'S VOICE (off-screen)

You work hard, you know that?

> HARPER

Yeah, I'm a beaver.

> MIRANDA'S VOICE (off-screen)

Harper?

CUT TO

MIRANDA. She is lying on the bed. Her skirt is raised, not enough to be indecent, more than enough to be inviting. She is wearing a blouse unbuttoned at the throat. A very sexy girl.

> MIRANDA

Don't you ever feel the need to relax?

CUT TO

A SHOT FROM BEHIND THE BED. In the next room, TAGGERT is clearly visible sprawled on the couch. During this —

> HARPER'S VOICE

You want to get me over there so beauty in the next room will get all hot and bothered. Lady, if you can't make him hot and bothered, I'm sure not going to do it for you.

> MIRANDA

You don't think I'm attractive?

CUT TO

HARPER, going through the clothes. He stops.

> HARPER

You're rich, young, beautiful, and my wife is divorcing me; what the hell do you think I think? *(Abruptly he starts toward her as she lies there.)* Now if you really want to play, we'll send beauty off somewhere and douse the lights.

CUT TO

MIRANDA. She jumps off the bed, fast.

CUT TO

HARPER. He laughs, turns back to the closet, puts his hand in a pocket. Then —

HARPER

Bingo! *(He takes a handful of money from a pocket, together with a photo. HARPER shows photo to MIRANDA.)* You know her?

MIRANDA

No.

HARPER

Hey Beauty —

CUT TO

THE LIVING ROOM. TAGGERT is asleep on the couch. HARPER enters, shakes him roughly awake.

HARPER

You ever seen this woman with Sampson? Fay Estabrook's her name.

TAGGERT
(blinks sleepily)

Nope.

HARPER drops him back down on the couch, moves back into the bedroom and toward MIRANDA.

CUT TO

MIRANDA, as HARPER approaches.

MIRANDA

Is she a friend of yours?

HARPER

Never met her. But if she's still in town, and if I can spread some money around, by tonight we may be bosom buddies.

MIRANDA

Who is she?

INSERT: A photograph of an enormously attractive young blonde. On the photo is written clearly:

> "To Ralph:
> my dear friend now,
> as I was then.
> Fay"

HARPER'S VOICE (off-screen)

Fay Estabrook? She was a very hot young starlet once upon a time.

MIRANDA'S VOICE (off-screen)
(the CAMERA is still holding on FAY's face)
What happened to her?

HARPER'S VOICE (off-screen)
She got *fat.*

On the word "fat" —

CUT TO

FAY ESTABROOK'S FACE. IT IS INDEED FAT.

PULL BACK TO REVEAL

FAY walking from the parking lot of a restaurant into the restaurant, SWIFT'S. It is evening. The sun is going down.

FAY ESTABROOK is still blonde, but she is twenty years older and forty pounds heavier than when the picture was taken. Girdled heavily, she moves into SWIFT'S.

CAMERA PANS TO

HARPER, across the street, watching.

CUT TO

INSIDE SWIFT'S.

HARPER enters. There is a bar to the left of the door. He moves to it, looks around.

CUT TO

PAN SHOT of restaurant tables. In one corner, alone, menu in hand, is FAY ESTABROOK.

CUT TO

HARPER at the bar. BARTENDER comes up.

HARPER
Beer.

BARTENDER
Bass Ale, Black Horse, Carta Blanca or Guinness Stout. We don't serve domestic beer after six o'clock.

HARPER
Bass.
(BARTENDER gets a bottle and glass. HARPER takes out a dollar bill, hands it over)
Keep the change.

BARTENDER
(setting down beer and glass, taking the bill)
There isn't any change.

HARPER
(annoyed)
Keep it anyway. *(He pours himself a glass, looks out.)*

CUT TO

DWIGHT TROY *moving through the tables of* SWIFT'S. *When he gets to* FAY's *booth, he sits down immediately.*

DWIGHT TROY *is a tall, slender man in his forties, the kind who is usually in the company of young women. The perennial aging chorus boy.*

A waiter comes up to the table, bringing FAY *a drink.* TROY, *talking earnestly and rapidly to* FAY, *shakes his head at the waiter, who goes away.*

CUT TO

HARPER, *sipping his beer.*

DISSOLVE TO

HARPER, *finishing his beer, ordering another.*

DISSOLVE TO

TROY *at the booth. He stands, nods to* FAY, *then turns and walks out of the restaurant.*

CUT TO

HARPER, *sipping his beer. He is watching* FAY *closely and, after a moment, he crosses the restaurant to her booth. When he talks, his entire speech pattern has altered.*

HARPER
Miss Estabrook?
(FAY looks up)
Miss Fay Estabrook?

FAY
What is it, dumpling?

HARPER
*(the words machine gun out of him — he
seems to be enormously nervous and shy)*
Please. *(he shoves a pen and paper at her)* For my daughter — she watches all your old movies on the television — she just thinks you're wonderful, Miss Estabrook and I'm sorry to bother you but — *(he gives an embarrassed smile)*

FAY

No bother, dumpling. *(she signs the paper, hands it over)*

HARPER

Thank you. *(he takes the paper, starts to turn away, stops, turns back — then, faster than before)* The truth is — the truth is I'm not married and I don't have a daughter and it's me, Miss Estabrook, me who watches you on the television and I don't know how many fans you have, millions probably, but I'll bet there isn't one more faithful than I am and could I buy you a drink, Miss Estabrook?

FAY

*(squints up at him a moment, then reaches
into her purse, takes out glasses and looks up
at him, holding the glasses to her eyes)*

When were you born?

HARPER

The second of June.

FAY

Geminian. Geminis have no heart. You cold-hearted, dumpling?

HARPER

Dogs are all the time licking my hand.

FAY

(laughs, gestures to the seat opposite)

You believe in the stars?

HARPER

Doesn't everybody?

CUT TO

*FAY, smiling at him. She picks up her glasses again, holds them in her hand and looks
through them at HARPER. The smile broadens.*

DISSOLVE TO

HARPER AND FAY DANCING.

*It is a hotel type place where they are, and their bodies are not close. (IN THE FOLLOWING
BRIEF MONTAGE; THE DEGREE OF FAY'S DRUNKENNESS CAN BE MEASURED BY THE CLOSE-
NESS OF THEIR DANCING BODIES.)*

DISSOLVE TO

HARPER AND FAY DANCING. A LATIN PLACE.

They dance by a ringside table, HARPER picks up FAY's drink, hands it to her.

DISSOLVE TO

HARPER AND FAY DANCING. BEHIND THEM, A JUKEBOX.

FAY is starting to go now. She leans her heavy body more on HARPER. She thinks she is terribly sexy. Publicly, he thinks so too. Privately, his thoughts are different.

DISSOLVE TO

HARPER AND FAY DANCING. A DIFFERENT JUKEBOX.

FAY's pretty smashed by this point.

DISSOLVE TO

HARPER AND FAY DANCING ALONE IN A BAR.

He is practically carrying her as they move. Suddenly, she pushes herself away from him.

> FAY
>
> Where are we, the morgue? *(she staggers toward him)* Maybe you better take me home, Harper.

> HARPER
>
> Not 'til we have another drink. *(He signals the BARTENDER.)*

> FAY
> *(into his arms)*
>
> You're nice to me.

They move to the bar. The BARTENDER puts down the drinks. FAY downs her shot without a chaser. HARPER looks at his drink a moment, then glances up.

CUT TO

HARPER staring at himself in the mirror. The look he gives himself is a good deal less than kind. With a quick flick of his hand, he knocks his drink flying. His hand is cut slightly.

CUT TO

The glass shattering on the floor.

CUT TO

The BARTENDER, glaring at HARPER, who is licking his cut hand. The cut is not severe.

> HARPER
> *(putting some money on the bar)*
>
> Sorry. Accident. *(he turns to FAY)* Hey, there's this great place up the street we just gotta go to.

FAY

The Valerio?

HARPER

I think that's the name of it

FAY
(managing to push away from the bar)
OK. (she looks around)

CUT TO

PAN SHOT of the empty bar.

CUT TO

FAY
(starting to the door, she stops,
throws her head back and cries out)
Where are the merrymakers?

CUT TO

HARPER. He takes a deep breath, then moves up beside her.

HARPER

Here we are.
(He helps her stagger out the door.)

DISSOLVE TO

THE VALERIO BAR.

HARPER AND FAY enter, go to a booth. She sits heavily.

FAY

I like this place. I got a friend stays here.

HARPER

A good friend?

FAY
(smiles)
You're getting jealous I can tell. What is it with men, always trying to possess me? Hey what happened to your hand?

HARPER

I cut myself shaving.
(FAY roars. A WAITRESS approaches.)
Two double Scotches. (back to FAY) He here now?

FAY
(pleased with the interest)

You really are jealous, arencha, dumpling? (She reaches out, chucks him under the chin.)

CUT TO

HARPER. He manages to make a big smile.

CUT TO

The two of them. Different angle. The entrance to the bar is visible.

FAY

Ralph's in Vegas. He's got a home in the desert. I just help him with his astrology charts. An' a little interior decoration. I done his room; wish you could see it. I got this fabulous taste.

HARPER

You got everything, dumpling.

> (TAGGERT AND MIRANDA appear in bar
> entrance, look around. Before they can
> start for him, HARPER is on his feet.)

Back in a sec'.

> (He nods to TAGGERT AND MIRANDA
> to get out of sight. They retreat back
> through the doorway entrance.)

CUT TO

HARPER, coming through the door. The three stand very close together. The following takes place quickly, voices soft and serious.

MIRANDA
(upset)

I've been trying to find you for hours. You're supposed to be looking for Ralph —

HARPER
(to TAGGERT)

— get her out of here before she spoils a night's work —

TAGGERT

— but Mrs. Sampson's been calling — she wants your advice —

MIRANDA

— she got a special delivery letter from Ralph. He told her to get some money ready; a half a million cash.

> **HARPER**
> Can she get that much?

> **MIRANDA**
> *(nodding)*
> Albert has father's power of attorney. The letter said to cash some bonds
> and then wait with the money 'til she heard from him again.

> **HARPER**
> She's sure it's his writing?
> *(MIRANDA nods)*
> Then have Albert get the money but don't hand it over to anyone with-
> out proof that Sampson's alive.

CUT TO

MIRANDA, upset, starting to protest.

CUT TO

HARPER, cutting her off.

> **HARPER**
> I'm sorry, it's a possibility, so face it.

CUT TO

The three of them.

> **HARPER**
> Albert will know how to handle things up there. *(starting to go — to TAGGERT)*
> Get her to bed.

CUT TO

*HARPER, coming back into VALERIO BAR. He sees FAY standing and talking to a Mexican
looking waiter.*

CUT TO

FAY and the waiter, as HARPER moves up behind her. She is terribly smashed now.

> **FAY**
> *(indignantly)*
> Yer no Mexican. No yer not foolin' me. Yer a phony Mexican. *(to HARPER)*
> He's a phony Mexican.

> **HARPER**
> *(steering her back to their booth)*
> What's the trouble, dumpling?

FAY

He won't play "Babalu." I can sing "Babalu" like nothin', but he won't play it. A real Mexican wouldda played it.

HARPER

He's just a waiter; he doesn't have a guitar.

FAY

If he was a real Mexican, he wouldda had a guitar.
(they are at their booth)

HARPER

Quick, where do you live?

FAY

118 Woodlawn Lane in the Palasades. Why?

HARPER

I'm gonna drive you home.

CUT TO

FAY sitting down in the booth.

FAY

I'm great now. Ready to roll. *(she grabs her double shot, downs it in a gulp)* See?
(She smiles. But only for a moment. Then the whisky starts to take effect. She begins to pitch forward. HARPER grabs her. In a whisper)
Hellllppppp . . .

CUT TO

HEADLIGHTS CUTTING THROUGH DARKNESS,

passing over a street sign saying Woodlawn lane.

CUT TO

FAY's car driving slowly along a street, then turning into a driveway; the motor cuts off.

CUT TO

HARPER, getting out of the car, walking around, opening the door.

CUT TO

FAY. She is lying sprawled on the seat, solid dead weight.

CUT TO

HARPER. *He gives a sigh. Then moves toward her.*

DISSOLVE TO

HARPER, *dragging* FAY *under the arms toward the front door. Reaching it, he manages to prop her against him, grabs for her purse, manages to find the front door key. She starts to slip but he grabs her, finally stabs the key into the lock, pushing the door open. He drags* FAY *forward into the dark house.*

CUT TO

HARPER *throwing the lights on in the foyer. Beyond is the living room and a visible couch. He starts to drag her toward it.*

CUT TO

THE LIVING ROOM *and* FAY's *body hitting the sofa like the rock of Gibraltar. The sudden activity rouses her and she opens one eye.*

> **FAY**
> *(barely able to speak)*
> Don't try to do anything to me tonight. I'm dead tonight. Some other time, huh dumpling? Any other time . . . *(And she is out.)*

CUT TO

HARPER. *He reaches down and raises an eyelid. A marbled eyeball stares whitely at nothing. In a moment, she is snoring. He turns, rapidly begins walking about the room In one corner is a desk and he moves to it, opens the drawers, looks inside, closes the drawers again.*

CUT TO

HARPER, *moving into the kitchen of the house, looking up, down, anywhere.*

CUT TO

HARPER, *moving faster now, flicking on the lights of a bath room, opening the medicine chest. It is filled with feminine beauty aids.*

CUT TO

HARPER, *in what is obviously* FAY's *bedroom. There are astrology books and astrological signs and he starts into her dresser, the top drawer, then the next one down, then the next one down, then — suddenly, he stops dead.*

CUT TO

The drawer. At first what is seen is simply piles of nylon stockings. But then HARPER's HANDS *shove the stockings aside. The drawer is crammed with money, fives, tens, etc. The money is greasy and dirty, soiled as hell, tied in almost endless bundles.*

CUT TO

HARPER. *He stares and stares at the money. He starts to reach in and pick some up when*

The telephone rings with shocking loudness. HARPER *starts in surprise. The phone rings again.* HARPER *hesitates, then closes the dresser drawer and moves toward the sound.*

CUT TO

THE FOYER *and the ringing phone.* HARPER *approaches, picks it up. He sticks his hand across the mouthpiece.*

CUT TO

The foyer, another angle. Beyond, snoring blissfully, FAY *is visible.*

> **HARPER**
>
> Hello.

> **A VOICE ON THE PHONE** (BETTY)
>
> Mr. Troy? This is Betty. Is Fay there?

> **HARPER**
>
> No.

> **VOICE**
> *(she is terribly nervous)*
>
> Listen — Fay was in the Valerio awhile ago fried — with some guy — we don't want him there when the truck goes through — so get rid of him —

> **HARPER**
>
> — right. Where are you?

> **VOICE**
> *(There is a pause. In the
> background is the babble of voices.)*
>
> The Piano; where would I be?

> **HARPER**
>
> Is Ralph Sampson there?

> **VOICE**
> *(Another pause. The voice is hard now.)*
>
> All right, who is this?
> *(HARPER hangs up. He stands for a moment
> over the phone, his hand on the receiver.)*

CUT TO

DWIGHT TROY, *standing in the doorway, a gun in his hand.*

TROY

I beg you not to move. *(He speaks with a British accent acquired at great effort and cost.)*

CUT TO

HARPER, turning slowly. He looks terribly frightened and when he speaks, it is as he spoke when he first approached FAY in the restaurant — nervous and very fast.

HARPER

I demand to know who you are.

TROY

Age before beauty, old stick.

HARPER

I happen to be Miss Fay Estabrook's escort for the evening and this happens to be Miss Fay Estabrook's house.

TROY

And the light happens to be on in Miss Estabrook's bedroom; what were you doing there?

HARPER

Nothing. I didn't go in there. Miss Estabrook did when we arrived.

TROY
*(moving out of the FOYER
toward the BEDROOM)*

Come along.

                 (HARPER follows.)

CUT TO

TROY moving into the bedroom.

TROY

Turn around, old stick.

HARPER

Going to shoot me in the back, aren't you?

TROY
(impatient)

Turn around.

CUT TO

HARPER. He is standing in the doorway, facing out of the bedroom.

HARPER

This is shocking treatment. Typical Los Angeles hospitality.
*(Behind him there is the clear sound of
the dresser drawer opening and closing.)*

CUT TO

FAY, dead to the world on the couch. She is snoring magnificently now.

The CAMERA tips up to catch TROY's face, scowling down at her.

TROY

She never could hold her liquor.

CUT TO

HARPER, TROY, and FAY.

TROY

Why should you be interested in an old bag of worms like this?

HARPER
(starting to protest)
Miss Estabrook is not an old —

TROY

— Miss Estabrook is my wife so I know whereof I speak. I'm Dwight
Troy. I don't believe you ever specified your name.

HARPER

I'm Lewis Harper. I sell insurance. I had no idea she was —

TROY
(waving the pistol — urbane as always)
— relax, old stick, I'm not the jealous type. But on the other hand —

CUT TO

TROY. CLOSE UP. He means this.

TROY

I don't like strangers either. So I think you'd better never see us again.

HARPER'S VOICE (off-screen)

Is that a threat?

TROY

Is it ever, old stick. *(A very cold smile plays across his face.)*

FADE OUT

FADE IN ON

HARPER, WALKING ALONG A HIGHWAY.

A cab appears, he flags it down.

CUT TO

HARPER, getting in, sitting back.

> **HARPER**
> You know a place called The Piano?

> **CAB DRIVER**
> Yeah, yeah, sure; but I don't think you want to go there, mister.

> **HARPER**
> *(leaning back, closing his eyes — he is tired)*
> I'm a swinger.

DISSOLVE TO

THE CAB PULLING UP IN FRONT OF A BAR.

The sign "The Piano" is visible in front.

CUT TO

HARPER, standing on the street as the cab drives off. HARPER rubs his hands over his face, goes to the front door, opens it.

CUT TO

PAN SHOT OF THE PIANO.

It is a tourist trap, garish and dark (if that's possible). There are negro waiters and several "hostesses." In the rear, on a slight platform, a woman is playing the piano. The music is slow and bluesy and it underscores the scene.

CUT TO

HARPER, following a negro waiter to a table in a corner. Near the table is an exit door. HARPER sits, mimes something to the waiter who nods, goes to the bar.

CUT TO

CLOSE UP of HARPER, looking around the place.

CUT TO

A "hostess" moving away from the bar toward HARPER. She is very made up and built well enough but the face is neither young nor fair.

> **HOSTESS**
> *(standing by HARPER's table)*
Buy me a drink, Handsome?

> **HARPER**
I should buy you a pair of glasses.

> **HOSTESS**
What about it?

> **HARPER**
> *(gesturing for her to sit)*
I've always been a sucker for classy broads.

> **HOSTESS**
> *(sitting — pleased)*
You really think I'm classy?

> **HARPER**
If my heart didn't belong to Betty, I'd give it all to you.

> **HOSTESS**
> *(pointing)*
Her you want?

CUT TO

BETTY at the piano finishing a jazz number. Her eyes are closed. She is not young and she hasn't lived easy.

> **HOSTESS' VOICE** (off-screen)
> *(as we watch BETTY play)*
Her you want more'n me? Boy, are you sick.

DISSOLVE TO

The waiter putting a large glass on the piano, whispering into BETTY's ear. BETTY looks over at HARPER, nods, goes right on playing.

DISSOLVE TO

BETTY, turning the switch that controls the spotlight that bathes the piano. The light goes out. She picks-up her drink, hesitates a moment, then starts down towards HARPER. The "hostess" at HARPER's table gets up and leaves.

CUT TO

HARPER, He rises, smiles at her approach.

> **HARPER**
Lew Harper.

                              BETTY
Betty Fraley.

                              HARPER
                    (as they sit — every inch the hipster)
Betty; I know who you are. I got every side you ever cut.

                              BETTY
You're putting me on; you're probably tone deaf.

                              HARPER
Don't fight it, baby; you're something else.

CUT TO

BETTY. She looks at him a moment. Then she smiles.

                              BETTY
I believe you. *(the smile dies)* Except you got cops' eyes.

CUT TO

HARPER. After a moment, he nods.

CUT TO

BETTY.

                              BETTY
                          (frightened now)
Narcotics? I did my time.

CUT TO

HARPER.

                              HARPER
Private.

                              BETTY
I know you now. You said you were Troy. What are you after?
                    (This next goes very fast.)

                              HARPER
Ralph Sampson —

                              BETTY
— I don't know him —

                              HARPER
— I think you do —

BETTY

—all right, I do—he comes in here sometimes and gets drunk—he's a drunk and all drunks look alike—

HARPER

—what else do you know?—

BETTY

—nothin'—

HARPER

—tell me—

BETTY

—nothin,' nothin'—

HARPER

—*tell me*—

BETTY
(very soft and even)

—take him, Puddler.

CUT TO

HARPER, looking around, momentarily confused—he starts to rise—

CUT TO

PUDDLER. A giant with a cruel, battered face.

As HARPER starts to rise, PUDDLER slams down with his fist and HARPER, taken by surprise, cannot avoid the punch. It is a terrible blow, and it smashes flush against the side of his face.

CUT TO

BETTY. Hurrying up from the table.

BETTY

He's fuzz; work him good.

CUT TO

HARPER, groggy, trying to rise again. Again, a terrible blow crashes against his face and he is only semi-conscious now.

CUT TO

PUDDLER. He reaches down, grabs HARPER roughly, starts to drag him toward the exit door.

CUT TO

THE EXIT DOOR OPENING.

We are in an alley beside The Piano. It is dark and PUDDLER *braces* HARPER *against the wall and hits him in the stomach.* HARPER *grunts, starts to fall, but* PUDDLER *grabs him.* HARPER's *coat is open and* PUDDLER *sees* HARPER's *gun in his shoulder holster.*

CUT TO

PUDDLER, *taking the gun out, holding it momentarily in his hand. He contemplates using it to beat* HARPER, *then shakes his head, drops the gun and kicks it down the alley.*

CUT TO

The pistol, skittering through the darkness. In the background there is the sound of a heavy punch. The gun comes to a rest. Someone walks up to the gun.

CUT TO

ALAN TAGGERT, *standing over the gun. He stoops, grabs it, creeps forward. In the background there is the sound of another punch.*

CUT TO

TAGGERT, *moving up behind* PUDDLER *who has* HARPER *braced against the wall.* TAGGERT *hesitates only a moment. Then with great grace and style, a la Douglas Fairbanks Senior, he reaches high with the gun and brings it crashing down on the back of* PUDDLER's *head.*

CUT TO

PUDDLER, *crumbling.*

CUT TO

TAGGERT, *looking down at him.*

TAGGERT
*(smiling — just as pleased
with himself as can be)*

Hot damn, I did it!

CUT TO

HARPER. *Semi-conscious.* TAGGERT *hurries to him.*

TAGGERT
(his mood has not changed)

Harper, Harper, you see that? *(He begins slapping* HARPER *in the face.)* How are you? Harper. Come on now. You all right?

HARPER
(he is miserable)

I ... have ... been ... better, thank you.

CUT TO

Traveling shot of TAGGERT *helping* HARPER *along the alley.*

TAGGERT

Hey, you know this detective work is really fun.
(HARPER gives him a look)

HARPER

Where'd you come from?

TAGGERT

I got Miranda bedded down and I was restless. So, you really think Sampson was kidnapped? Who'd do it?

HARPER

How would I know? A woman named Estabrook maybe. Maybe a man named Troy. Ever hear of him?
(They are at the sidewalk now. HARPER
manages to stand by himself.)

CUT TO

TAGGERT. *He points to a car.*

TAGGERT
(crossing to it)

That's me over there.

CUT TO

HARPER, *nods, makes it to the car, gets in.*

CUT TO

TAGGERT, *getting in behind the wheel.*

TAGGERT

Sampson mentioned a Troy once. I think he was a buddy of that nut Claude Sampson gave the mountain to. *(he starts the car)* Where to?

HARPER

Follow the yellow brick road.

DISSOLVE TO

A SHOT FROM THE STREET OF FAY ESTABROOK'S HOUSE.

CUT TO

HARPER and TAGGERT in the car.

> **TAGGERT**
> *(whispering — excited)*
> Doesn't look to me like there's anybody home.

> **HARPER**
> *(normal voice — he is feeling better)*
> Drive in.
>> *(TAGGERT does)*

CUT TO

The car driving in the driveway, stopping, the lights going out.

CUT TO

HARPER and TAGGERT in the car.

> **HARPER**
> Turn 'em back on.
>> *(TAGGERT does)*
> Kind of big, don't you think?

CUT TO

THE OPEN GARAGE. It is enormous, much larger than would be normal for a house like FAY's.

> **HARPER'S VOICE** (off-screen)
> Big enough to hide a truck in, wouldn't you say?

> **TAGGERT'S VOICE** (off-screen)
> And then some.

DISSOLVE TO

HARPER and TAGGERT by the front door. HARPER, his gun in his hand, is knocking loudly on the door. After a pause —

> **TAGGERT**
> Want me to break it down?

> **HARPER**
> Easy, Tiger. *(He starts to walk around the house.)*

DISSOLVE TO

HARPER, approaching the back door. TAGGERT is a step behind. HARPER tests the door a moment with his hand, then steps aside.

HARPER

Sic 'em.

TAGGERT

You really want me to?

(*HARPER nods*)

Hot damn.

Without warning he throws himself against the door. It splinters, gives way. HARPER moves into the darkness. TAGGERT rubs his shoulder tenderly and follows along.

DISSOLVE TO

The FOYER. HARPER unlatches the door, opens it a crack.

HARPER
(*holding out his gun*)

Can you use this?

TAGGERT

I prefer a tommy gun, naturally.

HARPER

Shut up, Alan.

TAGGERT
(*softer*)

Yessir.

HARPER
(*hands him the gun*)

If anybody comes, let me know. But don't show yourself.

TAGGERT nods. HARPER moves off into the darkness. TAGGERT stands by the door peering out, nervously biting his lip.

DISSOLVE TO

HARPER. The lights come up abruptly. He is in FAY's bedroom. He goes to dresser, opens the money drawer.

CUT TO

THE DRAWER. It is empty except for a pile of nylons. In the distance, the growl of a heavy motor is heard.

CUT TO

HARPER. He stands still a moment. The motor grows louder. HARPER dives to the wall, flicks out the light, stands in darkness as the motor sound continues to grow.

TAGGERT'S VOICE (off-screen)
(a frantic whisper)

Harper. *Harper.*

CUT TO

HARPER, *moving through the darkness.*

CUT TO

TAGGERT, *standing behind the door. The motor sound is at a peak now and a great splash of light cuts through the crack in the door.*

TAGGERT
(throwing the door open suddenly)

I'll take him for you, Harper.

HARPER

Don't!

(But too late. TAGGERT is out the door.)

CUT TO

TAGGERT, *standing in a blaze of light on the steps of the house. HARPER moves into the doorway as TAGGERT aims the pistol and fires.*

The sound explodes in the quiet night.

CUT TO

HARPER, *elbowing TAGGERT aside as the roar of the truck grows.*

CUT TO

An army surplus truck painted blue backing rapidly down the driveway. It has a closed van.

CUT TO

HARPER, *streaking across the lawn.*

CUT TO

The truck, backing into the road.

CUT TO

HARPER, *running.*

CUT TO

The truck, stopping, changing gears.

CUT TO

HARPER, *approaching the end of the lawn.*

CUT TO

The truck, starting to move slowly forward.

CUT TO

HARPER, *leaping through the air, landing on the driver's side of the cab. He starts to hook his arm through the open window.*

CUT TO

The driver. A thin-faced man, cadaver-pale. Frantically, he stomps on the brake.

CUT TO

The truck screeching down. HARPER *falls hard into the street. The truck backs away from him.*

CUT TO

HARPER, *dazed, kneeling in the road. The roar of the truck is deafening now.* HARPER *looks up.*

CUT TO

The truck, picking up speed as it comes toward him, the lights blinding.

CUT TO

HARPER, *forcing his body into a sideways dive.*

CUT TO

The truck, turning toward HARPER.

CUT TO

HARPER, *rolling frantically out of the way as the truck roars by.*

CUT TO

The truck, really moving now, taking a sharp turn around a corner and disappearing into the night.

CUT TO

HARPER, *sprawled out. He manages to force himself up into a kneeling position.*

CUT TO

The ground the truck rolled over. It is soft, and the tracks of the truck are plainly visible in the mud.

CUT TO

HARPER, staring down at the tracks. Muddy, bloody, and beat, he cannot stop shivering.

DISSOLVE TO

HARPER, GETTING OUT OF TAGGERT'S CAR AND MOVING UP A WALK.

> TAGGERT'S VOICE (off-screen)
Pick you up at nine.
> *(HARPER nods, continues walking*
> *to the front door, inserts a key.)*

CUT TO

HARPER, coming into his house. On the mantel over the fireplace is a picture of HARPER and SUSAN. He passes it by, goes into the bedroom, flicking out the living room lights as he goes. The house is lit by moonlight. After a pause, in the darkness, he reappears, moves to the mantel, takes the picture, flicks it backhanded into a dark corner of the room, where it falls. He turns, reenters the bedroom and closes the door. After a beat, the door reopens, he comes out, moves to the corner of room where we cannot see him but hear him muttering to himself, bumping into things. Then he reenters the shot, puts the picture back on the mantel, carefully, in the moonlight, straightens and dusts it, then quickly exits into his bedroom and shuts the door. The door stays shut.

FADE OUT

FADE IN ON

THE SAMPSON PLANE LANDING IN SANTA BARBARA.

FELIX is visible, standing by the Rolls.

DISSOLVE TO

HARPER AND ELAINE SAMPSON.

She is in the sunshine, applying oils to her body. HARPER, a cup of coffee beside him, looks at a piece of paper.

> HARPER
You're sure this is your husband's writing.

> MRS. SAMPSON
> *(nodding)*
That moronic scrawl is unique.

> HARPER
> *(glancing at the envelope now)*
Sent from Buena Vista. *(he puts it down)* Albert take care of everything?

MRS. SAMPSON

He's getting the money; he ought to have it here now. But I couldn't let him inform the police, I'm afraid. *(She puts down the oil, picks up the aluminum reflector.)* You see, I'm not the least sure that my husband's business dealings are remotely legal. Not all of them anyway. He has an absolutely morbid fear of police —

HARPER

— I think he's in big trouble, Mrs. Sampson.

MRS. SAMPSON
(not remotely upset)

Come now; for all we know he's gettin' ready for a round-the-world jaunt with some harlot and needs spending money.

HARPER

I think he's been kidnapped. I think this note was dictated. Your husband keeps lousy company, Mrs. Sampson; as bad as there is in Los Angeles and that's as bad as there is.

MRS. SAMPSON
(she seems almost pleased)

I knew it! He loves playing the family man but he's never fooled me. Water seeks its own level which should put Ralph bathing happily somewhere in some sewer —

CUT TO

MIRANDA, *in the doorway. Blind mad.*

MIRANDA

— Father may be dead and you're crowing —

CUT TO

The three of them, MIRANDA *moving in toward her stepmother.*

MRS. SAMPSON
(airily waving her away)

— I don't believe it's the children's hour yet, darling.

MIRANDA
(stung)

You have such an advantage in emotional scenes, Elaine, being frigid —

MRS. SAMPSON

— puss, puss, puss, did Alan brush you off again?

CUT TO

HARPER, *glancing from one of them to the other.*

> **HARPER**
> *(very quietly)*
> Excuse me, ladies. *(And he turns and leaves. As he goes —)*

> **MRS. SAMPSON'S VOICE** (off-screen)
> I should think you'd be accustomed to not being wanted by now.

> **MIRANDA'S VOICE** (off-screen)
> I love your wrinkles. I revel in them!

> **MRS. SAMPSON'S VOICE** (off-screen)
> Puss, puss, puss . . .

DISSOLVE TO

HARPER, *standing in front of the SAMPSON house as ALBERT GRAVES drives up and hurriedly gets out of his car. ALBERT carries a large briefcase which he clutches.*

> **ALBERT**
> *(starting into the house)*
> What happened to that which, for want of a better term, I choose to call your face.

> **HARPER**
> *(following him in)*
> I changed cosmeticians.

DISSOLVE TO

The Sampson study. ALBERT, still holding the briefcase clutched to him in one hand, is opening the wall safe with the other. HARPER sits on a desk close beside.

> **HARPER**
> You have any friends left on the Los Angeles police from when you were D.A. up here?

> **ALBERT**
> I have some favors left uncollected, yes. *(The wall safe opens. ALBERT unlocks the briefcase, begins stuffing money into the safe.)*

> **HARPER**
> Tell them to run a check on any black limousines rented or stolen the last three days. And have them stick someone at a hole called The Piano.

> **ALBERT**
> *(turns — momentarily stops putting in money)*
> Dwight Troy's place?

HARPER

How do you know Troy?

ALBERT
(putting in money again)
I had to take some papers to Las Vegas once for Sampson to sign. He and Troy were gambling. I checked on Troy. He seemed elegant enough but people have a habit of dying around him. I tried telling Sampson, but— *(and he shrugs, stuffs in one last packet of money, then, with an enormous sigh)* —thank heavens. *(He closes the safe, gives dial a twirl.)* I was so nervous bringing that out here I got this out of mothballs. *(He reaches awkwardly into a coat pocket, brings forth a pistol. He looks at it and laughs a little.)*

HARPER

You better get a Santa Barbara cop out here to watch it.

ALBERT

Aren't you staying?

HARPER
(shaking his head)
I feel like visiting the mountain Sampson gave away. If someone will tell me where it is.

CUT TO

ALBERT. *He is abruptly standing very straight trying to smile and look his best.*

CUT TO

HARPER, *squinting at* ALBERT. *Then he turns, looks toward the study door.*

CUT TO

MIRANDA, *coming across the outside hall toward the study. The door frames her approach.*

CUT TO

ALBERT
(awkwardly moving forward)
Miranda. Hello. How are you?

CUT TO

MIRANDA, *moving through the study door.*

MIRANDA

Suicidal. I've just had the nicest chat with Elaine.

CUT TO

ALBERT. Fidgeting.

> **ALBERT**
> Would you be so good as to instruct Mr. Harper on how to get to the temple.

CUT TO

MIRANDA. She starts to laugh.

CUT TO

HARPER.

> **HARPER**
> What's so funny?

CUT TO

MIRANDA. Still laughing.

> **MIRANDA**
> Albert's holding a gun.

CUT TO

ALBERT. And so he is. Embarrassed, he makes a little smile then with some difficulty manages to stuff the gun into the nearest pocket.

> **ALBERT**
> I suppose it is funny.

> **HARPER**
> When we were in the Army, Albert was a dead shot. Didn't you ever tell her you done good in the Army?
> > *(ALBERT almost manages*
> > *to shake his head once)*

> **MIRANDA**
> You're kidding me.

> **HARPER**
> Sure I am. All heroes look like John Wayne, don't they, Miranda? It's an army regulation.

> **ALBERT**
> This is all dreadfully beside the point—

> **MIRANDA**
> *(to HARPER)*
> —I'll keep you company, all right? Just wait 'til I change. *(She turns, leaves the room.)*

CUT TO

ALBERT. He hurries to the doorway, watches MIRANDA's retreating body. HARPER moves up beside him.

HARPER

Now don't forget about that local cop. Don't leave until he's in this room, got it?

> *(ALBERT still stares after MIRANDA)*

Albert—

> *(He forces ALBERT to pay attention.*
> *Then—his voice low)*

—whoever sent that note knew you had Sampson's power of attorney. This whole case, if it is one, feels like an inside job.

ALBERT
(very hopefully)

Taggert maybe?

HARPER

Poor Albert.

> *(ALBERT turns for a last glimpse*
> *of MIRANDA who is just moving*
> *around a corner and out of sight.)*

Poor nice Albert.

ALBERT
(staring out at where MIRANDA was last seen)
I am nice. *(he turns to HARPER)* Wouldn't you think she'd notice?

CUT TO

HARPER.

HARPER

The bottom is loaded with nice people, Albert.

> *(CAMERA moves into CLOSE UP)*

Only cream and bastards rise.

> *(CAMERA holds a moment, then—)*

FADE OUT

FADE IN ON

HARPER'S CAR, ROARING ALONG A MOUNTAIN ROAD.

The road, seen from above, is like a white worm and the car is clearly moving faster than it ought.

CUT TO

HARPER at the wheel, his eyes on the road, his right hand clenched tight around the steering wheel. The cut on his right hand — gotten when he broke the glass during his time with Fay Estabrook — is plainly visible. MIRANDA SAMPSON sits beside him. She is wearing a matching sweater and skirt, the sweater unbuttoned at the throat. She looks marvelous.

CUT TO

The car, executing a sharp curve, then picking up speed again.

CUT TO

HARPER and MIRANDA.

> **MIRANDA**
> Why so fast, Fangio; trying to impress me?

> **HARPER**
> You've got a way of starting conversations that kills conversations.

> **MIRANDA**
> You're right, I'm sorry.

CUT TO

The car, executing another turn. The mountain they are climbing is gorgeous, the scenery below fresh and clean.

CUT TO

MIRANDA.

> **MIRANDA**
> Let's try it over. Why so fast?

CUT TO

HARPER.

> **HARPER**
> I don't mind a little tame danger now and then.

> **MIRANDA**
> Tame?

> **HARPER**
> Danger controlled by me.

CUT TO

MIRANDA watching HARPER for a moment. Then —

> MIRANDA

Is that why your wife is divorcing you?
> *(HARPER gives her a look. She hurries*
> *on, excitedly; for once she acts her age)*

Because of the danger? Because she loved you desperately except she was afraid that every time the telephone rang it would be someone telling her you'd been shot down in the dust or knifed in the back or something?

CUT TO

HARPER. He shakes his head.

> HARPER

She felt ... used. *(He spins the wheel of the car.)*

CUT TO

The car roaring into then out of another turn. Below, the mountain falls away sharply.

> HARPER'S VOICE (off-screen)

She said I only needed her when I was out of work. When I was on a case she claimed it was like being married to a madman.

CUT TO

HARPER and MIRANDA.

> MIRANDA

Was she right? Why didn't you get different work? What do you do this for?

> HARPER

I inherited the job from another man.

> MIRANDA

Your father?

CUT TO

HARPER. CLOSE UP.

> HARPER

Myself when I was younger. I used to think that evil was something you were born with, like a harelip. There were good people and bad people and all I had to do was walk around and judge. Except the more I walked, the more I found that everybody's harelipped.

CUT TO

HARPER and MIRANDA.

                              MIRANDA
You judge everybody?

                         (HARPER *nods*)
Me?

                       (HARPER *nods again*)
Well? What do you think of me?

                              HARPER
The evidence isn't in. Provisionally I'd say you had nearly everything and
could develop into nearly anything.

                              MIRANDA
Why "nearly"? What's my big deficiency?

CUT TO

HARPER.

                              HARPER
You need a tail on your kite — something to slow you down. So you'll stop
acting like a bitch in heat every time something pretty in pants wanders by.

CUT TO

MIRANDA. Stung.

                              MIRANDA
You judge yourself too?

                    HARPER'S VOICE (off-screen)
Why not?

                              MIRANDA
What about last night? With that woman?

CUT TO

HARPER.

                              HARPER
You think that bothers me? *(He gives a smile. He is very casual but intensely
aware of the scar on his right hand.)* Just feeding liquor to an alcoholic to get
information. *(he shrugs)* All part of the job. *(He looks at the speedometer. It
reads 70.)*

CUT TO

The road, starting to straighten a bit.

CUT TO

MIRANDA. *Still angry.*

> **MIRANDA**
> I drive fast when I'm bored—I pretend I'm on my way to meet something—something utterly new. All naked and bright—a moving target in the road. I've driven 105 along here.

> **HARPER'S VOICE** (off-screen)
> Trying to impress me?

> **MIRANDA**
> Do it, old man.

CUT TO

HARPER. *He shakes his head.*

CUT TO

MIRANDA.

> **MIRANDA**
> You're just as stuffy as Albert; same Victorian hang up. You still probably think that woman's place is in the home.

CUT TO

HARPER, CLOSE UP.

> **HARPER**
> *(evenly, emotionless)*
> Not my home.

FADE OUT

FADE IN ON

A SIGN BY A RATHER PRIMITIVE ROAD LEADING OFF THE HIGHWAY.

The sign reads: The Temple In The Clouds. HARPER'S CAR pauses momentarily at the sign, then turns off onto the primitive road.

DISSOLVE TO

THE CAR CLIMBING SOME MORE.

DISSOLVE TO

THE CAR REACHING THE CREST OF THE MOUNTAIN.

Blocking the car is a barbed wire fence and gate. HARPER gets out of the car, moves to the gate, looks down.

CUT TO

THE TEMPLE IN THE CLOUDS.

It is set in a saucer-shaped depression in the top of the mountain. It is a square, one-storied structure of white-painted stone and adobe built around a central court. There are a few outbuildings and from one of them, black smoke can be seen trailing from the chimney. No one is visible, yet from somewhere, a voice calls out.

> VOICE
> Have you come to seek salvation?

CUT TO

HARPER. Surprised. He looks down at the Temple again.

CUT TO

The temple. Slowly, something motionless begins to come alive. A man has been sitting on the roof of the building. He rises now. A great, white-haired prophet of a man, clad in the inevitable sheet. He has a rich, mellifluous voice and it rises and falls in almost poetic cadence.

CUT TO

MIRANDA, moving up behind HARPER.

> MIRANDA
> It's me, Claude; Miranda Sampson.

CUT TO

CLAUDE.

> CLAUDE
> Of course it is; the Sun God told me of your coming. *(he hurries down from the roof)*

CUT TO

HARPER and MIRANDA, as CLAUDE approaches.

> HARPER
> Ask him what the Sun God knows about your father.

> MIRANDA
> *(loudly, then softer as CLAUDE gets nearby)*
> This is a Mr. Harper; we're looking for Ralph. Has he been here?

> CLAUDE
> To my sorrow, no.
> *(HARPER has the barbed wire gate open by*

this time and turns to get into the car)
You may not bring the machine onto holy ground. Neither it nor you have been purified.

CUT TO

CLAUDE. Going on; passionately.

> **CLAUDE**
> I was a lost and evil man, blind-hearted and sinful. But then the sword of the blessed Sun slew the black beast of the flesh and I was purified.

CUT TO

The three of them.

> **HARPER**
> I'd like to look around.

> **CLAUDE**
> You'll be risking the wrath of the Sun God.

> **HARPER**
> *(moving through the gate)*
> I'm lionhearted.
> *(he moves away from CLAUDE;*
> *MIRANDA follows)*

DISSOLVE TO

HARPER and MIRANDA walking through the front door of the main building.

CUT TO

HARPER and MIRANDA coming through the door, looking around.

CUT TO

The living room. It is empty. THE CAMERA BEGINS TO MOVE out of the room, down a hall.

DISSOLVE TO

A small bedroom. It is empty, save for a couple of straw beds on the floor. THE CAMERA KEEPS MOVING.

DISSOLVE TO

Another bedroom, similarly furnished. THE CAMERA KEEPS MOVING.

DISSOLVE TO

HARPER and MIRANDA leaving the main house, going to the small building with th
smoking chimney. HARPER opens the door.

CUT TO

A Mexican girl. Startled, she glances up from stirring a large pot of beans.

CUT TO

HARPER, moving toward her. She retreats.

HARPER
Relax.
> *(She continues to retreat.*
> *He goes on but in Spanish)*
Relax. Have you seen a man called Sampson?

MEXICAN GIRL
> *(in Spanish)*
Nothing. No one.

HARPER
> *(in Spanish — taking picture from his pocket)*
This man.

MEXICAN GIRL
> *(in Spanish — shaking her head)*
No one. No one.

CUT TO

CLAUDE, suddenly in the doorway.

CLAUDE
I told you Sampson was not here.

CUT TO

The four of them.

CLAUDE
> *(in Spanish, to the girl)*
Go back to your labors.
> *(she hurries to the pot)*

HARPER
> *(indicating pot)*
Expecting the disciples for supper?

CLAUDE

Whoever comes to the Temple In The Clouds may be sure of some warm beans and a bed of straw. Where is the harm?
(HARPER shrugs, starts out of room)

CUT TO

HARPER moving outside, CLAUDE and MIRANDA following.

CLAUDE
(catches up to HARPER)

May we speak?

*(he steps close to HARPER, MIRANDA
moves on back toward the car)*

CUT TO

CLAUDE. EXTREME CLOSE UP.

CLAUDE
(softer, less flamboyant, terribly honest)

I know you think me a charlatan. I can only say that if you were correct, then death could not claim me too quickly. You obviously have some strong connection with the Sampsons; don't deride me to them, I beg you. The gift of this temple was the beginning of my life. I know to you I look ridiculous but I only want to increase the amount of love in this world. Where is the harm?

CUT TO

HARPER. CLAUDE's honesty has not gone unnoticed.

CUT TO

The two of them.

CLAUDE

You believe me?

HARPER

Maybe.

CLAUDE

That in itself is a victory. *(he turns, indicates roof)* I must return to contemplation. Please don't laugh.

HARPER
(not laughing)

I only laugh at what's funny. Stupidity usually. *(With a nod, he turns and starts to walk up to the car.)*

CUT TO

HARPER *walking along, his hands thrust roughly into his pockets. He kicks at a stone. Then he stops suddenly, staring down. He drops to his knees. Then—*

CUT TO

CLAUDE. *On the roof where we first saw him. The sound of laughter is heard. The sound bothers him.*

CUT TO

The ground in front of HARPER. *The pattern of a truck tire is plainly visible; the same pattern as that of the truck that tried running him down the night before.*

CUT TO

HARPER *staring down at the tire marks.*

CUT TO

CLOSE UP *of* HARPER'S *face. He cannot stop laughing. It builds and builds and—*

FADE OUT

FADE IN ON

HARPER'S CAR,

driving slowly up to the open gates of the Sampson estate.

CUT TO

Inside the car. MIRANDA *is asleep, her head on* HARPER'S *shoulder. Abruptly something catches his eye and he stops the car.*

CUT TO

The Sampson mailbox. A large white envelope is plainly visible.

DISSOLVE TO

The Sampson kitchen. HARPER *enters, carrying the envelope carefully, holding it in a handkerchief.* MIRANDA *follows.* MRS. KRONBERG, *in the kitchen, turns at their entrance.*

HARPER
*(putting the envelope on the kitchen
table, hurrying for a long knife)*

Mr. Graves here?

MRS. KRONBERG

He went back into Santa Barbara. But there's a deputy or something in the library.

HARPER

Get him.

(She goes. He carefully slits the envelope, then, using the handkerchief with quick skill, he removes and unfolds the envelope. Staring at it)

Bingo.

INSERT: *We do not see or take the time to read the entire note, but what we do see are large printed letters pasted almost childishly to a white piece of paper:*

DEPOZIT 250 THOU AT NINE TO NITE. ON GRASS. IN MIDDLE OF ROAD. SOUTH END OF HIGHWAY DIVIZHUN. OPPOZITE FRYER'S ROAD. ONE MILE SOUTH OF SANTA BARBARA. TOO BAD FOR SAMPSON IF YOU SCREW UP.

CUT TO

HARPER *and* MIRANDA *looking at the note.*

MIRANDA
(starting to panic)

What're you gonna do?

HARPER

Whatever I can.

MIRANDA

You better. *You better.*

(She goes. As she exits, DEPUTY SHERIFF enters.)

DEPUTY SHERIFF

What's going on?

HARPER

Nothing much. Kidnapping and extortion.

It might be well to note at this point that the DEPUTY SHERIFF is very young-looking. Fresh out of the police academy, he is not dumb. But he is infinitely inexperienced.

DEPUTY SHERIFF

That the note?

(He reaches for it. HARPER grabs his hands.)

HARPER

It's hard to do cutouts with gloves on.

DEPUTY SHERIFF
(disgusted with himself)
Fingerprints. Now I knew that, they taught that at the academy — what's the matter with me?

HARPER
You got an evidence case?

DEPUTY SHERIFF
Yessir. You want me to get it?

HARPER
Quick thinking.
(The DEPUTY SHERIFF *turns and dashes out of the room, passing* ALAN TAGGERT *who stands in the doorway.)*
The long arm of the law; good luck. *(he sits down wearily in a chair)* Hello, Alan.

TAGGERT
Miranda said kidnapping.
*(*HARPER *nods slowly)*
You must be beat; I slept all day and I'm still tired.

HARPER
(softly, rubbing his eyes)
You have a gun, Alan?

TAGGERT
A .32 I use for target practice.

HARPER
Better get it ready.

TAGGERT
Whatever you say, Lew.

CUT TO

HARPER. For just a moment, he closes his eyes, exhausted. Then he pushes himself to his feet and goes to the BUTLER'S PANTRY, *closes the door and dials.*

ALBERT'S VOICE (off-screen)
Yes?

HARPER
It's a snatch. The note's here. Get the Sheriff and pay me a visit.
(During the above, there may or may not have been a click on the line. If there was, HARPER *takes absolutely no notice of it.)*

ALBERT'S VOICE (off-screen)

Right. When's the money to be delivered?

HARPER

Nine tonight.

ALBERT'S VOICE (off-screen)

Nothing yet on the limousine but we're checking. *(A brief pause. Then—)* Lew? How do you suppose they knew the money was ready?

HARPER

Either they're gambling or they've got friends inside the castle. You think?

ALBERT'S VOICE (off-screen)

I think.

(ALBERT hangs up. HARPER does not.)

CAMERA MOVES IN ON HARPER. He stands still, holding the phone in his hands, waiting.

CAMERA CONTINUES TO MOVE IN, tighter as he stands there, biting his lip now, trying not to breathe. He waits and as the wait becomes increasingly unendurable, the biting of the lip becomes more and more agitated. Then—

—there is the faint metallic rustle of a receiver being replaced somewhere in the house.

At the sound, HARPER slams his own phone back in its cradle. There is a wild smile on his face as he rips the pantry door open and races into the empty kitchen and dashes out without a moment's hesitation.

CUT TO

The library. MRS. KRONBERG stands by the safe. On the desk is a phone. HARPER tears in—

HARPER

What are you doing in here?

MRS. KRONBERG
(nervous)

I thought someone — *(she gestures toward the safe)* — the money . . .

HARPER

How many extensions in the house?

MRS. KRONBERG

Five — six. Three up, three down.

HARPER
(turns away, angry)

Too damn many.

CUT TO

HARPER's FACE. CLOSE UP. The anger glows.

FADE OUT

FADE IN ON

HARPER, STANDING IN FRONT OF THE SAMPSON HOUSE.

It is dark. Two cars are pulling up to the front door. There is the start of fog and everything looks the least bit eerie. The lead car comes to a halt; it is ALBERT's Cadillac.

CUT TO

ALBERT getting out of his car. In the background, a uniformed man gets out of the second car

> **ALBERT**
> *(indicating the second car)*
I've brought Sheriff Spanner.

CUT TO

ALBERT moving to HARPER. Still in the background, the DEPUTY SHERIFF hurries up to the SHERIFF and gives him the ransom note.

> **ALBERT**
> *(almost in a whisper)*
I've been pondering all this and it's my opinion we give them the money clean and hope they come through with Sampson. Then, if they don't, we'll hunt them down. You think?

> **HARPER**
> *(nodding)*
I think.

> **SHERIFF SPANNER**
> *(A slight, intellectual looking man, he*
> *speaks in a beautifully modulated voice,*
> *like a radio announcer. Ransom note*
> *clearly held in his hands, he approaches.)*
This says to drop the money and drive north, meaning he'll be making his getaway south. I'll set up a roadblock down the highway —

CAMERA BEGINS TO MOVE around the three men as they stand in the gathering darkness.

> **ALBERT**
— you do and we can kiss good-bye to Sampson —

> **SHERIFF SPANNER**
— Whoever I catch, I guarantee I'll make him talk —

> HARPER

—if we obey everything there's better than a fifty-fifty chance Sampson won't come out alive—he might be able to identify the guy who picked him up at Burbank. That's bad enough but you'll make it worse if you trip the money man. You'll have a kidnapper in the county jail and Sampson with his throat cut somewhere—

> SHERIFF SPANNER
> *(to ALBERT)*

—who is this clown?

> HARPER

I'm a private detective but I used to be a sheriff until I passed my literacy test—

> ALBERT

—gentlemen, please—

> MRS. SAMPSON'S VOICE (off-screen)

Are you going to rescue my Ralph for me?

CUT TO

ELAINE SAMPSON in a wheelchair, framed in the front door to the house. Even though it is not cold, she has a heavy coat thrown across her shoulders.

CUT TO

ALBERT, going to her.

> ALBERT

Now Elaine, I don't want you to worry.

> MRS. SAMPSON

How can I worry with men like you on the job?

CUT TO

HARPER and SHERIFF.

> SHERIFF
> *(softly)*

That's a brave woman.

CUT TO

HARPER. Nodding, deadpan.

> HARPER

Gutty as hell.

DISSOLVE TO

THE LIBRARY.

The safe is open and ALBERT is taking the last of the money out, putting it into a plain black satchel.

ALBERT

I do hope we're right about no road-blocks. *(He closes the safe, then zips the satchel shut.)* What are you going to be doing while I make the deposit?

HARPER

Wait a little south of you, see what I can see.

(ALBERT nods, takes the satchel.
They start out of the room.)

CUT TO

HARPER and ALBERT crossing the foyer and going out the front door.

CUT TO

HARPER and ALBERT coming out of the front door. ALBERT stops, confused.

CUT TO

ALAN TAGGERT standing by ALBERT's Cadillac. He is all chipper and smiling and magnificently attired in an obviously imported trench coat, collar up. He twirls a pistol around his index finger.

TAGGERT
(throwing off a sharp salute)

Private Taggert ready for duty sir.

CUT TO

HARPER and ALBERT.

HARPER

I want Alan to go with you.

ALBERT
(smiling at TAGGERT, whispering to HARPER)

Why?

HARPER

He can use a gun; you might need him.

CUT TO

ALBERT. He sighs enormously, then nods his head.

ALBERT

God bless us, every one.

DISSOLVE TO

HARPER, SITTING IN HIS DARKENED CAR BY THE SIDE OF A DIVIDED HIGHWAY.

The fog is worse now, coming in patches. The car clock reads nine.

CUT TO

The highway. It is empty . . .

CUT TO

HARPER. He fondles the ignition key nervously.

CUT TO

The highway. Still empty.

CUT TO

HARPER. He turns on the ignition. The car clock reads a little bit after nine.

CUT TO

The highway. A great black limousine roars out of the fog, passes by and then is quickly lost in the fog again.

CUT TO

HARPER. He jams his car forward after the limousine, turning onto the highway. He drives for just a moment. Then there comes the sound of the squealing of tires as if a car has made a sudden turn.

CUT TO

HARPER's car, driving into the fog.

CUT TO

HARPER, in his car, as he comes to a side road veering off the highway. He hesitates, slowing the car. Then there are three muffled sounds coming right after each other: the screech of brakes, the sound of a gunshot, the roar of a car motor. They all emanate from a slight distance up the side road and HARPER turns his car onto it and starts to drive when —

CUT TO

A blinding pair of lights as another car roars down at HARPER.

CUT TO

HARPER's car, pulling over.

CUT TO

HARPER in his car, watching as we —

CUT TO

A WHITE CONVERTIBLE, *roaring down the side road and turning onto the highway, getting lost in the fog. The top is covered and it is impossible to see who is driving.*

CUT TO

HARPER's car moving forward, then stopping again.

CUT TO

HARPER, getting out of his car, gun in hand. He peers ahead through the fog.

CUT TO

The black limousine, half off the side road.

CUT TO

HARPER. Moving quietly, he approaches it from the rear, slowly moves around the car, gun in position.

CUT TO

A dead face. It belongs to the driver of the limousine and it is the same man that the night before tried killing HARPER *with the truck. There is a bullet hole above his left ear. The eyes are open.*

CUT TO

HARPER reacting to the sight. He finds it repellent and it shows. He takes a breath, opens the front door.

CUT TO

The body starting to topple out.

CUT TO

HARPER, shoving it back into an upright position. With his free hand, he grabs the ignition keys, walks to the trunk.

CUT TO

The trunk opening. It is empty. The door slams shut.

CUT TO

HARPER, moving to the side of the car away from the driver. He opens the door, looks briefly in the back, then checks the glove compartment. It is empty. Then, with a grimace, he begins going through the pockets of the corpse. The corpse is clad in a windbreaker and jeans. The eyes are still open. HARPER reaches into a pants pocket.

CUT TO

HARPER'S HAND. It holds some change and a book of matches on which is visible: "THE CORNER. The place in Buena Vista."

CUT TO

HARPER shoving the stuff back into the pocket, starting to reach into another as —

> **ALBERT'S VOICE** (off-screen)
> *(in the distance, calling out)*

Lew. *Lew.*

> **HARPER**
> *(going on with what he's doing, shouting back)*

Up here!

CUT TO

HARPER'S HAND. It holds a comb and a handkerchief.

CUT TO

HARPER, shoving the stuff back into the pocket as car lights pierce the fog. HARPER tries reaching across the corpse to get at the far pockets but it brings him into too close contact with the body so he quickly gets out of the car and starts around it.

CUT TO

ALBERT and TAGGERT getting out of their car as HARPER crosses around the limousine. The body in the limousine is invisible to them at this point.

> **ALBERT**

This is the car that picked up the money, I'm positive. A man grabbed it as soon as we'd tossed it out—

> **TAGGERT**
> *(excited)*

— I wanted to take off after him but old Al here, he didn't see it my way. If I'd been driving we'd have had him by now.

> **HARPER**
> *(opening the car door—again the body starts
> to topple and again HARPER grabs it)*

You really think so?

CUT TO

ALBERT and TAGGERT. ALBERT is horrified at the dead, staring face but TAGGERT is even more upset. The excitement drains from his features and, obviously about to be sick, he turns and hurries into the darkness.

> **ALBERT**
> Who killed him?

> **HARPER**
> Someone in a white convertible. *(reaching into a pocket while supporting the corpse with his free hand)* The money's gone.

INSERT: HARPER'S HAND. It contains a wallet. HARPER examines it briefly. It contains a few small bills, nothing else. During this —

> **HARPER'S VOICE** (off-screen)
> It was a heist or his partners double-crossed him. Either way, it's bad for Sampson.

CUT TO

ALBERT. He is standing close to HARPER now but his back is turned to him. He maintains that position for the rest of the scene, looking away.

> **ALBERT**
> OK. Now, we take the wraps off the case, call in the police, post a reward, agreed?

> **HARPER**
> Agreed. *(he is at the last pocket now)* Get as many men on it as you can.

INSERT: HARPER's HAND. It contains another book of matches from "THE CORNER. The Place in Buena Vista" and a few cigarettes wrapped in brown paper.

> **HARPER'S VOICE** (off-screen)
> Marijuana; why not.

CUT TO

HARPER, shoving the stuff back into the pockets, propping the body up behind the wheel, closing the door. ALBERT still looks away.

> **HARPER**
> Call Sheriff Spanner first. He won't be able to do much but it's a nice gesture.

> **ALBERT**
> Where are you going?

HARPER

On a wild goose chase. Things look so bad for Sampson now I might as well. *(he raises his hands up high, fingers spread wide)* All the perfumes in Arabia, eh Albert?

CUT TO

A NEON SIGN FLASHING IN THE NIGHT: "THE CORNER" ON AND OFF, ON AND OFF.

CUT TO

HARPER, *walking in the front door of "The Corner," letting the door shut behind him. There is the sound of band music.* HARPER *looks around.*

CUT TO

Some middle-aged people twisting in front of a glowing jukebox.

CUT TO

HARPER, *still standing by the door, glancing around as if looking for somebody. A waitress comes up to him. She, like the rest of the place, is a bit faded.*

WAITRESS

Like a nice table?

HARPER
*(he speaks throughout this from
the side of his mouth and very nervously, almost as if he had facial tics)*
Later, maybe. You can help me though. I'm lookin' for a guy. I met him at the ball park. He said he'd meet me here only I don't see him.

WAITRESS

What's his name?

HARPER

Sees that's the trouble: I don't know it. I owe him some loot on a bet's the thing. He's maybe 40, very thin, pale. Wears a windbreaker and Levis. Drives a blue truck.

WAITRESS
(vaguely suspicious; not cordial)
Come again on why you wanna find him?

HARPER

I owe him money on a bet.

WAITRESS

An' you're just eaten up with honesty, is that it?

HARPER
You know what happens to bookies that don't pay off?

WAITRESS
(pleased with herself)
I knew you was a bookie the minute you come in.

HARPER
No kiddin'?

CUT TO

WAITRESS. She is smiling now, the vague suspicions gone.

WAITRESS
You been waitin' tables as long as I have, you get to know the types.

CUT TO

HARPER. He is smiling too.

HARPER
I didn't know I was that obvious.

CUT TO

The two of them.

WAITRESS
Eddie's who you want. Eddie somebody. Comes in here a lot for coffee.
Ain't been here for two, three nights now. Three nights it was; I remember 'cause he wanted to make a long distance call and the boss didn't like
that 'cause sometimes he gets stung when it's over three minutes so Eddie
made it collect. I don't know where to. How much you owe Eddie?

HARPER
(ignoring the question)
Where's the boss?

WAITRESS
Behind the bar.

CUT TO

BARTENDER. He is very old. HARPER walks up and sits.

HARPER
Bottle-a-beer.
(the BARTENDER nods, goes to get one)
I'm looking for a guy called Eddie. See, I owe him a little money. He phoned
me long distance from here three nights ago.

> BARTENDER

You from Las Vegas?

> HARPER
> *(nods)*

Just came from there.

> BARTENDER
> *(putting a bottle of beer and a glass on the bar)*

I wouldda guessed you were from Vegas.

> HARPER
> *(handing over money)*

You're physic.

> BARTENDER

Psychic you mean.

> HARPER

Know where Eddie lives?
> *(BARTENDER takes the money, shakes his head)*

Then I guess I'll have to wait until he gets here.

CUT TO

HARPER, moving across the bar. All the tables are empty but he keeps moving until he gets to the window and looks out into the darkness.

CUT TO

The parking lot, which is what HARPER sees outside the window.

CUT TO

HARPER nodding, sitting down, pouring himself a glass of beer.

DISSOLVE TO

HARPER AT THE TABLE. THE BEER BOTTLE IS EMPTY.

He abruptly sits up, leans forward, looks out the window.

> HARPER

Nuts!

CUT TO

The parking lot. The DEPUTY SHERIFF who forgot about the fingerprints is getting out of his police car.

CUT TO

HARPER, getting hurriedly up from the table, looking around. Then he begins to move quickly toward the dancers.

CUT TO

A door with GENTLEMEN printed on it. HARPER opens the door, walks inside.

CUT TO

HARPER coming into the men's room. It is clean, but it is still a men's room. There is a phone high on one wall. HARPER takes it all in.

HARPER

Swell.

HARPER begins to pace the room. Then he stares at the phone a moment, reaches into his pocket for a handful of change.

CUT TO

SUSAN HARPER lying in bed. She wears a negligee and is reading a book, her glasses perched on the end of her nose. She is also eating candy — there is a huge box of it on her bedtable. If it has not been mentioned thus far, it should be noted that she is possessed of a splendid body. The telephone rings as she plops a chocolate into her mouth.

SUSAN
(picking up the phone)

Hello?

HARPER'S VOICE (off-screen)
(it is very breathy and excited and sounds not at all like his regular speaking voice)

Mrs. Harper?

SUSAN

Yes.

HARPER'S VOICE (off-screen)

Mrs. Lewis Harper?

SUSAN

That's right...

HARPER'S VOICE (off-screen)

Oh, thank heavens. You see, we picked your name from this enormous drum full of names only you had to be there to win, and you are, so you have.

SUSAN

Win?

HARPER'S VOICE (off-screen)

Yes, yes — six one hour frug lessons absolutely free. I'm Austin Marmaduke of the Austin Marmaduke Center for Ballroom Education. We're just off Wilshire and —

SUSAN

— I don't want them —

HARPER'S VOICE (off-screen)

— oh, of course you do, dear lady. Just think of the confidence you'll have the next time you and your husband go stepping. Think how proud and happy you'll feel, how endlessly feminine.

SUSAN
*(She has whipped her glasses off and
dropped them on the bed beside her. Now,
with the phone tucked under her chin, she
reaches for and manages to light a cigarette.)*
My husband is dead.

HARPER'S VOICE (off-screen)

Of course I didn't know; that's too bad —

SUSAN

— no, as a matter of fact you're wrong. His death did nothing but serve the cause of mankind. *(beginning to enjoy herself)* He was a fool, a sadist, a pathological pervert —

CUT TO

HARPER, listening to the insults.

HARPER

— I'm sure you don't mean —

SUSAN'S VOICE (off-screen)

— I do mean. He was grotesque in all ways. Can a soul be atrocious? His was. He was a degenerate's degenerate —

HARPER is more than a little hot under the collar.

HARPER

— I almost feel compelled to defend him —

CUT TO

SUSAN. She is really enjoying herself now.

SUSAN

— you won't believe this, Mr. Marmaduke, but he used to call me up on the phone sometimes, pretending to be other people. He actually thought it was funny.

CUT TO

HARPER.

> **HARPER**
> I'm hiding from a moron cop in a men's room in Buena Vista. That *is* funny.
> *(There comes the sound of SUSAN's laughter.)*

> **SUSAN'S VOICE** (off-screen)
> You're right. *(She laughs a little more, then pauses. When she speaks again, her voice is warm, soft, intensely personal.)* Lew?

> **HARPER**
> Yes, Susan.

> **SUSAN'S VOICE** (off-screen)
> Lew?

> **HARPER**
> What is it?

CUT TO

SUSAN. *Almost a whisper.*

> **SUSAN**
> Go to hell, Lew.

> **HARPER'S VOICE** (off-screen)
> Don't hang up—

> **SUSAN**
> —I never could resist you. *(She hangs up, puts out the cigarette, picks up her glasses and book. Then after a moment, she takes her glasses off again and stares at the silent phone.)*

CUT TO

HARPER. *He slowly hangs up. Then he almost smiles.*

> **HARPER**
> She loves me.

> **DEPUTY SHERIFF'S VOICE** (off-screen)
> Put 'em up!

HARPER
(*sighs wearily, turns to face other man*)

Put what up?

DEPUTY SHERIFF
(*he is very nervous*)

Your hands, your hands.

HARPER
(*His hands are not raised. Shaking his head*)

I just couldn't.

DEPUTY SHERIFF
(*his gun is very much on* HARPER)

How'd you get here?

HARPER

Same way you did — I found the matches in Eddie's pocket.

DEPUTY SHERIFF

How'd you know his name was Eddie?

HARPER

You're as alert as they come, you know that? The waitress told me. Now why don't you bug out?

DEPUTY SHERIFF

If anybody's leaving, you are. I'm waiting here. Sheriff said to stay on the job.

HARPER
(*starting to go to door*)

Then we're all safe.

DEPUTY SHERIFF

Just hold on. The bartender said this Eddie called you long distance in Las Vegas.

HARPER

I was trying to pump the bartender, get it? It was a gag.

DEPUTY SHERIFF

What'd you find out?

HARPER

That three nights ago Eddie phoned Las Vegas. Sampson was in Vegas three nights ago.

CUT TO

DEPUTY SHERIFF. Really excited now.

DEPUTY SHERIFF

Hey — it all fits.

CUT TO

HARPER. A look of pure astonishment on his face.

HARPER

Hey — you're right.

CUT TO

The two of them. HARPER moves to the other man, claps him on the back.

HARPER

Thanks for pointing it out to me.

CUT TO

The DEPUTY SHERIFF. He just looks at HARPER.

FADE OUT

FADE IN ON

THE NEON SIGN OF "THE CORNER" AS SEEN FROM SOME DISTANCE.

CUT TO

HARPER, sitting alone in his car, watching the neon sign. He yawns, rubs his eyes, then abruptly stops.

CUT TO

A blue truck pulling into the parking lot of "The Corner." It has a covered cab.

CUT TO

HARPER, leaning forward, peering out.

CUT TO

PUDDLER, getting out of the blue truck. He worriedly looks around, sees the DEPUTY SHERIFF's police car.

CUT TO

PUDDLER, running back to the truck, getting in, driving off with a roar. As he moves onto highway and picks up speed, a car pulls out and begins to follow him. The car is HARPER's.

CUT TO

The truck roaring down the highway. A good distance behind comes Harper.

CUT TO

The truck turning off the highway onto a less decent road. Harper follows.

DISSOLVE TO

The truck turning off the second road onto a third. This road is much narrower and rises sharply. There is no other traffic. HARPER's car follows along but as he makes the turn, he douses his headlights.

CUT TO

The truck, continuing to move upwards along the narrow road.

CUT TO

HARPER, squinting out through the windshield as he follows the truck upwards. After a moment, he looks up.

CUT TO

The moon, emerging from behind some thickening clouds.

CUT TO

The truck moving slowly up the mountain road.

CUT TO

HARPER, leaning forward. Then abruptly, he twists the wheel to the right.

CUT TO

The edge of the road. Below is a sickening dropoff. HARPER's car rims the edge, then swerves back onto the road.

CUT TO

HARPER, starting to sweat.

CUT TO

A LONG LONG SHOT *from above. The truck, lights on, cuts through the dark night. Trailing safely behind it comes the shadow of a car.*

CUT TO

PUDDLER, driving the truck, spinning the wheel at a particularly sharp curve.

CUT TO

HARPER, *sweating more now, driving.*

CUT TO

The moon, skimming through clouds.

CUT TO

HARPER, *braking and spinning the wheel as he comes to the same curve.*

CUT TO

HARPER'S CAR, *rimming the edge of the highway again and again, below is the sickening dropoff.*

CUT TO

HARPER, *breathing a little heavily, sweating profusely now, continuing to drive.*

DISSOLVE TO

A SERIES OF SHOTS,

one melding into the next, of hairpin turns and below, the drop into space as HARPER *continues to drive through the darkness. The screech of brakes and of wheels spinning accompanies this, adding to the feeling of vertigo. Through all the shots,* HARPER'S *eyes are visible, burning bright . . .*

FADE OUT

FADE IN ON

HARPER, CROUCHED BESIDE HIS CAR,

staring down at the Temple In The Clouds. The blue truck is parked below, its back door open. There is no sound from below. HARPER *moves to the barbed wire gate, opens it softly.*

CUT TO

HARPER, *moving quietly toward the truck.*

CUT TO

The rear of the truck. It is empty. There is a wooden bench padded with burlap along each side.

CUT TO

HARPER, *staring at the inside of the truck. Then there is the sound of a door creaking open.* HARPER *turns.*

CUT TO

CLAUDE, *dressed as before, coming out of the Temple.* HARPER *moves toward him.*

CLAUDE
(seeing him)

What are you doing here?

HARPER

I got the call; I've been converted.

CLAUDE

Is there no end to your sacrilege?

HARPER
(his gun in his hand — to PUDDLER, who
stands in the doorway CLAUDE came out of)

Stay right there.
(PUDDLER starts to run toward
HARPER. HARPER FIRES.)

CUT TO

The bullet kicking up dust at PUDDLER's feet.

CUT TO

The three of them.

HARPER

Please, don't make any trouble.
(PUDDLER stops dead. HARPER is watching
him as CLAUDE jumps at HARPER. HARPER
moves a step closer, then delivers a vicious
swipe with his elbow into CLAUDE's stomach.
CLAUDE gasps and drops to the ground)

I said please. Now where is Sampson?

CUT TO

CLAUDE, on the ground. He raises his arms to the sky and begins chanting in Spanish.

CUT TO

A door across the court, springing open as if it knew Spanish.

CUT TO

HARPER, watching.

CUT TO

The open door. A tiny, half-naked Mexican man appears in the doorway. CLAUDE's wild chanting continues. Another Mexican man appears. Another. Now there are half a dozen, now ten. Now more than a dozen. Now close to twenty. CLAUDE's chanting goes up in pitch and the tiny Mexican men begin moving through the darkness. They are jammed together in a clump and might be some kind of animal.

CUT TO

HARPER, watching, gun in hand, as the MEXICANS come closer to him.

> **HARPER**
> *(to CLAUDE)*
>
> Tell them to get back!

> **CLAUDE**
> *(in English — his voice even*
> *now, the phony sing-song gone)*
> On the contrary, Mr. Harper. *(And then he is screaming in Spanish —)*
> Attack! Attack! Attack!

CUT TO

HARPER. Moving back.

> **HARPER**
> *(to CLAUDE)*
>
> They'll die. Tell them!

> **CLAUDE**
> *(still on his knees — in English)*
> Shoot unarmed men? I don't think so, Mr. Harper,

CUT TO

HARPER and the MEXICANS. For a moment, no one moves. Then the MEXICANS charge. HARPER swings out with his gun, clubs one, another, another. But they keep coming, surrounding him, grabbing at him and no matter how hard he fights, how many he hits, more of them keep coming and coming and finally, inevitably, he disappears in their midst, falling before their kicking feet, their clubbing arms . . .

FADE OUT

FADE IN ON

HARPER, LYING IN A DARK ROOM IN THE TEMPLE.

He is severely bound, his hands tied behind his back, his feet tied together too.

CUT TO

A hand holding a knife. The hand slices through the darkness, rests for a moment on the ropes tying HARPER's feet, then cuts through them.

PULL BACK TO REVEAL

DWIGHT TROY, *immaculate as always. He rises, goes to the wall, turns on the light.*

> **TROY**
>
> Do get up, old stick.

> **HARPER**
> *(not moving)*
>
> I like it here.

> **TROY**
> *(prodding HARPER with the knife)*
>
> You mustn't give way to the sulks, Mr. Harper. Come, come.

> **HARPER**
> *(forcing himself up to his knees)*
>
> I'm shocked, Troy—a man of your eminence involved in something as seamy as smuggling in immigrant labor.

> **TROY**
>
> You couldn't be more right, you know; it is beneath me. But it pays so well. The poor idiots pay me to smuggle them in. They're wonderfully cheap workers so once I've got them it's no problem to dispose of them to farm owners and ranchers and they pay me too. It's all disgustingly lucrative but as you've suggested, hardly enriching to the soul.

CUT TO

TROY. CLOSE UP.

> **TROY**
> *(as charming as ever)*
>
> What about your soul, Mr. Harper?

CUT TO

The two of them. HARPER's on his feet.

> **HARPER**
>
> It'll pay you to let me go.

> **TROY**
>
> You're rather low on bargaining power, aren't you, old stick?

> **HARPER**
>
> Not necessarily. Where's Sampson?

> **TROY**
> *(absolutely honest)*
>
> Ralph Sampson? Dear boy, how should I know?

> **HARPER**

And the 500 thousand?

> **TROY**
> *(he takes out his gun)*

No more riddles, old stick.

> **HARPER**
> *(angry)*

Your driver kidnapped Sampson two days ago. Tonight he picked up a half
million in ransom money —

> **TROY**
> *(amused)*

— Eddie? He hasn't the brains.

> **HARPER**

Enough brains for a fall guy. He's dead and whoever killed him got the
money.

> **TROY**

And you suspect me, old stick?

> **HARPER**

I do if you drive a white convertible.

CUT TO

TROY. For the first time, the elegance is gone. Stunned, he stands still for a moment. In
CLOSE UP, he begins to shout.

> **TROY**

CLAUDE! PUDDLER!

CUT TO

TROY, in a fury now, starting to pace the room.

> **TROY**
> *(big)*

I am surrounded by knaves and fools.
> *(CLAUDE and PUDDLER hurry into doorway)*

We're leaving the temple. Claude — take our latest truckload to that ranch
in Bakersfield. Get the cash, then lose the truck. Meet me at my place afterwards.
> *(CLAUDE goes)*

Puddler, was Betty at the club tonight?

> **PUDDLER**

No sir.

TROY

Is she still driving the same car?

PUDDLER

The convertible? Yessir.

TROY
(he is still moving back
and forth across the room)
Is she still living in the same place?

PUDDLER
(shakes his head)
She moved to some cabin somewhere a couple of weeks ago.

TROY

Then I shall have to find that cabin, Puddler; no matter what the cost. I want you to take Mr. Harper to the pier. Keep him there until you hear from me.
(PUDDLER goes to HARPER,
grabs him roughly)
Knaves and fools who can't keep out of trouble. Well, we'll show them trouble, won't we, Puddler.

CUT TO

PUDDLER. CLOSE UP. *His moronic face manages to make a smile. The effect is not remotely pleasant.*

FADE OUT

FADE IN ON

A LONG PIER BUILT OUT OVER THE OCEAN. OIL DERRICKS IN THE SKYLINE. THE SOUND OF THE OCEAN.

CUT TO

HARPER's *car driving up to the start of the pier.* PUDDLER *is driving. He opens the car door, carefully puts* HARPER's *ignition key in his pocket, and gets out. Then he reaches in for* HARPER *who is wedged, arms tied behind his back, on the floor of the back seat. Roughly,* PUDDLER *jerks* HARPER *free of the car and puts him on his feet.*

CUT TO

PUDDLER *slamming the car doors, pushing* HARPER *out along the pier.* HARPER, *terribly stiff, does what he can to get the kinks out.*

CUT TO

HARPER, *peering through the darkness in the direction he will be walking.*

CUT TO

The far end of the pier. There is a large oil pump rising and falling like a mechanical teeter-totter. Beside the pump is a tool shed. Nothing but ocean beyond.

CUT TO

PUDDLER, shoving HARPER along. Below them, black water gleams through the planks of the walk.

CUT TO

A LONG SHOT of the two dark figures moving through the dark night toward the end of the almost endless pier.

CUT TO

The shed at the end of the pier. PUDDLER takes out a key, opens it, shoves HARPER inside.

CUT TO

Inside the shed. It is dark. Then PUDDLER lights a lantern. Throughout the following, the shed is never bright, always shadowy. There is a bench along one wall. At the end of the bench is a vise. Beside the vise are a few tools: pincers, wrenches of various sizes, a dull, rusty file. HARPER notices these. PUDDLER shoves HARPER toward the bench.

PUDDLER
Make yourself t' home. *(He moves to close the door of shed.)*

HARPER
Leave it open. I need the air; you stink.

CUT TO

PUDDLER. He looks at HARPER a moment.

CUT TO

The two of them. PUDDLER backhands HARPER viciously across the mouth, spinning HARPER into the wall. HARPER's mouth begins to bleed.

CUT TO

HARPER. CLOSE UP. Eyes bright.

HARPER
Your brains are rotting and I can smell it.

CUT TO

PUDDLER. He looks at HARPER, a bit confused.

CUT TO

The two of them. PUDDLER backhands HARPER again across the mouth. Again HARPER spins against the wall. This time he loses balance and slips to his knees.

> **PUDDLER**
> I c'n give it more'n you c'n take it.

> **HARPER**
> *(smiles)*
> Can you? We both know what you're afraid of, don't we, Puddler?

> **PUDDLER**
> What?

> **HARPER**
> Of everything. Mostly me.

PUDDLER laughs, then goes to close the door of the shed. The minute his back is turned, HARPER simultaneously makes a noise with his feet and screams loudly. PUDDLER jumps, frightened, whirling around.

> **HARPER**
> *(now he is laughing)*
> I rest my case.

CUT TO

PUDDLER. He closes the door. Then, angry, he begins to whisper.

> **PUDDLER**
> They got a 'spression. Kill the body an' the head dies. You ever hear that?

PUDDLER begins slowly to walk toward HARPER.

CUT TO

HARPER, watching him come.

CUT TO

The two of them. PUDDLER grabs HARPER, holds him with his left hand.

> **PUDDLER**
> *(digging his right hand viciously
> into the pit of HARPER's stomach)*
> Kill—
> *(HARPER gasps. PUDDLER swings again.)*
> —the *body*—
> *(Again HARPER gasps and his knees buckle.
> PUDDLER holds him upright with his left*

> > *hand, swings his right a third time.)*

—an' the *head*—

> > *(PUDDLER pauses for just a mo-*
> > *ment. Then he swings a final terrible*
> > *punch at HARPER's stomach.)*

—*dies.*

> > *(He abruptly releases his grip with his left*
> > *hand and HARPER, gasping, falls to his knees.)*

CUT TO

HARPER. On the floor, managing to stay on his knees, bent over, the side of his bleeding face against the cold wooden floor.

> > > > **HARPER**
> > > > *(gasping)*

You're...afraid of...me.

CUT TO

PUDDLER, standing over him.

> > > > **PUDDLER**

Like hell.

CUT TO

HARPER, as before.

> > > > **HARPER**

Untie me then...untie me and I'll tear your head off.

CUT TO

PUDDLER. He starts to really laugh.

> > > > **PUDDLER**

Now I get it. Yer tryin' t' get me t' untie you so's you can trick me.

CUT TO

HARPER. Starting to rise.

> > > > **HARPER**

You smelly, feeble minded—

CUT TO

The two of them. HARPER is still on his knees when PUDDLER swings. The punch lands flush on HARPER's mouth. He falls.

> PUDDLER
> *(laughing)*

—yer tryin' to trick me.

CUT TO

HARPER. *He slowly starts to rise.*

CUT TO

The two of them. PUDDLER *all but leaps forwards, grabs* HARPER, *slams him in the face again, knocking him against the wall. Again* HARPER *falls.*

> PUDDLER

Tryin' to trick Puddler. *(he laughs)*

CUT TO

HARPER. *More slowly, he rises. When he gets to his knees,* PUDDLER *kicks him in the stomach.* HARPER *gasps, doubles up, falls sideways to the floor.*

CUT TO

The two of them.

> PUDDLER

You can't trick Puddler.
> *(he reaches down, grabs* HARPER,
> *lifts him to his feet)*

> HARPER
> *(he can hardly talk)*

You fish-eyed faggot—

PUDDLER *brings his leg up, knees* HARPER *in the stomach. As* HARPER *doubles over,* PUDDLER *clasps his hands, smashes them down on the back of* HARPER's *neck.* HARPER *crumbles, lies on the floor face down.* PUDDLER *grabs into one of his pockets, brings out a clasp knife, opens it and roughly cuts through* HARPER's *bonds.*

> PUDDLER

OK. Trick me.
> *(*HARPER *barely moves.* PUDDLER
> *starts to laugh.)*

Trick me!
> *(*HARPER *forces himself up onto all fours.*
> *He crawls to the bench to help himself up.*
> *Before he reaches the bench,* PUDDLER *softly*
> *prods* HARPER *on the shoulder with his foot.*

> HARPER *topples over sideways, immediately*
> *forces himself to all fours again.)*

I'm waitin'.

CUT TO

HARPER, *crawling to the bench.*

CUT TO

The bench. There are, as before, tools beside a vise: wrenches, pincers, a rusty file.

CUT TO

PUDDLER. *He is watching from across the shed as* HARPER *manages to crawl to the bench and start to force himself up.*

PUDDLER
I'm really quakin' in my boots.

CUT TO

HARPER, *pushing himself to his feet, using the bench for support.*

CUT TO

The bench. Everything is as before except the file is gone.

CUT TO

PUDDLER *watching as* HARPER *finally makes it to his feet.* HARPER *holds to the wall for support. Then he lets go, stands wavering on his own two feet.*

PUDDLER
You gonna tear my head off now?

CUT TO

The two of them. HARPER *staggers across the shed toward* PUDDLER *who moves to meet him.* PUDDLER *grabs* HARPER *in a bear hug, lifts him off the ground.*

CUT TO

HARPER *and* PUDDLER *in* CLOSE UP. HARPER, *the file gripped in one hand, rakes it hard across* PUDDLER's *face, cutting from temple to temple.* PUDDLER SCREAMS, *shoves* HARPER *away.*

CUT TO

PUDDLER. CLOSE UP. *For a moment he just stands there, blanking. Then a great red curtain of blood descends across his face and be is momentarily blind.*

PUDDLER
(as his hands fly to his face)

You ... tricked me ...

CUT TO

The two of them. HARPER lunges forward, throws a punch at PUDDLER's stomach. PUDDLER drops his bloody hands. HARPER slams him in the face and PUDDLER staggers back and falls.

CUT TO

PUDDLER, scrambling to his feet. The blood still flows down across his face. He lunges toward HARPER who steps aside, then throws a punch as PUDDLER goes by. PUDDLER falls again, gets to his feet. He rushes at HARPER and this time grabs him. His arms go around HARPER's back.

CUT TO

HARPER, caught, hitting down at PUDDLER's face.

CUT TO

The two of them. PUDDLER lunges like a bull toward the wall of the shed. He smashes HARPER into the wall, then backs away as HARPER continues to hit him. Again PUDDLER charges blindly forward. This time their bodies smash into the door of the shed. The door splinters before the force of their bodies.

CUT TO

The pier outside the shed as the door splinters. The two men come spilling out onto the pier. As they fall, HARPER tries to scramble away but PUDDLER holds on to him, his arms still circling HARPER's body. PUDDLER drags them both to their feet. Then he staggers forward. HARPER smashes harder and harder at his face and finally PUDDLER is forced to let him go. HARPER, loose, tries to move but PUDDLER CHARGES AGAIN. He grabs HARPER blindly and they begin to fall.

CUT TO

The two bodies in midair, toppling from the edge of the pier toward the black water below. There is a tremendous splash as they hit. Then they are both gone. Slowly, the water begins to smooth over. CAMERA HOLDS ON the black water.

DISSOLVE TO

HARPER, struggling to surface. He swims to ladder of pier, grabs it.

HARPER

Puddler? Puddler? I didn't mean for you to drown. Puddler? *(he dives under water, comes up a little later)* I can't see anything down there, Puddler. I didn't mean for you to drown. Puddler?

.

CUT TO

HARPER, gripping the ladder. His body starts to shiver from the cold. Then he begins to climb the ladder.

CUT TO

HARPER staggering to his car, opening the door.

CUT TO

The ignition of the car. There is no key.

CUT TO

HARPER. He scrambles around the pier, finds a piece of copper wire attached to a pole holding a tarpaulin. He rips it free.

CUT TO

HARPER, crouched under the wheel of the car, wiring ignition terminals beneath the dash.

HARPER
(muttering as he works at the wiring)

I didn't mean for you to drown. I didn't mean for you to drown.

His body is shaking terribly.

FADE OUT

In the ensuing darkness there is the sound of someone knocking wildly on a door.

FADE IN ON

SUSAN HARPER AS SHE SWITCHES ON THE LAMP BESIDE HER BED.

The knocking is louder now. She gropes for her glasses, gets them and, clad in her negligee, gets out of bed.

CUT TO

SUSAN, crossing from the bedroom of her apartment and entering the living room. The living room is dark, the only light coming from the bed lamp in the next room. As she approaches the door —

SUSAN

Who is it?

HARPER'S VOICE (off-screen)

Me.

SUSAN

What do you want?

HARPER'S VOICE (off-screen)
(the knocking becomes louder, more urgent)

Susan—

(SUSAN moves forward, opens the door
to the limit of the chain latch)

CUT TO

HARPER, *as seen through the slit in the door. His clothes are dry and crumpled. His hair goes in all directions. His face shows the effect of the battle with* PUDDLER. *He looks wild.*

CUT TO

SUSAN. *She unhooks the chain lock, opens the door.*

SUSAN

What happened?

HARPER
(pushing into the room, closing the door)

I killed someone, I drowned him and I'm cold.

(He moves toward her. She retreats a step.)

CUT TO

A SHOT FROM ABOVE *them in the darkened room. For the remainder of the scene, the* CAMERA *stays above them, looking down at them, eavesdropping. The only light still comes from the lamp in the next room.* HARPER *and* SUSAN *talk very softly and all the dialogue is overlapping; they know each other very well. As they move in the darkened room, the* CAMERA *moves above them, circling, as if this were a prize fight and we were watching the fighters down below.*

SUSAN

Why'd you come here—?

HARPER

—I'm cold, Susan—

SUSAN

—*why did you come here*—?

HARPER

—you know why—

SUSAN

—I can't help you—

HARPER
(reaching for her)

—yes—

SUSAN
(retreating)

—we're not going to get involved again—

HARPER

—we *are* involved—

SUSAN

—were. We've been there. It didn't work—

HARPER

—I need you—

SUSAN

—now you do; what about later—?

HARPER

—later too—

SUSAN

—like hell; you'll take off—

HARPER

—no—

SUSAN

—yes; on whatever lousy case you're on—

HARPER

—I'm through. I mean it—

SUSAN

—you'll leave me—

HARPER

—I'm cold, Susan; can't you get that?—

SUSAN

—*you'll leave me*—

HARPER
(he reaches for her, brings her close,
buries his face in her neck; his hands
commence to move across her body)

—I hate this case—everything about it stinks—I'm done with it Susan,
I swear—

SUSAN

—you just want a warm body beside you, someone you can use for awhile—

HARPER

—no more—

SUSAN

—I want you to go—

HARPER

—like hell you do—

SUSAN

—*go*—

HARPER

—not when I'm cold—

SUSAN

—*what do you want from me?*—

HARPER

—a few kind words—

SUSAN

—what else?—

HARPER

—anything I can get—

SUSAN
(hesitates a moment)

—at least you're honest. *(She takes off her glasses. Then her arms go around him tight.)* I'm not even sure I like you.

HARPER
(indicating bedroom)

Come on.

SUSAN

Aren't you going to carry me? You used to carry me.

HARPER

That was when I was younger. And before you put on weight.

SUSAN

Go to hell.

HARPER
(nodding)

Eventually.

They move toward the light.

FADE OUT

FADE IN ON

AN ENORMOUS FRYING PAN FILLED WITH COOKING BACON.

PULL BACK TO REVEAL

SUSAN cooking. She has her glasses on, wears a robe. It is morning. After a long moment, HARPER enters, dressed. SUSAN quickly glances up at him, then back to the bacon. Throughout what follows, she is concentrating completely on her cooking and her voice, except for once, is just as casual as she can make it.

SUSAN

I thought we were just going to lounge around all day.

HARPER
(This is not something he is looking forward
to either. Honest and businesslike throughout)

I'll call you as soon as I can.

CUT TO

SUSAN, cooking, turning bacon.

SUSAN

Oh? Going back on the case?

CUT TO

HARPER.

HARPER

That's right.

CUT TO

SUSAN.

SUSAN

And what you said last night —

CUT TO

HARPER.

HARPER

— forget what I said.

CUT TO

SUSAN. *She glances up, smiles.*

SUSAN

OK. Sure, I understand; last night you were cold.

CUT TO

HARPER. *He says nothing.*

CUT TO

HARPER *and* SUSAN. SUSAN *concentrates on turning over some bacon.*

SUSAN

You're really ending things this time, you know that?
>   (HARPER *nods. She does not see.*
>   *Then, looking up at him, the one*
>   *time her voice goes — Big*)

You know that?

HARPER
(softly)

Yes.

CUT TO

SUSAN. *Quiet again.*

SUSAN

Why do you have to go back?
>   (*There is no sound from* HARPER.)

Why? Will you tell me?

CUT TO

HARPER. *Stands there, starts to talk, changes his mind, says nothing.*

CUT TO

SUSAN. *She shakes her head.*

SUSAN

All this bacon; I feel like such a fool. Sort of a wedding breakfast. *(she shrugs)*
Bye, Lew.

CUT TO

HARPER

HARPER

Bye. *(he starts to go; stops momentarily)* Wish me luck?

CUT TO

SUSAN.

SUSAN
(she looks at him, shakes her head)
Just an infinitely lingering disease.

CUT TO

HARPER. He turns, goes.

CUT TO

SUSAN. She continues cooking the pan full of bacon.

FADE OUT

FADE IN ON

ALBERT GRAVES, RUNNING DOWN THE WALK OF THE SAMPSON HOUSE.

CUT TO

HARPER, moving around his car toward ALBERT. The sun is very hot.

HARPER
Anything new on Sampson?

ALBERT
(shaking his head)
We know who the murdered man is though; I copied the high points of his record down. *(reaching into a pocket, pulling out paper)* Named Eddie Lassiter. Usual truancy stuff. Worked up to car thief. Then narcotics. Arrested with sister Betty Lassiter by the Narcotics Bureau. After he got out he —

HARPER
(taking paper, looking at it)
— how are the Sampsons?

ALBERT
Mrs. Sampson's fine, of course; chipper as can be. Miranda's not so good.

TAGGERT'S VOICE (off-screen)
(it comes from a great distance)
Hey Lew.
(HARPER looks up.)

CUT TO

From HARPER's point of view, a LONG SHOT of TAGGERT standing atop the diving board.

> TAGGERT
> *(waving)*

Top o' the mornin'.

CUT TO

HARPER and ALBERT. HARPER smiles, waves back.

> HARPER
> *(glancing back at EDDIE's record; casually)*

Where's Alan stay?

> ALBERT

Guest house way off in the back. *(He looks toward house. Then —)* Uh oh.

CUT TO

SHERIFF SPANNER leaving the Sampson house, hurrying down toward them.

> ALBERT'S VOICE (off-screen)

The sheriff's a bit put out with your behavior.

CUT TO

HARPER and ALBERT, watching SPANNER come.

> ALBERT

He feels you haven't quite let him in on everything.

> SPANNER
> *(moving in close on HARPER)*

OK. Where were you after you left "The Corner?"

> HARPER

Looking for Sampson.

> SPANNER

There's a half million missing and you were looking for Sampson; you expect me to take your word for that.

CUT TO

HARPER. Angry.

> HARPER

I don't much care if you take my word or not, baby. I'm not working for you.

CUT TO

SPANNER. Angry.

SPANNER

If I wanted to be ugly I could put you away this minute.

CUT TO

HARPER.

HARPER

Don't look now, but you are ugly.

CUT TO

SPANNER.

SPANNER

You know who you're talking to?

CUT TO

HARPER.

HARPER

A sheriff with a tough case on his hands and no ideas in his head so he's looking for a fall guy.
(CAMERA MOVES IN tight on HARPER'S FACE)
Well if you'd come on like a human being instead of the son of Frankenstein I'd have given you a couple right off. (the words tumble out) Such as Betty Fraley—put out a state-wide alarm—she plays at the "Piano" and put her down for suspicion of the murder of Eddie Lassiter. And put another alarm out for Dwight Troy and Fay Estabrook and a religious nut named Claude for smuggling in immigrant workers. They've been using Sampson's Temple In The Clouds and they dumped a bunch last night in Bakersfield.

CUT TO

SHERIFF SPANNER. He just looks at HARPER.

CUT TO

The three men.

HARPER

And don't bother thanking me; I'm just a law abiding citizen performing his duty.
(He turns, starts away.
ALBERT moves after him.)

CUT TO

HARPER and ALBERT.

> ALBERT
>
> You sure of all that?

> HARPER
>
> All of some, some of all. You better give King Kong a hand with it.
> (*ALBERT nods. HARPER grabs
> him, shakes him hard*)

CUT TO

HARPER, CLOSE UP.

> HARPER
>
> (*He is up!*)
> It's breaking, Albert. The whole shooting match. Wide wide open!

FADE OUT

FADE IN ON

A ONE-STORY WHITE FRAME HOUSE.

HARPER *moves to the front door, quickly opens it, steps inside, closes the door again.*

CUT TO

HARPER, *inside the house. He looks around.*

PAN SHOT. *The guest house. Clearly,* TAGGERT *lives here. There are pictures of him on a desk in various poses: playing tennis, swimming, piloting a plane. There is an unmade bed. There is a large, obviously expensive hi-fi set. There are stacks and stacks of records.*

CUT TO

HARPER. *He crosses to the records. Ignoring the 33's and 45's, he reaches for a stack of old 78's and begins going through.*

INSERT: *HARPER's hands holding a record done by Betty Fraley. He flips to the next record and again the recording is by Betty Fraley. He goes through another and another and—*

CUT TO

ALAN TAGGERT *standing in the doorway, watching HARPER go through the records.*

> HARPER
>
> (*very calmly; his back to* TAGGERT)
> I didn't know you liked jazz, Alan. (*he turns, looks up*)

CUT TO

TAGGERT. *He shrugs, smiles.*

TAGGERT

Some kinds; not all. *(He is wet from swimming. A towel thrown around his shoulders.)* What can I do you for?

CUT TO

HARPER. *He smiles.*

HARPER

You're very polite; what you mean is: what the hell are you doing sneaking around my cabin?

CUT TO

HARPER *and* TAGGERT.

HARPER

I thought maybe I could borrow a shirt from you. Mine's — *(he indicates rumpled clothing)* — not as neat as it might be. *(He takes a record now, turns on hi-fi.)* You believe me? *(He puts record on machine. An old piano begins to play. It is the same song* BETTY *was playing that night at "The Piano.")*

TAGGERT

Sure.

HARPER

Well, don't. I was really here to see if I could tie you and the Fraley broad and Lassiter into the kidnapping.

CUT TO

TAGGERT. *Stunned, he looks at* HARPER. *Then he sits in a chair.*

TAGGERT
(innocent)
Lew, I didn't do it. I didn't do anything.

CUT TO

HARPER. *He starts to saunter around the room.*

HARPER

Eddie called you in Las Vegas. You told him when you were flying Sampson to L.A. You probably told him to rent the limo. Then the next day, you got Sampson plastered — which isn't hard, I'm told — and when he phoned the Valerio —

CUT TO

TAGGERT. *Bewildered, he listens, shaking his head slightly.*

HARPER'S VOICE (off-screen)
—you canceled the call and phoned for Eddie instead. That canceled call's important. Nobody else knew that Sampson was going to call the Valerio. Do me your Sampson imitation, Alan; I bet it's good.

TAGGERT
I'm on your side, Lew. Who saved you at "The Piano"? —

CUT TO

The two of them.

HARPER
You went there to see Betty. And later, when you fired at the blue truck I put it down to stupidity. But you were just warning Eddie to take off.

TAGGERT
(Rises, crosses to the desk, opens a
drawer. What you expect is he's going
to take out a gun but what he takes out is
a comb. Nervously, looking at himself in
the mirror, he begins combing his hair)
You saying all this just because I've got a couple of records? There's hundreds of people with records of Betty Fraley.

HARPER
The first day I met you said you had a woman. I bet she's Betty Fraley even though it makes me sick to think of it.

CUT TO

TAGGERT. *Pleading.*

TAGGERT
I don't even know her. Not even to say hello to.

CUT TO

HARPER

HARPER
You must have been seen together plenty.

CUT TO

TAGGERT. *Terribly upset now.*

TAGGERT
I'll tell you the truth—I go there—to "The Piano"—half a dozen times

maybe — just to hear her — half a dozen times at the outside but that's all —
I don't know her, Lew. I don't.

CUT TO

HARPER. He looks at TAGGERT for a long time.

CUT TO

TAGGERT. He is scared and upset but innocent.

CUT TO

HARPER. He stares a moment more. Then —

> **HARPER**
> *(very soft — sincere)*

OK, Alan, I believe you.

CUT TO

TAGGERT. He manages to nod his head, make a little smile.

CUT TO

The two of them. The tension is broken. HARPER walks back to hi-fi and starts the record over again. TAGGERT walks back to the desk and drops comb in the open drawer. During this —

> **HARPER**

I'm really glad that's over, Alan, but I had to push you to see. You understand?
(TAGGERT nods)
I like you, and the idea of you and her — *(he indicates the hi-fi where record is playing)* — not only is she old and ugly and overweight and untalented, she's damaged goods, kid. There's a big crack somewhere deep inside her. She tries to use dope to cover it but it can't. She's man crazy, Alan. The night I was there, she was begging me to take her with me. *Begging me.* But I couldn't go near a thing like that. You'd have to be damaged your-self to go near a thing like that, wouldn't you say so, Alan?

> **TAGGERT**

You can be very cruel, you know that? *(He has taken a gun from the drawer and holds it level, pointed at HARPER's stomach.)*

> **HARPER**
> *(nodding)*

Alas.

CUT TO

TAGGERT, CLOSE UP. He is just as handsome as ever except that now what shows in his face is what HARPER has said: he is damaged.

> TAGGERT

What Betty and I have you'd never understand; but your ignorance doesn't give you the right to sully it either.

CUT TO

HARPER.

> HARPER

If you think she's Aphrodite, that's your business; I just want Sampson, if he's alive.

CUT TO

TAGGERT.

> TAGGERT

He is. So far.

CUT TO

HARPER. *He stares at* TAGGERT'S *gun. Then he glances around for something; anything.*

> HARPER

Then give him to me. Keep the money. I won't talk. I mean that. Killing me gets you nothing.

> TAGGERT'S VOICE (off-screen)

Wrong, baby; it guarantees me freedom of action.

> HARPER

It guarantees you death by gas. What kind of freedom you think you'll have running with an addict on your back?

CUT TO

TAGGERT. *He smiles.*

> TAGGERT

Nobody's running. We'll be sitting very happily in Buena Vista, in our lonely little cottage by the sea. While everybody *thinks* we're running.

CUT TO

HARPER. *He is sweating now, tensing up, getting ready.*

> HARPER

You can have your lousy little cottage — *just give me Sampson.*

CUT TO

TAGGERT.

TAGGERT

Top o' the mornin', Lew. *(The gun points like a finger at* HARPER'*s head.)*

CUT TO

HARPER. *He launches into a desperate dive toward* TAGGERT.

CUT TO

TAGGERT. *Smiling, the gun raised. There is an explosive sound.*

CUT TO

HARPER. *In midair, his body buckles at the sound.*

CUT TO

TAGGERT. *The gun arm drops.*

CUT TO

HARPER, *reaching out.*

CUT TO

The two of them. TAGGERT'*s body falls.* HARPER *catches him in his arms. A great red spill of blood stains the white towel around* TAGGERT'*s shoulders.*

CUT TO

ALBERT GRAVES, *gun in hand, standing in the doorway.*

CUT TO

HARPER, *slowly lowering* TAGGERT'*s body to the floor.*

CUT TO

ALBERT. *There is a dazed tone in his voice as he starts to talk.*

ALBERT

Do you know . . . that . . . I almost stopped off in the kitchen for a glass of water? *(He takes a step forward, then another.)*

CUT TO

HARPER, *kneeling over* TAGGERT.

ALBERT

How could you get caught like that?

HARPER
(taking TAGGERT's gun, looking at it)
I don't know; I guess I hoped he wasn't guilty. *(putting the gun in his pocket)*
He was in on the kidnapping; he and the Fraley broad. She was in love
with him. *(almost sadly)* Fool.

CUT TO

The two of them. HARPER rises, starts for the door.

ALBERT
Everybody was in love with him. I wonder how Miranda's going to take it?

HARPER
Guess.

ALBERT
*(following HARPER — nervous,
the words come hard)*
If I tell her . . . she might not — I mean there's a strong chance she won't
see the way it was — really was . . . and I was sort of wondering if — I mean
I know it's not strictly within your province but —

HARPER
— you want me to tell Miranda?
(ALBERT manages a nod)
You're getting to be a real nuisance, asking favors all the time; what have
you done for me lately?
(ALBERT smiles.)

CUT TO

*The two men walking together toward the main house. BETTY's record on the hi-fi comes
to a close . . .*

DISSOLVE TO

MIRANDA IN THE MORNING ROOM OF THE SAMPSON HOUSE.

She is arranging fresh cut flowers. Her movements are very slow.

CUT TO

HARPER in the doorway, watching her.

HARPER
I've got some moderately good news.

CUT TO

MIRANDA. *She looks slowly up at him.*

CUT TO

HARPER, *moving inside.*

> **HARPER**
> There's reason to think your father's alive.

> **MIRANDA**
> How do you know?

> **HARPER**
> I just talked to one of the kidnappers. He's dead now. His name was Alan Taggert.

CUT TO

MIRANDA. *Noiselessly, she sits down heavily in a chair, her hands folded in her lap.*

> **HARPER'S VOICE** (off-screen)
> He didn't say where your father was, but with a little luck—

> **MIRANDA**
> *(looking slowly up at HARPER)*
> —you killed him?

CUT TO

HARPER.

> **HARPER**
> *(shaking his head)*
> He was about to kill me. Albert got him.

CUT TO

MIRANDA. *She smiles and for a moment it seems possible that she is going to laugh, but she doesn't.*

> **MIRANDA**
> *(dully)*
> Alan was so beautiful you'd think he'd be type cast for the hero. And Albert; well tell me now have you ever seen a man as overlookable as Albert Graves? I'm dumb. *(she starts to shake her head)* I keep getting fooled by appearances.

CUT TO

HARPER. *Starting toward her.*

> ### HARPER
> Go ahead — let it out.

CUT TO

MIRANDA. Eyes bright and for the first time her voice has power.

> ### MIRANDA
> You're as dumb as I am, Harper. Alan's the Galahad and Albert's the clown
> and I'm the grieving daughter, right?
> > *(CAMERA MOVES TO EXTREME CLOSE UP)*
> Except I don't care a damn about Ralph. He's a terrible man and what he gets
> he deserves. Yesterday, when the note came, I realized I just didn't care so I
> thought, "You better quick hibernate, Miranda, before everyone discovers
> what a horrid little thing you are." *(abruptly her face brightens)* Galahad —

CUT TO

*ALBERT, peeking in through the doorway. Embarrassed and confused, he glances around
behind him to see who MIRANDA is addressing.*

CUT TO

MIRANDA. She stands.

> ### MIRANDA
> Do you think I'm horrid, Albert?

CUT TO

ALBERT. In the doorway.

> ### ALBERT
> Horrid? No. no, certainly not. Quite the contrary, actually —

CUT TO

MIRANDA. She breaks into a run across the room.

CUT TO

HARPER. Watching.

CUT TO

*ALBERT and MIRANDA as she runs into his arms. Hesitantly, after a beat, ALBERT holds
her gently. Then tighter. Tighter still. The look on his face is one of astonishment coupled
with disbelief coupled with joy. CAMERA MOVES IN ON ALBERT'S FACE.*

FADE OUT

FADE IN ON

THE CITY LIMITS OF BUENA VISTA AND A SIGN SAYING SO.

DISSOLVE TO

HARPER ROARING INTO A GARAGE.

As the attendant starts toward him, HARPER calls out.

> **HARPER**
> You got a road that runs along the ocean?

> **ATTENDANT**
> *(nodding)*
> All the way. You house hunting?

> **HARPER**
> Something like that.

> **ATTENDANT**
> You can see most of 'em from Fremont. Take a left at the first light down to the water. Starts there.

HARPER drives off, burning rubber.

CUT TO

THE OCEAN.

HARPER's car comes into view, takes a right, starts following the ocean road.

CUT TO

PAN SHOT FROM THE ROAD of a house. The house appears, then disappears as a neighboring house comes into view. These are small places, and soon a third house is visible.

THIS BEGINS A MELDING SEQUENCE, OF HOUSE AFTER HOUSE.

CUT TO

HARPER, driving along the road, staring out at the houses.

CUT TO

Another melding shot of houses. They are more remote now; not so close together.

CUT TO

HARPER, driving faster down the road.

CUT TO

Another house, and then another, and then some bushes, and then another house, and then

CUT TO

HARPER, stopping the car, suddenly jamming it into reverse, backing up to the row of bushes, getting quickly out.

CUT TO

HARPER, forcing his way through the bushes, looking out toward the water.

CUT TO

An isolated cottage by the sea. There is no garage. Two cars are parked. One is Fay Estabrook's car; the other is a white convertible.

CUT TO

HARPER, running back to his car, backing it off the road. He opens the door, and before he gets out we can see him working with the pieces of copper wire he has to use to start and stop the car. After a moment, the car motor dies.

DISSOLVE TO

The cottage from fairly close. From inside comes the terrible sound of a scream.

PULL BACK TO REVEAL

HARPER, TAGGERT's gun in hand, crouched between the two cars. He reaches into one, then the other, and removes the ignition keys. Then he begins quietly to approach the cottage.

CUT TO

Inside the cottage. BETTY FRALEY is spread-eagled and bound across the bed. Her shoes are off, her feet bloody. DWIGHT TROY sits beside the bed. He is debonair as always. FAY ESTABROOK stands beside him. Across the bed stands CLAUDE dressed now in a regular business suit.

TROY

Now Betty, I wish you'd listen to reason. I bribed a number of fine respectable citizens in order to find you here. You should know I hate throwing money away.

FAY
(impatient)

Tie a can to it; we all know you swallowed the dictionary.

TROY

I must make Betty see my point, darling. *(to BETTY)* Now it should be clear to you that I enjoy inflicting pain just as it's clear to me that you don't enjoy enduring it. So Betty dear, it's only sensible to tell me where the money is.
(BETTY bites her lip, shakes

her head. TROY sighs.)
Very well; but I warn you, this next little trick is absolutely unendurable.
(We do not see what he does, but it is done to
BETTY's feet and legs. The ensuing scream
makes the preceding one seem like a cry of
joy. In the background, HARPER's taut face
appears briefly at a window, then it is gone.)

CUT TO

BETTY. The scream stops. She lies still, breathing heavily, all color gone from her face.

BETTY
(a whisper)

What about me ... if I tell?

CUT TO

TROY. He smiles.

TROY

What about you *when* you tell I think is what you mean. Claude will get
you to picturesque Mexico. I have contacts for that as you're well aware
(bending forward) Shall we have another go?

CUT TO

BETTY. As TROY starts to hurt her, she again starts to scream. Then —

BETTY
(screaming out)

Buena Vista! The bus station. A locker. The key's in my bag.

CUT TO

Shot of all of them.

TROY
(reaching for her bag,
starting to go through it)

Excellent. *(rummaging)* You're going to be furious with me, Betty, but I
never said you'd be alive when you got to Mexico, did I? *(pulling out the key)*

CUT TO

HARPER, gun in hand, battering through the front door.

CUT TO

TROY, whirling, deftly taking a gun from inside his coat —

CUT TO

HARPER, *firing.*

CUT TO

TROY, *grabbing at his stomach. The key falls from his grasp.*

CUT TO

Shot of the room. HARPER *runs to the key, stoops, grabs it as* CLAUDE *dives for him.* FAY *starts for him too as we —*

CUT TO

HARPER, *whirling from* CLAUDE's *grasp, bringing his gun crashing down across* CLAUDE's *temple.* CLAUDE *crumples. Then* FAY *is on him, scratching for his eyes.*

> **FAY**
> *(screaming)*
> You shot Troy! You shot him!

> **HARPER**
> *(shoves her across the room — he means this)*
> I'll kill him if you don't shut up!

CUT TO

FAY. *About to scream, she looks at* HARPER, *abruptly closes her mouth.*

CUT TO

HARPER, *getting* BETTY *loose from the bed.*

> **HARPER**
> Can you walk?

> **BETTY**
> Maybe.
> *(*HARPER *moves toward* FAY*)*

CUT TO

FAY. *Retreating.*

CUT TO

HARPER, *advancing on her.*

> **FAY**
> I'll give you anything I've got.

HARPER
That's a rich choice. Take off your shoes.
> *(She does. There is a closet door behind her.*
> *He shoves her into it, closes the door, locks it.*
> *Inside, she starts to bang on the door and yell.)*

CUT TO

BETTY. *Free, she is trying to walk, but can't. The pain from the effort is evident.*

CUT TO

HARPER. *He scoops up* FAY's *shoes, goes to* BETTY, *scoops her up too, starts to carry her out.*

BETTY
(looking at his face closely)
Who are you?

HARPER
The local scoutmaster. *(And he carries her out the door.)*

CUT TO

HARPER, *carrying* BETTY. *They are almost to the road. The terrain, it should be noted, is rocky and hard.*

BETTY
Fay'll get out.

HARPER
(glancing back)
She already has.

CUT TO

FAY ESTABROOK. *Barefoot, she is doing her best to hurry away from the cottage. But even from this distance, the terrain is clearly giving her trouble: she keeps grabbing first one foot as it hits a rock, then takes a step, then grabs the other foot.*

CUT TO

HARPER *and* BETTY *approaching car.* HARPER *pitches* FAY's *shoes into the deep woods across the road.*

BETTY
She'll get away.

HARPER
A fat barefoot alcoholic? Sure she will.

CUT TO

FAY, stumbling comically along. The CAMERA HOLDS ON *her slow, erratic progress.*

FADE OUT

FADE IN ON

HARPER'S CAR DRIVING BACK DOWN ALONG THE OCEAN FRONT ROAD.

CUT TO

Inside the car. HARPER *and* BETTY.

> **BETTY**
>
> You're Harper, right?

> **HARPER**
> *(nods)*
> And I'm still looking for Ralph Sampson. Where is he?

> **BETTY**
> I tell you what I think: you got the key to the locker; well, you can have the money. But I know where Sampson is, and that's gonna buy me my one last ticket for happiness.

CUT TO

HARPER.

> **HARPER**
> The happiness market's crashed, baby; Taggert's dead. Now where's Sampson?

CUT TO

BETTY. She shakes her head. Again and again.

> **BETTY**
> *(very quietly)*
> You're just tryin' to get me to talk.

CUT TO

HARPER.

> **HARPER**
> You're right. But I'm not lying. Taggert's dead.

CUT TO

BETTY. She stares at HARPER'S FACE, *doing what she can to disbelieve him. Then she seems almost to shrivel. Her head lolls to one side. She does not cry. After a moment, she begins to talk in a dead voice.*

BETTY

The far side of Santa Barbara. About forty miles. The main highway. There's
a deserted beach club. The Sundown. That's the name of the place...the
Sundown...

CUT TO

HARPER

*standing in the phone booth of the Buena Vista service station where he had previously
stopped to ask about the ocean road. BETTY is visible in the front seat of the car, slumped
and motionless. The ATTENDANT hovers around, making himself useless.*

HARPER
(in the midst of conversation)
...the Sundown, Albert; can you find it?

ALBERT'S VOICE (off-screen)
I can try. You know my sense of direction.

HARPER
You should beat me there. And get Spanner down to Buena Vista. Fremont
Drive. There are some bushes in front of the house and a black Chrysler
sedan and a white Chevy convertible — even he might find it. With any
luck, we'll all be bombed by suppertime. *(He hangs up.)*

CUT TO

HARPER'S CAR with HARPER at the wheel, roaring back onto the highway.

CUT TO

Inside the car.

HARPER
I took care of your playmates for you.
                    *(BETTY does not move. HARPER reaches over,
                    with one hand, turns her head toward him.)*

CUT TO

BETTY. She is crying soundlessly. The tears pour down her face.

DISSOLVE TO

HARPER'S CAR — RACING DOWN THE HIGHWAY.

It is afternoon now; the sun is much lower in the sky.

CUT TO

Inside the car. HARPER is driving. BETTY has stopped crying.

BETTY

Did you kill him?

HARPER
(shaking his head)

He was trying to kill me.

BETTY

Don't I wish he had. *(Against her will, she starts to cry again.)*

HARPER

I'd feel a lot more sympathy for someone as tender hearted as you except I keep remembering you shot your brother in the head last night.

CUT TO

BETTY. *She forces herself to stop crying.*

BETTY
(a quiet, sing-song voice)

That's right; my own baby brother. I brought him up. I taught him about music, he taught me about cars and narcotics. Then they caught him pushing. He helped the Feds—he fingered me as a user. That time in jail just about killed me, it did kill my career. Eddie never knew I knew he fingered me but I always swore to myself I'd get him. *(pause)* I got him.

CUT TO

The two of them.

HARPER

And Taggert you sucked in cause you needed an inside man for the Sampson job.

BETTY
(violently shakes her head)

No, no, we *loved* each other, we *cared*. But we needed money.

HARPER

So naturally you had to kidnap Sampson.

BETTY

We couldda blackmailed him—he was getting a cut from Troy on the immigrants—but with him and his lawyers we figured it was too much for us, they were too smart. Sampson's kid wouldda married Alan, but Sampson wouldn't let her. And Alan and me, we hadda be together—

HARPER

—I don't buy love's old sweet song from you, Betty.

                                    BETTY
                                  (desperate)
It's true. You're jealous. Everybody was jealous of Alan and me. Were you
there when he died? I bet his last words were about me. I bet he died saying my name. Tell me. The truth now. *Tell me.*

CUT TO

HARPER. He hesitates only a moment. Then —

                                    HARPER
You're right, I am jealous. He died saying your name.

CUT TO

BETTY. Smiles suddenly, eyes bright with tears.

                                    BETTY
Don't you think I knew that...
                          (CAMERA HOLDS on her face. Then —)

DISSOLVE TO

HARPER'S CAR MOVING SLOWLY ALONG THE HIGHWAY.

The sound of the ocean is heard. It is later in the afternoon.

CUT TO

Inside the car. HARPER and BETTY.

                                    BETTY
Pretty soon now. Just past this sign.

CUT TO

*An old tattered sign. Visible are the words: "This fabulous piece of oceanfront property
available for subdividing..." The car moves on. The rest of the sign is lost.*

CUT TO

*Another sign, in terribly frayed shape. It proclaims: "THE SUNDOWN: AMERICA'S
MOST ELEGANT OCEANFRONT SPA." Below the sign, the road drops away and
far below, a long deserted building is visible.*

CUT TO

*HARPER, starting down the long long rickety flight of steps leading to the beach house.
Behind him, his car is visible. The motor is turned off. BETTY sits dolefully in the front
seat staring out at HARPER.*

CUT TO

A LONG SHOT OF HARPER *running down the stairs.*

> **HARPER**
> *(his voice comes from the appropriate distance)*
Mr. Sampson? Mr. Sampson?

CUT TO

Another shot of HARPER *running down.*

> **HARPER**
> *(still calling)*
Albert? Mr. Sampson?

CUT TO

HARPER *taking the last of the stairs two at a time. He reaches the bottom and looks around. It is a very eerie place.*

CUT TO

The beach club. There is a men's room sign and a ladies' room sign and off of each are a number of doors.

CUT TO

HARPER, *starting toward the men's room side.*

> **HARPER**
It's Lew Harper, Mr. Sampson. Your wife hired me.

CUT TO

HARPER, *sticking his head into the first door.*

> **HARPER**
Albert? Mr. Sampson? *(he moves to second door)* Mr. Sampson?

CUT TO

HARPER *opening the second door. He barely has it open when a gun appears clubbing down at his skull.* HARPER *falls without a cry.*

CUT TO

ALBERT GRAVES HURRYING DOWN THE FLIGHT OF STEPS TO THE BEACH CLUB. HE REACHES BOTTOM, LOOKS AROUND.

> **ALBERT**
> *(almost in a whisper)*
Lew? It's Albert.

There is a GROAN. ALBERT jumps at the sound, then turns to face it.

CUT TO

HARPER. He is on his knees, trying to rise.

> ALBERT
> *(running to him)*

What happened to you?

> HARPER
> *(rubbing his head)*

The usual. *(He reaches into his pocket, pulls out the key to the locker where the ransom money is. He stares at it a moment, then stuffs it back.)*

> ALBERT

Can you get up?

> HARPER
> *(Nods, slowly forces his way
> to his feet. His head is cut from the
> blow he received. As he rises)*

There must have been a fourth member of the gang guarding Sampson. He suckered me. You should have been here years ago, Albert. What kept you?

CUT TO

ALBERT. He is embarrassed.

> ALBERT

I just knew you'd ask that. *(dropping his voice)* I couldn't find the silly place — I kept driving around and around — I remembered you said it was a beach club so I knew it had to be on the water but that didn't stop me from driving past this place half a dozen times. I'm sorry, Lew.

CUT TO

HARPER, moving toward the row of doors beside the men's room. He opens one, then the next —

> HARPER
> *(during this)*

Didn't you see my car parked up top?

> ALBERT
> *(a step behind HARPER like a shadow)*

Your car's not there. I didn't see it anyway.

> HARPER
> *(scowls; begins moving much faster)*

Whoever mugged me must have wired the terminals —

ALBERT continues to follow HARPER as he opens various doors. Then —

HARPER stops abruptly.

CUT TO

RALPH SAMPSON in one of the small dressing rooms. He is sitting on a bench, bound hand and foot. One end of a rope is tied in a hard knot under his left ear. The other end is strung through a staple in the wall. His open eyes are suffused with blood.

CUT TO

HARPER. Grimacing, he approaches SAMPSON. Hesitantly, he reaches out for SAMPSON's wrist.

> **HARPER**
> *(softly)*
> Dead and warm. (*He turns away, rubbing his hands across his coat.*)

CUT TO

ALBERT, in the doorway, making room for HARPER to exit.

> **HARPER**
> *(starting to hurry up the stairs)*
> Hit it, Albert.

> **ALBERT**
> *(hurrying along behind)*
> What about Sampson?

> **HARPER**
> The cops'll want him just that way.

> **ALBERT**
> Where are we going?

> **HARPER**
> After Betty Fraley —

CUT TO

HARPER at the top of the stairs. ALBERT's Cadillac is visible behind him. HARPER is all but screaming down at ALBERT who is hurrying up the stairs as fast as he can.

> **HARPER**
> — move it! Move it!
> *(as ALBERT comes close to the top)*
> Gimme your keys!

ALBERT
(Panting. He is exhausted.)
You don't know which way they went. *(He hands keys over.)*

HARPER
(grabbing the keys, diving for the car)
I know the ransom money's in Buena Vista.

CUT TO

ALBERT'S CADILLAC ROARING DOWN THE HIGHWAY.

It is approaching dusk. The sunset is going to be blinding.

CUT TO

Inside the car.

ALBERT
Then why are we going away from Buena Vista?

HARPER
*(He stares straight ahead. The
car is traveling terribly fast.)*
I'm guessing she wants to get as far from the money as possible. And the
locker key's still in my pocket.

ALBERT
If we find her it will just be luck.

HARPER
(his voice surprisingly loud)
I'm due!
(ALBERT glances at HARPER, then away.)

CUT TO

HARPER. He is driving like a madman.

DISSOLVE TO

THE CADILLAC ROARING ALONG THE HIGHWAY.

It passes a few other cars literally as if they were standing still. It is very close to sunset now.

DISSOLVE TO

THE CADILLAC AGAIN.

*It must be going over a hundred miles an hour and sunset is still closer. Everything is suf-
fused with a soft red light.*

DISSOLVE TO

THE CADILLAC MOVING FASTER THAN EVER.

It is sunset now.

CUT TO

HARPER. He looks as wild now as he has ever looked. The beatings, the lack of sleep, the emotional pounding; all these are covered by a final terrible burst of animal energy. He reacts to something up ahead.

HARPER

Bingo!

CUT TO

HARPER'S CAR. It is quite a ways ahead but it cannot travel nearly as fast as the Cadillac.

CUT TO

The two cars. HARPER starts closing the gap.

CUT TO

HARPER at the wheel. He stares ahead. ALBERT, concerned, looks at him.

CUT TO

The two cars. HARPER pulls closer to the lead car.

CUT TO

BETTY FRALEY in the lead car. There is the sound of a car horn and she whirls to face it.

CUT TO

HARPER, banging on the horn of ALBERT's car. He is even with her now. HARPER starts to scream.

HARPER

PULL OVER! *OVER!*

CUT TO

The two cars roaring along side by side.

CUT TO

HARPER. Screaming.

HARPER

PULL OVER!

CUT TO

BETTY. *She just shakes her head.*

CUT TO

The two cars shooting down the highway. HARPER *begins moving a little ahead. Then —
deliberately* BETTY's *car turns, turns off the highway onto the shoulder, skirts along that
for a moment, then continues away from the road down a hill toward some trees.*

CUT TO

HARPER, *frantically shaking his head.*

CUT TO

HARPER's *car. It hits a glancing blow against the first tree.*

CUT TO

*The car careening on. It rockets into another tree, off that. The sounds are horribly loud.
The car begins to roll now, over and over as its pace slows. Doors fly off. It seems like some
gigantic toy being pulled to pieces.*

CUT TO

HARPER *and* ALBERT. *They stare at the holocaust; they cannot look away.*

CUT TO

The car slamming into one final tree. It seems almost to shudder. Then it lies still.

CUT TO

HARPER, *driving off the highway toward the wreck.*

CUT TO

HARPER, *throwing the door of the Cadillac open, jumping out, running full tilt toward
the other car.*

CUT TO

The wreck. HARPER *dashes up, reaches inside for Betty Fraley. He carries her a short distance away, lays her down.*

CUT TO

The lower half of BETTY's *body. She is barefooted.*

CUT TO

HARPER. He takes his coat off, kneels down, gently covers her bare bloody feet. ALBERT comes up behind him. HARPER stays down on his knees, over the body.

FADE OUT

FADE IN ON

THE SAME PLACE,

except now there are dozens of cars in the area, many of them police cars. It is dark, and the piercing headlights create an atmosphere altogether weird. HARPER leans against ALBERT's Cadillac. The strain of the preceding days are showing fully now; the string is played out and there is no energy left. His face is streaked with dried blood; his shirt is bloody too.

> **ALBERT**
> *(walking over to HARPER)*

The sheriff says we can go now. He sent some man after Sampson.

> *(HARPER does not move.)*

Want me to drive?

> *(HARPER nods, gets in the car.*
> *ALBERT walks around the car.)*

Where to?

> *(HARPER removes the locker key*
> *from his pocket, holds it high.)*

CUT TO

THE KEY STILL HELD IN HARPER'S HAND.

PULL BACK TO REVEAL

The Buena Vista bus station. It looks like any other. HARPER moves alone across the half-deserted floor toward the lockers. He reaches the lockers, pauses, then inserts the key and pulls.

CUT TO

The locker. Inside is a plump satchel.

CUT TO

HARPER. Almost angrily, he reaches for the satchel, yanks it out, flicks the zipper open a little, then zips it shut. Then he turns, starts slowly to walk away.

CUT TO

HARPER moving to the exit of the bus station. A porter leaning on a broom watches him approach. As HARPER draws near —

> **PORTER**
> *(quietly)*

Hey Mister, you got blood on your shirt.

> **HARPER**
> *(nods; without breaking stride)*
It's one of those Italian imports.

CUT TO

ALBERT waiting in his Cadillac as HARPER leaves the bus station. HARPER opens the car door, tosses the satchel on the seat between them, gets in.

> **ALBERT**
The grieving widow next?
> *(HARPER nods. ALBERT starts to drive.)*

CUT TO

THE CADILLAC CRUISING THROUGH THE DARKNESS.

CUT TO

HARPER and ALBERT. ALBERT drives as one would suspect: cautiously.

> **ALBERT**
> Sheriff Spanner seemed very confident he'd pick up the fourth man.

> **HARPER**
> *(he had been staring dully out)*
What? I'm sorry, I wasn't listening.

> **ALBERT**
The fourth man — the one that mugged you. Spanner says there's a bartender at "The Piano" who hasn't been seen the last few days. He's the fourth man; the one who got Sampson. That's what Spanner thinks.

> **HARPER**
Whatever Spanner thinks I'll bet against on principle. *(He grabs the satchel, plops it in his lap, starts to unzip it.)*

CUT TO

The satchel. It is stuffed like a Christmas goose with money.

CUT TO

HARPER. He brings out a bundle of bills perhaps two inches thick. They are held together with the usual paper that banks use to hold large numbers of bills. He riffles the bills as if they were cards. Then he rips the binding paper.

CUT TO

ALBERT, watching, amused.

CUT TO

HARPER. He throws the bills up to the roof of the car.

> **HARPER**
> *(like a drunk — as the money flutters down)*
> Happy New Year. *(reaching back into the satchel)* Encore, encore. *(He rips the binding again, throws these bills up. They flutter down all over the inside of the car. HARPER starts to laugh, reaches into the satchel again.)*

CUT TO

ALBERT, starting to laugh.

CUT TO

HARPER, roaring with laughter.

CUT TO

ALBERT, likewise.

CUT TO

HARPER. He smashes out with the next bundle of bills, slapping ALBERT hard across the face. ALBERT's glasses are knocked askew.

CUT TO

ALBERT, groping for his glasses, putting them back on, turning to look at HARPER.

CUT TO

HARPER.

> **HARPER**
> *(dead)*
> You're the fourth man, fink.

CUT TO

ALBERT.

> **ALBERT**
> You think I kidnapped Sampson?

CUT TO

HARPER.

> **HARPER**
> Of course not; I only think you killed him.

CUT TO

The two of them.

> **HARPER**
> What do you think was killing me when I pulled her from the wreck? The car was empty, Albert.

> **ALBERT**
> They split up. He took a different car.

> **HARPER**
> Sure; and she stayed in a car she knew would identify her.

> **ALBERT**
> You said something about wiring terminals. That's man's work.

> **HARPER**
> Any two bit car thief knows the trick; she had one in her family.

> **ALBERT**
> Keep your damn accusations —

CUT TO

HARPER. CLOSE UP. He lies back, his eyes closed.

> **HARPER**
> *(very soft)*
> — we don't lie to each other, Albert. Save it for the cops. Please, huh? Lies are for those other people, not us, OK?
> > *(CAMERA stays on HARPER. There is a pause.*
> > *Then ALBERT's voice is heard, also very soft.)*

> **ALBERT'S VOICE** (off-screen)
> Sampson's no loss to anybody.

CUT TO

ALBERT. He is concentrating very hard on just driving.

> **ALBERT**
> I hadn't meant to, actually; not in any premeditated way. But when I got there and saw him — it seemed that he had to die. *(he manages to shrug)* It was no loss, I assure you.

CUT TO

HARPER. He is enormously upset now, and the feeling does not leave him.

> **HARPER**
>
> But you were doing so good with Miranda. Today. At last. She might have married you.

CUT TO

ALBERT. His eyes are bright.

> **ALBERT**
>
> He never would have let her. It was a game with him. He found out how I felt and he pushed us together but he never would have let her. Just laughs for the client, that's all I was supplying. You going to turn me in?

CUT TO

HARPER. He manages a nod.

> **HARPER**
>
> After I make my report to Mrs. Sampson.

> **ALBERT'S VOICE** (off-screen)
>
> You don't have to.
>
> *(HARPER says nothing.)*

CUT TO

ALBERT.

> **ALBERT**
> *(big)*
>
> You were hired by a bitch to find scum!

CUT TO

HARPER. Nodding.

> **HARPER**
>
> Yes.

CUT TO

ALBERT. Softer now.

> **ALBERT**
>
> You got a better friend than me?

CUT TO

HARPER. He shakes his head.

> **HARPER**
>
> None near as good.

CUT TO

ALBERT

He was scum Lew, I swear.

CUT TO

HARPER. As he starts to talk, he leans back. It is not inconceivable that he might weep, and his eyes close. CAMERA moves in very close.

HARPER

When we first met — *(he manages a little smile)* you were gonna be Governor and I was gonna be the greatest defender of justice in the history of the State of California. *(the smile is gone, the eyes close)* Well, these days I make three-fifty a week on a good week and last year there were six good ones. I haven't got much, Albert; all I got is me. You hire Lew Harper, you get Lew Harper. And I'll get cut up and kicked and lied to and loathed but I'll do my job. And if a bitch hires me to find scum, well, I'd rather it was Prince Charming asking me to scout out Cinderella, but everything isn't the way I'd rather it was. Susan doesn't get this and I don't guess you will either, but I got to do my job, Albert. All the dirty way.

CUT TO

ALBERT. He reaches down into a coat pocket, feels to see that his gun is there. It is. With a sideways glance at HARPER, he resumes driving.

DISSOLVE TO

THE LONG SAMPSON DRIVEWAY.

ALBERT's Cadillac pulls up. HARPER gets out.

CUT TO

HARPER and ALBERT.

ALBERT
(he means what he is saying)
I don't understand why you have to do this. Do you understand why I can't let you?

HARPER
(He nods slowly. Then —)
You still got your gun?
(ALBERT nods)
Then you better do it before I hit that door.

CUT TO

The front door of the SAMPSON house. It stands open.

CUT TO

HARPER and ALBERT.

> **HARPER**
> The way I feel now, if I never make it to that door, it wouldn't be the worst thing that ever happened. So long, Albert.

CUT TO

THE START OF A LONG LONG TRAVELING SHOT. CAMERA stays right on HARPER's FACE as he starts slowly walking toward the front door. Behind him, ALBERT gets smaller and smaller as HARPER continues to move. HARPER's FACE almost fills the screen as ALBERT takes out his gun, rests his arm on the window of the car, begins to take aim. HARPER keeps walking away. ALBERT raises the gun slowly, carefully, until it is pointed at the back of HARPER's head. HARPER is almost at the door as ALBERT's fingers tighten around the trigger. Then HARPER reaches the door; ALBERT's gun arm drops.

> **HARPER AND ALBERT**
> *(together)*
>
> Aw hell.

THE PICTURE FREEZES.

FADE OUT

THE END

THE GREAT WALDO PEPPER

DIRECTOR	GEORGE ROY HILL
PRODUCER	GEORGE ROY HILL
CINEMATOGRAPHER	ROBERT SURTEES
EDITORS	PETER BERKOS
	WILLIAM REYNOLDS
ART DIRECTOR	HENRY BUMSTEAD
COMPOSER	HENRY MANCINI
SCREENPLAY	WILLIAM GOLDMAN
	(FROM A STORY BY
	GEORGE ROY HILL)

THE BIGGEST CHANGE

In *Adventures in the Screen Trade*, I wrote a chapter about *The Great Waldo Pepper*, the thrust of which was that *Waldo* was a quality picture undone commercially because the audience would not follow where we wanted them to go.

Looking back now, two things stand out: 1) It seems even more remarkable than ever that it was a commercial disappointment, because nothing like that has happened ever since. 2) Today, the movie we released back then would never have seen daylight, and the movie we would have released would have been the giant success everyone expected it to be.

To understand the first point, it is necessary to alter the time frame. George Roy Hill, the director, whose love of old airplanes had been the creative pulse of the film from the beginning, was, in 1975, along with David Lean, one of the two hottest directors in the world. Not only was he on fire, as Marv would say, he was also brilliant and gifted — still by far the greatest director with whom I have ever worked. Hill's three most recent films at the time were:

1969 – *Butch Cassidy and the Sundance Kid*

1972 – *Slaughterhouse Five*

1973 – *The Sting*

Slaughterhouse was an extremely fine version of Kurt Vonnegut's famous and fantastical anti-war novel, well received at the time. *Butch* and *Sting* were both Oscar nominated (Hill won for *The Sting*, as did the movie), and were two of the most commercially successful films of all time.

Both co-starrring Robert Redford.

Redford's career began in 1962 and in the next half a dozen years he was in a dozen movies, none of which took off. That all ended when *Butch Cassidy* opened in '69. He followed that success with five more movies which did not connect commercially, though at least two of them, *Downhill Racer* and *The Candidate*, both of which he produced, were wonderful then and are better now. Then came this quartet:

1972 – *Jeremiah Johnson*

1973 – *The Sting*

1973 – *The Way We Were*

1974 – *The Great Gatsby*

Jeremiah Johnson, one of the great westerns, was a hit but a much bigger hit when it was re-released. *The Sting* we know about. *The Way We Were* was one of the most popular romantic movies then or ever. And *The Great Gatsby* was arguably the most hyped movie of its time. When we started work on *Waldo*, then, Redford was not just the number one box-office attraction in the world, he was more — *the* romantic hero of the era, and probably the biggest since the golden days of Clark Gable, generations before.

I guess it's as if today Spielberg and Cruise announced they were going to make a swashbuckler.

And they made a good one.

And people did not come running.

Frankly, I cannot conceive of this happening. I also can't come up with anytime that it's happened since *Waldo*. *The Last Action Hero* was certainly a disappointment. (I tried to salvage it.) But the movie that was rushed into distribution wasn't such a terrific movie. *Cable Guy* was certainly a disappointment. But it was not Jim Carrey in his wheelhouse. What makes *The Great Waldo Pepper* so unusual is that it *was* a terrific movie and it *was* in the star's wheelhouse.

I thought then and still do that it was as fine as any performance he's ever given. Redford has been dogged forever as has Paul Newman as is Tom Cruise with what I call the "Cary Grant Syndrome." The camera loves them so much and they are such gifted actors that you never catch them acting. As Clint Eastwood said, he likes working with actors who don't have anything to prove. So the assumption, say, on *Rain Man* is that Hoffman is the actor, because he looks like he's working, Hoffman made it a hit, while Cruise was just this cute guy the camera happened to catch a couple of times as he wandered by. For me, Cruise made that movie. He provided the rock of belief any picture so needs. (Just as Morgan Freeman was the rock of *Seven*.)

At any rate, we finished *Waldo Pepper* and, with tremendous expectations, had our first major sneak preview in Boston.

Death.

Sneaks, I suspect, have been with us since the first Neanderthals wondered should they have less blood during the Brontosaurus sequence and if they did, would the tribe in the next cave give then two sabertooth tiger skins instead of the usual one. And although today sneaks are remarkably "scientific," they have always entailed the same basic premise: having strangers in to judge you.

Sneak previews are more controversial now than at any time in my memory — a lot of people rebel at the faith put in the "numbers" which supposedly foretell your fate. They don't. *The Princess Bride*, for example, was sensationally received in sneaks and was only a middling success upon release. Speaking for myself, I think sneaks can be a positive learning tool in one way — *they let us know if we have confused the audience.*

For the rest, I pay little attention to the "numbers." I sit in the back corner seat if I can, and I pay some attention to the movie, and some attention to the audience, and some to myself. *Am I bored?* Is this funny, was it supposed to be funny? Is this sad? Is this constructed properly — Jesus, those people are leaving — are they running or walking? If they are running up the aisle, fine, I know they just have to pee and we haven't lost them. If they are walking, that means they are gone and we have failed.

During the first sneak of *The Year of the Comet* — another flick of mine you never saw—*fifty* people—a simply amazing number—out of five hundred stormed out in the first five minutes. Think about that; I sure did. It meant I had failed as a storyteller so horribly I could not keep those nice folks in their seats FOR FREE ENTERTAINMENT! They preferred reentering the reality of their lives, anything rather than go where I wanted to send them. (The opening scene then was a snooty Bordeaux wine tasting in a snooty London auction house. The movie itself was a caper/chase after a legendary bottle of wine. And boy, did nobody give a shit.)

Today, audiences are recruited by the company you hire that is setting up the sneak. And they come and they are given a little speech by the recruiter where he welcomes them and thanks them and asks would they please fill out the questionnaire that will be given to them at the film's completion and he has alerted two dozen or so people to stay after the preview and talk with him, a focus group.

Then on with the show.

The *Waldo* audience was blissfully happy for almost two thirds of the flick. Then came the climactic moment when Susan Sarandon freezes on the wing of the plane and Redford makes a sensational midair plane-to-plane transfer to the opposite end of the wing of her plane, then moves slowly toward her, getting even closer and closer and finally when he reaches out for her she falls to her death.

Which is when we died in Boston.

Back then, we did not have the questionnaires or focus groups that are used today. But I know if we did, they would have made an overwhelming difference. Questionnaires are essentially filled with all kinds of preference material. "How did you like Robert Redford's performance. Would you rate it excellent, very good, good, fair, or poor, check one."

The focus group is twenty-something folks who are asked to stay after and talk to a man from the sneak company. And he is supplied with questions the movie makers are curious about. "How many of you liked the beginning? Show of hands please." (It is taped.)

And I know this—when the question came about did you like it when Susan Sarandon fell off the wing, there would have been a very sullen silence. And no hands. And soon they would have been asking, no, demanding to know this: *why did she have to die?*

The truth? She didn't.

All we had to do was reshoot the sequence.

You read a lot these days in the media about a movie being in trouble because it is reshooting the ending or some such. The truth? Totally fucking backwards. If a movie is a real stiff, the studios throw it out there as fast as they can and spend as little as they can to do it so as to keep their losses as low as possible. You only reshoot if the studio thinks you have a hit. It ain't a sign of weakness, folks, *it's a sign of strength.*

Reshooting is, I think, the biggest change since I started.

Some people now provide for it in the original budget. Woody Allen is famous for reshooting and he hasn't done all that badly, has he? Once he reshot *an entire film*, totally recasting it first. Reshooting can be just a tremendous help. Because when you do it the first time, everyone is flying blind. You *think* this might work, you *hope* it will work—but you never know and I am sure even an Olympian figure like Spielberg is constantly bedeviled by uncertainty. *The Princess Bride*, for example, ends with the kid asking his grandfather to come back and read him more tomorrow and the grandfather (Peter Falk) turns and says, "As you wish." Well, in the original, he didn't just turn and say it, he crossed the room to the sick kid's bed and kissed him and then said the line.

Upon inspection, Rob Reiner felt it a bit treacly. So the single shot was redone. The most famous example of course is *Fatal Attraction*. The entire ending was altered totally. In the original Glenn Close kills herself and frames Michael Douglas who goes off to jail. What we saw was Glenn Close attacking the house and getting killed by Douglas' wife and the family all warm and toasty together at the fade out.

What could we have done with *Waldo*? Easy. Pick up when Redford's coming close to her and have a shot of the plane—only now, guess what, we hadn't realized it but it's flying low to the ground—and look, up ahead there's the lake—and when Sarandon falls, wait for it—

—she falls into that convenient lake.

And starts to swim ashore. (So we'll know she's alive.)

And Waldo maybe waves down to her.

And furious and spunky, she shakes her fist back up at him.

End of reshoot. Could have maybe done it in a day.

See how helpful a reshoot can be?

Now, there are other problems to be dealt with—namely, would Hill, the Giant Ape of Hollywood at the time, go along with the change. We will never know, but I think he would have thought a lot about it. And I know the studio would have applied tremendous pressure.

And I think Hill would have gone this far: he would have done the reshoot, cut it into the film and had another sneak. If the reaction was the same as that first lethal night in Boston, he would have stayed with her dying. But if they had loved us—and we were sensational til Sarandon's death—I don't think any sane person could have resisted that evidence.

I remember having these thoughts riding back to the hotel with Hill. About how easy it would have been to get rid of the death. But I didn't bring it up because Hill liked the movie as it was, as did I, and reshooting then was just not done, at least it hadn't been in the few movies I'd been connected with.

Now this question: if we had done the reshoot and if the audience had loved us—and you must trust me, they would have, they sure loved *Butch* and *Sting*—*would it have been a better movie?*

I think not. It would have been even more a fun and games thing, kind of a trifle, with far fewer echoes. Would *Fatal Attraction* have been a better movie if they had kept the original ending? I can't say, I never saw the original ending, but it might have been more ironic, more thought provoking, more true. But then, who knows if anyone would have seen it.

This quandary haunts us all in the movie business. If you have a clear-cut choice between a softer version that's a hit and a tougher one that fails commercially, *your decision depends on the budget.* By which I mean if I am the Coen Brothers or John Sayles — for me the most important figures in American independent film — I absolutely go with the tough version. That's the side of the street they have chosen to work and bless them. But if I am involved with a major studio effort, if tens and dozens of millions of dollars are at stake, well, I hate to say this but I believe there is no moral or financial reason for Mr. Warner Brothers or Mr. Viacom to go bankrupt.

There is a sadness involved here though. One of the reasons I feel so gloomy about studio product now is that more and more, as costs rise, movies are showing a thinner and thinner slice of the entirety of human experience. Comic bloodbaths are what that studios want today. And the flood is just beginning.

CAST LIST

ROBERT REDFORD	WALDO PEPPER
BO SVENSON	AXEL OLSSON
BO BRUNDIN	ERNST KESSLER
SUSAN SARANDON	MARY BETH
GEOFFREY LEWIS	NEWT
EDWARD HERRMANN	EZRA STILES
PHILIP BRUNS	DILLHOEFER
RODERICK COOK	WERFEL
KELLY JEAN PETERS	PATSY
MARGOT KIDDER	MAUDE
SCOTT NEWMAN	DUKE
JAMES S. APPLEBY	ACE
PATRICK W. HENDERSON, JR.	SCOOTER

NOBODY LIVES FOREVER

There is the sound of an absolutely glorious tune, played by a cornet. (We are in black and white now; color doesn't come until the end of the song.)

The cornet goes on playing, the sound stays lovely; sweet and sad.

And now we see still photographs of young men. Pilots. Some of them smiling, most of them handsome. All of them dead.

Still the cornet plays, even more beautiful than before.

Interspersed with the faces now come still pictures of crashes. Nothing shocking, just old photos of planes scattered across the landscape, and by now one thing should be evident: in the 1920s, at least, if you flew long enough, chances were you didn't die of old age.

As we go into color, the words "Nebraska, 1926" come on the screen.

The cornet song comes to an end...

THE WAY IT WAS

A boy named SCOOTER *sits fishing by a country stream. Suddenly he cocks his head, listens a moment, looks skyward, then takes off running.*

We are in a really small rural midwestern town in the 1920s — unless otherwise indicated, all of this movie takes place in really small, really midwestern towns in the 1920s. SCOOTER *runs on through the town. We are looking down at the whole place now, all of it visible to us with* SCOOTER *at first the only one running. But as the motor sound gets louder:*

A man outside the gas station looks up toward the sky.

A fat woman carrying laundry out behind her house does the same.

A MINISTER *in a horse and buggy in front of the general store also looks up.* SCOOTER *runs by.*

The motor sound is louder now.

A couple of other children run out from inside houses to the middle of the street, turn around and around, then stop, pointing skyward.

A couple of clerks run out of the general store, wiping their hands on their aprons. They look skyward too as SCOOTER *runs by.*

The sound is louder still.

Windows open at a couple of houses along the street and families can be seen crowding in, leaning out, looking up.

A bunch of dogs start jumping around, barking, and now —

—all the people down below begin following the flight of the airplane (which we haven't seen). It is very easy, looking down on them, to tell that the airplane is heading for a large field by a farmhouse just outside town. SCOOTER is still the only one running.

The motor sound is very loud now.   .

Then a couple of other kids take off in the direction of that field, the pack of dogs running right along with them.

Now the MINISTER in the buggy starts after the kids.

Now the two clerks from the general store start after the buggy.

It's like the Pied Piper down there, as practically everybody in sight, old, young, and in between, hurries down the road in search of adventure, SCOOTER ahead of them all.

SCOOTER clambers over the fence, runs a few steps, then stops, suddenly confused, because with no warning, the motor sound is gone. As SCOOTER hesitates, he turns to see a great big beautiful airplane coming in for a landing dead at him, flying just above the ground.

The plane lands way way across the field. It comes to a stop and the moment it does, the pilot jumps out. He is a young man in his middle twenties. He wears beautifully shined boots and a white scarf and an airman's jacket and he looks, believe it or not, dashing. People don't look dashing anymore, but they did then, some of them anyway, and WALDO does. The town's folk are starting to reach him now, and he gives them a little wave, a little smile.

WALDO
Hey, good people. *(He raises his goggles and smiles as winningly as possible at the gathering crowd.)* You better all grab your courage, everybody, because this is flying weather. Now, I'm talking five dollars for the best five minutes of your lives.

He moves toward them, urging them in.

The townspeople move around, splitting their attention between WALDO and his Standard. It must be remembered that most of them have never seen an airplane before, not this close. Some of them hesitate, anxious to run their hands along the wings, but clearly not too confident about the whole thing.

WALDO
*(to the people by the wings,
all reassurance and charm)*
When you die and St. Peter says to you, "Hey, when was you happiest down there?" you're going to say, "Well, it was OK the day I got married and I didn't much mind the day I first fell in love. But seeing the sky with The Great Waldo Pepper — *(a long theatrical pause)* — that beats them all."

As some of the townspeople run their hands over the plane, WALDO moves toward them, letting them see him close. The townspeople are with him now and WALDO says this next loudly.

WALDO

But first, who wants a free ride?

SCOOTER has been tearing all the way across the field, and bursts through the crowd shouting:

SCOOTER

Meee — meee — meee —

WALDO

— usually, I try to pick somebody that shows more enthusiasm, but in your case, I'll make an exception. What's your name?

SCOOTER

Scooter.

WALDO gets a five-gallon can from his cockpit and takes it to SCOOTER.

WALDO

Well, you look big and strong to me, Scooter, and that's the main thing. Because I'm gonna need a lot of gas. I can tell there's a lot of riders here today. I'll tell you what, you go take this to the nearest gas station every time I need it, and when we're all done, at the end of the day, I'll give you a free ride. How's that?

SCOOTER takes the can and starts off for town.

WALDO

Atta boy.

The credits begin here and continue through the scenes of WALDO taking the townspeople flying.

In the crowd, several men reach for their wallets.

SCOOTER with the empty five-gallon can is hurrying to town. There is the sound of the airplane motor again and he looks longingly up to the sky.

SCOOTER returns along the dirt road. The can is full now, and it's heavy. There are shrieks and sounds of laughter coming from the field.

WALDO helps an excited woman out of the plane on the ground, immediately taking some money from the next person in line, a MINISTER, helping him up into the plane.

MINISTER

Praise the Lord!

SCOOTER puts down his gasoline can and runs up a long driveway to his family's farm. A woman and a girl are standing on a porch. He speaks animatedly to them a moment and then runs back down the drive. He watches the plane as the shadow of it passes him on the ground.

WALDO helps a FARM BOY into the front cockpit.

WALDO

Go ahead. Get in.

FARM BOY

What if I don't like it?

WALDO

If you really hate it, I'll give you a second ride free. Go on. Go ahead.

It's later in the day now. SCOOTER's got the can full again, and he's lugging it back toward the field. But slower than the last time.

WALDO

OK. Atta boy, Scooter. Keep her coming.

The line of people standing in the field wait their turn, all of them pleased and talking away. A young couple hold hands and laugh nervously at the front of the line.

WALDO pushes a very large LADY in a very colorful print dress onto the wing.

LADY

Oh, no. I changed my mind.

WALDO
(determined not to lose this one)
No. Keep going. It's OK. *(straining)* No, no. Go ahead. Go on.

It's the end of the day now, and SCOOTER is really whipped. WALDO is helping the last passenger out of the plane. He nods, smiling good-bye; then reaches into a jacket pocket, takes out a roll of bills. He is engrossed in counting it as SCOOTER staggers to him with the last can of gas.

SCOOTER

Here 'tis.

WALDO
(counting)
Just put it anywhere, Scooter.

SCOOTER

I asked my mom, Mr. Pepper, and she said sure you could come for supper. We live just the other side of them trees.

WALDO

I'll be up later. *(peeling off a bill and handing it to SCOOTER)* And thanks. *(He puts the rest of the money in an envelope.)* Go on now; I gotta secure the plane good, and mail this off.

SCOOTER
(he's really very brave and not close to tears;
but that sound you hear is his heart breaking)

My free ride though.

WALDO

I just said that to get you to work for me. I never take kids up alone.

SCOOTER makes a quick nod, turns, starts walking away.

WALDO

I paid you a buck; that's enough.

SCOOTER walks away. His hands jam into his pockets. His shoulders sag. WALDO looks after him, finally breaking into a great smile, and as he does —

— the scene dissolves to something, but we can't tell what it is. But it's orange kind of, with some other colors mixed in, only the colors seem somehow to be shifting and there are slants of yellow light and white things too, and accompanying it is the sound of motor roar and then without warning, it all shifts into focus. We've been looking at clouds —

— the tops of clouds with sunset slanting through and it's so gorgeous you can only stare and that's what SCOOTER is doing, staring, thrilled, as WALDO is smoothly flying the plane down through the clouds and then back up again, taking SCOOTER on a guided tour of sky.

The CREDITS come to an end...

THE SECOND BEST FLIER IN THE WORLD

The scene shifts to a farmhouse in late afternoon. WALDO sits having dinner. SCOOTER, the little kid, sits right beside him. The FARMER is forty but looks fifty-five, gnarled and tough. He's at the head of the table. The FARMER'S WIFE, whom we saw on the porch earlier, drained and faded in looks but still bright behind her eyes, sits across from WALDO. Dinner has been cooked and served by the FARMER'S DAUGHTER, who hardly says a word. She's maybe eighteen, and with half a day at Elizabeth Arden she'd knock your head off. But even now, even with no make-up and hot from cooking, she ain't bad. WALDO has noticed her. And she is very much aware of, and flustered by this.

FARMER

You musta done pretty good today, if what Scooter says is right.

WALDO
(nods, eating)

Best in over a year.

He finishes his plate, and the second he puts his fork down, SCOOTER jumps up, grabbing the plate, streaking for the stove to refill it.

WALDO

Right when the war finished, barnstorming was like this all the time; nowadays though, I guess people have just got used to airplanes

FARMER'S WIFE

Head up to Hickory, why don't you? Little place, over to the northern part of Nebraska. My sister lives there and she'd have said if there'd ever been an airplane come to town.

WALDO

I was going for the air show in Lincoln, but I'll just make a detour, thanks.

SCOOTER is at the stove, filling WALDO's plate. The FARMER'S DAUGHTER is nearby, standing at the sink. There's a water pump by the sink, and she's working the handle up and down; but all the time, her eyes are on WALDO. SCOOTER catches her doing this. She suddenly begins pumping very hard.

WALDO notes it all. As SCOOTER brings back the filled plate, he stares up at WALDO for a moment.

SCOOTER

Are you the best flier in the world, Mr. Pepper?

FARMER'S WIFE

Hush up, Scooter —

WALDO
(laughing)
— wouldn't I like to be. *(he shakes his head)* But there's so many amazing pilots around that've done so many incredible feats with their airplanes; sorry to disappoint you, Scooter, but if I'm gonna be honest, there's just no way I can tell you I'm the best flier in the world. *(pause)* I'm the second best flier in the world.

FARMER'S WIFE
(really interested)
Who's better?

WALDO

Well, in first place, I'd have to put the German ace, Mr. Ernst Kessler. He shot down seventy planes and lived to tell the tale.

FARMER

Don't seem right. Shooting down Americans don't make a man a hero to me.

WALDO

Maybe not, but Kessler was special.

FARMER

An honest day's work is what I call special.

SCOOTER

Were you in the war?

WALDO

The last part of it.

SCOOTER

Did you fight Kessler?

WALDO

(there is a pause for a
moment, then to SCOOTER)

Once, just after dawn on the morning of August fifteenth, we were on patrol over Hürtgen Wood. There were five of us, Curtin, Landis, Swaab, and MacKinnon. We were on our way back when we saw Kessler flying below us with one escort plane. He didn't see us, and we dove on them. On the first pass we shot down the escort plane, but Kessler was too fast. I followed the escort down to make sure he was finished. Then I started climbing back up — I figured that with those odds Kessler'd make a run for it. But he didn't, he took them all on — one against four, and he was doing the attacking. By the time I'd climbed back up, he'd shot down three of them.

SCOOTER

How?

WALDO

They were kids — Landis and Swaab were nineteen and Curtin not much more. They panicked, I guess — they were flying against Ernst Kessler and they knew it.

SCOOTER

How could they tell?

WALDO

Well, the German pilots were all allowed to decorate their planes the way they wanted. Richthofen had an all-red Fokker triplane. Kessler's was black with yellow stripes — like a wasp. And he painted his girl's name on it. "Lola." Anyway, by the time I'd climbed back up, he was after Mac-Kinnon. I tried to help, but Kessler was behind him and put a burst into him and Mac's plane caught on fire. Mac had always said he'd never die in flames, so he jumped.

SCOOTER

Didn't he pull his parachute?

WALDO

Nobody had parachutes then, Scooter. He'd just rather fall to his death than burn on the way down. Then Kessler dove down on me.

FARMER'S DAUGHTER

Weren't you scared?

SCOOTER

Oh, don't be dumb.

WALDO

It was crazy, but I was happy. It was just me against him. I was in a Camel, so I was faster and I could get height. But the Fokker could turn inside me, and he had that working for him. And he was all over the sky. He could snap around on the head of a pin. One second I'd have him and the next he'd be coming right at me, and then, I don't know, he was behind me and my guns jammed. I pounded on the handle until my fists were bleeding, but I couldn't unjam them, and I was there in his gunsights and helpless. *(pause)* And he didn't fire. He had seen me pounding on my guns, and he came right up alongside me, almost as close as you are to me now, and looked at me. And then he did it. *(WALDO makes a salute.)* Like that. Over Hürtgen Wood Ernst Kessler saluted me. Then he peeled off and dove back toward his lines.

There is silence for a long moment. Even the FARMER has stopped eating. SCOOTER stares at WALDO in awe.

A SURPRISE FOR THE STUNT KING

It is dawn. A gasper of a morning. There is the sudden roar of WALDO's motor as he starts to take off into the mist. WALDO flies on past the farmhouse and past a steeple. The midwestern countryside is glorious. Eventually he flies toward a farm field and a crowd around an airplane. WALDO heads in that direction fast.

As he approaches he sees a bunch of rural type people standing in the field. This is a beautiful field, by the way, with a large pond at one end of it. The CAMERA PANS past a brightly painted sign saying "CAPTAIN AXEL OLSSON, U.S.A., THE STUNT KING."

AXEL'S VOICE

I can take you high or low, fast or slow, any way you want to go.

CAMERA PANS to AXEL seated on the side of his plane.

AXEL

I can land you as soft as an old maid getting into a feather bed. If you're feeling in a morbid mood, I'll fly you past the cemetery; for the jealous ones among you, I'll take you over your house so you can see who's visiting your wife.

AXEL himself is quite visible now, affable and gangling. And the sound of WALDO's approaching plane is getting to be quite evident.

BOY

Hey, look!

WALDO is flying toward the crowd.

AXEL
(smiling at his crowd)
All right, folks. Never mind. He's just passing through. Passing through. Now, for the bravest of the brave, I'm going to do some stunts first for free.

AXEL, a trifle disconcerted, watches WALDO land close by.

AXEL

Excuse me, friends, a fellow lover of the blue may be in trouble.

AXEL jogs to WALDO, who is getting out of his plane.

AXEL

Before we get started, son, I want you to know I consider your presence here an act of aggression.

WALDO

Aggression? This is my territory.

AXEL
(claps a friendly hand on WALDO's shoulder)
Smile, son, never disconcert the masses.

WALDO
(smiling)
Then fly your crate the hell out of here.

AXEL
(jovial as can be)
For what conceivable reason?

WALDO

Nebraska's mine. I've been working it for two years.

AXEL

Then you just got yourself a new partner. But these people are mine.

WALDO

Then you're not leaving?

AXEL

You grasp things very well, I can see that. But don't you leave, either. If you'll carry my gas can into town for me, I'll give you a free lesson at the end of the day. Judging from that landing, you'll need all the help you can get.

WALDO watches as AXEL goes back to the crowd. As this happens, WALDO saunters over to AXEL's plane and kneels out of sight by the undercarriage. During this AXEL goes on talking to the crowd.

> **AXEL**
>
> Forgive the intrusion, fellow adventure lovers. *(gesturing them around him)* Now let's remind ourselves just where we were. Some people would say that you're about to see the greatest exhibition of aeronautical skill in the history of the world. I myself wouldn't go that far. It is probably the greatest since the invention of the airplane. Now this'll be the order, folks. First, the falling leaf— *(he makes his hand flip so that it's going upside down)* — then the barrel roll— *(he moves his hand in a circular motion)* — then an inside loop— *(appropriately mimed)* — and finally a daring low level pass. *(He makes his hand shoot quickly off to one side.)*

AXEL prepares to take off. The crowd watches as he adjusts his helmet and calls out to WALDO kneeling in the front of the plane.

> **AXEL**
>
> Son! Son!

WALDO pops up from under the plane, smiling serenely.

> **AXEL**
>
> I'd be obliged if you propped me, son.

> **WALDO**
> *(smiling)*
>
> Happy to.

> **AXEL**
>
> Ah, you're a good loser, son, I like good losers. But then you've probably had lots of practice. Contact!

> **WALDO**
> *(stepping up to the prop)*
>
> Contact!

WALDO spins the prop and it catches, and the engine roars into life. The crowd is really excited.

As the plane starts trundling out to takeoff position, AXEL stands dramatically in the back cockpit at attention, facing backward, and salutes. The crowd, including WALDO salute back. Now AXEL lets it out full, starts across the field, the motor roaring in his ears, and faster and faster he goes, pushing his Jenny expertly along. And then it's takeoff time and the plane rises gracefully up into the air. Well, most of the plane rises gracefully up into the air; actually, the vast majority of the plane rises. Just the wheels don't. They have been un-

screwed from the rest of the plane and they continue to roll down the field, bumping along on their own. AXEL's a little confused, staring down at what looks like his wheels rolling along down there. Finally he realizes those <u>are</u> his wheels rolling along down there.

WALDO dashes forward, clapping his hands for attention.

> **WALDO**
>
> Little change in the program, folks — my partner and I have a little surprise planned for you. How would you folks like to see the famous Axel Olsson crash?

The crowd clearly would love it.

AXEL has circled and now comes toward them flying low.

> **WALDO**
> *(as if AXEL could hear; calling out)*
> Pond's the safest spot, Axel — plenty deep enough.

AXEL flies low past WALDO, leans out and shakes his fist. WALDO shakes his fist right back, turns to the crowd.

> **WALDO**
>
> That's his sign that he's just raring to go! *(points to the field)* OK, everybody down to the pond!

AXEL circles above the pond, furious. WALDO is nearing the pond.

> **WALDO**
>
> Here's the thing, folks — it really makes Axel feel appreciated if when he's done, assuming he's alive, there's a reward waiting — *(taking out his hat)* — in Wichita folks usually put in fifteen, twenty bucks to see a crash this close up — but you all decide whatever you feel like — *(out at the pond now, he starts passing the hat)* — thank you — thank you — *(as more bills get put in, he calls out again)* — they love it, Axel. They're good people.

AXEL circles still lower now . . . maneuvering closer. WALDO shouts out his final instructions as he moves even more swiftly in the opposite direction from the surging crowd.

> **WALDO**
>
> Now, stay by the pond, everybody. That's the best spot to see it. And be sure and give the Captain a nice round of applause when he's finished. It just means the world to him, knowing you care.

AXEL starts into his descent. And as he does, WALDO heads fast for his nearby plane, pocketing the money.

The crowd stands strung along the edge of the pond, gradually starting to clap as AXEL flies down toward it. The clapping grows louder now, faster.

WALDO props his plane and watches AXEL a moment, unaware that his own plane, propeller turning, has started off without him. He tears after it, manages to catch it, clambers in.

The pond explodes as AXEL crashes down into it. The splash would register on the Richter scale; you never saw so much water — for a moment the splash obliterates the plane. Then the water subsides and the plane is visible, floating but damaged.

The crowd applauds like crazy now. It's all madness. AXEL gets out of the cockpit, his left leg held at a somewhat unusual angle. His wrath, at the moment, is Homeric.

WALDO flies over AXEL, saluting his defeated opponent, the same way we saw him salute earlier when he was talking about Kessler. As he flies on, AXEL bangs on his plane, shouting

AXEL

Come back here!

THE GIRL WHO LOVED ADVENTURE

The printed word "MEANWHILE . . . " fills the screen. The CAMERA pulls back to reveal —

— a movie theater . . . and the words were a title card. Now the card is gone and it's a Rudolph Valentino picture, The Son of the Sheik.

WALDO watches happily. A chase is going on. He studies the screen intently, his concentration wavering only to MARY BETH who sits just in front of him to the right. It's hard to tell because it's dark, but maybe she's got the best body on the North American continent. WALDO stares at her hard. His eyes flash like Valentino's in the darkness. MARY BETH glances around and looks away. But not too quickly.

Valentino embraces a beautiful maiden, and removes his gun which is getting in the way of his amorous advances.

MARY BETH intently watches the screen. Her eyes stay riveted on it. She has, by the way, a white summer sweater on the seat beside her.

WALDO
(leaning forward and speaking softly)

That was a mistake.

MARY BETH

What?

WALDO

He shouldn't have taken off his gun.

MARY BETH

Why not?

WALDO

Arabs behind those rocks. Do you like movies?

> MARY BETH

Uh huh. If the clothes are nice.

> WALDO

Is this your sweater?

> MARY BETH

Uh huh.

And WALDO climbs over the seat, and hands the sweater to MARY BETH as he sits alongside.

On the screen Arabs are sneaking up behind Valentino. One jumps him. He reaches for his gun, which is gone.

WALDO and MARY BETH watch. MARY BETH moans.

> WALDO

Don't worry. Don't worry. You know what I'd do if I was him?

> MARY BETH

What?

> WALDO

Throw sand in their eyes. Blind them.

Valentino reaches down and throws sand in the Arab's face. MARY BETH turns at last away from the screen. Quietly, she studies WALDO's face, her eyes bright.

AXEL'S REVENGE

The scene shifts to a classy (for Lincoln, Nebraska) restaurant. In a far corner, WALDO and MARY BETH sit at a table, very close. WALDO has a bottle in a brown paper bag. He hands it to MARY BETH, who takes a quick drink, hands the bottle back. Neither she nor he is totally sober.

> WALDO

You could tell it was Kessler because he had this black and yellow plane that had three wings and it looked like a wasp—

> MARY BETH

—oo-o-o . . . That could sting you, you mean.

> WALDO

Right. And he had the name of his girl friend Lola painted on the side of the plane.

> MARY BETH

Honest? Did you all do that? What I wouldn't have given for that, seeing my very own name flying through the sky—that would have been the

highlight of my life — *(looking over her shoulder)* — look, there's Axel —
(As the name registers on WALDO, she waves.)
— hello, Axel.

AXEL looms in the restaurant entrance. One leg is in a cast and he moves with the aid of a crutch. WALDO's back is to him as he moves toward their table.

MARY BETH
(sees that AXEL has a crutch)
Oh, my gracious, he's gone and hurt himself again, poor thing...

MARY BETH jumps up from the table and goes to AXEL as we HOLD on WALDO, who has not turned around yet, knowing full well what's behind him.

AXEL
Hi, honey. Oh, it's a long story.

MARY BETH
Oh, don't tell me. I'd be too upset. I want you to meet a friend of mine.
Now, he's a pilot, too. And he's been telling me one exciting thing after
another. Waldo, this is Axel. Axel, this is Waldo Pepper.

WALDO
(still not really looking at AXEL)
Smile, son, never disconcert the masses.

AXEL stares long and hard at WALDO and finally takes a seat.

MARY BETH
Oh, I can't hardly believe it. Me sitting here with two aces. Oh, you two
must have heaps to talk about.

AXEL doesn't answer, just sits and watches WALDO. MARY BETH is Pearl Mesta suddenly and she wants her party to be a success, in spite of the strange looks that are going across the table.

MARY BETH
(brightly)
Tell Axel how you fought that black and yellow German, Waldo.

WALDO
He wasn't black and yellow, his plane was.

MARY BETH
That's right, and it had "Lola" on it. — *(to AXEL)* — Lola was Kessler's
truest love.

AXEL
Ernst Kessler?

MARY BETH

Uh huh and —

AXEL

— you fought Ernst Kessler?

MARY BETH

He sure did and was it ever exciting, just wait'll you hear what happened. Tell him, Waldo.

WALDO
(trying a shrug; drinks)

Later maybe.

AXEL

Now, please.

MARY BETH

Oh, do it, Waldo. *(to AXEL)* He coulda killed Waldo but he let him go on account of Waldo's gun jammed. When he and Waldo tangled, Kessler had such respect he just gave a salute and off he went.

AXEL stares silently at WALDO, a knowing look on his face.

AXEL
(slowly)

That must have been some thrill.

WALDO
(he knows what's coming; we don't but he does)
Well, things were going awful fast at the time, but looking back on it, I guess I'd have to agree it was kind of exciting.

MARY BETH

He's just being modest, Axel. It was a very dangerous thing — that German had shot down four other planes before Waldo could stop him.

AXEL
(nods)
Landis, Swaab, Curtin, and MacKinnon.

MARY BETH

That's right, and Waldo — *(stops suddenly)* — how'd you know?

No one answers for a moment. Then —

AXEL
(eyes burning)
Because they were all in the Fourteenth Scouts, Mary Beth, and so was I.

And when they took off that morning, I didn't see any Waldo Pepper taking off with them.

> WALDO
> *(a long beat)*

You didn't, uh?

> AXEL
> *(indignation mounting)*

There were five of them in the flight. Kessler shot down four of them that morning, but he let their leader live. And his name was Captain Frank Madden. He died only a couple of years ago.

> MARY BETH
> *(flustered)*

I don't get it.

> AXEL

You been sitting here with a four-flusher, Mary Beth. He's been telling you stories and getting you drunk so's he can work his way with you. C'mon.

AXEL stands, while MARY BETH looks at WALDO in confusion. The CAMERA keeps moving in to him and it is clear that what AXEL said is true. MARY BETH and AXEL desert WALDO, who looks after them for a moment.

> WALDO
> *(pauses, yells)*

It shoulda been me!

WALDO takes a long pull on the bottle.

KESSLER

This scene opens at the Lincoln air show, on a man we have never seen before. It is DOC DILLHOEFER. He looks fifty; tough, canny, wiry, and totally untrustworthy.

> DILLHOEFER

Ladies and gentlemen — *(pause)* — it is my privilege as the head of the Dillhoefer Flying Circus — *(pause)*

A word about DILLHOEFER's pauses. He uses them, expertly, mainly to manipulate the crowd. And it's during these pauses that we cut away to show just what's going on. We're at the Lincoln air show that's been talked about. ERNST KESSLER is going to perform, and the crowd is already excited. WALDO is there alone, watching. AXEL is with MARY BETH in a different part of the gathering. Out in front of everybody, orchestrating, is DILLHOEFER holding his security blanket, his megaphone. He never uses it and has no need, his lungs being what they are.

                    DILLHOEFER
                    (building now)
— on his first, foremost and final American tour — *(faster now)* — exclusively — *(still faster)* — the greatest flyer — *(hurrying)* — the most courageous ace of aces — *(going for climax)* — the most foolhardy aerial stunt performer — *(big)* — in the entire history of the civilized world, and so now, without any introduction, let me just give you — *(looong pause)*

Dillhoefer gestures toward the sky and as he does —

                    DILLHOEFER
                    (huge)
— The Black Knight of Germany, Ernst Kessler!!!

We see a begoggled ERNST KESSLER *in his biplane, upside down and literally inches off the ground and headed directly toward* DILLHOEFER, *who is panicking.* KESSLER *swoops over the announcing booth as* DILLHOEFER *dives clear into the dirt.* DILLHOEFER *lifts himself up and scowls after the departing plane.*

                    DILLHOEFER
Goddam Kraut.

KESSLER'S *plane pulls up now into a wingover and starts coming back in front of the stands again, gathering speed. He performs another low-level maneuver.*

                    DILLHOEFER
All right now, he's made his turn out there, ladies and gentlemen — *(pause)* — and now, he's coming back so keep your eyes on him. He's about to perform — *(pause)* — a spectacular vertical roll.

The CAMERA *cuts to this guy who is bulling his way through the crowd. As he forces his way along, what you expect him to say is "oops" or "pardon me" or "sorry, my fault." In point of fact, what he does is just the reverse.*

This guy's movement is pretty noticeable now, and everyone around is watching him. Not WALDO, *though, who is staring dead ahead, concentrating on* KESSLER. *The approaching guy is in the row behind* WALDO *now, not slowing his pace. He steps over the row, squeezing aside a baffled lady who is sitting next to* WALDO.

                    APPROACHING GUY
                    (to the staring lady, as he sits in her seat)
Thank you.

Nobody wants trouble with a loony, not at an air show outing, and so, grumbling, the others in the row squeeze together, making a place for the displaced lady.

WALDO *is staring out, watching* KESSLER. *He has never varied, the only one who paid no mind to the nut who is now sitting beside him. There is a moment of silence.*

> WALDO
> *(without turning)*

What are you doing here, Ezra?

> EZRA
> *(leans across, whispers)*

It's going to be a monoplane.

WALDO is stunned. He makes a desperate and successful effort to keep everything under control.

> WALDO
> *(softly; still staring front)*

A monoplane...you mean you are building me a plane with only one wing?

> EZRA

That is correct. I thought you'd like to know. The biplane is as dead as a dodo bird.

The CAMERA switches back now to the aerial action as KESSLER goes into a new set of stunts.

> DILLHOEFER'S VOICE

And now he comes, gaining speed and pulling up, and there it is, it's a roll going straight up into the heavens, and now he comes out of it on the top.

> WALDO

In case you hadn't noticed, Ezra, that was a biplane.

> EZRA
> *(with a note of frustration)*

Exactly. It's an antique.

> DILLHOEFER'S VOICE
> *(describing the aerial action)*

Another death defying maneuver, a precision four point roll a few feet off the ground.

> WALDO

Monoplanes fall apart.

> EZRA

Mine is cantilevered. It can't fall apart.

> WALDO

It can't pull high g's.

> EZRA

Absolutely untrue.

WALDO'S VOICE

It's unstable, unmaneuverable and . . . and they can't do *that*.

The "that" is KESSLER's famous four point roll.

EZRA
(going on unperturbed as
if nothing had happened)

When we were ten, who built a glider that soared one hundred and thirty-eight feet off the old Jorgensen barn?

WALDO

You did, but—

EZRA

—and that same day who busted his butt jumping from a second story window with a parachute made of old bedsheets that refused to open?

WALDO

I did but—

EZRA

—then don't lecture me on aerodynamics!

Suddenly DILLHOEFER's voice breaks in.

DILLHOEFER'S VOICE

Now, ladies and gentlemen—a combat maneuver invented by a great German ace and used by Ernst Kessler to escape his pursuers in the late, great war—the Max Immelmann turn.

The CAMERA follows KESSLER, into this striking maneuver, but EZRA has other things on his mind, and he continues to show WALDO his plans and sketches which he is unfurling in his lap, and WALDO's.

EZRA

Waldo, take a look at this. Just take a look at this. Now it's got a perfect span to chord. Morane was absolutely right ten years ago. But nobody would listen— *(pause)* —except me.

WALDO

Wait a minute.

WALDO and the crowd concentrate on KESSLER's next feat, which DILLHOEFER attempts to describe for the rapt audience.

DILLHOEFER'S VOICE

Now, keep your eyes on him, folks—because he's at altitude now—and there he goes. He's going into—into an inverted—he's actually performing — *(even* DILLHOEFER *can't find the words to describe what we're see-ing)* — folks, what you're seeing up there — it's really —

We see KESSLER's *plane tumbling wildly in space.*

DILLHOEFER'S VOICE
— well, maybe he'll tell us when he gets down.

KESSLER *smoothly recovers his plane from the spin and starts up again.*

DILLHOEFER'S VOICE
He's going up for altitude, ladies and gentlemen. That means — *(a very pregnant pause)* — he's almost ready — *(on his stand, holding his megaphone)* — OK — remember this so you can tell your grandchildren — *(gesturing toward* KESSLER*)* — from an altitude of three thousand feet, the only man alive to do ten complete revolutions without crashing — *(huge and fast)* — the Death Spin of Ernst Kessler.

We see KESSLER's *plane climbing directly overhead.*

Meanwhile EZRA *is still trying to hold* WALDO'S *attention to his plans.*

EZRA
It really is a brilliant concept, Waldo.

WALDO
Wait a minute.

EZRA
(doggedly going on)
Now, look, Waldo, if you're worried about maneuverability—

WALDO
(ignoring EZRA*)*
— shut up!

EZRA
(in pursuit)
Look at the size of that aileron.

WALDO
(almost angry)
Shut up!!!

EZRA
(not really understanding)
Huh.

KESSLER'S *plane pulls up and over into a spin. The crowd watches. There is dead quiet now.*

A few people are moving their lips and at first we can't quite get it but then we do: they're counting, counting the spins... "One"... "Two"...

KESSLER's *plane spins down.*

WALDO AND EZRA
(starting to count)
... Two... Three... Four... Five...

KESSLER *spins down even faster and now the earth is rising, rising fast to meet him and—*

—the crowd, watching, is starting to shout: "Six"... "Seven"...

And now the ground is really getting close.

WALDO *stops counting, just watches.*

WALDO
Enough. Enough. He's running outta room.

KESSLER *is doing the ninth spin. The crowd is loud now, yelling "Nine"...* KESSLER *still holds it going into the tenth spin, but the ground is so close, there's no way he's gonna make it—*

—the crowd shrieks— KESSLER'S *going to die.*

But KESSLER *comes out of the tenth spin and damned if he hasn't almost miscalculated, but he has it under control as he adds throttle and zooms back skyward.*

WALDO *breathes deeply, turns to* EZRA.

WALDO
He is the best. Isn't he?

EZRA
You can beat him, Waldo... with my monoplane.

WALDO *continues to look off at* KESSLER's *plane.*

DILLHOEFER
Here he is, folks. He's coming in to land... The greatest aviator in the world... Ernst Kessler.

KESSLER's *plane comes to a stop several yards from* DILLHOEFER's *tent. The air show continues, but reporters and a group of people move toward it as it rolls to a stop. The plane is painted in show colors, with a sunburst on the top wing, only it is in black and red, without, of course, any German crosses on it. It is a Jungmeister or period equivalent.*

DILLHOEFER'S VOICE
Ladies and gentlemen. A short intermission. During which time, for a nominal fee you can take a ride in one of our own modern airplanes.

WALDO, with EZRA, watches from a distance. He is unable to see KESSLER except as a vague helmeted figure obscured by the reporters who crowd around him as he gets out of the cockpit.

WALDO

Have you test-flown it yet?

EZRA

The minute it gets an engine.

WALDO

Oh, Christ. *(reaches for his wallet)*

EZRA

I got a surplus Liberty lined up. All it takes is money.

WALDO
(fishing the AXEL money out of his pocket)
Here. I got lucky up north this week.

EZRA
(looks at it doubtfully)
That'll make a down payment.

WALDO

Don't worry. I got a line on more.

WALDO goes down from the stands and when he sees DILLHOEFER approaching, he hurries over to intercept him.

WALDO

Mr. Dillhoefer?

DILLHOEFER
(doesn't slow down)
Yeah.

WALDO

I'd like to introduce myself. I'm Waldo Pepper.

DILLHOEFER
(doesn't break stride)
Pleased to meetcha, Pepper, and the answer is no.

DILLHOEFER barges right on past WALDO, who then catches up and walks alongside him.

WALDO

I thought we might discuss —

DILLHOEFER

— it's still no.

WALDO
(getting angry)

Hey now, look, I —

DILLHOEFER
(stops abruptly)

— OK, I've heard of you. You're a damn good pilot, right? And barnstorming ain't bringing in much these days so you want a job flying in my circus,
right? But do you got an act? No. Right? Well, the answer is no unless you
got an act. Look over there. You think that pack of jackals come out here to
see good pilots? It's blood they want to see. Sudden death is my business,
Pepper, not good pilots.

(he starts walking again, WALDO alongside)

Now I'll do the same for you as for anyone else. I'm gonna lose the Kraut at
the end of the month to a western outfit. That leaves an act open. You dream
up a stunt that makes people think you're gonna die, no, that makes people
sure you're gonna die, I'll take you on. You might try wing walking — they
say it's pretty popular down South. Good luck.

*Without waiting for a reply, DILLHOEFER turns and strides into the tent. WALDO looks
after him angrily, then looks toward KESSLER. KESSLER remains obscured by the reporters
around him. Except for glimpses of his back and the back of his helmet through the crowd,
neither WALDO nor we have seen the man's face or know what he looks like.*

OOPS

*The scene is an empty airfield. There's a dirt road running past the place. There's an old
barn that passes for a hangar. And right now that's all.*

*Except for WALDO. He stands alone by his plane in a corner of the field by the road. There
is a sign stuck in the ground beside him in which the key words are: "LESSONS. RIDES.
STUNTS. Lowest Prices in the area."*

*AXEL and MARY BETH drive up in an open touring type car. As they reach WALDO, they
stop. AXEL gets out of the car, hobbles on his crutch past WALDO and over to his plane.
MARY BETH stays seated.*

MARY BETH
(from the car)

Yoohoo. Hiya, Waldo. How are you doing?

AXEL

It's an inferior model, but it will suit my purposes.

WALDO

What's that mean?

AXEL

I'm gonna borrow your plane, son. You wrecked mine and it won't be ready for a month.

WALDO

I don't lend my plane!

AXEL

Dillhoefer has promised me employment provided I come up with an act. I need a plane to improvise.

WALDO

You're not improvising with mine.

AXEL

Why not? Seems the least you can do for someone who was in combat while you were sitting it out in —

WALDO

— I was *in* combat! With the Sixth Pursuit in the Calais sector! I just got there late because I was an instructor in —

AXEL
(holds up his hand)
— son, I'm not a vindictive man. You learned your lesson the other night. There's no need to apologize.

WALDO
(furious)
Who's apologizing! I just said —

MARY BETH is shouting at them from the car.

MARY BETH

— you're both starving. Well, you are, practically, so why not try helping each other?

WALDO and AXEL look back at her. A moment's silence.

WALDO
(looks at AXEL)
Well, what could we do anyway? You're half crippled and my engine's giving me fits.

AXEL

Actually, I've got some ideas on that subject. *(calling out)* Can you drive, Mary Beth?

MARY BETH

Why?

On that question we pull back to see MARY BETH *driving. Fast. We pull back farther to reveal* WALDO, *half sitting, half standing, in the seat of the touring car, drying his hands, over and over, drying his hands.*

Pull back farther to reveal just what the hell's going on and what this is all about: MARY BETH *is driving the car straight across the empty airfield.* WALDO *sits/stands beside her. And above them,* AXEL *flies the plane. From the center of the plane a rope ladder dangles.* WALDO *moves more into a standing position.*

WALDO

Go straight, Mary Beth.

MARY BETH

Got it. Going straight.

WALDO
(looking up at the plane)

To the left.

MARY BETH
(looking at WALDO)

You want me to go to the left?

WALDO

No, you go straight — *(to the plane)* — slow down.

MARY BETH

You want me to slow down?

WALDO

No, go faster.

MARY BETH

Faster. Oh —

WALDO

— right.

MARY BETH

Huh?

WALDO

Right. Turn to the right... Wait, you go straight. To the left.

MARY BETH *at this point is totally confused and the ladder hits the side of the car.*

WALDO

What the hell are you doing?

MARY BETH

Why, you told me to go fast. Don't you want me to go fast?

WALDO

Not you. You're fine.

MARY BETH

That's what you said.

WALDO

Here. Here.

But MARY BETH turns back and keeps driving, heading toward the hangar in the distance. We see AXEL flying the plane toward the car. What WALDO is about to try is a car-to-plane transfer. He crouches, tense, ready to spring, steadying himself as well as he can, and he watches the ladder whiz by way over his head.

AXEL's flying too high and too fast.

WALDO, AXEL, and MARY BETH confer in the middle of the field. AXEL is in the plane, engine running. WALDO and MARY BETH shout to him.

WALDO

You got to slow it down!

AXEL

Hell, I'll stall out if I get any slower!

WALDO

No, you won't. Just come across the field and hold steady at fifty. Let us do the adjusting to you!

MARY BETH

I hope I don't go and ruin everything!

AXEL

Don't you worry, Mary Beth — we're doing a great stunt!

WALDO

I hate to be a stickler for accuracy, but you're just flying and she's just driving — I'm the one doing a great stunt!

AXEL

True, son; and that's why you'll get all the glory!

AXEL guns the engine and the plane takes off. MARY BETH and WALDO steam across the field again. Really fast now. AXEL flies above them, jockeying his plane into position.

WALDO

Dammit — *(and he gestures)* — get over to the right —

Now AXEL *is low enough and he's not too fast either, but he's slightly misjudged the approach angle and the ladder dangles uselessly off to the left of the speeding car.*

MARY BETH

— to the right you want me to go?

WALDO

What? — No — you go straight —

MARY BETH
(turning)
— I couldn't hear — straight or right or what am I supposed to do?

WALDO

You're doing great — you're the only one doing great — just don't worry —

AXEL *maneuvers the plane.* WALDO *watches — the ladder is still too far left, but getting closer.* MARY BETH'S *a gutsy girl, belting straight along toward the hangar, which is getting kind of close now.*

MARY BETH

— Waldo?

WALDO
(concentrating on the ladder)
Not now, Mary Beth —

AXEL *works the plane.* WALDO *focuses on the ladder — it's above him now and almost in perfect position. But the hangar is looming dead ahead.*

MARY BETH

— I really think you ought to listen to me, Waldo —

WALDO'S *body is ready — the ladder is just a hair too high to attempt the transfer —*

WALDO

— dammit, I said not now —

— MARY BETH *guns straight at the side of the hangar.* WALDO *makes his move! He leaps clear of the car, grabs for the ladder, holds on, and he's timed it perfectly.*

MARY BETH *swerves the car sharply to avoid the hangar and* AXEL, *with* WALDO *on the ladder, pulls up sharply now to avoid the hangar. But of course it's too late.*

WALDO *smashes into the hangar; the sound is deadly.* MARY BETH *fights the car, turns it back toward* WALDO, *and* AXEL *looks back helplessly.*

REUNION

The scene is a lovely midwestern farm. There is a barn close by and farm equipment. After a moment, we hear the sound of a truck, and EZRA *drives up to the side of the farmhouse. With him is* WALDO, *with a collarbone cast which suspends his left arm out straight from his shoulder. He also has a crutch with him which he uses for his leg, also in a cast. They pull up to the side of the barn.* WALDO *is clearly nervous, and sits in the front seat with* EZRA *after the truck has stopped.*

EZRA

Go on, it'll be OK.

WALDO

You shoulda told her.

EZRA

In case you hadn't noticed, my sister is the worrying kind. Now go on.

WALDO *reluctantly gets out and starts painfully around the side of the house. He hesitates again.*

EZRA

Go on!

WALDO *limps on.*

Inside the side porch is a lovely GIRL, *in a faded house dress, sorting tomatoes from a basket, putting them on the sill to ripen. The door opens, she doesn't turn.*

GIRL

Ezra, if you want lunch, better get it now.

WALDO'S VOICE
(softly)

Guess who's back?

The GIRL *whirls, an expression of joy on her face which suddenly turns to dismay. Now we see* WALDO's *face for the first time since the accident, in all its glory. It is the color of an over-ripe plum, his left eye swollen completely shut, and his lip would make a Ubangi wild with envy. His smile, an attempt to be winsome, is perfectly hideous. He opens his arms. The* GIRL *shrieks.*

GIRL

You bastard! You rotten bastard! . . . Every time you come home you do this.

She dives into the tomatoes and starts flinging them at him. WALDO *hobbles out, yelling protestations in a complete rout.*

A LITTLE MORE TENDERLY

The scene is a bedroom in the farmhouse late at night. WALDO *is in bed.* MAUDE *is with him. They are under the covers, probably naked, and are as deep in each other's arms as the cast will allow.* WALDO's *left arm cast sticks straight up, and his leg cast is on the footboard.*

MAUDE

I don't know what got into me, Waldo. *(silence)* I guess it was seeing you all bandaged up again that did it. *(silence)* I just never get to see you except when you're all banged up. *(silence)* Still it's mean to throw things at a crippled man. *(giggles, then silence)* I'm sorry, Waldo. *(She kisses him gently.)*

WALDO

Ouch!

A further silence, then

WALDO

Scratch my back.

MAUDE

What?

WALDO

Scratch my back and I'll forgive you. The itching's driving me nuts. Higher. Oh, that's it.

MAUDE snuggles to him.

WALDO

You're forgiven.

MAUDE

Is it only going to be when something's broken?

WALDO

Me coming back home, you mean?

MAUDE

You coming back home, I mean.

WALDO

You could fly with me.

MAUDE

Waldo, I get *sick*.

WALDO

You think still?

MAUDE

The last time I went up with you all I saw was the inside of a paper sack.

WALDO
(sadly)

Yeah, I guess.

MAUDE

Besides, it wouldn't look proper.

WALDO

We could always get married.

MAUDE

The only smart thing we ever did was not get married.

WALDO

You ever did.

MAUDE

It would never work, Waldo. Think of all the girls you'd be missing.

WALDO

I'd try very hard to cut down.

MAUDE

That's sweet of you, but, no thanks. If I'd ever done it, it would have been before you went off to war. You were awful cute in those days.

WALDO

I'm still awful cute.

MAUDE

And you practically as much as promised me you'd get killed.

WALDO

I know, I know, I'm sorry about that.

MAUDE

Well, I guess you're still trying.

WALDO
(looking at her now)
I really do love you, Maudie.

MAUDE
(softly, rubbing his body now)
Except in flying weather . . . Oh, Waldo . . .

WALDO

. . . Hey, Maudie . . .

Gently, they begin making love . . .

THE STILES SKYSTREAK

We are back outside around the Stiles farm. EZRA is in work clothes, dusty and oily, and

more than that, for the first time in our acquaintance with him, he is nervous. He ges-
tures to WALDO and MAUDE, who stand on the porch, gestures again and again for them
to follow him. MAUDE helps WALDO down the porch steps and as EZRA leads them around
the corner of the building, he never once stops chattering on.

EZRA

OK, I got it all outside and set up and hurry it up you two.

MAUDE

We're hobbling the best we can.

EZRA

Now you got to understand this thing is so different and genius-like that
some amongst us might not think it was perfect— *(quickly)*— it is perfect,
I'm not saying that, but some might think it needed a coat of paint or some
kind of little touching up here and there and, dammit, if you two don't
hurry it up I'll just call the viewing off— *(talking on again)*— I haven't had
exactly an unlimited budget so don't expect it to look like something you
might see in a museum, all dusted and clean—I'm a designer and I don't
give a damn for clean—and what makes this the greatest thing of its kind
is the design, so concentrate on that— *(At a corner, he stops. He is desperately*
nervous now and to cover it, he does a quick imitation of DILLHOEFER.)— ladies
and gentlemen— *(pause—then gesturing)*— the Stiles Skystreak!

WALDO and MAUDE walk around the corner and look at EZRA's plane. We don't see it
yet, just their faces as they stare. EZRA watches them closely, about to come apart with ten-
sion. WALDO leaves MAUDE and starts walking around the plane. Finally we see it and
it's nothing. Well, maybe not nothing, but it sure as hell isn't a recognizable airplane. It
looks like Rube Goldberg gone mad. WALDO and EZRA survey the chaos. MAUDE is be-
hind them. It's impossible to know what WALDO's thinking, except we know he spent a lot
of money assembling this mess, or rather, enabling EZRA to assemble it.

WALDO
(quietly—stepping into the pieces)

Don't you think it might be a little nose heavy, Ezra? *(This might be a joke—*
there isn't any plane nose.)

EZRA
(quietly back)

This—this elevator tab trim adjustment should take care of that. *(He holds*
up a part.)

WALDO
(staring at where the motor would go)

How much horsepower?

EZRA

Eighty.

WALDO
(louder now — something strange is going on)
Could it take one hundred twenty?

EZRA
One hundred twenty? Well —

WALDO
(big)
— could it take one hundred twenty?

EZRA
(bigger)
If you get me the money to buy a one hundred twenty it'll take one hundred twenty. Hell, it'll take one hundred eighty — do you like it?

WALDO
What about the wings with one hundred eighty?

EZRA
I'll buttress the wings, I'll attach an extra set of flying wires to the wings. Don't worry about the goddam wings. DO — YOU — LIKE — IT?

WALDO
*(he is clearly wildly excited
and he hobbles to EZRA)*
Ezra — I could do the outside loop with this plane, couldn't I? ... Couldn't I?

EZRA
Of course, you could. With a plane like this even I could do an outside loop but then, I'm a superb pilot.

MAUDE
What's an outside loop?

WALDO
It's the last great stunt — Even Kessler hasn't done it — *(to EZRA)* — if you build the first plane to do it and I'm the first guy to fly it, we'll both get rich and fat and famous, Ezra — think you'd mind that?

EZRA
I need more money.

WALDO
I'll get more money.

EZRA
(yelling to MAUDE)
He likes it!

WING WALKING

In this scene we see WALDO and AXEL flying along. WALDO is now completely healed. As he levels off the plane:

> **WALDO**
> *(leaning forward to the front*
> *cockpit and poking AXEL)*
> Anytime you're ready!

AXEL appears lost in thought.

> **WALDO**
> Dammit, we flipped and you lost — now you go first!

> **AXEL**
> *(shouting back)*
> I really have this terrible problem with heights, Waldo, believe me —

> **WALDO**
> — Dillhoefer won't give us a job unless we can wing walk. We gotta find out if we can do this, now move!

Suddenly AXEL stands up in the cockpit and we're into the wing walking sequence. AXEL leaves the cockpit and, careful not to look down, he makes his way toward the wings. WALDO keeps the plane steady as AXEL takes a step onto the lower wing. WALDO makes sure the plane stays perfectly level and even. AXEL loses his balance, nearly falls, curses, grabs hard for the nearest strut, puts his foot too hard on the wing and it goes right through, the fabric ripping under his weight. WALDO stares helplessly as AXEL fights for balance, fighting for his life, making it, finally lying flat across the lower wing, eyes wide, staring at the ground. It's the first time we've seen it from up here, and the ground is several thousand feet away and it's chilling, and there are no parachutes. Pale, drained, weak, AXEL closes his eyes, blotting out the ground, opens them again, turns, and begins frantically scrambling off the wing. WALDO watches him come. When he's close enough, AXEL grabs WALDO, hangs on with everything he's got. Finally, he gets a little composure back. Then, to WALDO, in a masterpiece of understatement:

> **AXEL**
> I didn't like it much.

> **WALDO**
> All right. Get back here and we'll switch.

WALDO puts one leg out, AXEL lifts one leg in, and they try to keep it smooth, but it's not easy and there are times when no one has the stick, and the plane zigzags all the hell around. WALDO and AXEL shout at each other constantly during this: "Watch it." "Don't tell me watch it, you watch it." "I'll tell you any damn thing I want, move your leg." "It's stuck, gimme a minute." They go on like that until the switch is done and AXEL is flying from the back cockpit. WALDO carefully tries to make his way. The plane shifts suddenly, almost pitching WALDO off. He manages to grab hold, turns, glares back at AXEL.

WALDO moves down the fuselage toward the wings, gets there, grabs a strut, starts onto the lower wing, and now it's really getting hairy, the ground visible beneath him as he makes his way along the lower wing, then begins the terrible climb to the naked upper wing. AXEL fights to keep the plane level. WALDO won't look down, and he's half way onto the upper wing, making it slow, but making it, and now he's got most of his body on the upper wing and then all of his body is on. He lies there a beat before he wraps his feet in some wires on the wing and begins slowly edging into a crouch. The wind is ripping at his clothes and he still hasn't looked down, but when he's finally crouched and balanced, he takes a deep breath, looks out at the world.

> AXEL
> *(worried, staring out at*
> *WALDO who hasn't moved)*

Hey? Are you all right?

WALDO rises slowly to a standing position and throws his arms to the winds. Excitement courses through his body. But AXEL thinks that WALDO may have frozen up in fear.

> AXEL

Come back here. *(as soothingly as possible, considering he's shouting)* I can't land with you out there. Waldo, you freeze, we're both done. Now just come on back here, you've been gone long enough.

Suddenly WALDO's in motion, retreating down off the wing and back along the fuselage and then he's at the cockpit and holding tight.

> WALDO
> *(and he couldn't be more surprised)*

I love it.

HARD TIMES

The following scenes are a quick montage of various small towns starting with a sign which reads: "THE GREAT DILLHOEFER FLYING CIRCUS WELCOMES THE GOOD PEOPLE OF LITTLE FALLS." (The "Little Falls" has been tacked on.) Over this we hear:

> DILLHOEFER'S VOICE

They won the wing walking championship of Asia — *(pause)* — they took the European title, too — *(pause)* — the unbeaten — untied — unethical wonders of the wing walking world — Olsson and Pepper!

DILLHOEFER gestures toward the sky, where a plane is seen swooping down low past the grand-stand. WALDO is standing on the wing waving as they go by. The crowd is not too impressed.

> FARMER

Guy came through here last week did that standing on his head.

DISSOLVE TO the entire Dillhoefer Air Circus in the air flying in loose formation. They

*go by a water tower. The water tower has "POTH" on it. DILLHOEFER, is sitting in the
front cockpit of ACE's plane and points down, after a moment's thought.*

*We next see Dillhoefer's Flying Circus sign. This time "POTH" has been added for the
name, only it has been obviously hastily improvised.*

DILLHOEFER'S VOICE
I have always had a warm spot in my heart for the town my grandmother
was born in, and I heard of as a child at her knee... The lovely village of
Poth. *(he pronounces it "Pawth")*

The people of Poth are there... a dozen strong.

MAN
Poth. *(he pronounces it "Poe-th")*

DILLHOEFER
Powth! And because of that we have a special guest, the world famous opera
singer, the renowned Madame Jessie Lund who has agreed to fly with us...

The scene switches to the inside of the tent where we see WALDO close up.

WALDO
I just hate this.

AXEL
It's not a bad stunt.

WALDO
Not the stunt, the dress!

*WALDO stands and we see that he is wearing an enormous long gown. He picks up a purse,
jams a hat and wig on his head and stomps out of the tent to applause, off, very thin.*

*We DISSOLVE TO another CLOSE UP of the sign. Only this time the last part of the sign has
been changed to read "... GOOD PEOPLE OF GREAT RAPIDS." But they are few
in number, listening to DILLHOEFER's voice.*

DILLHOEFER'S VOICE
Folks, I always tell our boys that our annual sojourn to Great Rapids is the
climax of our year, so just crowd right in...

No one is interested; no one moves.

THE "IT" GIRL OF THE SKIES

*The scene shifts to the inside of DILLHOEFER's tent. Everyone is present and there is ten-
sion. DILLHOEFER is painting a new sign. WALDO, AXEL, DUKE, and ACE are all clearly
trying to think. MARY BETH is there.*

DILLHOEFER

Now, dammit, is she gonna help us or not, yes or no? What we need is sex —
real sex — *(this has been directed toward MARY BETH)*

AXEL

— it's dangerous —

DILLHOEFER

— we gotta come up with some new stunts, that's all. *(to WALDO)* When
the hell is this new plane of yours going to be ready?

WALDO

It'll be ready by the Muncie fair.

DILLHOEFER

That's not for weeks. Meantime we could starve. We *got* to come up with
something to tide us over. *(to DUKE)* Hey, Duke, how about "legendary"?
(This pertains to adjectives DILLHOEFER has been painting on his sign.)

DUKE
(handsome and vain)

I been legendary all month, Doc.

DILLHOEFER

OK — I'll make you "unprecedented."

WALDO

I could go roller skating on the wings.

DILLHOEFER

No good. Gates done that this season —

AXEL

— I could parachute off and play harmonica all the way down.

DILLHOEFER
(louder)

No good. Gates done that too, only they tooted a flute. *(whirling toward
MARY BETH)* It's sex gonna pull us out.

MARY BETH
(little pause; then)

Well, I am all the time saying how I just crave adventure —

DILLHOEFER
(excited; going to her)

— then it's yes?

AXEL
(worried)
Don't let him bully you into anything you don't wanna do —

DILLHOEFER
(really up)
— she's gonna do it, I knew she'd come through. We'll just stick her out
on the wing —

DUKE
— and she'll fake being afraid — and the wind'll blow her clothes off —

WALDO
— now why in hell would the wind blow her clothes off? When I'm wing
walking, the wind don't blow my clothes off.

DILLHOEFER
(to WALDO)
Nobody wants to see you with your clothes off; her, they'll come running
to see what happens — (to ACE) — it's a good gimmick, leave it in, we'll
just shred her clothes beforehand . . . and you're a good girl.

MARY BETH
(very softly — almost forgotten in all this)
And I get to pick the clothes.

AXEL
Huh? What was that, honey?

MARY BETH
(moving in toward the sign now)
I get to pick the clothes, I said. And I get to pick what words you use about
me in the sign. And I want my name the very highest on the sign and I
want my name bigger than anybody's —

The group begins to realize what they've wrought.

MARY BETH
— "The 'It' Girl of the Skies." I think I'll be that. (thinking) No — that's
good but it's not enough.

DUKE
Stop her, Doc!

MARY BETH
(to ACE, and sharply)
Nobody's stopping me, Buster Brown. (to DILLHOEFER) This is what you'll
write. I want it higher than anybody's and I want it bigger than anybody

else's name on the sign: "Fabulous Fantastic Mary Beth McIllhenny, the It Girl of the Skies!!!"

DRAWING A CROWD

This scene opens on the plane flying along with AXEL *piloting in the rear seat and* MARY BETH *busily putting on fresh lipstick in the front seat. She is dressed to the nines. Finally,* AXEL *reaches forward and taps her on the shoulder.*

> MARY BETH

All right! All right!

MARY BETH rouges her cheeks, then stands up and starts climbing out on the wing. A piece of her dress blows off into AXEL'S *face.* AXEL *pushes it aside as* MARY BETH *cautiously moves out to the edge of the wing and grabs hold of one of the struts.*

The plane approaches a small town and AXEL *swoops down. The* CAMERA *pans to a single main street. Quiet. Early morning. There is a roar from somewhere. The roar gets louder and, as a few heads peer out a few windows, we see* AXEL *flying dead down the center of the main street at maybe second-story level. And way out on the edge of one wing is* MARY BETH.

> AXEL
> *(nodding, gesturing)*

Now, honey.

> MARY BETH
> *(nods back, starts to scream)*

Help — help me, somebody — Hellllllpppp . . .

MARY BETH is hollering away, calling out "Help" and "Help me" and "Puh-leeze won't somebody help me" and she looks just as frightened as she's supposed to and wonder of wonders, the wind is ripping her clothes off. As AXEL *flies along, the windows are filling, people staring bug-eyed at this gorgeous girl in jeopardy and her blouse coming slowly off, trailing behind her and then it's gone.* AXEL *flies along, pleased.* MARY BETH *kneels there, calling out "Help, help, help" in a kind of mindless way.*

As the plane flies by, people are streaming out of their houses now, staring as the half-naked girl on the wing begins to grow smaller and smaller in the distance. AXEL *begins to go for altitude.* MARY BETH *kneels exactly as before.*

> AXEL

C'mon back now, honey. *(smiling, and just as gently as possible)* Now, honey, you don't want to go and freeze on me, do you? No. So come on in before you catch cold.

MARY BETH is frozen . . . absolutely unmoving. AXEL *isn't smiling anymore.*

> AXEL

Mary Beth!!!

Meanwhile, WALDO, DILLHOEFER, and ACE are putting up the tent in a nearby field as AXEL's motor sound grows louder. They pay very little attention as AXEL appears low on the horizon, with MARY BETH as before on the end of the wing.

> **WALDO**
> *(looking up now)*

What the hell's he trying to do? He can't land with her out there — he'll cartwheel.

Slowly, they realize what has happened.

> **WALDO**

She's frozen. *(to ACE)* C'mon!

> **ACE**

I knew she wasn't worth any top billing —

> **WALDO**
> *(louder)*

— move!

As they start for the other DILLHOEFER plane, AXEL circles the field, talking to MARY BETH. Her eyes are staring off, vague and distant and deeply afraid. AXEL bursts out yelling:

> **AXEL**

We're both gonna die if you stay there — *(softer again)* — just crawl to the center, sweetie — I can land then, huh? OK? Yes?

MARY BETH is frozen. There doesn't look as if there's any way the lady's going to budge.

Meanwhile, ACE is taking the other plane up with WALDO in the front seat.

> **DUKE**

What are they doing?

> **DILLHOEFER**

How the hell do I know what they're doing? They don't know what they're doing.

AXEL, seeing them now, starts to fly closer. Half standing in the cockpit, WALDO makes a series of gestures to AXEL, first pointing to himself, then to AXEL's wing. We don't know quite what WALDO means by his gestures, but evidently AXEL does, because he nods, begins to maneuver his plane.

DILLHOEFER and DUKE and other members of the circus watch attentively down by the tent. DILLHOEFER gets a large bottle of liquor, takes a gigantic swallow, staring toward the sky. What the two planes are starting to do now is tricky: they are trying to fly wing to wing, AXEL's plane directly above, and just a few feet away from WALDO's.

DILLHOEFER and DUKE watch as gradually the two planes start to close the gap. DILL-HOEFER takes another drink.

WALDO is out of the cockpit now — and moving along the wing. And all the time, AXEL's plane is coming closer, closer, and suddenly we realize what's about to happen, and there isn't much in this world that's more dangerous or deadly than a midair plane-to-plane transfer but that's what's about to happen as WALDO swings onto the top wing and stands waiting to grab for AXEL's wing, which is coming in closer. His hands grab AXEL's wing strut as it sails past. He tries to pull his body up and safely over as ACE in the other plane pulls away. WALDO continues his battle, finally manages to get a knee over the edge of the wing and at last manages to pull his body up on the wing, on the side opposite MARY BETH.

DILLHOEFER is drinking really heavily now watching as WALDO rests a moment. WALDO moves quickly along the wing, passes rapidly past the front cockpit and starts out on the other wing toward MARY BETH. AXEL watches as WALDO begins the traverse but as he edges away from the center, the combined weight on the one side of the plane makes it a bitch for AXEL to fly.

AXEL
(shouting to WALDO)

I can't keep it level —

WALDO
(shouting back)

— put her in a shallow dive . . .

AXEL nods and starts into a shallow dive. ACE, while still flying, is staring up now, tense and panicked as AXEL's plane tilts badly, then is righted. But WALDO keeps slowly crawling to MARY BETH. Eighteen feet away. Now fifteen. MARY BETH does not move.

AXEL uses everything he knows to keep the plane from tilting too far over. WALDO is now just ten feet from her, but going slow, because the tilt is worse now, and for one horrible moment his balance is gone and he drops flat to the wing, holding tight for life, looking at the desperate girl only ten feet away on the wing edge. She kneels as always; not a muscle has moved.

AXEL fights for balance, staring ahead as WALDO pushes himself to his knees, slowly begins the final desperate crawl toward the wing edge. Every time he slides a leg forward, the balance gets that much more impossible to keep. Each time he stops and stares at AXEL, who nods when he's got the plane balanced enough to try another foot out again. And now WALDO's only seven feet away and now only five and that's almost but not quite enough to touch her and the balance is really precarious now.

WALDO

Here, take my hand. I'm going to help you back, Mary Beth. Take my hand.

MARY BETH reacts slightly and turns her frightened eyes toward WALDO.

WALDO

Mary Beth. Take it . . .

WALDO holds onto the wing with one hand, slowly, tentatively starts to reach out toward MARY BETH with the other and the plane is really tilting now.

Meanwhile, AXEL is doing every trick in the book to keep the plane near level. As WALDO asks MARY BETH once more to take his hand, she reaches out, letting go of the strut she's been clinging to with such determination. But her balance is gone and her hand never reaches WALDO as she slips off the wing into space.

WALDO looks down, his hand still extended, almost frozen in his kneeling position on the wing, in despair.

NEWT

This scene opens on a man in a blue uniform. He's a POLICE CHIEF and we are in the waiting room of a police station. He's talking to DILLHOEFER. WALDO and AXEL sit off in a corner, dazed.

> **POLICE CHIEF**
> You'll notify her family?

> **DILLHOEFER**
> Yes sir — we know exactly what to do, don't worry — *(a little embarrassed)* — I hate to say this, but I *am* in business, and an accident really brings out the people, so if you'll just excuse us —

> **POLICE CHIEF**
> — nobody's going no place unless he says so.

> **DILLHOEFER**
> Unless who says so?

The POLICE CHIEF nods toward a door and leads DILLHOEFER past AXEL and WALDO into a nearby office.

> **WALDO**
> I almost had her, Jesus, I came so close.

> **POLICE CHIEF**
> *(to the three of them)*
> In here.

Inside the office a man waits, a Pat O'Brien type — gentle-tough, going to flesh. His name is NEWT POTTS and we'll be seeing more of him. As the group enters, WALDO suddenly shows recognition.

> **WALDO**
> Hey, Newt.

> **NEWT**
> Hey, hot shot, how are you?

WALDO

Doc, this is Newton Potts. He was my squadron leader in France. He got eleven planes — Doc, he really got eleven planes!

DILLHOEFER
(shaking his hand)
I've heard of you, Mr. Potts. What brings you here?

NEWT

You do, Mr. Dillhoefer. I'm the Regional Air Inspector here for the Department of Commerce. I'm afraid I'm going to have to shut you down.

DILLHOEFER

On who the hell's authority?

NEWT

The Air Commerce Act has passed Congress. Your air circus is operating in direct violation of the Civil Aeronautics code.

WALDO
(stunned)
Hey, come off, Newt. What is all this?

NEWT

The fun and games are over, Waldo. You guys been scaring the hell outta people for too long. Flying is becoming big business, and people gotta figure it's safe.

DILLHOEFER
(outraged)
You think you can walk in here, wave a piece of paper and take away our livelihoods just like that?

NEWT
(hands him a small brochure)
You meet the requirements in there, you can fly again. Your planes got to be licensed, pilots licensed, no stunting over congested areas, no wing walking — it's all in there. *(he picks up his hat)* When you're ready for inspection, let me know and I'll come back. Until then, you're grounded.

WALDO

If I study real hard you think I'll pass, Newt? You gonna license the clouds, the rain, you gonna make highways up in the sky for us all to follow?

NEWT

Yup. All of that is coming, along with airlines, airmail, and there's going to be big money in it, if you're smart.

WALDO

I'm not a chauffeur, and I'm not a mailman — I'm a flier!

NEWT
(pause, then quietly)
I'm afraid not anymore, Waldo. Not until an investigation is held on the death of that girl. *(silence)*

DILLHOEFER
(shocked)
Hell, Waldo and Axel were only trying to save her!

NEWT
Then that will come out in the investigation. But until then everyone involved in the incident will not be issued licenses.

DILLHOEFER
When's it going to be held?

NEWT
The regional board convenes in six weeks in Wichita.

DILLHOEFER
I got a contract at the Muncie fair in two weeks. I need Waldo and Axel to fly — you can't do this to me!

NEWT
I got nothing to do with it. It's Congress. And you guys. You done it to yourselves. Why don't you all grow up? *(he starts to the door and pauses a little)* Waldo, you're the greatest natural flier I've ever seen in my life. If the war'd gone on a little longer, you might've proved that to everyone. But that kind of flying is finished. You're gonna have to learn to live with it. I'm sorry, hot shot. *(turning to DILLHOEFER)* Dillhoefer, I'll be in touch.

NEWT *goes out.* WALDO *is genuinely confused.*

WALDO
I don't understand — he was a great squadron leader. What the hell happens to people?

AXEL
(studying the pamphlet)
Kid stuff.

WALDO
(going to him)
What's it say?

AXEL
(folds the pamphlet)
Not it. Us. What we been doing. He's right. It's kid stuff.

WALDO's world is starting to come apart.

> **WALDO**
>
> We can still work the Muncie fair. Newt's an old pal. Give him time and he'll come around. We'll only ask to fly that one job.

There is a pause.

> **AXEL**
>
> My heart isn't in it, Waldo. *(long pause and he starts to leave)* You take care.

THE OUTSIDE LOOP

The scene shifts to the Muncie fair. WALDO is standing alongside one of those concessions where you toss baseballs at milk bottles. He is as tense as we've ever seen him. He looks around the corner and out toward the field where EZRA's plane is parked. Walking around the plane are EZRA and NEWT. They are engaged in a conversation we cannot hear. NEWT peers at the engine, tests the wires, sticks his head in the cockpit, with EZRA talking a blue streak all the time. WALDO watches them anxiously, but stays out of sight. He paces back a couple of times and looks again. NEWT has stopped examining the plane and is engaged in what seems like a heated conversation with EZRA. NEWT seems to be shaking his head adamantly. WALDO is trying to interpret what's happening, very worried. The tide seems to be turning. EZRA is gesticulating and NEWT seems passive. WALDO is hopeful.

EZRA and NEWT are both silent for a moment. Finally NEWT nods his head affirmatively. They shake hands and EZRA starts for the stands. WALDO, excited, steps out to greet EZRA.

> **WALDO**
>
> Well, do I fly? Or are we finished?

> **EZRA**
>
> Neither. I fly.

WALDO, stunned, says nothing.

> **EZRA**
>
> Newt says you already asked him three times, and he can't let you. Waldo, somebody's going to do the outside loop any day now. If I do it first, you'll still have the plane later on. Newt says you might even get by with a couple months' suspension. Then you can do it in exhibitions all over the country. You can follow Kessler around and show him up.

> **WALDO**
>
> All I did was try to save her.

> **EZRA**
>
> Newt's gotta go by the rules. Half the local C.A.A. is sitting out there. *(pause)* Look, we've been together all our lives. Tell me to fly and I'll fly, tell me to skip it, I'll skip it. But they want to know now.

WALDO is silent. Then he picks up a baseball and takes aim at the pyramid of milk bottles. He scores a bull's eye.

The CAMERA shifts to the Muncie fair action.

> DILLHOEFER
> *(big)*

Are you ready?

A deafening "yessssss" is heard.

> DILLHOEFER

Are you sure you're ready?

The crowd is enormous. The size of it is startling. Again comes the answering "yessssss."

> DILLHOEFER

Down from the heavens— *(he pauses; the crowd is dead silent)*—all—for— you— *(and now he gestures dramatically toward the skies, then, bursting his lungs)* —the *Stiles Skystreak!*

The crowd scans upward. EZRA in the monoplane zooms just over their heads. The crowd yells with excitement. They've never seen a plane quite like EZRA's. DILLHOEFER turns to address the crowd again; as always, he carries his megaphone; as always, he relies on lung power.

> DILLHOEFER
> *(shouting)*

Can you stand it? *(pause—quietly)* Now for the first time in the history of the U.S. of America!—the most difficult and dangerous aerobatic maneuver in the world—never before even attempted! *(building to a roar)* Mr. Ezra Stiles will now perform an outside loop!

The crowd is really screaming. WALDO is standing quietly with ACE by the Dillhoefer Jennies. WALDO takes a few steps out, watching as EZRA goes for altitude. He is nervous as hell.

EZRA is flying, very high above the crowd. Then he dives. That's how you start an outside loop. You dive and then curve out of that so that you're flying inverted, parallel to the ground, and then comes the hard part, going from that inverted position with enough speed to come out of it and begin the steep climb that will eventually allow you to fly level, the pilot on top, completing the maneuver, and when you're flying fast inverted, trying for power for the climb, it's tough, but when you're actually into the climb, that's murder because not only is the strain enough to pull the wings off, it can damn near kill the pilot, the pressure enough to black him out and send him all the way down. And EZRA moves out of the dive into the second part, the inverted part, and as he's flying along—

> WALDO

Power on. Put the power on— *(watching)*—wait! Wait!

The following dialogue is intercut with the action of the crowd watching, WALDO watching, ACE and the others watching, as well as shots from the cockpit of EZRA in the plane.

DILLHOEFER

He's into it—he's into his dive and that doesn't look so tough, does it, folks? Well, it isn't, not compared with what's coming. So keep your eyes on him, that's a brave man up there and he only wants to make history for you so just you keep watching. Now he's coming out of the dive and he's flying inverted—that's right, inverted. And you've seen that before, but what you haven't seen is that what he's got to do now is pick up speed—really pick it up, all the way, more power than any plane's ever generated, any plane that size, because once he's done he's got to power his way into a climb and he could black out any second, folks, that's the kind of pressure's being forced onto his brain. He could go just as I'm standing here talking to you so *don't—you—take—your—eyes—away.* He's trying the climb—he's trying it—he's giving it everything he's got—he's almost there, almost there—

We see EZRA's face close up, and it's the only time we've seen it like this and he's starting to make the attempted climb and his eyes are out of their sockets and the pain on his face is unendurable.

WALDO is watching as EZRA aborts the first attempt, unable to get sufficiently into the climb. He rights the plane, goes again for altitude.

DILLHOEFER carries his megaphone. He glances at the crowd a moment, then hurries over to WALDO. Above them now, EZRA is again trying to force his monoplane into the climb— the strain on the man and the machine is terrible.

DILLHOEFER
(who has walked over to WALDO's side)
He's not gonna make it, is he?

WALDO

He'll make it!

DILLHOEFER
(into his megaphone)
It's all right, folks. He's under control.

EZRA starts the second try on the outside loop. He makes the dive, flies along inverted. But then he aborts this attempt too, and immediately begins to prepare for another.

DILLHOEFER
(to WALDO and ACE by the tent)
Well, if he don't, we'll go right into the opera star routine. *(to ACE)* Ace, get the plane ready.

ACE nods.

EZRA is leveling, starting into an outside loop again. WALDO is staring up.

WALDO
(big)

Piece of cake, Ezra!

EZRA pulls over now into a straight dive. We see his airspeed building as he goes straight down. Then he pushes the nose forward.

WALDO
(watching)

Hold back. That's it. That's it.

EZRA adds power and the plane strains to come up the back side of the loop.

WALDO
(willing it around)

Don't let it slide back. Don't... That's what it's doing. It's sliding back.

EZRA, under enormous strain, pushes forward with stick and throttle. The plane is slowing, the strain builds and builds. Suddenly, WALDO, without warning, breaks into a wild run. From the beginning he is going full out even though nothing has really happened, he's going on some kind of nameless sense. But then something does happen, something very terrible. At the moment of greatest stress, the wings fold, the plane starts to fall and we're into nightmare.

WALDO runs on, as sounds begin building all around him — screams and motor roars and louder and louder and then the inevitable crash and there is metal ripping and the screaming sounds are worse and as his best friend for all his life in the world has had his dreams and probably his existence shattered, we see it all reflected in WALDO's eyes as he runs and runs.

Finally, WALDO reaches what's left of the plane. EZRA is inside, vaguely alive, eyes open, mouth open, bloody.

WALDO jumps over wreckage, forcing his way to the cockpit, starting to try to pull EZRA out, but all kinds of things are jammed up and EZRA is stuck so WALDO begins pulling and wrenching and kicking to get EZRA free.

WALDO
(as he works)

Let me get the belt.

(no response)

Can you move your legs?

EZRA

Not much.

WALDO

Well, try.

EZRA

They're jammed.

WALDO

Goddammit, Ezra.

EZRA

Son of a . . .

WALDO

Hey, one of you guys give me a hand, will ya?

And we don't expect this, not the thought or the fear or the noise as EZRA *shouts:*

EZRA

Christ — Waldo — they're smoking!!!

Hundreds of people stream out from the grandstand, some of them pulling at the wings some distance away, but the majority of them are circling around the wreck, grabbing at this, poking at that, pulling anything they can get, some of them with cigarettes in their mouths, some of them with children in their arms. Part of the crowd is still seated in the stands, just as aghast as WALDO *is at the behavior of their fellows.*

WALDO
(wading in, shoving and hitting)
Put that away, goddammit. Put those cigarettes away. Get away.

EZRA'S VOICE

Waldo.

WALDO

Get away from the plane, dammit . . . Get away!

Suddenly the crowd starts shrieking and WALDO *whirls around to see flames explode all around the plane. The crowd backs away from the fire as* WALDO *charges it.*

EZRA
(crying out)
Don't let me burn —

WALDO *is by him now.*

EZRA

— please just don't let me burn —

WALDO *cannot wedge him loose;* EZRA *is caught and the flames are higher.*

EZRA

— *please* —

WALDO

Come on, help me. Help me. Don't just stand there. Help me get him out.

EZRA

Waldo — I'm burning — I'm burning!

And EZRA is. WALDO is scorched now, too. He reaches out, grabs a two-by-four from the wreckage of the plane, clubs EZRA with it, knocks him unconscious.

WALDO

Get away. Get away. *(charging into the crowd)* Get away from here, you goddam vultures. Get away. Go on. *(hitting out everywhere)* Get back... Go back. Go on. *(almost crazed now)* Go back. Go on. Get away.

WALDO suddenly turns and starts into a run. The people still in the stands are horrified. ACE, with the Dillhoefer plane, is set and ready to fly as WALDO practically vaults into the cockpit.

The crowd is circling the flames, picking at the wreckage, grabbing whatever they can as the sound of a motor gets suddenly loud. WALDO cuts across toward them in the plane at great speed. He's flying with his wings on the ground and as he gets closer, he rises into the air, banking, coming back down toward the crowd.

WALDO
(screaming it out)

Get away — get away!

The crowd by EZRA'S plane starts to panic as WALDO dives on them, pulls up, gets set to do it again. WALDO, diving down, scatters the people, brushing by just a few feet away, rising up again. The crowd backtracks, not knowing just what to do as WALDO begins herding them like a pack of wolves, cutting them off here, heading them off there, turning them back. WALDO dives again, closer than ever, and you can hear them screaming in fear.

The crowd, really panicked now, bolts, some of them toward the amusement area beyond.

DILLHOEFER

What the hell is he doing?

WALDO roars across the field just above the ground and the people dive helpless as he flies by. It's looking like a battlefield now, with the flames and the people scrambling and stumbling as WALDO dives straight down on them and there is sudden silence as his engine sputters and conks out.

Wherever you look, people are running, running and hiding and slipping and ducking and they're getting their money's worth today, all the bloodthirsty people, and beyond EZRA's plane is the amusement area with rides and concessions and stands, and WALDO tries pulling out but he doesn't quite make it, and he crashes in the concession area, and everything breaks, plane and banners and running people, the chaos total, the holocaust complete...

HOME AGAIN

We are back at the Stiles farm. WALDO is sitting in the yard on a lawn chair. From the distance a car approaches, and stops beside the house. NEWT gets out and starts toward WALDO. WALDO is wrapped in a blanket so it is hard to tell precisely what his wounds are but they are grievous. MAUDE comes to the screen door, carrying a pitcher of lemonade, and watches NEWT approach. NEWT goes directly to WALDO and sits. MAUDE comes out and watches. NEWT is silent for a moment. He is sympathetic and obviously does not relish this moment.

NEWT

It's permanent, Waldo. The regional board met at Wichita and you're permanently grounded. It's a federal offense now if you ever fly again. Jail, that means.

WALDO doesn't say anything. Not a nod. NEWT is the more clearly upset of the two.

NEWT

I put in my pitch for you, I did everything I could — I couldn't budge 'em. It's a miracle no one was killed. If they had, you'd've been up on manslaughter. As it is, they figure they're letting you off easy.

WALDO is silent, his face turned toward the sun.

WALDO
(finally)
Yeah, well, they did the right thing. No doubt about it.

NEWT glances at MAUDE a second. She remains silent. After a moment, NEWT stands.

NEWT

You can work for me if you want. It's the best I can do. It'd be clerking, sure, but you'll still be in aviation.

WALDO
(after a moment)
I used to think I'd die if I couldn't see a cloud from above. *(smiles and looks at the sky)* They're awful pretty from down here, if you take the time to look up. Thanks, Newt, but, no thanks.

MAUDE watches WALDO. Their eyes meet for a moment.

NEWT

Ever change your mind, let me know. *(starts to go)* Did you hear about Kessler?

WALDO looks at him.

NEWT

He did the outside loop last week over in St. Louis. First time ever.

WALDO
(pauses; then)
Oh? Well, someone was bound to do it sooner or later. Doesn't really make much difference who's first.

NEWT
See you around, hot shot.

NEWT leaves. WALDO stares off in silence.

WALDO'S SOLILOQUY

Later that night, in the bedroom, MAUDE stirs and turns to find the space beside her empty. She sits up and looks at the clock.

MAUDE
Waldo?

There is no answer. MAUDE puts on a wrapper, gets up, and walks outside. It's very late at night. WALDO sits under a tree, holding a bottle of liquor. He is very drunk, and has no intention of stopping there.

WALDO
Looks bad, folks — looks real bad —

We realize now that WALDO isn't exactly talking to himself — his right hand is held in front of his mouth and it's a microphone. MAUDE steps out on the porch, but he doesn't see her.

WALDO
—I guess the Arctic wastes was too much for any man, even Pepper— *(drinks from bottle)* — it was a crazy idea, folks. No man can fly alone around the world — *(drinks again)* — it woulda made Lindbergh's solo flight across the Atlantic look like a puddle jump, but I guess it ain't to be — *(a really long swallow)* — we might as well return you to the studio — *(cocks his head)* — wait a sec — *(looks around)* — any of you fellas hear what I heard? *(they didn't)* Just imagination, folks, sorry; anyway — *(breaks off again)* — I could have sworn I heard — *(shrugs)* — must be getting old and — *(he makes a little rumble)* — no — dammit, that is a motor — *(more rumble)* — hear that, you fellas? *(really makes a loud motor sound now)* Good people, I got tears in my eyes — *(he does)* — it's him, folks he's done it. *(big)* That's Waldo Pepper up there, everybody!

MAUDE stands on the porch. She is crying. WALDO turns and suddenly sees her. He just stares.

STILL TRYING

This scene takes place in a dirty room, filled with mementoes, and, perhaps for that reason, we won't recognize DILLHOEFER immediately. He's reading in bed, wearing glasses, new to us. The point is this is the man's room, it's his home, and somehow, it's sad. He gets up off the bed as there is a knock on the door.

> DILLHOEFER

Who is it?

> WALDO'S VOICE

It's me, Doc. Waldo Pepper.

> DILLHOEFER

Good-bye.

> WALDO'S VOICE

Just for a second, OK?

DILLHOEFER takes off his glasses as he opens the door halfway. WALDO's healed reasonably well. They neither of them look as young as they used to.

> WALDO

Howdy, Doc. Looking good, Doc — real good. What you been doing?

> DILLHOEFER
> *(cutting through)*

Get to it, Pepper.

> WALDO
> *(he had not expected this much hostility)*

Well, I'm healing pretty fast so I was wondering about getting back into flying.

> DILLHOEFER

I can't advise you on that. You want to go to jail, go to jail.

> WALDO

Oh, I'd use another name, of course. I wouldn't want star billing or anything.

> DILLHOEFER

With me? You get me the worst publicity a man could ever ask for, you get me suspended for a year, and here you are now, asking me for a job.

> WALDO

Come on, Doc.

> DILLHOEFER

You're crazy. Pepper, there's not an outfit in this whole part of the country that'll even touch you. *(resignedly)* Ah, it's all gone, anyway. They don't want to see stunting anymore. They want speed. Records. Fast — Faster. Get yourself a bug, hit two hundred, and you're home free.

WALDO

I — I can do that.

DILLHOEFER

Good-bye, Pepper. *(pause)* Your friend Olsson's doing pretty good in Holly-wood. Maybe the C.A.A. hasn't set itself up in the West yet. Try California. *(opens the door)*

WALDO

C.A.A. . . . See ya, Doc.

DILLHOEFER

You're not a bad sort, Waldo, but you're dangerous. People die around you . . .

SCROUNGING

The scene takes place on a Hollywood film set. A sword fight is in progress between, let's say, Zorro and Basil Rathbone. Zorro is doing great until in one flourish Rathbone attacks and Zorro's sword goes flying. We see WALDO speaking with AXEL dressed up like the Rathbone character.

WALDO

How's the pay?

AXEL

It's good. The people are kinda nutty, but you get used to them. I haven't been out of work since I got here.

WALDO

Who do I see about getting a job?

AXEL

Don't worry about it.

Rathbone sneers, as Zorro backs against the wall, helpless. Rathbone toys with him a moment before moving in for the kill.

DIRECTOR

Good. Cut. Axel, move in. Come in, Axel.

AXEL
(to WALDO as he rises)

Be right back.

DIRECTOR
(to AXEL)

Now, you'll be in that position over there. All right, gentlemen. All right, stand by, everybody. Roll 'em.

AXEL, dressed as stunt double, moves into the position vacated by the "villainous Rathbone."

DIRECTOR
OK, roll. Action!

Zorro has been backed against the wall where there is a large rope cleated. He quickly whips out a small dagger and cuts the rope. An enormous chandelier drops from about fifteen feet right on top of AXEL, creaming him.

DIRECTOR
Cut. Have you got that? OK for you? OK, Joe? Good.

Cut to a western saloon where, on the second floor, white-clad hero WALDO is grappling with black-clad villain AXEL. The villain picks up the hero and just heaves him over the banister and the hero flies all the way down and crashes into a poker table, crushing it, everything splattering every which way.

DIRECTOR'S VOICE
That was a good one. Very good. Let's put the camera on this.

The DIRECTOR turns away as his star, dressed in white like WALDO, approaches him.

STAR
Frank, just a minute. I'm just too catlike to fall that way. Every fan I have will know in his heart it simply isn't me. I have too much natural grace. Couldn't we club me with a wrench or something like that, anything. My reflexes are just too quick to be taken off guard that way.

DIRECTOR
(acquiescing)
One more time, please. And, Axel, will you use the gun butt on him this time. Props, will you move the debris out of the way so the men can bring in the table.

And here we go again.

NEWS OF GENERAL INTEREST

The scene shifts to an open car. AXEL and PATSY, his girl, are in front, WALDO sits in the back. They are driving along the ocean; it was blue then. There is a silence during which AXEL watches PATSY with quick glances.

AXEL
What's up?

PATSY
Werfel asked me to give you a message. He'd like you to reconsider.

AXEL

I thought they had all their pilots.

PATSY

Not after this morning.

AXEL

Another midair?

PATSY nods.

AXEL

We been through this before. Tell him no.

PATSY

I'm glad, because I already did.

WALDO has leaned forward, listening eagerly.

WALDO

Let's us do it!

AXEL

You're talking to an airplane pilot, son. Western's promised me an opening the end of the month, once my application passes C.A.A. review.

WALDO

Who'd approve you?

AXEL

I'm clean — I took my year's suspension.

WALDO

You really want to get thrown to the lions.

AXEL

It's better than getting creamed by a Fokker. I can't do that kind of stunt work anymore. I'm outta practice.

WALDO

We can work back. I could never get the job myself but Werfel knows you, Axel; you can vouch for me and I'll use an assumed name. How about it?

AXEL
(to PATSY)

You think we could?

PATSY nods.

AXEL

God knows, Werfel pays his pilots big.

PATSY

All their next of kin agree on that.

MR. BROWN AND MR. KESSLER

The scene is a movie screening area in a tent. On the screen an airplane is coming in low over a battlefield. It is silent, and under the footage we can hear a narrator (WERFEL), whom we cut to occasionally.

WERFEL'S VOICE

This is the out-takes on the crash where Dick had that piece of bad luck.

The screen shows a plane coming in low over a small creek and crashing violently, wrapping into a ball.

WERFEL'S VOICE

Dick's gonna be fine, more or less, thank God. And thank God we had two cameras on it because we got it from such different angles I think we can use it for both Curtin's crash and Landis's. I'm positive the audience will never notice they're the same.

On the mention of Curtin and Landis, we cut to WALDO, who takes sharp interest. Another plane flies over the wreck onscreen.

WERFEL'S VOICE

That's supposed to be Madden's plane flying over, but we'll probably cut that part out and start him going back up to help MacKinnon.

WALDO starts looking around him, now very excited. He gets up and slips away toward the entrance, which is a tent flap. He is practically running.

The picture starts over again.

WERFEL'S VOICE

Here's the same crash again from a different angle, so you'll see what I mean. I'd say Dick was lucky to get out of it alive. As it is, he'll be in the hospital for at least a couple of months, and no use to us. All right, that's enough. Let's have some lights, please.

WALDO goes out of the tent where they have been showing the movie. There are several aircraft around, which he looks at, but he still looks around, searching for something. He runs around the corner of the tent and comes up short because on the edge of the field is a black and yellow Fokker triplane, painted to resemble a wasp, and on the side is the name "Lola." WALDO just stares at the plane; he cannot look away. It is simply magnificent.

WALDO turns and hurries back to the tent. The movie is over and WERFEL is standing talking to AXEL. Other pilots and members of the cast are standing in small groups. WERFEL is explaining what's needed to AXEL, as WALDO approaches them.

> WERFEL

We've shot everything up to where Madden comes back up and Kessler is on MacKinnon's tail. We need MacKinnon's plane to flame, and see him jump to his death, and then the final dogfight between Madden and Kessler. Do you think you can handle it?

> AXEL
> *(all confidence)*

No problem.

WALDO has reached them.

> AXEL

George, I'd like you to meet Mr. Werfel. This is the famous George Brown from back East.

> WALDO
> *(hardly containing the excitement)*

Excuse me. What is this picture?

> WERFEL

So far I'm calling it "Eagles Over France." It's about the Fourteenth Air Squadron.

> WALDO

But this is Kessler's battle.

> WERFEL

That's right. The Fourteenth Squadron flew against Kessler, it's all true.

> WALDO

True? But you've got it all wrong. *(pointing out)* The Fourteenth had Spads, and they didn't have Newports or SES's.

> WERFEL

Mr. Brown...

> WALDO

And there was a different insignia.

> WERFEL

Mr. Brown, anybody can supply accuracy. Artists provide truth.

> WALDO

But, Mr. Werfel, I know this battle. And they were stationed much closer to the front line. There was no phony farmhouse. And they didn't have...

> NEW VOICE

He is quite right.

This balding guy is sitting alone on the side.

> **BALDING GUY**
> It didn't look like that. *(quick smile)* But then, perhaps a little poetic license is justified.

> **WERFEL**
> *(to the balding guy)*
> You're learning. *(to AXEL)* Now, look here. Are you sure you can handle these stunts?

> **WALDO**
> *(stopping by the balding guy's chair; nervously)*
> You're Ernst Kessler, aren't you?

> **KESSLER**
> *(nods, holds out his hand)*
> And your name is Brown.

> **WALDO**
> I'm sorry I went on about what an expert I was on your battle.

> **KESSLER**
> No need. You probably know more than I. I was there, of course, but there wasn't much time for me to study.

> **WALDO**
> Well, anyway, I'm glad to be on your movie, Mr. Kessler.

> **KESSLER**
> Hardly mine. I'm just the technical adviser. They let me do my own flying — publicity, I suppose.

> **WALDO**
> Aren't you playing yourself?

KESSLER smiles and points. And as WALDO looks, he sees WERFEL talking with a fabulous looking guy dressed in a German airman's uniform.

> **KESSLER**
> Ernst Kessler shot down seventy planes. If you were casting the part, who would you pick?

KESSLER stands up now — he's maybe all of five foot two, balding and going to flab.

> **WALDO**
> I'd pick you.

> **KESSLER**
> It doesn't matter; it's all lies anyway, Mr. Brown.

WALDO

Forget that Brown stuff; my name's Waldo Pepper.

KESSLER
(a long pause)

You're Waldo Pepper.

WALDO nods.

KESSLER

You were Ezra Stiles' friend.

WALDO watches KESSLER, again nods yes.

KESSLER

You were at Muncie when he tried the outside loop.

WALDO nods.

KESSLER

You were in some trouble, yes?

WALDO doesn't answer.

KESSLER

It's over now?

WALDO shakes his head no. KESSLER pauses again.

KESSLER

Very nice to have met you. *(starts away; stops)* Perhaps we will have the chance to fly together.

WALDO

I'd like that.

KESSLER

Good-bye, Mr. Brown.

WALDO

Good-bye.

A LEGEND IN THE NIGHT

It is night in the hangar where the planes for the film are kept. In the center of a pool of light stands a biplane with Allied markings. It looks beautiful but somehow ominous. Presently we hear voices, not entirely sober, but we do not as yet see the speakers. The CAM-ERA moves slowly during the entire scene, first toward the plane, then over the top of the plane to see both WALDO and AXEL sitting on the hangar floor, staring at the plane mo-

rosely, a half finished bottle between them. They are more than a little drunk. The CAM-
ERA *keeps moving toward them.*

> AXEL
>
> You got any sound notions on how to set this goddam thing on fire in
> midair, and then jump out without singeing your ass off?

> WALDO
> *(he doesn't)*
> Did you find out how much Werfel's gonna pay for this stunt?

> AXEL
>
> Yeah. Five hundred.

> WALDO
>
> Five hundred. You mean, he's gonna pay me five hundred dollars just to
> set this thing on fire and jump?

> AXEL
>
> No, not you. He's paying me five hundred. You're flying the Madden plane.

> WALDO
>
> How do you know?

> AXEL
>
> Kessler talked to Werfel. Said he wanted to do the dogfight with you.
> *(turning back to the plane)* You know, if I place a charge under the cowling,
> if I run some wires back under the floorboard to a switch here . . . when I
> hit the switch, a smoke pot goes.

During this, the CAMERA *has moved away from them toward the entrance of the hangar's
half-open doors. A figure is standing there in the shadows watching silently.*

> AXEL
>
> When I jump clear, the plane will be going —

AXEL stops, looking beyond WALDO *to the entrance.* WALDO *follows his gaze. There is a
silent beat and then* ERNST KESSLER *steps into the light.*

> KESSLER
> —I was not spying. I did not wish to be an intrusion.

WALDO watches KESSLER *approach.*

> KESSLER
>
> So tomorrow we do the MacKinnon jump. Who is doing it?

> AXEL
>
> I am.

> KESSLER

May I ask why? Others have refused.

> AXEL

I'm thirty-two and I've been flying since I was twenty, and I'm getting married and they're paying me five hundred dollars for this jump and that makes my total worth close to two hundred fifty bucks. *(pause)* I need the money bad.

> KESSLER

I understand the need for money, Captain, believe me. I myself am in debt for slightly less than forty thousand dollars. I still would not like to make that jump.

WALDO and AXEL are both watching KESSLER now.

> WALDO

How can someone like you be in debt forty thousand dollars?

> KESSLER
> *(a small, sad smile)*

I ask myself that from time to time... All I can tell you is that life is clear for me up there alone. *(He takes a drink from their bottle.)* In the sky I found, even in my enemies, courage and honor and chivalry... *(he pauses)* On the ground... *(he shakes his head)*

The three of them do not move.

WALDO AND KESSLER ON THE GROUND

The scene shifts to the airfield at dawn. WALDO and AXEL are working on AXEL's plane, stringing a wire from inside the cockpit to fasten on the tail of the plane.

> AXEL

Is it secure?

> WALDO

Huh?

> AXEL

Is it secure?

> WALDO

Yeah.

> AXEL

OK. I'll put the switch in back here, now.

WALDO

Yeah.

AXEL

Are you sure?

WALDO

Sure about what?

They are suddenly sprinkled with kerosene from the can a mechanic is pouring over the tail of the plane. AXEL jumps up, enraged.

AXEL

Hey! Goddammit to hell. Don't be a moron. That thing is already a fire hazard, just sitting there. Get me a three-eighths end wrench...Never mind, I'll get it myself.

AXEL gets up and goes to him, berating more. WALDO stands and looks beyond to where the Fokker is being rolled out of the tent. He glances around.

KESSLER is standing on a small bridge over a lake that runs through the landing field, next to a movie set of a Normandy type farm house. WALDO walks over to him and stands for a moment.

WALDO

You let them get height on you that day.

KESSLER turns and looks at him.

WALDO

They were up in back of you and they had the sun behind them. How come?

KESSLER
(smiles)

You are quite correct—I was heading back home—cold, and, I'm afraid, careless. I flew much better missions than this one. Nobody knows about them, but I did. This one only took eight minutes; someone down below told me that once. I was surprised; you see, nothing in my life has been the same since, and eight minutes seemed too little, like a cheat. *(drinks from a small flask)* The five of them came at us out of the sun and on the first pass, Madden shot down my escort planes which left it four to one against me and, of course, I wanted to run but they had the angles on me, so I closed with them and that they did not expect. I could see how young they were. So frightened. They already knew my plane.

WALDO

Who was Lola?

> **KESSLER**
> *(another swallow)*

My first wife — *(explaining)* — I've had three.

WALDO nods

> **KESSLER**

She left me soon after the war. All three have left me but Lola is the only one I still seek out in crowds. *(Hands the bottle to WALDO.)* Where was I?

> **WALDO**

They recognized your plane.

> **KESSLER**

They forgot everything — they made such final mistakes. I kept firing until the babes were gone, and the last was MacKinnon and he flamed. I don't blame him for jumping. I would have done the same. But I never saw him go because Madden was on me.

> **WALDO**

Did you know it was Madden?

> **KESSLER**

I think so, yes. I wanted it to be, I know that. Madden, they said, was a wonder, and I was Ernst Kessler. But not against children, that proved nothing. You see, I keep track of talent — *(he looks at WALDO now)*

> **WALDO**

— Madden tried going under you first, didn't he? He really surprised you.

> **KESSLER**
> *(he nods)*

I thought I was done, but I maneuvered free. But before I could breathe, he was on me again and I thought, oh, my God, is he better than I am? — Is there someone who can beat me in the sky?

> **WALDO**

Were you scared?

> **KESSLER**
> *(searches for a word)*

No — everything was in order; the world made total sense. We battled. No lasting advantage. He was brighter, I was smarter, he was faster, I was quicker — until he hesitated coming out of a turn — *(another drink)* — his guns had jammed; I could see his fists pounding, trying to make them regain function, and I thought, "Run, Madden, try for the clouds." But he didn't. He came straight for me instead, and I thought, "You are very stupid, but you are very brave, so someone else will have to kill you."

WALDO

Is that when you saluted?

KESSLER

Yes.

WALDO

What did you do then?

KESSLER

Wept.

AXEL'S LAST FALL

A while later, WERFEL is addressing WALDO, AXEL, and KESSLER. Behind them are the planes, their engines already turning over. Wardrobe people fuss around AXEL, trying to mask a parachute under his large flying jacket.

WERFEL

I want you to pull your smoke pot and keep it going for a full ten seconds — then set your plane on fire. Got it?

AXEL

Got it.

WERFEL

And make goddam sure it's flaming good before you get out. Then you jump, and I'll follow you down all the way. You can't open your chute too soon or you'll spoil the whole effect. I don't want to have to do this shot again. Got it?

WALDO
(helping AXEL)

Of course, you could not open the chute at all — that way he'd be sure to get the effect.

AXEL, unamused, stares at him. WALDO shrugs.

WALDO

Only the artist provides truth.

And then we are in the sky. Four planes, the three fighters and the camera plane, are flying in formation. At a signal from the cameraman, the others peel off. KESSLER fires a dummy burst from his machine guns and we're into the stunt itself. AXEL reaches down and pulls a toggle switch in the floor of his cockpit, black smoke pours out. He starts counting. KESSLER is right behind him firing bursts continuously. AXEL reaches ten (in about two seconds) and triggers another switch. The rear part of the plane bursts into flame. He kicks the stick forward and gets out with no more ado.

WALDO pulls in after KESSLER, letting the camera ship dive on past them to follow AXEL down. AXEL is falling free from the plane, but close to it. The chute still hasn't opened. The people on the field are watching, and we see now the burning plane outdistance AXEL, whose chute still hasn't blossomed. WALDO is worried as hell now and noses down into a sharp dive following the burning plane, with KESSLER right with him.

The plane crashes and explodes. AXEL's body comes hurtling after it, and when it seems it could not be any longer, AXEL's chute blossoms. It breaks his fall, but he hits the ground hard and lies still.

WALDO lands and vaults out of his plane, tearing toward a crowd of people who surround the area where AXEL came to earth. WALDO forces his way through, stops as he sees AXEL, who has never looked happier. Someone has slipped him a whiskey bottle and he drinks long and deeply while white-clad medical men tend him.

> **AXEL**
> Guess who's still alive — me.

NEWT AGAIN

The scene shifts to the front porch of AXEL's and WALDO's rooming house. It's night, and there is a figure sitting on a rocker. A pipe flares up occasionally, but we don't see who it is. A car comes down the street, stops, and WALDO and AXEL get out. Or try to. They are both drunk now and it takes them awhile because of that and also because AXEL has various wounds, all of them bandaged. The figure on the porch watches. We can tell now it is NEWT and he is kind of amused at the two of them. As they approach the house, he stands.

> **AXEL**
> Ah, we got it. We got it, folks.

> **WALDO**
> Steady. Steady as we go. You want to be a movie star.

> **AXEL**
> *(slurring badly as they weave up the steps)*
> We got it. There. Oh, boy.

> **WALDO**
> Who's that? Is that Newt? *(squinting)* Newt? *(louder)* Whatcha doin' in California?

> **NEWT**
> Working. I'm regional head of the C.A.A. now. Western's sent me Axel's pilot application and I'm here to check out a few things, say a few words about his character —

> **AXEL**
> — I got a stupendous character, the world agrees on that.

NEWT

Good, good. Any bad habits I should know about? Drinking, for example?

WALDO
(they can barely stand up)

No problem there.

NEWT
(laughs)

Well, if Western's dumb enough to want you, they won't be in business long enough for you to do them any lasting harm. *(coming closer, moving slowly)* Hey, what do you think about Kessler?

WALDO looks at him.

NEWT

He's in town — they're doing the Madden dogfight for some movie.

WALDO

That's right, I read that — next week, I believe the papers said.

NEWT

No, tomorrow.

WALDO
(shrugs)

I must have got it wrong. *(changing the subject)* Hey, you gonna come in and have a drink with us?

NEWT

No. Thanks. But I can't. I gotta get up early tomorrow. Betcha every pilot in town's gonna try to sneak in on this one. I don't know about you guys, but I wouldn't miss it for the world . . . *(He looks at WALDO, then slowly walks away.)*

WALDO AND KESSLER IN THE SKY

It's the next morning at the hangar. And there is a lot of activity around the hangar, a lot of people milling around — all the excitement and buzz that surrounds a major film sequence about to be shot. WALDO is inside half-dressed. AXEL stands by one window watching outside.

WALDO

See him?

AXEL
(testily)

Waldo, don't you think if I saw him I'd at least grunt or something . . .

An ASSISTANT DIRECTOR type appears in the hangar entrance.

ASSISTANT DIRECTOR

Ready?

WALDO'S VOICE

Coming...

ASSISTANT DIRECTOR

I'll tell Mr. Werfel. *(And he goes.)*

WALDO emerges wearing the costume of an American officer in the war. He's as nervous and excited as we've ever seen him — the uniform glistens. His white silk scarf makes him look more dashing than ever.

WALDO

Well?

AXEL

Well what?

WALDO

How do I look?

AXEL just smiles.

ERNST KESSLER looks terrific, too. He's wearing the uniform of a German officer and it shines. Behind him, the great black and yellow Fokker triplane stands ready. WERFEL is standing alongside. WALDO hurries up.

WERFEL

All right, we'll start with the independent passes over the camera plane. When I've got enough I'll signal and we'll get some head-on passes — but close; remember that. Close to the camera at all times.

WALDO is struggling with his parachute.

WERFEL

And I know those are uncomfortable and I know you didn't really wear them in the war, but there's two dead on this picture already and you'll wear them now. Any questions?

KESSLER looks at WALDO, shakes his head. WALDO does the same. WERFEL throws off a salute. WALDO and KESSLER don't salute him back. Turning, they start jogging toward their planes.

We see NEWT's car coming down the road, fast.

WALDO reaches his Camel. KESSLER, nearby, stands beside his Fokker. He looks at WALDO a moment. Then looks after WERFEL. WALDO sees WERFEL has gone. He turns back to

KESSLER, who does a strange thing: he slips out of his parachute, tosses it to the ground. WALDO smiles and nods, quickly tosses his parachute aside, and gets into his plane.

AXEL stands with PATSY.

PATSY

Why are they doing that?

AXEL doesn't answer, but is beginning to guess something.

NEWT's car swirls to a stop. He leaps out and hurries across the parking area.

The Fokker starts to move. The Camel starts to move also. They taxi along together, graceful, lovely, the sun bouncing off their wings. The camera plane moves out, much larger, bulkier, graceless. The three planes go for altitude.

NEWT comes up behind PATSY and AXEL, watching.

NEWT

Who's flying against Kessler?

AXEL

Brown. *(long pause)* New guy.

NEWT
(after a long pause)
I'll get him when he comes down . . .

PATSY and AXEL just look at each other, then back to the sky. The camera plane is circling around. The cameraman is gesturing. WALDO is flying high now, leveling off; he peers toward the camera plane. The cameraman is gesturing bigger now. WALDO squints, looks around and sees KESSLER flying exactly alongside.

WALDO nods. KESSLER nods. And like that WALDO peels off, and KESSLER, at the same second, breaks off in the opposite direction. The maneuver done, WALDO glances back to see KESSLER turning inside and getting on his tail. KESSLER rides WALDO's tail, only closer, and wham, WALDO executes a snap, just like that.

On the ground, AXEL, PATSY and NEWT look up.

PATSY

I don't understand. What are they doing?

AXEL again doesn't answer. Nearby WERFEL looks up in growing dismay and disbelief.

Back in the air, WALDO comes out of his maneuver. And KESSLER's right with him, still right on his tail. KESSLER, enjoying himself, rides WALDO's tail closer than ever, until suddenly, WALDO starts to really put on a show, controlling the Camel as if it were part of his body, dodging with it, feinting, a loop from out of nowhere, and as he comes out of it and looks back, KESSLER's still there, still enjoying himself. And now WALDO's starting to smile, too. KESSLER, happy as a goddam clam, is smiling right back.

Suddenly, WALDO's gone, diving for safety, and KESSLER can't quite keep up as WALDO banks, gets free, goes for altitude, suddenly turns, flies toward KESSLER now. KESSLER is stunned that WALDO is coming dead for him.

AXEL'S VOICE
(as the planes veer off)

They're actually fighting, for chrissakes.

KESSLER is getting ready as again WALDO comes straight for him, and they're close together, frighteningly close, but then KESSLER makes a move, and has him, because the Fokker is dead on top of him now, and as WALDO maneuvers, he cannot shake the other plane. And slowly, inexorably now, KESSLER begins forcing WALDO down, and the ground is close, too close to try diving for freedom, and up ahead, beyond the battlefield set, is a ravine and it is there that WALDO is being forced, and no matter how he tries, he cannot shake free. And just before he smashes into the ravine he does a great thing: flips his plane ninety degrees so that his wings are at right angles with the ground and like that he skims safely through the pass, comes out alive and well on the far side. KESSLER is watching WALDO's maneuver and as WALDO survives, KESSLER in his cockpit claps his hands together a few times in genuine appreciation.

WALDO starts back up, soaring for altitude. KESSLER follows. The planes circle, getting ready. Once over Lierval, Udet was flying alone and found Guynemer and for eight minutes they fought and they were both legendary when they clashed and probably there was more sheer talent in the sky that morning than any other time in the war. These are different skies, and it's a different war, but there's no less talent on display, here and now, in the blue of California.

WALDO and KESSLER charge dead at each other as the ultimate dogfight begins, WALDO feinting, KESSLER countering, coming back with a maneuver of his own.

On the ground, the crowd is frozen, staring, and if you don't know a thing about flying, you can still sense that something pretty good is going on up there, and if you do know something about flying, then all you can do is watch and say, "Thank God, I'm here, I'd rather be here than anywhere else in the world."

In the sky the two planes are flying dead at each other and then, when it doesn't seem as if there's time enough to avoid the crash, KESSLER goes one way, WALDO maneuvers the other, and breaks KESSLER's strut with his wing tip.

AXEL

Jesus, he rammed him.

In a matter of minutes, the two planes come together again, too close, and again there is contact and now the fabric on one of WALDO's wings is cut, starts to tear.

The two planes circle each other, like some wounded prehistoric beasts. The two pilots just couldn't be happier. The planes keep fighting and for a moment KESSLER has WALDO but WALDO slips free.

On the ground, WERFEL realizes at last what it's all about.

WERFEL
Well, get a camera on them, will you? If those stupid bastards are gonna kill each other, I want it on film.

WALDO comes down on the Fokker. KESSLER dives free, then banking, comes up at WALDO, knocking his wheels away. But WALDO recovers and turns back on his assailant, joyously.

NEWT
(the words just burst from him)
Beat him, Waldo! *(embarrassed, trying to explain)* Well, as long as he's up there he might as well win.

WALDO climbs away from KESSLER, doubling back suddenly, as KESSLER dives clear. KESSLER climbs again, and again the two great planes circle, waiting, gathering strength, until suddenly we see them charging, and WALDO cuts one way, KESSLER makes a countering move but too late, because again there is the terrible sound of contact in midair and as they manage to pull apart, another wing is torn on KESSLER's plane, the fabric beginning to weaken and strain. KESSLER knows he's in trouble so he charges; WALDO turns into the charge, accepts it, and it seems like a head-on is inevitable, but KESSLER passes over WALDO by inches and WALDO pulls up sharply, taking a piece out of KESSLER's tail with his propeller. WALDO pulls up, his propeller gouged, his plane vibrating. He looks down on KESSLER. KESSLER is in worse trouble. He looks at his top wing. It's close to pulling loose. KESSLER looks back up at WALDO. One fast evasive maneuver and he's done for and he knows it.

On the ground, NEWT is shouting.

NEWT
You got him! One more pass and you got him!

WALDO peels off and dives screaming down on KESSLER. KESSLER, helpless, his controls soft, tries to maneuver but is barely able to keep his plane under control. WALDO plunges down to the attack and, at the last moment, pulls up and skids deftly into position alongside KESSLER. KESSLER watches and waits.

KESSLER raises his goggles and slowly, as he once did to Madden over the Hürtgen Wood, he salutes. WALDO stares at him a moment, then acknowledges KESSLER's gesture with one of his own. The salutes hold.

Suddenly the planes separate, KESSLER dropping down, WALDO soaring toward the clouds.

WALDO's plane goes into one giant joyous roll. He flies into a cloud. The white covers him.

Stay with the cloud.

Now the lovely cornet song from the start of the picture is heard again.

WALDO never comes out of the cloud.

The cornet song is softer.

Now we see a still photo of WALDO *in black and white. He sits on a plane wing, arms raised, naturally, to the skies. He looks wonderful. Beneath the photograph comes the following legend:*

WALDO PEPPER
(1895–1931)

Stay with WALDO.

Listen to the cornet song.

Fade out . . .

ALL THE PRESIDENT'S MEN

DIRECTOR	ALAN J. PAKULA
PRODUCER	WALTER COBLENZ
CINEMATOGRAPHER	GORDON WILLIS
FILM EDITOR	ROBERT WOLFE
PRODUCTION DESIGN	GEORGE JENKINS
MUSIC	DAVID SHIRE

SCREENPLAY	WILLIAM GOLDMAN
	(FROM THE BOOK BY
	BOB WOODWARD
	AND
	CARL BERNSTEIN)

With all the hype surrounding new movies today, I no longer think it is possible to judge them as art objects when they come out. All you can answer with certainty on initial release is this: do they work at the box office?

Two movies have opened in the past two weeks, both of which got many terrific reviews, *A Time To Kill* and *Emma*. And if you were alive on earth lately (not necessarily the same thing, alas) you could easily be forgiven for forgetting those titles. Because all that has been talked of is their two young stars, Matthew McConaghey and Gwyneth Paltrow.

McConaghey is a bright young Texan of twenty-six who until two years ago, wanted to be a director, while Paltrow is a bright young local of twenty-three who probably two years ago wanted to be a good actress. Rarely has the hype been as relentless as has the publicity surrounding these two — he is the new Paul Newman, she is suddenly and from nowhere, the greatest actress of her generation, a better and younger Meryl.

Everyone I have talked to is sick to death of them both. And the reviews, particularly of *A Time to Kill*, have not so much reviewed McConaghey's performance as they have his entire career. ("He will never be Paul Newman." "He is clearly the next Paul Newman." "Is not." "Is too.") All this for his very first lead role. Now this is good for their agents when they come to negotiating their next contracts, but it is not very good for either of their performing careers.

It is, in point of fact, sad.

The greatest acting explosion in this country took place at the Ethel Barrymore Theatre in this town, in December of 1947, when a twenty-three-year-old actor opened in a play whose fame subsequently went around the world. As did his.

It was Brando, of course, in *A Streetcar Named Desire*.

I saw that performance.

It is amazing to me how much of that December matinee I still remember. Where my seat was, the color of some of the costumes, the placement of some of the actors when they said some of the lines.

I was a sixteen-year-old in from Chicago and I knew nothing of what I was about to witness. It was, I think, one of sixteen shows my family saw in two weeks. (You could do that then. I guess, technically, you could do that now. The difference was that then, you wanted to.)

The play started and then a sound started that I have only heard two times in the theatre. (Al Pacino in *The Indian Wants the Bronx* and George C. Scott in *Children of Darkness*.) I wish I could tell you precisely what that sound was but thinking back, I cannot. It was not whispering. Or anyway, not just whispering. And it was not just gasps. I guess the closest I can come is this: some kind of visceral recognition of greatness.

No one had ever seen anything like Marlon Brando before.

And soon after the opening the hype started. At last we had someone who might be the American Olivier. Within a half dozen years, Brando was the most famous actor in the world.

Now, class, how have things changed for the worse? Think about that. (While you're thinking, a hint: the key word is in the first sentence of the paragraph above.)

The word is *after*. The fame started *after* the performance. *Brando had done something*. Today, we can't be bothered with anything time consuming like that. Paltrow and McConaghey are famous for this: *they got cast*. That's it, folks. Are they talented? Oh yes. Enormously. Hopefully they will be giving us pleasure for years. Are they good in their roles? That's for you to decide but I can tell you this much: *they ought to be*.

They are not, either of them, playing the maid. He snared the most sought after male ingenue lead of the year, and she got arguably the most appealing lady ever written by the greatest female writer of them all.

So how is any of this even remotely sad?

Because these two performers are being denied the two greatest gifts any performer can have.

(1) The ability to surprise us.

(2) The right to fail.

When the hype hit Brando, it was, of course, such a different tiny world in terms of publicity. He could still work at his craft eight times a week — and he could still surprise us. He could do things we didn't know an actor could do, let us ride his talent to places we had never been.

But McConaghey and Paltrow have been denied that. We know too much about them. The name of his dog, the name of her boyfriend. Several critics have wondered if she would have even been cast in the part if she had not been living with Brad Pitt. Doesn't matter in the long run. We do not live in the long run, so when we see *Emma* we think, "*That's* the girl that nailed Brad Pitt? I wonder what he sees in her."

In twenty years, that won't matter. They will either be married in which case we will be tired of them, or they will have broken up, in which case those of us with short memories will have forgotten that they ever cohabitated. (But right now, as the movie starts its run, that is what we think about.)

So they can't surprise us because we are too knowledgeable.

Worse, they cannot be allowed to fail.

Which everyone in the public eye needs to do. Tim McCarver feels that athletes must fail and must fail as early as possible. Because in the beginning, they have gotten by on their talent alone. But with failure comes thought, and greatness needs the combination of talent and mind.

If Paltrow and McConaghey's next ventures stiff at the box office, the media will be filled with "Whatever happened to?" stories. And their failure will be what we see when we see them, not their work.

In other words, the world is too much with us. How really gifted are they? I hope we get the chance to find out.

Fred Rosen, the head of Ticketmaster, said something that goes a long way towards explaining the explosion of hype today. "I know there's rock concerts and movies and books and television and computers and CD's and CD ROM's and the Internet — but I also know this: *Everybody's only got the same two hours.*"

Those same two hours are at the basis of so much of what we are bombarded with today. In the case of movies, there is a simple and basic problem: there are waaaay too many movies being made. Only Disney, of the major studios, has done something about this and decided to cut back on production. The other studios are involved in one of Hollywood's great intellectual pursuits: dick swinging.

All the studios are engaged in a totally moronic contest that involves market share. If my market share of gross at the end of the year is bigger than yours, I win. Never mind what it costs to achieve that share.

Let's say four movies are opening this Friday. At a total cost, counting prints and advertising, of a quarter of a billion dollars. (In today's world, low budget films.) Those four studios face the same basic problem: how do I make my movie stand out? Well, most obviously and expensively, a major star will do that. We know who they are, we have memories of them in earlier work, probably we even like them. They are easy to get on Leno and Letterman and magazines fight to put them on the cover.

So a star generates hype easily.

But if I'm dealing with *Emma* or *A Time To Kill*, what do I do? (I understand one is a Grisham novel with Sandra Bullock. But she is not the lead and this was a serious flick, not a fantastical conceit about a Mafia law firm.) Well, you take the most salable performers you have, and hype the shit out of them. Because if you don't score on that first big weekend, you are dead in the water because next weekend, four more movies are going to open.

It did not used to be this way. Thirty years ago, a movie would open in maybe a dozen theatres in the entire country, and sit there for up to a year, while interest built across America. (Seems medieval, yes?)

The cost of money changed all that. And once television was seen as the crucial way to publicize a movie, everything went mad. Costs became brutal and money had to be brought in as quickly as possible. So now big movies open in over two thousand theatres. (I would guess in the near future, if a movie is a lock — let's say sequels to *Jurassic Park* or *Independence Day* — they will open in five thousand theatres. And maybe I'm guessing low.)

The scariest thing about hype today is this: as the hype artists get more and more skilled, and they are, pretty soon hype is going to be accepted as truth.

Who said I'm not an optimist?

Which brings me to *All the President's Men*. It was the most hyped movie of any

I've ever done. Woodward and Bernstein were so famous as having helped bring down Nixon and winning the Pulitzer and Robert Redford was the biggest star in the world, (sort of like Brad Pitt is today, only more so). And the book was so famous and Dustin Hoffman was so famous and the troubles of getting it off the ground were so famous and the troubles with the script were so famous and on and on.

Reading it now, I was shocked, after twenty years, to realize how small a picture it was. Maybe it should have been a little black and white movie with two unknowns in the leads. (Redford, no fool then or ever, knew this. Woodward and Bernstein had been unknown when the story happened. In their twenties when the Watergate break-in took place.) One of the great appeals of the material was these two little guys, with no fame and few connections, managed to do what they in point of fact did.

Another shocker was this: how hard I slaved to try and get it right and how it doesn't matter remotely as much as I thought it did. Let me explain that. Because we were dealing with a piece of material that actually changed the course of history, I felt this insane pressure to have it as dry dust authentic as I could.

Especially placing all those weird people with all those weird names. You probably have long forgotten them but those names are still with me.

Stans and Segrettis and Kleindienst and Abphanalp and Rebozo and most especially for me, Kalmbach. I remember being haunted trying to figure out how to get Kalmbach into the story. My life, during those crazed writing months, was filled with detritus like that. *My God, the earth will open and swallow me if I don't get Kalmbach in here.*

Having read the script over now, I see the story would have worked without my suffering. David and Goliath usually does...

CAST LIST

DUSTIN HOFFMAN	CARL BERNSTEIN
ROBERT REDFORD	BOB WOODWARD
JACK WARDEN	HARRY ROSENFELD
MARTIN BALSAM	HOWARD SIMONS
HAL HOLBROOK	DEEP THROAT
JASON ROBARDS, JR.	BEN BRADLEE
JANE ALEXANDER	BOOKKEEPER
MEREDITH BAXTER BIRNEY	DEBBIE SLOAN
NED BEATTY	DARDIS
STEPHEN COLLINS	HUGH SLOAN, JR.
PENNY FULLER	SALLY AIKEN
JOHN McMARTIN	FOREIGN EDITOR
ROBERT WALDEN	DONALD SEGRETTI
FRANK WILLS	FRANK WILLS
F. MURRAY ABRAHAM	1st ARRESTING OFFICER

PRE-REHEARSAL VERSION MARCH, 1975

THIS IS THE ROSS MACDONALD VERSION

Watergate looked at primarily as a mystery

It is too long.

It is not interested primarily in personal relationships.

It attempts to show, step by step, how the reporters got their story.

It does not have Woodward's social or personal life yet.

Whatever else it may lack—it was turned in *a week ahead of schedule*. The author would like that fact remembered.

Start with as few credits as possible. When they're over —

FADE IN ON

A TINY PIECE OF BLACK TAPE.

We see it in the center of the large, dimly lit screen. As the tape is pressed around a door —

BEGIN THE BREAK-IN SEQUENCE

It's a major piece of action, running maybe five minutes and it's all as detailed and accurate as we can make it, with as many "if only's" included as possible. ("If only" the tape had been attached up and down instead of around the door, Wills wouldn't have spotted it and alerted the police; "if only" the first police car called had gone to investigate, Baldwin, watching from the Howard Johnson Motor Inn, would have seen their uniforms and radioed Hunt and Liddy in time for them to have gotten to the five burglars and then safely away.)

The break-in ends when Leeper arrests the five men. He thought he only had one guy, so when ten hands were raised he was surprised. The hands are all encased in Playtex rubber surgical gloves. HOLD *on the hands a moment; then —*

GO TO

A DARK APARTMENT.

The phone rings. WOODWARD *fumbles for the receiver, turns on the bed light. He listens a moment.*

WOODWARD
No, no trouble, Harry, be right down. *(he hangs up)* Son of a bitch.

He lies back. The apartment is one room, a small terrace beyond. Not much of a place.

WOODWARD *lies still, staring at the ceiling. He blinks, blinks again.* HOLD . . .

CUT TO

THE ENORMOUS FIFTH FLOOR OF THE WASHINGTON POST.

It looks, early of a Saturday morning, pretty deserted. Those reporters that are around are young, bright, and presently involved in nothing more taxing than drinking coffee and thumbing through the papers.

HARRY ROSENFELD *surveys the scene from his office doorway as* WOODWARD *approaches, hangs his coat at his desk, not far from where* ROSENFELD *is standing.*

ROSENFELD
Where's that cheery face we've come to know and love?

WOODWARD
You call me in on my day off because some idiots have broken into local Democratic Headquarters — tell me, Harry, why should I be smiling?

> ROSENFELD

As usual, that keen mind of yours has pegged the situation perfectly. *(chomps on some Maalox tablets)* Except (a) it wasn't local Democratic Headquarters, it was National Democratic Headquarters —

> *(WOODWARD is surprised —*
> *he hadn't known.)*

— and (b) these weren't just any idiots, these were special idiots, seeing as when they were arrested at 2:30 this morning, they were all wearing business suits and Playtex gloves and were carrying — *(consults a piece of paper)* — a walkie-talkie, forty rolls of film, cameras, lock picks, pen-sized tear gas guns, plus various bugging devices. *(puts paper down)* Not to mention over two thousand dollars, mostly in sequenced hundred dollar bills.

> WOODWARD

Preliminary hearing at Superior Courthouse?

> ROSENFELD
> *(nods)*

Two o'clock, work the phones 'til you go.

CUT TO

THE CRIMINAL COURTS BUILDING.

WOODWARD hurries along, goes inside as we

CUT TO

A CORRIDOR INSIDE. WOODWARD comes down it, looks around, sees a door marked "Counsel's Offices" and heads toward it. Now —

CUT TO

A CLERK AT A DESK as WOODWARD comes up. Behind them, two lawyers are clearly angry about something, talking and gesticulating to each other.

> WOODWARD
> *(to the COUNSEL'S CLERK)*

Could you give me the names of the lawyers for the men arrested in the Watergate.

> CLERK

These two were appointed — *(indicates the angry men)* — only now it turns out the burglars got their own counsel. *(he starts to laugh)*

> FIRST ANGRY LAWYER
> *(to CLERK)*

When you gonna stop thinking it's so funny.

SECOND ANGRY LAWYER
(to CLERK*)*
We wouldda done a terrific job protecting those guys.
(neither lawyer, by the way,
is Clarence Darrow)

FIRST ANGRY LAWYER
You think we're not as good as some hotshot fancy lawyer? —

CUT TO

THE COURTROOM *and business is booming. Muggers, pimps, hookers, their families and friends. In the scene that follows, a constant counterpoint is what's going on up at the front as an endless succession of petty criminals caught the previous night, the aforementioned muggers, pimps, and hookers, are shuttled in, given a quick appearance before a* JUDGE *who sets bond, and then shuttled out.*

In the audience, one man stands out — DOUGLAS CADDY. *He is extremely well-dressed and obviously successful. Beside him sits another smaller man, who is unshaven and squints.* WOODWARD *moves in, sits alongside* CADDY.

WOODWARD
Mr. Caddy? My name's Bob Woodward, I'm from the *Post* and I wanted to ask about how you happened to come on this case —

CADDY
— I'm not here.

WOODWARD
(nods)
OK.

He takes out a small notebook, writes, muttering aloud as he does.

WOODWARD
Douglas Caddy, the attorney of record, when questioned about his presence in the courtroom, denied he was in the courtroom, "I'm not here," Mr. Caddy said.

CADDY
(impatiently)
Clearly, I *am* here, but only as an individual, I'm not the attorney of record. *(indicating unshaven man)* Mr. Rafferty has that position. Whatever you want, you'll have to get from him, I have nothing more to say.

And as he gets up, walks off—

CUT TO

THE WATER FOUNTAIN IN THE CORRIDOR. *There is a small line.* CADDY *waits at the end of it.*

> **WOODWARD**
> *(moving in behind him)*

Mr. Rafferty was very helpful. Four Cuban-Americans and this other man, James McCord.

> **CADDY**

Look, I told you inside —

> **WOODWARD**

— you have nothing more to say, I understand that.

CADDY turns away; WOODWARD goes right on.

> **WOODWARD**

What I don't understand is how you got here.

> **CADDY**

I assure you, there's nothing mysterious involved.

> **WOODWARD**

Probably you're right, but a little while ago, I was talking to a couple of lawyers who'd been assigned to represent the burglars.

> **CADDY**

So?

> **WOODWARD**

Well, they never would have been assigned if anyone had known the burglars had arranged for their own counsel. And that could only mean the burglars *didn't* arrange for their own counsel — they never even made a phone call. *(looks at CADDY)* So if they didn't ask for you to be here, how did you know to come?

Without a word, CADDY turns, leaves the line without getting a drink. Silently, WOODWARD watches. Now —

CUT TO

CADDY seated as before beside RAFFERTY. WOODWARD's voice comes from behind him, and as CADDY turns, WOODWARD is seated one row back.

> **WOODWARD**

Did you know to come because one of the other men involved in the break-in called you?

> **CADDY**
> *(turning)*

There is no reason to assume other people were involved.

> **WOODWARD**
> Your clients were arrested with a walkie-talkie; they didn't need that to talk among themselves.

CADDY looks at WOODWARD, turns back.

> **CADDY**
> *(turning back)*
> They are not *my* clients.

> **WOODWARD**
> You're a lawyer and you're here —

> **CADDY**
> — I met one of the defendants, Mr. Barker, at a social occasion once — *(stops himself)* — I have nothing more to say.

> **WOODWARD**
> *(leaning forward as CADDY*
> *turns away again)*
> A Miami social occasion? *(explaining)* Mr. Rafferty told me the Cubans were from Miami.

> **CADDY**
> *(sighing)*
> Barker's wife called me at three this morning; her husband apparently had told her to call if he hadn't called her by then.

> **WOODWARD**
> It was really nice of you to come, since you'd only met him once.

> **CADDY**
> Are you implying you don't believe me?

> **WOODWARD**
> I have nothing more to say.

> **CADDY**
> You don't mind getting on people nerves, do you?

WOODWARD considers this a moment. Then —

> **WOODWARD**
> Nope.

And on that word —

CUT TO

THE COURTROOM *as without warning, it quiets. There is suddenly a tremendous air of expectancy, you can feel it. Now we see why as five men in dark business suits are led in; they've been stripped of belts, ties, and shoelaces. MCCORD is taller than the others. They stand, facing the JUDGE, backs to the audience.*

WOODWARD sits watching as the proceedings start, but it's hard to hear. He concentrates as the JUDGE starts speaking.

> **JUDGE**
> Will you please state your professions.

The five men do not move or reply. Then, after a long pause, Barker says —

> **BARKER**
> Anti-Communists.

> **JUDGE**
> Anti-Communists? *(perplexed)* That, sir, is not your average occupation.

WOODWARD starts moving forward now, down an aisle, moving past kids and whores and all the rest, trying to hear what the hell's going on. At the front of the spectator's section is a fence-like wooden barricade about three feet high. As he approaches it —

The JUDGE indicates the bald burglar.

> **JUDGE**
> Your name, please.

> **MCCORD**
> James McCord.

> **JUDGE**
> Will you step forward, sir.
> *(MCCORD obeys)*

WOODWARD at the bench is leaning forward, trying to hear but it's hard.

> **JUDGE**
> And what is your occupation, Mr. McCord.

> **MCCORD**
> *(softly)*
> Security consultant.

> **JUDGE**
> Where?

> **MCCORD**
> *(softer)*
> Government. Recently retired.

JUDGE

Where in government?

MCCORD
(we can't really make this out)
...Central...Intelligence...Agency...

JUDGE
(he can't either)

Where?

MCCORD
(clearing his throat)

The C.I.A.

And on these words,

ZOOM TO

CLOSE UP — WOODWARD *leaning over the fence practically falling over it in a desperate straining effort to catch what's going on.*

WOODWARD
(stunned)

Holy shit.

Now from the courtroom —

CUT TO

THOUSANDS AND THOUSANDS OF *WASHINGTON POSTS.*

We are at the end of the press run, the papers are all assembled and being cabled and sent off by machine to various places. As the papers continue to roll past —

A UNION TYPE EMPLOYEE *grabs a paper, looks at the front page.*

The Watergate story, headlined whatever it was headlined, is visible. The byline was by Alfred E. Lewis. The union type Post employee glances at the article —

UNION POST EMPLOYEE
(reading half-aloud)
"Five men, one of whom said he is a former employee..." *(stops reading, gives a shrug)* Schmucks.

And as he turns happily to the sports section —

CUT TO

A CLOSE UP OF HUNDRED DOLLAR BILLS.

It's new money and looks as if it's been recently ironed. Someone is going through the cash, making a quick count. During this —

FIRST VOICE (v.o.)

Hurry it, huh, Bachinski?

BACHINSKI

You said I could look at it —

PULL BACK TO REVEAL

We're in a room in a police station and two men are present. One, a COP, *is nervous as hell and constantly aware of the door. The other,* BACHINSKI, *is taking hurried notes in a reporter's type notebook as he examines the evidence.*

COP

— I said look, not memorize —

BACHINSKI

— almost done, give it a rest, all right... *(and as he looks at an address book, he stops)*

CUT TO

THE ADDRESS BOOK. *Beside the name "Howard E. Hunt" is the notation "W. House." Now,* BACHINSKI *hurriedly opens the other book to the letter "H" and there is the same name, "Howard E. Hunt" and beside it, the letters, "W.H."*

COP (v.o.)

What'd you find?

BACHINSKI (v.o.)

Beats me. These notebooks belonged to Cuban guys?

COP (v.o.)

S'right.

BACHINSKI (v.o.)

It's gotta mean either White House or whore house, one or the other.

We HOLD *on the* HUNT *name, and the address notations. Then —*

CUT TO

WOODWARD'S APARTMENT — NIGHT.

The phone rings, waking him. He fumbles for the phone and the light, finally gets them both.

WOODWARD

Bachinski? *(reaches for a notebook)* What? — hold it — *(gets it open, starts to write)* — OK, go on, go on...

CUT TO

A BOX OF MAALOX TABLETS.

ROSENFELD is opening them, we're in his office, WOODWARD sits across the desk, holding the notebook we saw him writing in.

>   ROSENFELD
> ...go on, go on...

>   WOODWARD
> That's everything Bachinski had, I think it's worth following up.

>   ROSENFELD
> Don't know; who the hell's Howard Hunt? *(crunches tablets)* It's probably nothing but check it out. Just go easy, it could be crazy Cubans.

HOWARD SIMONS sticks his head in the office.

>   SIMONS
> Anything?

>   ROSENFELD
> Woodward's onto a new wrinkle with the break-in thing — absolute page one stuff —

>   SIMONS
> — in other words, you got nothing, you're thumbsucking.

>   ROSENFELD
>   *(shrugs)*
> Could develop.

>   SIMONS
> Let me see what you get, but don't jump — *The New York Times* thinks it's crazy Cubans.

He moves on. ROSENFELD turns quickly to WOODWARD.

>   ROSENFELD
> OK, get on this W. House guy and do a better job than you did on McCord.

>   WOODWARD
> I did all right on McCord.

>   ROSENFELD
> Then how come the Associated Press were the ones found out that Mr. McCord is security coordinator for the Committee to Re-elect the President, otherwise known as CREEP?

> WOODWARD
> *(getting it straight)*

The head of security for the reelection of a Republican President got caught bugging the national offices of the Democrats? What the hell does that mean?

> ROSENFELD
> *(hasn't the foggiest)*

Mr. John Mitchell, the head of CREEP, says it means nothing. *(reads)* "... This man and the other people involved were not operating on either our behalf or with our consent. There is no place in our campaign or in the electoral process for this type of activity, and we will not forget it or condone it."

> WOODWARD
> *(getting up)*

You can't believe that.

> ROSENFELD

As a rough rule of thumb, as far as I can throw Bronco Nagurski, that's how much I trust John Mitchell ...

Now —

CUT TO

A MOON-FACED MAN RINGING A TRIANGLE.

CUT TO

THE NEWSROOM *as the triangle sound echoes.*

HOWARD SIMONS *leaves large Managing Editor's office, walks past another office, knocks twice on the glass wall.*

Inside the Executive Editor's office, BEN BRADLEE *sits. As* SIMONS *knocks, he turns, nods. He appears, for the moment, deep in thought.*

HARRY ROSENFELD *on the opposite end of the room hurries out of his office, following a bunch of editors, all of them heading across the huge room. As he passes* WOODWARD's *desk* ROSENFELD *pauses.*

> ROSENFELD

What'd you get on W. House?

> WOODWARD
> *(massaging his neck)*

Lotsa hints —

> ROSENFELD
> *(not happy)*

I can't sell hints to Simons — *(stops, looks at piece of yellow paper)* — you called

everyone you know?
>   (WOODWARD *makes a nod*)
Call someone you don't know.

WOODWARD continues to rub his neck as ROSENFELD *hurries off, all the editors still moving toward the place where the moon-faced man intermittently rings the triangle.*

WOODWARD picks up the sheet of yellow paper from his desk. Lined, legal-sized, it is <u>crammed</u> *with names and numbers and addresses. They are in no neat order; looking at them it's almost like following a path; chicken tracks in ink.* WOODWARD *mutters "to hell with it" and reaches for a thick book, flips it open.*

NOW WE SEE THE BOOK: it's the Washington Phone Directory and we're in the W's. As WOODWARD'S *finger stops, we can see he's looking at the White House entry number. There it is, just like your name and mine. Listed.*

Now WOODWARD *starts to dial, visibly nervous, a fact he tries very hard to keep out of his voice tone.*

>   WHITE HOUSE OPERATOR (v.o.)
White House.

>   WOODWARD
>   (*casually*)
Howard Hunt, please.

Throughout the following call, we stay on WOODWARD'S *face, hear the other voices.*

>   WHITE HOUSE OPERATOR (v.o.)
Mr. Hunt does not answer.

WOODWARD is delighted he's even there.

>   WOODWARD
Thanks, anyway —

And he's about to hang up, when —

>   WHITE HOUSE OPERATOR (v.o.)
I'll bet he's in Mr. Colson's office. Let me connect you.

>   SECRETARY (v.o.)
Charles Colson's wire.

>   WOODWARD
>   (*a little more excited*)
Howard Hunt, please.   ‵

>   SECRETARY (v.o.)
Mr. Hunt isn't here just now.

                              WOODWARD
Thanks, anyway.

And he's about to hang up again when —

                          SECRETARY (v.o.)
Have you tried Mullen and Company Public Relations? He works at Mullen
and Company Public Relations as a writer. The number is 552-1313. I'm
sorry I couldn't be more helpful.

                              WOODWARD
Listen, forget it.

He hangs up, sits there. His hands are a little twitchy . . . HOLD. Now —

CUT TO

*ROSENFELD hurrying (he __always__ hurries) toward his office. WOODWARD, looking for some-
thing in his desk throughout this scene, speaks to him.*

                              WOODWARD
Who's Charles Colson?

                              ROSENFELD
                               (stops dead)
I would liken your query to being in Russia half a century ago and asking
someone, "I understand who Lenin is and Trotsky I got too, but who's
this yokel Stalin?"

                              WOODWARD
Who's Colson, Harry?

                              ROSENFELD
The most powerful man in America is President Nixon, probably you've
heard his name.

*WOODWARD, unfazed by anything, continues to open drawers, close them, as ROSENFELD
rolls on.*

                              ROSENFELD
The second most powerful man is Robert Haldeman. Just below him are
a trio: Mr. Erlichman is Haldeman's friend, and they protect the President
from *everybody* which is why they are referred to as either The German
Shepherds or the Berlin Wall. Mr. Mitchell we've already discussed. Mr.
Colson is the President's special counsel.

                              WOODWARD
                                (rising)
Thanks, Harry. *(looks at ROSENFELD)* Know anything about Colson?

ROSENFELD

Just that on his office wall there's a cartoon with a caption reading, "When you've got them by the balls, their hearts and minds will follow."

WOODWARD nods, heads back toward the files as we

CUT TO

WOODWARD AT HIS DESK dialing the phone.

He's got the Colson file spread out now, and we can see pictures of the man and articles the Post *had done on him. But basically what we see is* WOODWARD *plugging away on the goddamn phone and you'd think his finger would fall off from all the dialing and you know his voice is tiring as this montage goes on, you can hear it grow raspy. But a lot of what a reporter does he does on the phone, and that's what we're compressing here. The dialing never stops, the voices are continuous.*

WOODWARD

Hello, I'm Bob Woodward of the *Washington Post* and . . . *(beat)* Mullen and Company Public Relations? Could you tell me when you expect Mr. Hunt? *(surprised)* He is?

HUNT (v.o.)

Howard Hunt here.

WOODWARD

Hi, I'm Bob Woodward of the *Post* and —

HUNT (v.o.)
(impatient)

— yes, yes, what is it?

WOODWARD

I was just kind of wondering why your name and phone number were in the address books of two of the men arrested at Watergate?

HUNT (v.o.)
(blind panic)

Good God!

And as he bangs the phone down sharply —

— more dialing SOUNDS. Now snatches of conversation —

WOODWARD

I'm sorry to bother you, Mr. Bennett, but we're doing some investigating of one of your employees, Howard Hunt.

BENNETT (v.o.)

Well, if you've been doing some investigating then obviously it's no secret to you that Howard was with the C.I.A.

WOODWARD
(he hadn't known)

No secret at all.

More dialing. Then —

WOODWARD
(tired, voice deeper)

Hello, C.I.A. This is R. W. Woodward, of the *Washington Post* — get me Personnel —

Dialing again. WOODWARD's voice is showing genuine fatigue.

WOODWARD

Hi, I'm Bob Woodward of the *Washington Post* — and — what's that? — you've never heard of me? — I can't help that — you don't believe I'm with the *Post*? — what do you want me to do, Madam, shout "extra — extra"?

There is the SOUND of the phone being slammed down in his ear. Hard. Now —

CUT TO

ROSENFELD AND SIMONS approaching WOODWARD who is working at his desk. He has put in a lot of hours on this and looks it.

ROSENFELD

Whaddya, got, whaddya got?

WOODWARD

Hunt is Colson's man — *(to Simons, explaining)* — that's Charles Colson, Nixon's special counsel —
(SIMONS almost says something,
decides against it.)
— they both went to Brown University — *(consulting his notes)* — Hunt worked for the C.I.A. till '70, and this is on deep background, the FBI thinks he's involved with the break-in.

SIMONS

What else have you got?

WOODWARD

According to White House personnel, Hunt definitely works there as a consultant for Colson. But when I called the White House Press office, they said he hadn't worked there for three months. Then the P.R. guy said the weirdest thing to me. *(reading)* "I am convinced that neither Mr. Colson nor anyone else at the White House had any knowledge of, or participation in, this deplorable incident at the Democratic National Committee."

He looks up at them.

                    SIMONS
Isn't that what you'd expect them to say?

                    WOODWARD
Absolutely.

                    ROSENFELD
So?

                    WOODWARD
              (he's got something and he knows it)
I never asked them about Watergate. I only said what were Hunt's duties at the White House. They volunteered that he was innocent when nobody asked was he guilty.

                    ROSENFELD
                 (to SIMONS)
I think we got a White House consultant linked to the bugging.

                    SIMONS
                    (nods)
Just be careful how you write it.

CUT TO

WOODWARD TYPING LIKE MAD, makes a mistake, corrects it, types on muttering to himself, and—

CUT TO

ROSENFELD IN HIS OFFICE munching a handful of Maalox tablets and—

CUT TO

WOODWARD taking a sheet from his typewriter, hurrying off and—

CUT TO

ROSENFELD taking the sheet from WOODWARD—

                    WOODWARD
Here's the first take—

ROSENFELD nods, shows him out and—

CUT TO

WOODWARD BACK AT HIS MACHINE *typing faster than before, makes another mistake, starts to correct it, glances around and —*

CUT TO

ROSENFELD IN HIS OFFICE *gesturing to somebody but not* WOODWARD *and —*

CUT TO

WOODWARD *watching as* BERNSTEIN *appears in view from behind the wide pillar by* WOODWARD's *desk, heads toward* ROSENFELD's *office.* WOODWARD *shrugs, goes back to his typing, makes a typo immediately, glances over toward* ROSENFELD's *office, freezes as we —*

CUT TO

ROSENFELD *handing some papers to* BERNSTEIN. *They look, from this distance, suspiciously like* WOODWARD's *story.*

CUT TO

BERNSTEIN *hurrying out of* ROSENFELD's *office, and —*

CUT TO

WOODWARD *watching* BERNSTEIN *until he disappears out of sight behind the pillar.* WOODWARD *hesitates, finally goes back to his typing, makes another mistake, fixes it, makes still another, his temper is shortly to make itself known and —*

CUT TO

ROSENFELD *as* WOODWARD *hands him another sheet of paper.*

WOODWARD
This is all of it, Harry.

ROSENFELD *nods, takes it, immediately starts to read as we —*

CUT TO

WOODWARD AT HIS DESK *watching as* ROSENFELD *gestures again. There is a pause. Then* BERNSTEIN *appears from behind the pillar and —*

CUT TO

ROSENFELD *handing* BERNSTEIN *another sheet of paper.* BERNSTEIN *nods, takes it, walks back toward his desk, disappears behind the pillar again.* WOODWARD *is starting to steam. Now —*

CUT TO

BERNSTEIN AT HIS DESK *typing magnificently, his hands rising and falling like Rubinstein's. Behind him is the pillar and for a moment there is nothing — then, very slowly, a figure peers out from behind the pillar — it is* WOODWARD.

He watches. BERNSTEIN continues to type, then after a moment, rests, thinks, shifts around in his chair and as his glance starts toward the pillar —

CUT TO

THE PILLAR. *WOODWARD is gone.*

CUT TO

BERNSTEIN *typing madly away.*

THE PILLAR. *WOODWARD is visible again, eyes very bright . . . now —*

CUT TO

BERNSTEIN *finishing typing, his hands moving majestically. WOODWARD comes up behind him, stands looking a second.*

Then —

WOODWARD

We have to talk.

BERNSTEIN *nods, grabs the papers both that he's been typing and that he's been copying from.*

And as he rises —

PAN TO

WOODWARD AND BERNSTEIN walking silently out of the newsroom then turning left down a darker corridor, passing bulletin boards and wall lockers and it's all nice and quiet as they amble on, nodding to the few people they pass on their way and after a while they turn right and enter the coffee lounge which is empty; the walls are lined with Norman Rockwell re-productions and various kinds of vending machines are visible, selling coffee or milk or fruit or sandwiches and there are some plastic tables and chairs and the minute they are alone, the silence ends.

WOODWARD

What the hell were you doing rewriting my story —

BERNSTEIN

— I sure couldn't hurt it, could I? —

WOODWARD

— it was fine the way it was —

BERNSTEIN

— it was bullshit the way it was —

WOODWARD

— I have to stand here and listen to the staff correspondent from Virginia? —

> BERNSTEIN
> *(a sore subject)*

—what have you been here, nine months?—I been in this business since I was sixteen—

> WOODWARD

—and you've had some fucking meteoric rise, that's for sure—by the time you turn forty you might be the head of the Montana bureau—

> BERNSTEIN

—you only got the job because both you and Bradlee went to Yale—

> WOODWARD

—Bradlee went to Harvard—

> BERNSTEIN

—they're all the same, all those Ivy League places—they teach you about striped ties and suddenly you're smart—

> WOODWARD

—I'm smart enough to know my story was solid—

> BERNSTEIN

—mine's better—

> WOODWARD

—no way—

> BERNSTEIN
> *(handing them over)*

—read 'em both and you'll see—

And as WOODWARD *glances at the two stories—*

CUT TO

BERNSTEIN *watching. Now—*

CUT TO

WOODWARD. *He glances from one story to the other. Then, disconsolately—*

> WOODWARD

...crap...

And he sinks down in a chair.

> BERNSTEIN

Is mine better?

WOODWARD *nods.*

> **WOODWARD**
> *(handing the stories back)*
> What is it about my writing that's so rotten?

> **BERNSTEIN**
> *(as he exits)*
> Mainly it has to do with your choice of words.

And as he goes, leaving WOODWARD just sitting there —

CUT TO

BERNSTEIN, *re-entering the newsroom, returning to his desk. He starts to insert some papers into his typewriter, hesitates, lights a cigarette. He inhales, as, behind him, WOODWARD briefly is visible going to his desk behind the pillar.*

Finally BERNSTEIN inserts the paper, starts to type as

> **WOODWARD** (v.o.)
> *(from behind the pillar)*

Carl?

> **BERNSTEIN**
> *(turns)*

Yeah?

> **WOODWARD**
> *(pushing his chair briefly into view)*

Fuck you, Carl.

And as he rolls forward again, out of sight —

CUT TO

RICHARD NIXON ON THE TUBE.

(It's the June 22 Press Conference.) He talks on about something, it doesn't matter exactly what here, the point is, it should include that strange smile of his that kept appearing when the man should not have been smiling. Hints of pressure maybe, that's all, and once it's established —

PULL BACK TO REVEAL

WOODWARD *sitting alone, gloomily staring at the set. We're in the* Post *Cafeteria, it's the next morning, and the place is pretty much empty. He sips the coffee, it tastes rotten. BERNSTEIN moves up behind him, carrying a cup of coffee of his own. He stands by WOODWARD briefly.*

> **BERNSTEIN**

You heard?

> *(WOODWARD glances up)*

They put us both on the break-in thing. Simons liked the way we worked together.
                    (WOODWARD *nods,* BERNSTEIN *sits down*)
Listen, I'm sorry I said your story was bullshit.

WOODWARD
It's OK; I'm sorry I called you a failure.

BERNSTEIN
Forget it, the main thing — *(stops)* — did you call me a failure?

WOODWARD
I was sure trying.

CUT TO

WOODWARD, BERNSTEIN, AND NIXON. *The way it's shot, it's almost as if they're watching each other,* NIXON *staring out from the TV set, answering questions.* WOODWARD *and* BERNSTEIN *sip coffee. We don't know yet — or better, they don't know it yet, but these are our adversaries.*

CUT TO

WOODWARD AND BERNSTEIN, *without* NIXON *now. They sit at the table. Occasionally,* NIXON *is audible in the background.*

WOODWARD
All right, what do we know?

BERNSTEIN
Let me lay a little theory on you —

WOODWARD
                    (*cutting him off*)
— I'm not interested in theory. What do we *know*? For example, Hunt's disappeared.

BERNSTEIN
Well, Barker tried to get blueprints of the Miami Convention Center and the air-conditioning system.

WOODWARD
And McCord was carrying an application for college press credentials for the Democratic convention. *(to* BERNSTEIN) *The Times* has got to be full of it — it can't be crazy Cubans.

BERNSTEIN
What, though? *(points to* NIXON) It can't be the Republicans — he'd never allow something as stupid as this, not when he's gonna slaughter McGovern anyway.

WOODWARD

Right. Nixon didn't get where he got by being dumb — *(stops abruptly)* —
listen, that was a Watergate question —

CUT TO

NIXON ON THE TUBE. *Serious now.*

NIXON

The White House has had no involvement whatever in this particular incident.

CUT TO

WOODWARD AND BERNSTEIN *staring at the set, thinking . . .*

CUT TO

WOODWARD AND BERNSTEIN *walking toward* BERNSTEIN's *desk.*

WOODWARD

Hey?

BERNSTEIN

Hmm.

WOODWARD

What do you think he meant, this *particular* incident? Were there others?
How would we find out? You know anyone important?

BERNSTEIN
(sits, shakes his head)
I lived here all my life, I got a million contacts, but they're all bus boys and
bellhops.

The reporter KEN RINGLE *at the next desk watches them a moment. Then —*

RINGLE

What do you need?

BERNSTEIN

Someone inside the White House would be nice.

RINGLE
(writes down phone number)
Call her. She worked for Colson, if that's any help.

As BERNSTEIN *grabs for the phone —*

CUT TO

A SECRETARIAL POOL IN A LARGE OFFICE.

BERNSTEIN is talking off to one side with an attractive girl.

> GIRL
>
> Kenny's crazy, I never worked for Colson, I worked for an assistant. Colson was big on secrets anyway. Even if I had worked for him, I wouldn't have known anything.

> BERNSTEIN
>
> Nothing at all you can remember?

> SECRETARY
> *(headshake)*
>
> Sorry. *(pause)* Now if it was Hunt you were interested in —

> BERNSTEIN
>
> — *Howard* Hunt?

> SECRETARY
>
> Sure. Him I liked, he was a very nice person. Secretive too, traveled all over, but a decent man.

> BERNSTEIN
>
> Any idea what he did?

> SECRETARY
>
> Oh, the scuttlebutt for awhile was he was investigating Kennedy —

> BERNSTEIN
>
> — *Teddy* Kennedy?

> SECRETARY
>
> Sure. I remember seeing a book about Chappaquiddick on his desk and he was always getting material out of the White House Library and the Library of Congress and —

And as she goes on, quickly —

CUT TO

THE NEWSROOM.

BERNSTEIN is at his desk, telephoning. WOODWARD stands alongside.

> BERNSTEIN
>
> White House Library, please.

We hear the other end of this phone call clearly.

OPERATOR (v.o.)

One moment.

LIBRARIAN (v.o.)
(elderly-sounding lady)

Library.

BERNSTEIN

Hi. Carl Bernstein of the *Washington Post.* I was just wondering if you remember the names of any of the books that Howard Hunt checked out
on Senator Kennedy.

LIBRARIAN (v.o.)

I think I do remember, he took out a whole bunch of material. Let me just
go see.

SOUND *of the phone being laid down.*

BERNSTEIN

—what do you think?—

WOODWARD

—Hunt doesn't seem like your ordinary consultant.

BERNSTEIN

Maybe a political operative of some sort—

WOODWARD

—a spy, you mean?

BERNSTEIN

It makes sense; Hunt worked for the C.I.A. and the White House was
paranoid about Teddy Kennedy.

LIBRARIAN (v.o.)

Mr. Bernstein?

BERNSTEIN

Yes, ma'am.

LIBRARIAN (v.o.)

What I said before? I was wrong. The truth is, I don't have a card that Mr.
Hunt took out any Kennedy material.
(WOODWARD and BERNSTEIN listen,
and now there is something in her
voice that wasn't there before: fear.)
I remember getting that material out for somebody, but it wasn't Mr. Hunt.
The truth is, I've never had any requests at all from Mr. Hunt. *(beat)* The
truth is, I don't know Mr. Hunt.

There is the SOUND *of the phone being dropped into its cradle.* BERNSTEIN *continues to hold his. He and* WOODWARD *just look at each other. Now —*

CUT TO

THE LIBRARY OF CONGRESS.

Now, as WOODWARD *and* BERNSTEIN *get out of a cab, start inside —*

CUT TO

A MALE LIBRARIAN IN HIS OFFICE.

LIBRARIAN
You want all the material requested by the White House?

PULL BACK TO REVEAL

WOODWARD *and* BERNSTEIN *standing there. They nod. One of them maybe says "yessir," the other maybe "please." The* LIBRARIAN *moves out of his office into a corridor. They go with him. No one else is around. The* LIBRARIAN *looks at them, then, quickly —*

LIBRARIAN
All White House transactions are confidential.

And just like that, he's back into his office, and as he shuts the door —

CUT TO

WOODWARD AND BERNSTEIN *walking along through the Library of Congress.*

WOODWARD
You think they are confidential? I don't know anything about how this town works, I haven't lived here a year yet.

BERNSTEIN
We need a sympathetic face.

On the word "face" —

CUT TO

A BEARDED YOUNG-LOOKING CLERK. *We're in the reading room of the library, and* WOOD-*WARD and* BERNSTEIN *are with him.*

YOUNG CLERK
You want every request since when?

BERNSTEIN
(to WOODWARD)
When did Hunt start at the White House?

> **WOODWARD**

July of '71.

> **BERNSTEIN**

About the past year.

> **CLERK**
> *(starts to smile)*

I'm not sure you want 'em, but I got 'em.

Now —

CUT TO

WOODWARD AND BERNSTEIN seated at a table with from anywhere between 10 to 20 <u>thousand</u> slips of paper. In front of them, seated at a high desk, the bearded clerk looks down on them, shaking his head. It's a staggering amount of work to thumb through.

> **CLERK**

I can't believe you guys are actually doing this.

> **WOODWARD**
> *(to the clerk)*

You do a lot of things when you're on a story. *(to BERNSTEIN, quietly)* Can you believe we're actually doing this?
> *(BERNSTEIN can't)*

Now we have a series of shots of the two of them going through the slips; it took them hours and hours, and the afternoon darkened as they worked. And they tired. Now —

CUT TO

WOODWARD AND BERNSTEIN getting back into a cab.

> **BERNSTEIN**

That was fun. *(slams the door)* What now?

> **WOODWARD**
> *(rubbing his eyes)*

I met a Presidential aide once at a social occasion.

> **BERNSTEIN**
> *(stunned)*

And you haven't called him? —

As the taxi pulls off—

CUT TO

ROSENFELD

reading an article by BERNSTEIN'S *desk.* WOODWARD *sits on an adjacent desk.*

> **ROSENFELD**
> *(to* BERNSTEIN*)*
> You got accurate notes on the White House librarian?
> *(*BERNSTEIN *nods.)*
> OK, we'll leave space for the White House denial and we should be set.

Suddenly he gestures and we —

CUT TO

BRADLEE STANDING ACROSS THE ROOM. *Without a nod, he moves toward* ROSENFELD.

CUT TO

WOODWARD AND BERNSTEIN, *nervously watching* BRADLEE *come. As soon as* BRADLEE *is within earshot,* ROSENFELD *starts his sell.*

> **ROSENFELD**
> Benjy, we got a present for you. Above the fold on page one for sure. It may not change our lives one way or the other. Just a good, solid piece of American Journalism — *(beat)* — that *The New York Times* doesn't have.

BRADLEE *by this time has taken the story, grabbed an unoccupied chair, sat down, started to read. His only response to* ROSENFELD *is an intermittent "uh-huh, uh-huh."*

CUT TO

WOODWARD AND BERNSTEIN, *watching as the silence goes on.* ROSENFELD *too. He wants the story too, but he doesn't want it like* WOODWARD *and* BERNSTEIN *do. They were, as they said, proud of their work. The silence goes on. Finally* BRADLEE *looks up.*

> **BRADLEE**
> You haven't got it. *(before they can reply)* A librarian and a secretary say Hunt looked at a book. *(shakes his head)* Not good enough.

He begins editing the piece, slashing paragraphs out of it.

> **WOODWARD**
> I was told by this guy at the White House that Hunt was investigating Teddy Kennedy.

> **BRADLEE**
> How senior?

> **WOODWARD**
> *(edgy)*
> You asking me to disclose my source?

Other reporters are watching now. BRADLEE *is impatient, as always.*

> BRADLEE

Just tell me his title.

> WOODWARD

I don't know titles.

> BRADLEE

Is he on the level of Assistant to the President or not?

WOODWARD doesn't know. BRADLEE continues to hack at their piece. Done, he stands, walks away.

> BRADLEE

Get some harder information next time.

WOODWARD and BERNSTEIN watch him go, they are embarrassed, angry, crushed. HOLD on their faces. Then —

CUT TO

WOODWARD'S APARTMENT — MORNING.

He is in pajamas and lugging a flower pot out to the balcony, positioning it so it would be visible to anyone passing in the alley below. He takes a stick with a red flag, jams it into the flower pot. He's nervous and he makes several adjustments, making sure the red flag is secure and won't fall.

CUT TO

WOODWARD down in the alley, staring up at his apartment. The flag is clearly visible. It's early. He checks his watch, hurries out of the alley.

CUT TO

THE CITY ROOM — NIGHT

Deserted except for a few older Front Page types, reporters whose legs have given out, playing cards in a corner of the room. WOODWARD is working at his desk until he glances up at a wall clock. It's almost one on the button and as he rises —

CUT TO

WOODWARD racing down the stairway of the Post; *as he hits the lobby, he turns and we*

CUT TO

OUTSIDE THE POST *— NIGHT*

WOODWARD appears in the side exit, walks off. When he gets out of sight of the paper, he starts to run. Now —

CUT TO

WOODWARD *turning a corner, running on. Up ahead is a cab —*

CUT TO

WOODWARD IN THE CAB *sitting forward tensely. Occasionally, various monuments are briefly visible, lit up in the b.g.* WOODWARD *takes out some money as we*

CUT TO

THE CAB *stopping.* WOODWARD *pays, gets out. The cab pulls away. When it is out of sight,* WOODWARD *starts to run again.*

CUT TO

A STREET *as* WOODWARD *runs by. It's not the nicest area in the world. He is going faster now.*

CUT TO

A CAB GASSING UP AT A STATION. WOODWARD *hurries to it, gets in and —*

CUT TO

THE SECOND CAB *roaring along some Washington streets.*

CUT TO

WOODWARD INSIDE THE CAB. *He looks at his watch, tries not to seem nervous. But his fingers are drumming, drumming and —*

CUT TO

THE SECOND CAB *stopping, as* WOODWARD *gets out, pays. The cab starts off, but slowly.* WOODWARD *waits. The cab doesn't turn as the first one did.* WOODWARD *still waits. Finally the cab turns and the second it does,* WOODWARD *starts to run again and —*

CUT TO

WOODWARD *turning a corner, running on and —*

CUT TO

ANOTHER CORNER *as* WOODWARD *turns it, finally stops and catches his breath as we —*

CUT TO

A GIGANTIC UNDERGROUND TYPE GARAGE

CUT TO

WOODWARD ENTERING THE GARAGE. *It's an eerie place, and his heels make noise and if you wonder is he edgy, yes he's edgy. He comes to the ramp leading down to lower levels, hesitates.*

CUT TO

THE RAMP. *It seems to descend forever.*

CUT TO

WOODWARD *starting down.* HOLD *on him as he walks. Down he goes, the shadows deepening, then disappearing, then covering him again. He continues on. He must be at least at the first underground level now but he doesn't stop, and we don't stop watching him as he continues to go down, turning, the* SOUND *of his shoes softer now and he's a smaller figure as we watch him circle around and around until we —*

CUT TO

ANOTHER LEVEL UNDERGROUND. *Dimly lit. A few cars parked here and there.* WOODWARD *hesitates on the ramp, looks around.*

THE GARAGE. *Dark, dark, eerie.*

CUT TO

WOODWARD *quietly stepping off the ramp, continuing to glance this way, that way. Now —*

CUT TO

TWO CARS PARKED BESIDE EACH OTHER.

Nothing unusual about that. But then some cigarette smoke appears, trailing up and disappearing from between the cars. As WOODWARD *moves forward —*

CUT TO

A MAN SITTING ON HIS HAUNCHES BETWEEN THE CARS, *smoking. He leans with his back against the wall.*

> **DEEP THROAT**
> I saw the flag signal — what's up?

> **WOODWARD**
> Nothing, that's the problem — the story's gone underground.

> **DEEP THROAT**
> You thought I'd help out on specifics? *(headshake)* I'll confirm what you get, try and keep you on the right track, but that's all. *(looks at* WOODWARD*)* Are you guys really working?
> *(WOODWARD nods)*
> How much?

> **WOODWARD**
> I don't know, maybe sixteen, eighteen hours a day — we've got sources at Justice, the FBI, but it's still drying up.

DEEP THROAT

Then there must be something, mustn't there. Look, forget the myths the media's created about the White House — the truth is, these are not very bright guys, and things got out of hand.

WOODWARD

If you don't like them, why won't you be more concrete with me?

DEEP THROAT

Because the press stinks too — history on the run, that's all you're interested in. *(inhales)* You come up with anything?

WOODWARD

John Mitchell resigned as head of CREEP to spend more time with his family. That doesn't exactly have the ring of truth.
(DEEP THROAT nods)
Howard Hunt's been found — there was talk that his lawyer had 25 thousand in cash in a paper bag.

DEEP THROAT

Follow the money. Always follows the money.

WOODWARD

To where?

DEEP THROAT
(shakes his head "no")
Go on.

WOODWARD

This man Gordon Liddy — he's going to be tried along with Hunt and the five burglars — we know he knows a lot, we just don't know what.

DEEP THROAT
(lights a new cigarette)
You changed cabs? You're sure no one followed you?

WOODWARD

I did everything you said, but it all seemed —

DEEP THROAT

— melodramatic? *(headshake)* Things are past that — remember, these are men with switchblade mentalities who run the world as if it were Dodge City.

WOODWARD

What's the whole thing about — do you know?

DEEP THROAT

What I know, you'll have to find out on your own.

                            WOODWARD
Liddy—you think there's a chance he'll talk?

                          DEEP THROAT
                             (rises)
Talk? Once, at a gathering, he put his hand over a candle. And he kept it
there. He kept it right in the flame until his flesh was seared. A woman who
was watching asked, "What's the trick?" And he replied, "The trick is not
minding."

*DEEP THROAT shakes his head, walks off. WOODWARD stands alone now, watching. Now
the shadows have the other man. Just his footsteps are audible. WOODWARD stands there . . .
HOLD.*

CUT TO

BERNSTEIN.

It's morning and he's struggling to get his bike down the steps of his apartment building.

CUT TO

*WOODWARD driving up in his two-year-old red Karmann Ghia. He roars up alongside
BERNSTEIN, waving a folded-up newspaper.*

                          BERNSTEIN
What's that?

                          WOODWARD
The fucking *New York Times.*

CUT TO

*THE TIMES spread somewhat tentatively over a mailbox. A small headline is visible, with the
words "Barker," "Liddy," and "Telephone" in some kind of order. WOODWARD and BERN-
STEIN look at it the best they can.*

                          BERNSTEIN
Goddamnit—

                          WOODWARD
—see?—

                          BERNSTEIN
—I'm trying—

                          WOODWARD
—fifteen phone calls—

> BERNSTEIN

—fifteen or more phone calls from the burglars in Miami to Gordon Liddy at CREEP—

> WOODWARD

Why didn't we get that?

> BERNSTEIN

Christ, and I even *know* somebody at the phone company—

> WOODWARD

—you do?—with access to records?

As BERNSTEIN *nods—*

CUT TO

A LITTLE CITY PARK.

A guy shells peanuts. BERNSTEIN *hurries up.*

> BERNSTEIN

Why couldn't you have just dialed me from the office, Irwin?

> IRWIN

'Cause I'm not calling out from the phone company anymore— *(drops his voice)*—I think the place is bugged.

> BERNSTEIN
> *(taking some peanuts)*

So tell me about the *Times* article.

> IRWIN

What do you want to know?

> BERNSTEIN

No games, Irwin; give.

> IRWIN
> *(looks at* BERNSTEIN*)*

My big civil rights buddy— *(shakes his head)*—boy, if John Mitchell was after your phone records, would you be screaming. *(eats)* What're you onto?

> BERNSTEIN

Something maybe big.

> IRWIN

And that makes anything you do OK, is that it?

> BERNSTEIN

Just tell me about the goddamn article.

> IRWIN
> *(shelling away)*

It was accurate, but I can't get a fuller listing for you — all Barker's phone records have bean subpoenaed.

> BERNSTEIN

Who by?

> IRWIN

A Miami D.A. The guy doing the investigating is named Martin Dardis. *(finishes his peanuts, starts off)*

> BERNSTEIN

Irwin? I really feel bad, doing something like this — you know that, don't you?

Irwin looks at BERNSTEIN for a long time. Then —

> IRWIN

Don't give me any more of your liberal shit, OK, Carl?

He walks off, doesn't look back. Now —

CUT TO

ROSENFELD

at the water fountain on the 5th floor. He chews up a few Maalox tablets, notices BERNSTEIN steaming up.

> BERNSTEIN

Harry, I just talked to a Miami investigator about Barker —

> ROSENFELD

— so?

> BERNSTEIN

I think it might be helpful if you'd send me to Miami.

ROSENFELD heads for his office, BERNSTEIN pursuing.

> ROSENFELD

I'm the one sent you to Toronto, Bernstein —

> BERNSTEIN
> *(trying to head him off)*

— that was awhile ago —

> ROSENFELD

— "I think it might be helpful if you'd send me to Toronto." That was your spiel then. "The Lifestyles of Deserters." *(whirls on BERNSTEIN)* I'm still waiting for it.

He enters his office, BERNSTEIN follows.

> **BERNSTEIN**
> Down to Miami and back — how much damage can I do?

> **ROSENFELD**
> You're the fella who *forgot* he rented a Hertz car, do I have to tell you they didn't forget to send us the bill?

And as he looks unsympathetically at BERNSTEIN —

CUT TO

SIMONS circling around the 5th floor. ROSENFELD falls into step. They keep moving throughout.

> **ROSENFELD**
> I can predict the next words you're gonna say: "anyone but Bernstein."
> > *(SIMONS gestures for*
> > *ROSENFELD to continue.)*
> I want to send a reporter to Miami.

> **SIMONS**
> Anyone but Bernstein.

> **ROSENFELD**
> Howard —

> **SIMONS**
> — remember Toronto, Harry.

> **ROSENFELD**
> That was awhile ago.

> **SIMONS**
> I don't get it — you were the one who wanted to fire him.

> **ROSENFELD**
> I know, I did, but dammit Howard —
> > *(SIMONS looks at him)*
> For the first time since I've known him, I think he's really humping...

CUT TO

BERNSTEIN'S APARTMENT.

A shambles. He is busy doing two things at once, studying notebooks and packing. Music plays, lovely stuff; the Bach Brandenburgs. As the phone rings —

> **BERNSTEIN**
> *(answering)*
> Yeah? *(pause)* Yes, this is Carl Bernstein. *(stunned)* You're repossessing my bicycle? *(softer)* Listen, I'm sure I paid this month's installment, so why don't you check your records before you go around hassling people? *(pause)* Oh…

And as he stands there —

CUT TO

AN ATTRACTIVE, EFFICIENT-LOOKING YOUNG WOMAN of BERNSTEIN'S age. She has just entered the apartment. Vivaldi is playing now.

> **BERNSTEIN**
> Hannah, I never would have bothered you but I'm off to Miami and they're gonna take away my ten speed unless I get it straightened out fast.

> **HANNAH**
> *(glancing around the chaos)*
> Where are your bills, Carl?

> **BERNSTEIN**
> Oh, they're here. *(starts lifting debris from his desk)* I'm keeping much better records now, Hannah. *(grabbing a big manila envelope)* See? *(hands it to her)*

> **HANNAH**
> *(looks inside)*
> Carl, it's a jungle. *(sits at his desk, takes out a mass of papers — glancing at the top bill)* I suggest you either pay this immediately or lay in a large supply of candles. *(studies another bill)* You'd give a stranger the shirt off your back — except it wouldn't be paid for.

He smiles, gently begins massaging her shoulders as she studies his finances.

> **BERNSTEIN**
> Hey…very tense.

> **HANNAH**
> *(nods)*
> Lot of pressure at the *Star*. *(looking at the bills)* Carl, when we got married, you were four thousand dollars in debt; when we split, you were solvent. That may prove to be the outstanding single achievement of my life, and now look at this. *(sighs)* How much did the damn bike cost?

> **BERNSTEIN**
> Five hundred; six maybe.

> HANNAH
> *(looking at paper)*
> You're two months behind — you got enough to cover?

> BERNSTEIN
> I think.

> HANNAH
> Give me your checkbook then.

> BERNSTEIN
> It's right under that pile.

He indicates a mound of papers. She pulls it out as he continues to massage her, more sensually now. She reaches back, puts her hands on his.

> HANNAH
> I thought you had to get to Miami.

> BERNSTEIN
> There's always a later plane.

> HANNAH
> You're a sex junkie, you know that, Carl?

> BERNSTEIN
> Nobody's perfect. *(more rubbing now)* I'm glad you're out of it, Hannah —
> you're a terrific reporter and I turned you into a bookkeeper.

HANNAH looks at BERNSTEIN a moment; then she kind of smiles gently, shakes her head.

> HANNAH
> Aw baby, you can get it up . . . I just wonder if you'll ever be able to get it
> together.

And quickly from that —

CUT TO

BERNSTEIN

seated perspiring on a hard bench in a stifling office. Outside: palm trees; we're in Miami. And judging from the number of cigarette butts strewn around the bench, BERNSTEIN's been there a while. Waiting. Nervous. And maybe he never will be able to get it together, who knows.

At the front, a SECRETARY sits filing her nails. Behind her are a number of closed doors to offices. No one passes without her OK. The clock hits three in the afternoon as BERNSTEIN gets up from the bench, goes to the SECRETARY.

> BERNSTEIN
> Hi, it's me. I'm still here.

SECRETARY
(couldn't be nicer)

I'm so glad.

BERNSTEIN

I'd really like to see Mr. Dardis.

SECRETARY

And you will. *(smiles)* But not now.

BERNSTEIN

I called him from Washington. He's the one who asked me to be here at eleven in the morning.

SECRETARY

I told you, he had to go out on a case.

CUT TO

THE BENCH as BERNSTEIN slumps back down. He wipes his forehead with his sleeve, smokes a fresh cigarette, is kind of interested when a UNIFORMED COP walks up to the SECRETARY, who is now putting red polish on her nails.

UNIFORMED COP

Is it OK to go on back?

She nods.

CUT TO

BERNSTEIN watching as the COP walks past the SECRETARY, enters an office behind.

CUT TO

THE CLOCK ON THE WALL. IT'S QUARTER OF FOUR NOW.

PULL BACK TO REVEAL

BERNSTEIN, approaching the SECRETARY again. She is working on her right hand now.

BERNSTEIN

Could you reach Mr. Dardis by car radio?

SECRETARY

He is not in the car. *(Smiles; she's just so understanding.)* Sorry.

CUT TO

ANOTHER UNIFORMED COP walking by the SECRETARY's desk.

SECOND COP

Hey, Babe.

He enters the same office the first COP *did.*

CUT TO

BERNSTEIN. *He lights another cigarette, puts it out, then lights another.*

CUT TO

THE SECRETARY

finishing her manicure. It is almost five o'clock now. BERNSTEIN, *his bench a sea of cigarette butts, slowly gets up and goes to the* SECRETARY.

> **BERNSTEIN**
> Mr. Dardis does call in every so often?

> **SECRETARY**
> Well of course.

> **BERNSTEIN**
> *(quietly)*
> Good. Just tell him I was here, that I'm sorry I missed him —

He walks out the double doors.

CUT TO

BERNSTEIN IN HALLWAY. *He looks down the hall. At the end, opposite the* SECRETARY'S *reception room, is a big glass door with a sign reading: Office of the Dade County Clerk.* BERNSTEIN *goes into a phone booth in the corridor from which he can see both offices. He puts in a dime, and dials.*

> **BERNSTEIN**
> Mr. Dardis' office, please.

CUT TO

SECRETARY. *The phone* RINGS *and she punches the button on the phone console.*

> **SECRETARY**
> Mr. Dardis' office.

CUT TO

BERNSTEIN *in phone booth.*

> **BERNSTEIN**
> This is Mr. Tomlinson in the clerk's office. Could you come across the hall for a moment? We've got some documents your boss probably should see.

He hangs up.

CUT TO

BERNSTEIN watching from phone booth as the SECRETARY *hurries across the hallway. As we see her open the door of the clerk's office,* BERNSTEIN *bolts out of the phone booth and runs into the reception room heading straight for the* SECRETARY's *desk.*

CUT TO

BERNSTEIN at her desk, looking at the telephone console, receiver in hand. He punches the button marked Intercom and we can hear it BUZZ *somewhere.*

> VOICE (v.o.)
Dardis.

> BERNSTEIN
Carl Bernstein's here to see you — I don't know why, but he seems angry —

CUT TO

DARDIS emerging through one of the doors behind BERNSTEIN. BERNSTEIN *sees him.*

> BERNSTEIN
> *(to DARDIS)*
Look, you've been jerking my chain all day. If there's some reason you can't talk to me — like the fact that you've already leaked everything to *The New York Times* — just say so.

> DARDIS
Listen, I've got a dinner — can't we do this tomorrow?

> BERNSTEIN
> *(headshake)*
I'm on deadline.

CUT TO

DARDIS' OFFICE. He is fiddling with a combination lock at a filing cabinet. BERNSTEIN *is seated across* DARDIS' *desk.*

> DARDIS
You want Barker's phone stuff or his money stuff?

> BERNSTEIN
Whatever.

He hands BERNSTEIN some papers, glances at his watch.

> DARDIS
I'll never get out of here in time.

> BERNSTEIN
> *(flying through what he's been handed)*
> The telephone calls . . . we know about that.

> DARDIS
> The rest is Barker's bank records. It's mostly the eighty-nine thousand in Mexican cashier's checks —

> BERNSTEIN
> — yeah, that was in *The Times* this morning.

BERNSTEIN continues to fly through the papers.

> BERNSTEIN
> *(continuing stops)*
> What's this Dahlberg check?

And as it's mentioned —

CUT TO

CLOSE UP — CASHIER'S CHECK. It's drawn on the First Bank and Trust Company of Boca Raton, Florida, it's dated April 10 and it's for 25 thousand dollars, payable to the order of Kenneth H. Dahlberg.

> DARDIS' VOICE
> That the twenty-five grand one? — Don't know —

CUT TO

BERNSTEIN starting to copy the check in meticulous facsimile. DARDIS watches.

> DARDIS
> I never could figure just who this Dahlberg was. *(watching BERNSTEIN)* Think it might be anything?

> BERNSTEIN
> *(casually)*
> This? *(shrugs)* Naw . . .

And from here quickly —

ZOOM TO

BERNSTEIN IN A PHONE BOOTH in the lobby of the Justice Building. Wildly excited —

> BERNSTEIN
> — *Woodward* — Woodward, listen, I don't know what I got — *(holding the Dahlberg facsimile)* — and I think the *Times* has it too — *(big)* — but somewhere there's a Kenneth H. Dahlberg in this world and we've gotta find him —

And now comes

THE HUNT FOR DAHLBERG.

This is a compressed montage sequence in which we CUT *from one reporter to the other, both of them desperately trying to locate a man named* DAHLBERG.

WOODWARD *is maybe in the reference room of the* Post, *sweating, surrounded by* Who's Who *and* Dictionary of American Biographies *and phone books from dozens and dozens of cities* —

BERNSTEIN *is maybe in the phone booth of the* Justice Building, *sweating, with a pile of dimes as he dials away.*

This took them hours, and that effort should be visible to us. They tire, grow punchy, but they keep on, checking phone books and dialing numbers and God knows what else. The point is, we want to get to DAHLBERG *in a reasonably short amount of time, but we also want people to know there was* <u>effort</u> *involved.*

CUT TO

WOODWARD, *bleary, in the reference room, a girl comes in, a researcher librarian type.*

> RESEARCHER
> Were you after the Dahlberg articles from the files? *(*WOODWARD *nods)* There aren't any, sorry.

And now she drops a piece of paper, a photo —

> WOODWARD
> Whazzis?

> RESEARCHER
> *(shrugs)*
> Our Dahlberg file.

As she leaves —

CUT TO

The photo.

It is a picture of Hubert Humphrey standing next to another man. The caption identifies that other man as KENNETH DAHLBERG. *Now* —

CUT TO

WOODWARD AT HIS DESK.

The room is reasonably quiet. ROSENFELD *is visible in his office. As* WOODWARD *picks up the phone, gets Minneapolis information* —

CUT TO

ROSENFELD'S PHONE, RINGING. *He hurries in, grabs it.*

> BERNSTEIN'S VOICE (v.o.)
> Harry — I know how to get Dahlberg —

> ROSENFELD
> — Woodward's talking to him now.

CUT TO

BERNSTEIN, *drenched. There are no dimes left. He listens a moment more, then nods, hangs up, leans back against the glass, takes a deep breath, closes his eyes as we*

CUT TO

WOODWARD *on the phone.*

> WOODWARD
> — this should take only a minute, Mr. Dahlberg, but we're doing a follow-up on the break-in — *(pause)* — and I was kind of curious about your check.

> DAHLBERG (v.o.)
> ...check...?

> WOODWARD
> The twenty-five thousand dollar one.
> > *(silence)*
> The one with your name on it.
> > *(silence)*
> In Bernard Barker's Florida account.
> > *(still nothing)*
> Bernard Barker, the Watergate burglar —

> DAHLBERG (v.o.)
> > *(struggling)*
> ...you're definitely doing a story...?

> WOODWARD
> Yes, sir.

> DAHLBERG (v.o.)
> I'm a proper citizen, I'm a decent man, I don't do anything that isn't decent or proper
> > *(WOODWARD waits, pen ready; tense as hell.)*
> I know I shouldn't tell you this...

WOODWARD'S *lips are going "tell me, tell me."*

DAHLBERG (v.o.)
(continuing)
That twenty-five thousand dollars is money I collected for Nixon in this year's campaign.

WOODWARD
I see. And how do you think it reached Miami?

DAHLBERG (v.o.)
I don't know; I really don't. The last time I saw it was when I was in Washington. I gave it to the Finance department of the Committee to Re-Elect the President. How it got to that burglar, your guess is as good as mine.

WOODWARD
(trying to keep his voice level)
That checks out with our findings, thank you, Mr. Dahlberg.

CUT TO

AN ARTICLE WITH WOODWARD'S NAME ON THE BYLINE.

ROSENFELD holds it.

ROSENFELD
CREEP financed the Watergate break-in, Jesus Christ.

He starts off.

WOODWARD
One sec' —

WOODWARD takes the story, scrawls BERNSTEIN's name in front of his on the byline. ROSENFELD watches. As WOODWARD finishes, he takes the story again, hurries off. Now —

CUT TO

THE HEADLINE OF THEIR STORY:

Campaign Funds Found in Watergate Burglar's Account.

Now —

PULL BACK TO REVEAL

that it isn't exactly a gigantic headline piece. As a matter of fact, as more and more of page one appears, we see that their story is tucked away at the bottom and as bigger and bigger headlines are visible —

PULL BACK TO REVEAL

— the whole first page. Plastered across the top in giant letters is the following: EAGLETON

<u>RESIGNS</u>. *And as you look at the whole page now, you can barely make out the tiny pid-*
dling Watergate story. The point is abundantly clear: nobody cared a whole lot.

CUT TO

THE TRIANGLE

being rung like crazy. And as it SOUNDS —

CUT TO

THE BUDGET MEETING

> SIMONS
> — OK, last go-round. Foreign, anything else?

The foreign editor, an enormously thoughtful-looking and respected man, indicates "no."

> SIMONS
> *(to another editor)*

National?

> NATIONAL EDITOR
> I'll stand with the Eagleton follow-ups and McGovern not being able to
> get a replacement — that's your page one stuff right there, Howard —

> SIMONS
> — Metropolitan? —

> ROSENFELD
> — you are ignoring the importance of the Dahlberg repercussions —

> NATIONAL EDITOR
> — nobody gives a shit about the Dahlberg repercussions —

> ROSENFELD
> *(to* NATIONAL EDITOR*)*
> — quit equivocating, say what you mean — *(to* SIMONS *and* BRADLEE*)* — our
> story got Government Accounting to start an audit on CREEP's finances —

> BRADLEE
> — and we printed that, didn't we, Harry? And when the frigging audit's
> done, we'll print that too —

> NATIONAL EDITOR
> — let me tell what happened when I was having lunch today at the Sans
> Souci —

> ROSENFELD
> — correction — when you were *drinking* your lunch *at the bar* of the Sans
> Souci —

NATIONAL EDITOR

— this White House guy, a good one, a pro, came up and asked what is this Watergate compulsion with you guys and I said, well, we think it's important and he said, if it's so goddamn important, who the hell are Woodward and Bernstein?

ROSENFELD

Ask him what he's really saying — he means take the story away from Woodstein and give it to his people at the National Desk—

NATIONAL EDITOR

— well, I've got some pretty experienced fellas sitting around, wouldn't you say so? —

ROSENFELD

— absolutely — and that's all they do, sit sit sit — every once in a while, they call up a Senator, some reporting —

NATIONAL EDITOR

— well, what if your boys get it wrong —

BRADLEE
(after a beat)

Than it's our asses, isn't it?

SIMONS
(indicates the meeting is over)

And we'll all have to go to work for a living.

As the men rise and head for the door, the FOREIGN EDITOR moves toward BRADLEE and SIMONS who remain seated as before.

FOREIGN EDITOR

I don't think either Metropolitan or National should cover the story.
(BRADLEE and SIMONS look at him)
I don't think we should cover the story, period.

BRADLEE

Go on.

FOREIGN EDITOR

It's not that we're using unnamed sources that bothers me, or that everything we print the White House denies, or that almost no other papers are reprinting our stuff.

SIMONS

What then?

FOREIGN EDITOR

I don't believe the goddamn story, Howard, it doesn't make sense.

BRADLEE

It will, it just hasn't bottomed out yet, give it time.

FOREIGN EDITOR

Ben, Jesus, there are over two thousand reporters in this town, are there five on Watergate? Where did we suddenly get all this wisdom?

BRADLEE and SIMONS say nothing. They respect this guy.

FOREIGN EDITOR

Look—why would the Republicans do it?—my God, McGovern is self-destructing before our eyes—just like Muskie did, Humphrey, the bunch of 'em. *(sits on the table, talks quietly on)* Why would the burglars have put the tape around the door instead of up and down unless they wanted to get caught? Why did they take a walkie-talkie and then turn it off, unless they wanted to get caught? Why would they use McCord—the only direct contact to the Republicans?

BRADLEE

You saying the Democrats bugged themselves?

FOREIGN EDITOR

The FBI thinks it's possible—the Democrats need a campaign issue, corruption's always a good one. *(rises, starts out)* Get off the story, Ben—or put some people on McGovern's finances; fair is fair, even in our business.

He leaves. BRADLEE and SIMONS stay where they are, both of them flattened by what the guy's said. Because they're not sure he's wrong... HOLD. Now—

CUT TO

THE PAPERS POURING OUT OF THE ASSEMBLY LINE.

We're back with the UNION GUY from before. He pulls out a paper again, looks at a story on the front page—

CUT TO

THE WOODWARD/BERNSTEIN STORY that said the GAO found that CREEP has mishandled over $500,000 in campaign funds.

UNION GUY
*(to another UNION GUY who's
reading over his shoulder)*

What'd'ya think?

SECOND UNION GUY

Politics as usual, someone just got caught with his hand in the cookie jar, that's all.

UNION GUY
(he's not so sure)

Big fuckin' cookie jar.

As he turns to the sports section —

CUT TO

GETTING THE CREEP LIST SEQUENCE.

Either they get it as it is now, or as they really did, from a Post *researcher who knew someone. In any case, we see the list, with the columns of names and numbers meaning offices and phone extensions*

We also see the two of them working, first, making long attempts at figuring out who worked for whom at CREEP.

Then, once they have that, they begin using the cross-reference phone books, which are not familiar to moviegoers. And from these, they begin to get the home addresses of the various small-fry people who work for CREEP.

Near the end alphabetically, there is a common female name, Jane Smith or something like that. As BERNSTEIN runs his finger down the addresses, something strikes him as familiar, and as he reaches for the phone —

CUT TO

A CRUMMY-LOOKING BAR — MID-DAY.

BERNSTEIN enters, looks around, then smiles and moves to a lovely girl with a sweet face who probably weighs 200 pounds. She is sitting alone in a corner booth. She nods to BERNSTEIN, can't quite pull off a smile.

BERNSTEIN
(sits across)

This is practically a high school reunion for us, Jane — I would have sprung for a classier place.

JANE

Anyplace really public, they'd know about it — they know everything at the Committee, Carl —

BERNSTEIN

— you don't really think you're being followed?

                              JANE

This girlfriend of mine at the Committee, the other day she went back to
the D.A. to tell all the things the FBI didn't ask her. That night, her boss, he
knew what she'd done. They control everything; that's how they know it all.

                           BERNSTEIN

FBI too?

                              JANE

You don't believe me? Well, I was working the weekend of the break-in and
my God, all the executives were running around like crazy—you had to
practically wait in line to use a shredding machine—and when the FBI
came to investigate, they never even *asked* me about it.

                           BERNSTEIN

If you don't like it down there, why don't you quit?

                              JANE

I don't know what they'd do to me.

                           BERNSTEIN
                        (reaching over)

Hey, easy . . .

                              JANE
                         (headshake)

We're a long way from high school, Carl . . . *(she looks at him)* . . . and I'm
scared.

HOLD on her frightened face a moment. Then—

CUT TO

BERNSTEIN

riding home on his bicycle. He gets to his building, starts lugging it up when—

                    JANE'S VOICE (v.o.)

They found out I saw you—
                        (BERNSTEIN stops, glances around)
— they wanted to know everything. *(louder)* Don't call me again.

                           BERNSTEIN
                    (moving toward her voice)

I can help if you'll—

                           JANE (v.o.)

—*stay away from me, Carl!*

CUT TO

JANE IN THE DARKNESS. If she was scared earlier, it's panic-time now. She turns, hurries off.

BERNSTEIN watches her. Suddenly a SOUND comes from the darkness behind him. He whirls. It was nothing but from the way he jumped when it happened you can tell the fear is spreading.

Now from Washington, in darkness —

CUT TO

ESSEX HOUSE IN MANHATTAN — BRIGHT SUNSHINE.

WOODWARD comes hurrying along, and as he enters the hotel —

CUT TO

A DESK CLERK shaking his head at WOODWARD.

> CLERK
>
> We have no one by the name of Mitchell registered.

> WOODWARD
>
> My mistake, sorry.

And as he goes—

CUT TO

WOODWARD out on the street, in a phone booth near Essex House.

> WOODWARD
>
> Get me John Mitchell, it's urgent.

> OPERATOR (v.o.)
>
> That would be room 710, I'll connect you.

WOODWARD waits anxiously as the connection is made.

> MAN'S VOICE (v.o.)
>
> The Mitchells.

> WOODWARD
>
> Can I speak to Martha Mitchell, please.

> MAN'S VOICE (v.o.)
>
> Who is this?

> WOODWARD
>
> I've met Mrs. Mitchell in Washington, I'm Bob Woodward of the *Post* and tell her —

And as the phone clicks dead —

CUT TO

AN ELEVATOR, the numbers of the floors being lit as it rises. 4 — 5 — 6 — WOODWARD stands alone in the elevator. As it reaches seven and the doors slide open, he steps out and

CUT TO

THE MARRIOTT SUITE. It's numbered 710. WOODWARD approaches but as he does the door begins to open so he whirls, knocks on the door nearest him. Now 710 is wide open and several maids leave, watched by a large black man.

> **FIRST MAID**
>
> We'll be back after lunch.

> **BLACK MAN**
> *(it's the voice from the phone)*
>
> We'll be here.

WOODWARD waits by his door as 710 slowly closes. The maids look at him a moment. He knocks again, louder.

> **SECOND MAID**
>
> I think they went out.

> **WOODWARD**
> *(shrugs)*
>
> I don't mind waiting.

The maids nod, move out of sight. WOODWARD stands tense and still, watching the closed door numbered 710 . . . Now —

CUT TO

NATIONAL AIRPORT IN D.C. — LATE AFTERNOON.

People are getting off the shuttle, WOODWARD among them. BERNSTEIN waits.

> **BERNSTEIN**
> *(as WOODWARD reaches him)*
>
> See her?
> *(WOODWARD nods)*
>
> Get anything?

> **WOODWARD**
>
> For the paper, no; for us, plenty.
> *(The two of them head for the terminal.)*
> I waited a long time and finally this big guy — I guess a bodyguard — he left and I knocked and she remembered me, we talked awhile.

BERNSTEIN

And? — And? —

WOODWARD
(looks at BERNSTEIN)
— she was panicked, Carl — every time I mentioned Watergate, you could tell.

BERNSTEIN

Were you eyebrow reading?

WOODWARD
(shakes his head "no")
It was there. I just don't get it; a CREEP secretary being scared, that's one thing. But what does the wife of one of the most powerful men in America have to be afraid of...?

They look at each other; neither has a clue. HOLD. *Now —*

CUT TO

THE RED KARMANN GHIA

moving along a residential area in Washington. It's later that night.

CUT TO

INSIDE THE CAR — NIGHT. WOODWARD *and* BERNSTEIN *driving along.*

BERNSTEIN

Left up ahead.

WOODWARD *nods.*

WOODWARD

Who's first?

BERNSTEIN

Alphabetically, on the CREEP phone list, Miss Helen Abbott of South George Street.

As WOODWARD *turns left:*

BERNSTEIN
(continuing)
Now hang your second right — *(explaining)* — this was my turf when I was a kid.

And on those words —

CUT TO

A DEAD END SIGN. *We hear* BERNSTEIN *explaining* —

> **BERNSTEIN** (v.o.)
> I brought you over one street too many — go back and hang a left again.

Now on those *words* —

CUT TO

ANOTHER DEAD END SIGN

CUT TO

WOODWARD AND BERNSTEIN *pulled over to one side.* BERNSTEIN, *baffled, stares around;* WOODWARD *looks at a map with the aid of a flashlight.*

> **BERNSTEIN**
> I don't get it . . . this really was my turf . . .

> **WOODWARD**
> *(concentrating on the map)*
> You're not a kid anymore.

> **BERNSTEIN**
> *(shaking his head)*
> My first day as a copy boy I was sixteen and wearing my only grown-up suit — it was cream colored. At 2:30 the head copy boy comes running up to me and says, "My God, haven't you washed the carbon paper yet? If it's not washed by three, it'll never be dry for tomorrow."
> *(*WOODWARD *is getting interested in the story now.)*
> And I said, "Am I supposed to do that?" and he said, "Absolutely, it's crucial." So I run around and grab all the carbon paper from all the desks and take it to the men's room. I'm standing there washing it and it's splashing all over me and the editor comes in to take a leak, and he says, "What the fuck do you think you're doing?" And I said, "It's 2:30. I'm washing the carbon paper." *(*BERNSTEIN *looks at* WOODWARD.) Just wanted you to know I've done dumber things than get us lost, that's all.

WOODWARD *goes back to his map.* BERNSTEIN *continues to smoke, staring around at the night.*

CUT TO

WOODWARD — AT THE FRONT OF A HOUSE. *A sweet old lady is looking out at him.*

> **WOODWARD**
> Hi. I'm Bob Woodward of the *Washington Post* and I hate to bother you at home —

SWEET OLD LADY

—I already get the *Post*. I don't need another subscription.

WOODWARD

No, I'm a reporter. I wanted to talk to you about the Committee to Re-Elect.

SWEET OLD LADY

The what to what?

WOODWARD

You work there, Miss Abbott.

SWEET OLD LADY

I'm not Miss Abbott.

CUT TO

ANOTHER LADY—IN HER DOORWAY. This time both WOODWARD and BERNSTEIN are there.

WOODWARD

Miss *Abbott*?

MISS ABBOTT

Yes?

WOODWARD

We're from the *Washington Post* and we wanted to ask you some questions about the Committee.

ZOOM TO

CLOSE UP—MISS ABBOTT

MISS ABBOTT

I'm sorry—

And from nowhere, suddenly, she bursts into tears.

CUT TO

WOODWARD AND BERNSTEIN as her door slams in their faces.

They just look at each other, bewildered. And a little bit upset; their upset increases as the rejections go on.

CUT TO

A WHOLE SERIES OF FACES

in quick succession—they're all in various doorways, men, women, young, old. The only thing in common is their fear.

MIDDLE-AGED MAN
(literally trembling)
God, it's just so awful—

And as he closes the door

CUT TO

A YOUNG GIRL
—I can't—I'd like to but— *(that's all she'll say)*

And as her door starts to shut

CUT TO

OLD MAN
— go — you've got to go before they see you — *please* —

And as he almost starts to beg

CUT TO

OLD WOMAN
— no . . . good . . .

She stands there, shaking her head back and forth, back and forth, pathetic and sad. Now —

CUT TO

WOODWARD.

He is seated alone staring at his coffee cup, surrounded by junk food debris. We are in a Hot Shoppe, it's night, and as BERNSTEIN *comes up with food, they're dressed differently from before.* BERNSTEIN *puts more junk food and coffee down.*

BERNSTEIN
You had the Mighty Mo and the fries without gravy, right?
*(*WOODWARD *shrugs)*

BERNSTEIN *passes over some food. They both look bleary and in foul moods. Silently, they start to eat, something they continue doing throughout. They're not hungry, they just eat.*

WOODWARD
This is terrific work, if you like rejection.

BERNSTEIN
I never scared anyone before.

WOODWARD
It's not us, they were scared before we got there. *(looks at* BERNSTEIN*)* What do we know?

BERNSTEIN
Facts or theory?

WOODWARD
Anything you've got.

BERNSTEIN
We know there's got to be something or they wouldn't be so panicked.

WOODWARD
And that something's got to be more than just Hunt, Liddy, and the five burglars — those indictments are gonna be bullshit when they come down. What else do we know?

BERNSTEIN
I just wish we knew when someone would talk to us, that's all.

They continue to eat, bleary and numb, as we

CUT TO

A MIDDLE-AGED WOMAN —

— kind of an honest, hard-working face.

WOODWARD and BERNSTEIN are standing in her doorway.

WOODWARD
A friend at the Committee told us to contact you —

WOMAN
— who was it?

BERNSTEIN
We never reveal our sources, which is why you can talk to us.

WOODWARD
It's safe, try it, you'll see.

She doesn't talk at first, but she doesn't slam the door either.

BERNSTEIN
We understand your problem —

WOODWARD
— you believe in the President, you wouldn't ever want to do anything disloyal.

BERNSTEIN
We appreciate your position — really.

And now she starts, at last, to talk, and they expect it to be their first breakthrough, but when it turns out to be the most withering onslaught yet, they are stunned.

> ### WOMAN
> You people — you think that you can come into someone's life, squeeze what you want, then get out. *(to BERNSTEIN)* You don't appreciate a goddamn thing, mister. *(to WOODWARD)* And you don't understand nothing. *(voice rising)* But the Committee's briefed us on you — so get the hell out of here — *(big)* — do you like scaring the life out of decent people? — 'cause if you don't, *in the name of God — stop it!*

As she slams the door —

CUT TO

WOODWARD AND BERNSTEIN, *slowly walking in silence back to the car.*

> ### WOODWARD
> At Yale once, they held an auction. There was this woman and her name was Lulu Landis. Her postcards came up for sale. She had 1400 postcards written to her and I'd never heard of her before but I knew I had to have those cards, I had to know why anyone would get so many messages. I paid sixty-five dollars for them ... I got all crazy trying to work it out and at first it was just a maze but then I found that her husband killed himself in Dayton, and once I had that, it all began to open, an evangelist had come to Dayton and his horses hit Lulu Landis at the corner of 13th and Vermillion and she was paralyzed. Permanently, and her favorite thing til then had been traveling and all her friends, whenever they went anyplace, they wrote her. Those cards, they were her eyes ...

They continue to walk; slowly.

CUT TO

A MIDDLE-AGED MAN — IN HIS DOORWAY

> ### MIDDLE-AGED MAN
> I know who you are and I'm not afraid but that don't mean I'll talk to you either — you're just a couple Democrats out to stop Nixon getting re-elected.

CUT TO

WOODWARD AND BERNSTEIN, *staring at the man.*

> ### WOODWARD
> Democrats?

> ### MIDDLE-AGED MAN
> That's right.

                          BERNSTEIN
I hate both parties.

                          WOODWARD
And I'm Republican.

The middle-aged man looks at him.

                          BERNSTEIN
                 (surprised, turns to WOODWARD*)*
Republican?

                          WOODWARD
Sure.

                          BERNSTEIN
Who'd you vote for?

                          WOODWARD
When?

                          BERNSTEIN
'68.

                          WOODWARD
Nixon.

BERNSTEIN *stares at him in silence as we —*

CUT TO

ANOTHER SERIES OF CREEP EMPLOYEES.

Only they aren't slamming doors, they're sitting in various rooms of their houses and apartments. We don't see the reporters or hear their questions but the answers they receive make it all self-evident. We start with the middle-aged man seen above.

                       MIDDLE-AGED MAN
Mitchell never left the Committee — he resigned, sure, but he was there as much as before —

CUT TO

                        YOUNGER MAN
— oh, don't worry, Gordon Liddy will be happy to take the fall for every-one because, well, it's not that Gordon's crazy, he's . . . *(pauses, looking for the right word)* . . . weird. I'll give you some Committee people who know about him — only don't tell it was me —

CUT TO

YOUNGER WOMAN
— of course we were briefed on what to say — and never to volunteer anything —

CUT TO

OLD WOMAN
— oh, we were never alone with the FBI, there was always someone from
the Committee right there —

Smiles, talks on as we —

CUT TO

RICHARD NIXON'S SOMBER VISAGE.

NIXON
. . . No one in this administration, presently employed, was involved in
this very bizarre incident . . .

PULL BACK TO REVEAL

*BERNSTEIN and WOODWARD in a crummy cafeteria, watching the evening news on the
TV set high on the wall. WOODWARD eats a hamburger, BERNSTEIN smokes, sips coffee.
It is night, as usual now.*

CUT TO

NIXON — on the tube.

NIXON
. . . What really hurts in matters of this sort is not the fact that they occur,
because overzealous people in campaigns do things that are wrong. What
really hurts is if you try to cover it up.

CUT TO

*WOODWARD AND BERNSTEIN as the news commentator comes on, begins introducing an-
other story.*

WOODWARD
Did he just say what I think he said?

BERNSTEIN
You voted for him.

He gives WOODWARD a big smile. WOODWARD eats his hamburger in silence . . .

CUT TO

A DIFFERENT TIME, A DIFFERENT PLACE — EARLY EVENING.

BERNSTEIN gets out of his car, walks up, and knocks on the door of a small tract house in the D.C. suburbs. A woman opens the door.

> **BERNSTEIN**
> Hi, I'm Carl Bernstein of the *Washington Post* and —

> **WOMAN**
> — oh, you don't want me, you want my sister. *(calls out)* For you.

And we —

CUT TO

THE BOOKKEEPER approaching the door. She's younger than the cliché version of a book-keeper. As she looks at her sister —

> **BOOKKEEPER'S SISTER**
> This here is Carl Bernstein —

> **BOOKKEEPER**
> — omigod, you're from that place, you've got to go.

The sister is smoking and there is a pack on the dinette table.

> **BERNSTEIN**
> Could I bum one of your cigarettes? —

As the sister starts for the pack —

> **BERNSTEIN**
> *(continuing)*
> — don't bother, I'll get it.

And he crosses ten feet inside the front door.

> **BOOKKEEPER**
> You've really got to go.

> **BERNSTEIN**
> Just let me get a match.

He goes into the living room area, picks up a book of matches. This whole scene moves slowly, the tension building under it — it's not like news people talking, nothing overlaps here.

> **BERNSTEIN**
> *(continuing)*
> But I want you to know that I understand why you're afraid — a lot of good people down there at the Committee are afraid. I'm really sorry for what you're being put through.

BOOKKEEPER
All those articles you people write — where do you find that stuff?

BERNSTEIN
We don't tell anyone that. Which is why you can talk to us. And if we can't verify what you say someplace else, we don't print it. That's another reason you can relax.

BOOKKEEPER
(tense)
I'm relaxed — light your cigarette.

BERNSTEIN lights the cigarette.

BERNSTEIN
You were Hugh Sloan's bookkeeper when he worked for Maurice Stans at Finance, and we were sort of wondering, did you go to work for Stans immediately after Sloan quit or was there a time lapse?

BOOKKEEPER
I never worked for Sloan or Stans.

BOOKKEEPER'S SISTER
(out of the blue; to BERNSTEIN)
Would you like some coffee or anything?

As the BOOKKEEPER winces

BERNSTEIN
(like a shot)
Please, yes, thank you. *(he looks at the BOOKKEEPER)* Can I sit down for a minute?

He is by a couch.

BOOKKEEPER
One minute but then —

BERNSTEIN
— right, right, I've got to go. *(he sits)* Why did you lie just then?

The BOOKKEEPER kneads her hands together silently. BERNSTEIN watches.

BERNSTEIN
I was just curious — you don't do it well, so I wondered. Have you been threatened, if you told the truth, is that it?

BOOKKEEPER
... No ... never in so many words ...

> BERNSTEIN
> *(gently)*
It's obvious you want to talk to someone — well, I'm someone.

He takes out his notebook.

CUT TO

THE BOOKKEEPER. *And she does want to talk. But the notebook scares her terribly and she can only stare at it.*

> BERNSTEIN
I'm not even going to put your name down. It's just so I can keep things straight. *(beat)* Start with the money, why don't you?

> BOOKKEEPER'S SISTER
> *(returning with coffee)*
How do you like it?

> BERNSTEIN
Everything, please.

> BOOKKEEPER'S SISTER
> *(going again)*
I won't be a minute.

> BERNSTEIN
> *(to the BOOKKEEPER, quietly)*
The General Accounting report said there was a 350 thousand cash slush fund in Stans' safe. Did you know about that from the beginning?

> BOOKKEEPER
> *(about to fold)*
There are too many people watching me — they know I know a lot —

> BERNSTEIN
— it was all in hundreds, wasn't it?

> BOOKKEEPER
A lot of it was. I just thought it was sort of an all-purpose political fund — you know, for taking fat cats to dinner, things like that.

> BERNSTEIN
Could buy a lot of steaks, 350,000 dollars.

> BOOKKEEPER
> *(her words are coming faster)*
I can't be positive that it was used for the break-in but people sure are worried.

BERNSTEIN

Which people?

BOOKKEEPER

The ones who could disburse the money.

BERNSTEIN

Who were they?

BOOKKEEPER

There were a group of them — I think five, I don't know their names.

BERNSTEIN

Sloan knew which five, didn't he?
(She nods.)

BOOKKEEPER'S SISTER
(back with cream and sugar)

Here we are.

BOOKKEEPER

I don't want to say anymore.

BERNSTEIN
(indicating coffee)

It's awfully hot — *(smiles)* — and you haven't finished telling me about the money —

BOOKKEEPER
(long pause; then — in a burst)

— omigod, there was so much of it, six million came in one two-day period — six million cash, we couldn't find enough places to put it. I thought it was all legal, I guess I did, til after the break-in, when I remembered Gordon got so much of it.

BERNSTEIN
(heart starting to pound)

Gordon Liddy, you mean?

BOOKKEEPER
(nods)

It was all so crazy — the day after the break-in he gave us a speech, bouncing up and down on his heels in that loony way of his — Gordon told us not to let Jim McCord ruin everything — don't let one bad apple spoil the barrel, he said. You just know that when Gordon Liddy's calling someone a bad apple, something's wrong somewhere. *(more and more moved now)* . . . It's all so rotten . . . and it's getting worse . . . and all I care about is Hugh Sloan. His wife was going to leave him if he didn't stand up and do what was right. And he quit. He quit because he saw it and didn't want any part of it.

> BERNSTEIN

Think Sloan's being set up as a fall guy for John Mitchell? Sometimes it looks that way.

There is a pause. Then —

> BOOKKEEPER

If you guys...if you guys could just get John Mitchell...that would be beautiful...

And now, at long last, she begins to cry. HOLD *on her tears, then —*

CUT TO

A TYPEWRITER

clicking away. The words "INTERVIEW WITH X. SEPT. 14" are visible. There is music blaring in the background, really blasting away, Rachmaninoff or worse.

We are in WOODWARD'S *apartment and* BERNSTEIN *is dictating notes from the* BOOK-KEEPER *interview. It's very late, and* BERNSTEIN *has notes on everything, matchboxes, and it's hard for him to read. They're both really excited,* BERNSTEIN *from his coffee jag,* WOODWARD *by what* BERNSTEIN'S *dictating.*

> BERNSTEIN

I couldn't believe what she told me. Eight cups of coffee worth.

> WOODWARD

Go on, go on —

> BERNSTEIN

— we've got to find out who the five guys are — the five with access to the slush fund — they were aware of the break-in.

> WOODWARD

Then tomorrow's grand jury indictments *will* just be bullshit.

> BERNSTEIN

It goes way high — we've got to find out where —

> WOODWARD

— we will —

> BERNSTEIN

— she was really paranoid, the bookkeeper.

> WOODWARD

That happens to people. *(he goes over, turns the hi-fi on even louder. Shouts —)* OK, go on.

The noise blasts away as BERNSTEIN *and* WOODWARD *hunch over the typewriter. It's a moment of genuine exhilaration. Paranoid, sure, but for the first time, they're really on to something; it's all starting to split open . . .*

CUT TO

WOODWARD AND BERNSTEIN.

They are driving through McLean, Virginia, a development of identical imitation Tudor houses.

> BERNSTEIN
>
> How do you want to handle Sloan?

> WOODWARD
>
> You mean, who's going to play the mean M.P. and who's going to be the nice one?
>
> *(BERNSTEIN nods; WOODWARD shrugs)*
>
> Whichever.

> BERNSTEIN
>
> He's another Ivy Leaguer so he'll probably expect you to be understand-ing — might surprise him if you're not.

> WOODWARD
>
> You want me to be the bastard.

> BERNSTEIN
>
> *(nods)*
>
> And I'll just shitkick in my usual way.

As they drive on —

CUT TO

A PRETTY YOUNG WOMAN standing in the doorway of one of the Tudor houses. She is very pregnant. She knows instinctively who they are, and she dominates them in a genuinely proud female way. What I mean is, it's her scene, and they're suddenly embarrassed to be bothering her.

> WOODWARD
>
> To see Mr. Sloan.

> MRS. SLOAN
>
> He's out. *(There is a pause. She studies them —)* You're those two from the *Post*, aren't you.
>
> *(they nod)*
>
> I'll tell him.

> BERNSTEIN
> *(as she's about to step back inside)*
This must be a difficult time for the both of you.

> MRS. SLOAN

This is an honest house.

> WOODWARD

That's why we wanted to see your husband.

She studies them still; more silence.

> MRS. SLOAN

That decision is up to him.

> BERNSTEIN
> *(conspiratorially)*
Maybe you could put in a good word.

> WOODWARD

We've got another appointment tonight in this area — we'll just stop back later, all right?

> MRS. SLOAN

It's a free country — *(beat)* — in theory.

They nod, start back down the walk. She watches them.

> MRS. SLOAN
> *(calling out)*

Be careful —

They turn, look back at her.

CUT TO

CLOSE UP — MRS. SLOAN

> MRS. SLOAN

— *you can destroy lives.*

CUT TO

WOODWARD AND BERNSTEIN *watching her. She seems like a terrific girl. And maybe they've upset her. Or maybe what she has said, coming from her, has more impact than otherwise. Quietly, they turn back, walk in silence toward the red Karmann Ghia . . .*

CUT TO

THE MCLEAN MCDONALD'S — DINNERTIME. *Lots of very noisy, happy children. WOOD-WARD and BERNSTEIN sit surrounded by their usual array of junk food.*

WOODWARD

Think Sloan's back?

(BERNSTEIN *seems lost in thought*)

What's wrong?

BERNSTEIN

Nothing — I just found out that Jeb Magruder from CREEP is a bigger bike freak than I am. (*sips coffee*) I never like it when the other guy's human...

They continue to sip coffee; outside it continues to rain. Now —

CUT TO

A YOUNG, SLENDER GUY *answering his door.*

WOODWARD *and* BERNSTEIN *stand outside, their jackets over their heads, protecting themselves from the rain which is harder now.*

WOODWARD

Mr. Sloan?

SLOAN

(*nods*)

My wife told me to expect you. (*softly*) As you know, I haven't talked to the press.

BERNSTEIN

We were hoping that maybe now you could. We know why you left the Committee. We know you're not guilty of anything. But we know you know who is —

It has begun to rain even harder.

SLOAN

— look, come in. We'll have to be quiet — my wife's asleep.

CUT TO

A CHRISTMAS CARD *from the Nixons, they are standing in front of the White House Christmas tree. It is signed: "To Hugh and Debbie Sloan, with thanks, Richard M. Nixon, Patricia Nixon."*

PULL BACK

and we're in the living room. More coffee is being drunk; SLOAN *endlessly stirs his.*

SLOAN

I'd like to talk to you, I really would, but my lawyers say I shouldn't until after the Watergate trial.

WOODWARD

You handed out the money. Maybe there's a legitimate explanation for the way it was done—

BERNSTEIN

—then again, maybe things are even worse than we've written—

SLOAN

—they're worse. That's why I quit.

WOODWARD and BERNSTEIN wait as SLOAN is clearly going through a struggle with himself. Then—

SLOAN

Try and understand this. I'm a decent Republican. I believe in Richard Nixon. I worked in the White House four years—so did my wife. What happened on June 17 I don't think the President knew anything about. Some of his men I'm not so sure of.

BERNSTEIN

Do you think the truth will come out at the trial?

SLOAN

That's another of the things I'm not so sure of.

BERNSTEIN

Because people at the Committee were told to lie to the prosecutors?

SLOAN

We were never told flat out "Don't talk." But the message was clear.

BERNSTEIN

To cover up?

SLOAN

Well, they sure didn't ask us to come forward and tell the truth.

WOODWARD

Does "they" mean the White House?

SLOAN

As opposed to the Committee? The Committee's not an independent operation. *Everything is cleared with the White House.* I don't think that the FBI or the prosecutors understand that.

WOODWARD

The report on the cash in Maurice Stans' safe, the three hundred fifty thousand, that's true?

SLOAN

No. It was closer to seven hundred thousand.

WOODWARD

And as treasurer, you could release those funds?

SLOAN
(nods)

When so ordered.

WOODWARD

We're not sure we've got all the guys who could order you, but we know there were five.

(SLOAN is silent.)

BERNSTEIN
(ticking them off)

Mitchell, Stans, Magruder, they're obvious —

SLOAN stirs his coffee.

WOODWARD

— there had to be a White House overseer —

BERNSTEIN

— Colson.

SLOAN

Colson's too smart to get directly involved with something like that.

WOODWARD
(to BERNSTEIN)

Haldeman. (to SLOAN) Right?

SLOAN

I won't talk about the other two.

BERNSTEIN

But they both worked at the White House?

SLOAN
(softly)

I will not talk about the other two.

BERNSTEIN
(out of the blue)

Kalmbach — Nixon's personal lawyer.

SLOAN is shocked at the mention of Kalmbach.

SLOAN

I can't say anything, I'm sorry.

> *(He starts to rise.)*

WOODWARD

One thing I'm not completely clear on — when you gave out the money to Liddy, how did that work?

SLOAN

Badly. *(and now for the first time, he almost smiles)* You don't realize how close all this came to staying undiscovered — I gave Liddy the Dahlberg check and he gave it to Barker who took it to Miami and deposited it.

BERNSTEIN

Right.

SLOAN

Then Barker withdrew the 25 thousand in hundred dollar bills and gave it back to Liddy who gave it back to me and I put it in the office safe which was crammed.

WOODWARD

Go on.

SLOAN

Well, when Liddy came and asked for money for what turned out to be the break-in funds, I went to the safe and gave him — out of this whole fortune — I happened to give him the same hundreds he gave me — banks have to keep track of hundreds. If the money had been in fifties, or if I'd grabbed a different stack, there probably wouldn't have been any Watergate story.

BERNSTEIN

Ordinarily, though, what was the procedure.

SLOAN

Routine — I'd just call John Mitchell over at the Justice Department and he'd say "go ahead, give out the money."

WOODWARD and BERNSTEIN just look at each other — they hadn't known it, not remotely. SLOAN stands and as they head for the door —

CUT TO

THE THREE OF THEM *heading across the foyer.*

BERNSTEIN

What happens when the baby comes?

SLOAN

We're moving. *(beat)* I've been looking for a job but it's been ... hard. My name's been in the papers too much. Sometimes I wonder if reporters understand how much pain they can inflict in just one sentence. I'm not thinking of myself. But my wife, my parents, it's been very rough on them.

CUT TO

BERNSTEIN AND WOODWARD looking very uncomfortable as SLOAN goes on.

SLOAN

I wish I could put down on paper what it's like—you come to Washington because you believe in something, and then you get inside and you see how things actually work and you watch your ideals disintegrate. *(beat)* The people inside, the people in the White House, they start to believe they can suspend the rules because they're fulfilling a mission. That becomes the only important thing—the mission. It's so easy to lose perspective. We want to get out before we lose ours altogether.

SLOAN opens the front door. WOODWARD and BERNSTEIN pause, nod, almost an embarrassed pause. Then as they hurry out into the rain—

CUT TO

A NERFBALL

flying toward a basket cupped to a picture window. When we

PULL BACK

we're in BRADLEE's office, SIMONS and ROSENFELD are also there, along with WOODWARD and BERNSTEIN. BRADLEE plays nerfball mostly; he hasn't got the world's longest attention span.

BERNSTEIN

Look—five men controlled that slush fund at CREEP—three of them we've got, Mitchell, Stans, Magruder, and we're pretty sure of Kalmbach.

WOODWARD

We'd like to wait til we have all five before we print it.

BRADLEE

This is a daily paper, we'll explain it tomorrow. *(looks at them)* You're certain on Mitchell?

WOODWARD

He approved the payments to Liddy while he was still Attorney General—

And all this now goes __fast__—

ROSENFELD

—you got more than one source? —

BERNSTEIN

—yes—

SIMONS

—has any of them got an ax? —

ROSENFELD

—political, personal, sexual, anything at all against Mitchell? —

WOODWARD

—no—

SIMONS

—can we use their names? —

BERNSTEIN

—no—

BRADLEE

—goddamnit, when's somebody gonna go *on* the record on this story—

ROSENFELD

—who you got? —

WOODWARD

—well, Sloan—

BERNSTEIN

—and we got a guy in Justice—

BRADLEE

—Deep Throat? —

WOODWARD

—I saw him. He verifies.

BRADLEE

OK. *(now after the burst of talk, a pause)* You're about to write a story that says that the former Attorney General—the man who represented *law* in America—is a crook. *(throws the nerfball)* Just be right, huh?

As WOODWARD and BERNSTEIN leave the office—

BRADLEE

Leave plenty of room for his denial.

CUT TO

BERNSTEIN AT HIS DESK ON THE PHONE. He has some papers in front of him and a notepad and pencil in his free hand. He is tired and very, very nervous. It is dark outside. In what follows,. BERNSTEIN takes notes.

> **OPERATOR'S VOICE** (v.o.)

Essex House, can I help you?

> **BERNSTEIN**

John Mitchell, please.

There is a BUZZING SOUND. Then —

> **JOHN MITCHELL'S VOICE** (v.o.)

Yes?

> **BERNSTEIN**

Sir, this is Carl Bernstein of the *Washington Post*, and I'm sorry to bother you but we're running a story in tomorrow's paper that we thought you should have a chance to comment on.

> **MITCHELL** (v.o.)

What does it say?

> **BERNSTEIN**
> *(starting to read)*

John N. Mitchell, while serving as US Attorney General, personally controlled a secret cash fund that—

> **MITCHELL** (v.o.)

— *Jeeeeeeesus* —

> **BERNSTEIN**

— fund that was used to gather information against the Democrats —

> **MITCHELL** (v.o.)

— *Jeeeeeesus* —

> **BERNSTEIN**

— according to sources involved in the Watergate investigation. Beginning in the spring of 1971 —

> **MITCHELL** (v.o.)

— *Jeeeeeesus* —

> **BERNSTEIN**

— almost a year before he left the Justice Department —

> **MITCHELL** (v.o.)

— *Jeeeeeeeeesus* —

BERNSTEIN

— to become President Nixon's campaign manager on March 1, Mitchell personally approved withdrawals from the fund —

MITCHELL (v.o.)

— all that crap, you're putting it in the paper? It's all been denied. You tell your publisher — tell Katie Graham she's gonna get her tit caught in a big fat wringer if that's published. Good Christ! That's the most sickening thing I ever heard.

BERNSTEIN

Sir, I'd like to ask you a few —

MITCHELL (v.o.)

— what time is it?

BERNSTEIN

11:30.

MITCHELL (v.o.)

Morning or night?

BERNSTEIN

Night.

MITCHELL (v.o.)

Oh.

And he hangs up.

CUT TO

BRADLEE AND BERNSTEIN *at* BERNSTEIN's *desk.* BRADLEE *is going over* BERNSTEIN's *notes.*

BRADLEE

He really made that remark about Mrs. Graham?
(BERNSTEIN *nods*)
This is a family newspaper — cut the words "her tit" and run it.

And now suddenly —

THE PRESSES OF THE *POST*

rolling the story. They're modern and gigantic and

CUT TO

WOODWARD AND BERNSTEIN. *They're in the lobby of the* Post *at night and through a thick-pane of glass they're watching their story roll and on their faces is something you don't expect to see: panic.*

BRADLEE comes up behind them, looks down at the presses, starts to talk.

BRADLEE

Once when I was reporting, Lyndon Johnson's top guy gave me the word: they were looking for a successor to J. Edgar Hoover. I wrote it and the day it appeared Johnson called a press conference and appointed Hoover head of the FBI for life...And when he was done, he turned to his top guy and the President said, "Call Ben Bradlee and tell him fuck you." *(shakes his head)* I took a lot of static for that — everyone said, "You did it, Bradlee, you screwed up — you stuck us with Hoover forever — " *(looks at* WOODWARD *and* BERNSTEIN*)* — I screwed up but I wasn't wrong.

They all watch the presses now.

BRADLEE
(continuing)
You guys haven't been wrong yet, is that why you're scared shitless?
(as WOODWARD *and* BERNSTEIN
nod, BRADLEE *starts away)*
You should be...

CUT TO

THE PRESSES *continuing to roll. The* SOUND *is incredible. Now —*

CUT TO

A TELETYPE MACHINE

clacking away like crazy. We can read the words, "The Senator finished by saying that although he was..." and from there —

DISSOLVE TO

A SENATOR *and while the words "although he was" are still very fresh in our minds —*

SENATOR

Although I am a Republican, I would like to state in a pure bipartisan spirit that I feel only sadness that a once fine journal of record like the *Post* would have become merely the hysterical spokesman for the equally hysterical left wing of the Democratic Party —

The SOUND *of the teletype doesn't stop in this little part and we see three people and it's very important that their voices are immediately recognizable and distinct. One, the* SENATOR *is from the West and will have that twang. The next two whom we are about to meet are* PUBLIC RELATIONS PEOPLE *from* CREEP *and the* WHITE HOUSE*. The* CREEP *VOICE is very southern, the* WHITE HOUSE GUY *sounds like an NBC announcer. The* WESTERN SENATOR *will be seen in a corridor of the Senate office building, talking to reporters, the* CREEP P.R. SOUTHERNER *will be talking to reporters in front of the* CREEP *office doors* *and so identified. The* WHITE HOUSE SPOKESMAN *will be standing on a platform with a flag visible off to one side. As the teletype goes on —*

CUT TO

THE SOUTHERN CREEP P.R. MAN

> **CREEP P.R. MAN**
> *(in mid-sentence)*

— hearsay, innuendo, and character assassination. I can only conclude that the so-called sources of the *Washington Post* are a fountain of misinformation —

CUT TO

THE WHITE HOUSE SPOKESMAN

> **WHITE HOUSE SPOKESMAN**

— the White House has long since stopped being surprised at this type of reporting by certain elements of the Eastern liberal press —

CUT TO

BRADLEE'S OFFICE.

A lot of activity. BRADLEE *is at his desk reading the teletype dispatches.* SIMONS *and* ROSENFELD *are there,* WOODWARD *and* BERNSTEIN, *too. A kid comes in with more teletype stuff. The editors look at it*

> **SIMONS**
> *(reading)*

Same kind of crap —

> **BRADLEE**
> *(glancing through; nods)*

— all non-denial denials — we're dirty guys and they doubt we were ever virgins but they don't say the story is inaccurate.

> **BERNSTEIN**

What's a real denial?

> **BRADLEE**

If they ever start calling us goddamn liars — *(little pause)* — it's time to start circling the wagons.

CUT TO

THE UNION GUYS IN THE *POST*

looking at a new headline:

NIXON ELECTION AIDES CONCEALED
FACTS FROM GOVERNMENT PROBERS

FIRST UNION GUY

You think they know what they're doing on the fifth floor?

SECOND UNION GUY

I got eight kids to support — they better.

They start for the sports section, only this time, they stop, go back, stare at the headline again. From them watching —

CUT TO

SIMONS,

walking WOODWARD to the elevators.

WOODWARD

What do you think Mrs. Graham wants to see me for?

SIMONS

Maybe to fire you — since you two started on this story, the *Post* stock has dropped, what, 50 percent?
(WOODWARD *pushes for the elevator*)
And the word is some Nixon people are challenging her TV licenses. I'm not saying she's going on relief, but I don't think it's unreasonable for her to want to meet you.

WOODWARD

You think she wants us to ease up on the story?

SIMONS

(shrugs)

I don't know, but I don't think that's unreasonable either, do you?

The elevator opens. WOODWARD shakes his head "no" and steps inside as we

CUT TO

MRS. GRAHAM in her office as a SECRETARY lets WOODWARD in. He's nervous. She's standing by the window, he crosses to her.

MRS. GRAHAM

I'm so glad you could come, Mr. —

WOODWARD

— I'm Woodward.

She nods. There's a pause. He waits. She's trying to say something, get something started, but it's difficult. Silence. She stares out again, quietly starts to talk.

MRS. GRAHAM

You know, the paper was my father's and my husband's when they were alive and I was thinking back a year or two ago when Ben called me and said he wanted to publish the Pentagon Papers the next day. *The Times* had already been stopped from publishing any more of them and all my legal counsel said "don't, don't" and I was frightened but I knew if I said no, I'd lose the whole fifth floor. So we published, and that night, after I'd told Ben to go ahead, I woke up in the darkness and I thought, "Oh my Lord, what am I doing to this newspaper?" *(She looks at WOODWARD.)* I woke up again last night with that same question.

(WOODWARD says nothing, waits.)

Are we right on this story?

WOODWARD

I think so.

MRS. GRAHAM

Are you sure?

WOODWARD

No.

MRS. GRAHAM

When will you be, do you think? — when are we going to know it all?

WOODWARD

It may never come out.

MRS. GRAHAM

Never? Please don't tell me never. *(beat)* Ben says you've found some wonderful sources.

WOODWARD

Some Justice Department lawyers and an FBI man, and some people from the Committee to Re-Elect, yes ma'am.

MRS. GRAHAM

And the underground garage one.

(WOODWARD, more nervous now, nods)

Would I know him?

WOODWARD

I couldn't say.

MRS. GRAHAM

But it's possible.

WOODWARD
(throat very dry)

It is.

MRS. GRAHAM

You've never told anyone who he is?
(WOODWARD shakes his head)
But you'd have to tell me if I asked you.
(WOODWARD nods)
Tell me.

WOODWARD
(he is dying)

I would, if you really ever wanted to know.

MRS. GRAHAM

I really want to know.

CUT TO

WOODWARD *caught between a rock and a hard place. He is silent until there is the* SOUND *of light laughter and we —*

CUT TO

MRS. GRAHAM. *The laughter came from her.*

MRS. GRAHAM

I wasn't serious. I have plenty of burdens to carry around, I don't need another.

WOODWARD *tries not to exhale too audibly.*

MRS. GRAHAM

We're going to need lots of good luck, aren't we?

WOODWARD

Nobody ever had too much.

CUT TO

CLOSE UP — MRS. GRAHAM *as abruptly she reaches out, touches* WOODWARD *on the arm.*

MRS. GRAHAM

Do better.

WOODWARD *makes a nod.* HOLD. *Then —*

CUT TO

BRADLEE

in a state of controlled anger, pacing around the tiny teletype room. WOODWARD hurries in.

> WOODWARD

What?

BRADLEE says nothing, just points to the AP teletype. WOODWARD looks at it, clearly is upset.

> BRADLEE

I thought you guys were supposed to be working on this story —
> *(to BERNSTEIN who tears in —)*
— you think I like being aced out? —

> BERNSTEIN

— what? —

> WOODWARD

— The *L.A. Times* has a huge interview with Baldwin —

> BERNSTEIN

— the lookout in the Motor Inn? —
> *(WOODWARD nods)*
— he say anything we don't know? —

> WOODWARD
> *(headshake)*
— just that a lot of reports were sent to CREEP, but he doesn't name who, not here anyway —

> BRADLEE

— it would have been nice to have had this, I sure would have liked to have had this —

> BERNSTEIN

— there's nothing new in it —

> BRADLEE

— it makes the break-in *real* — it's a major goddamn story — *(starts out)* —
I'm not going to kick ass over this, but I'd like you to know I hate getting beat, I just hate it — *don't forget that I hate it —*

And he stalks out. WOODWARD and BERNSTEIN stand staring at the teletype which keeps on clacking and clacking as the L.A. Times *story keeps getting longer.*

> BERNSTEIN

God*damn*it —

> WOODWARD

— shit —

> **BERNSTEIN**
> —we gotta top the *Times*—

> **WOODWARD**
> —I know, I know—

> **BERNSTEIN**
> —if we could name the guys got the reports, we'd be ahead again—

> **WOODWARD**
> —shit, who do we know?—

> **BERNSTEIN**
> —I know a lawyer at Justice—

> **WOODWARD**
> —has he got an ax?—

> **BERNSTEIN**
> —almost every source we've used has been Republican, this guy's a card-carrying Democrat.

> **WOODWARD**
> Then he's got an ax. *(beat)* Call him anyway.

As BERNSTEIN *nods, takes off out of the room—*

CUT TO

THE UNION GUYS

studying the front page, on which one headline indicates that they've named the guys at CREEP who got the reports.

> **FIRST UNION GUY**
> Who is this Woodstein? *(points to paper)* Two stories on the front page.

> **SECOND UNION GUY**
> If he can't pick a winner at Pimlico, to hell with him.

CUT TO

A HOT SHOPPE.

WOODWARD *is stirring his morning coffee as* BERNSTEIN *comes in, spots him, hurries over* BERNSTEIN *is maybe more excited than we've yet seen him.*

> **BERNSTEIN**
> —I want you to shut up and listen to me—

> **WOODWARD**
> —I haven't said anything—

BERNSTEIN

—for the first time I'm beginning feel like a fucking reporter—Woodward, I got a tip. A guy called *me* up with a tip—*(carefully)*—someone named Donald Segretti contacted a bunch of lawyers and asked them if they'd like to go to work with him screwing up the Democrats, dirty tricks, shit like that. The FBI knows about Segretti—Howard Hunt made a bunch of phone calls to him—they interrogated him, but on account of Segretti wasn't involved with the break-in, they didn't follow through. But Segretti did a lot of traveling—he called these lawyers from different places, and he told them the Republicans knew what he was doing.

WOODWARD

How high up, which Republicans?

BERNSTEIN

That's what we've got to find out, but Segretti went to Southern Cal. and so did a bunch of Nixon men—

WOODWARD

—Haldeman I know; who else?

BERNSTEIN

Dwight Chapin, Nixon's appointments chief—he knew Segretti in school. Maybe I'm crazy, but this is the first time any of this starts to make sense. What were the three theories?

WOODWARD

The burglary was done by Cubans or Democrats or Republicans.

BERNSTEIN

Now the reason no one believed the Republicans is because there wasn't any reason, they were so far ahead. But Segretti was talking to these other lawyers a *year* before the break-in.

WOODWARD

So maybe Watergate wasn't really about Watergate—maybe that was just a piece—

BERNSTEIN

—because a year before, the Republicans weren't ahead, not in the polls, Muskie was running ahead of Nixon then. Before he self-destructed.

WOODWARD

If he self-destructed.

Now, from the two of them—

CUT TO

A MAZE OF CREDIT CARD RECEIPTS IN VARIOUS PILES.

There is the SOUND *of bad guitar music, which as we*

PULL BACK

we see is BERNSTEIN *playing. We are in his apartment, it's night, and the two of them, bleary, are studying the maze of receipts.*

> WOODWARD
> Segretti criss-crossed the country over ten times in six months — and never stayed anyplace over a night or two. *(glancing up)* Switch to another station, huh? You're driving me crazy with that.

> BERNSTEIN
> Segovia begged me for me secret but I said, "No, Andres, you'll have to try and make it without me."

He switches to another song which sounds a lot like the one he just finished playing.

> WOODWARD
> *(pointing to the thickest stacks)*
> California, Illinois, Florida, New Hampshire — all the major Democratic primary states. *(whirling) Why does everything you play sound the same?*

> BERNSTEIN
> — 'cause I only know four chords —

CUT TO

THE CREDIT CARDS. *The camera moves across the travels of Donald Segretti. There is the* SOUND *of* BERNSTEIN'S *guitar.* HOLD *for a moment, then —*

CUT TO

A TINY, BABY-FACED MAN

standing in his doorway.

> BERNSTEIN (v.o.)
> Donald Segretti?

> SEGRETTI
> That's right.

CUT TO

BERNSTEIN — OUTSIDE THE APARTMENT DOOR. *We are, it will soon be clear, in California now, Marina Del Rey.*

BERNSTEIN

I'm Carl Bernstein.

(SEGRETTI *nods*)

My paper sent me out to see if I couldn't persuade you to go on the record.

SEGRETTI

You can't.

BERNSTEIN

Mind if I try?

SEGRETTI *shrugs, and as they enter his apartment —*

CUT TO

INSIDE. *They walk across to a small terrace outside, where they sit. The terrace has a glorious view of the water and lots of girls in bathing costume, below.*

BERNSTEIN

According to what we've been able to verify, you've been busy.

SEGRETTI

I've got a lot of energy.

BERNSTEIN

Listen — we know you're involved in this — we're going to get the story, why not help?

SEGRETTI

They never told me anything except my own role — I had to find out the rest in the papers.

BERNSTEIN

By "they" you mean . . . ?

He waits; SEGRETTI just shakes his head.

BERNSTEIN

By "they" you mean the White House, don't you?

(SEGRETTI *makes no reply.*)

Your buddy from USC, Dwight Chapin — he works for the White House.

SEGRETTI

I know where Dwight works.

BERNSTEIN

When did he hire you?

SEGRETTI *shakes his head, stares out at the girls.*

BERNSTEIN

Do you feel much about the things you did?

SEGRETTI

I didn't do anything wrong.

BERNSTEIN

Tell that to Muskie.

SEGRETTI

Oh, maybe nickel and dime stuff.

BERNSTEIN

During the Florida primary, you wrote a letter on Muskie stationery saying Scoop Jackson had a bastard child. You wrote another that said Hubert Humphrey was out with call girls.

SEGRETTI

Sometimes it got up to a quarter maybe — *(to BERNSTEIN)* — off the record.

BERNSTEIN

You wrote the Canuck letter — the one where you claimed Muskie slurred the Canadians.

SEGRETTI

I didn't.

BERNSTEIN

But you know who did.

SEGRETTI

When you guys print it in the papers, then I'll know. *(closes his eyes)* I'm a lawyer, and I'll probably go to jail, and be disbarred, and what did I do that was so awful?

BERNSTEIN says nothing, waits.

SEGRETTI

None of it was my idea, Carl — I didn't go looking for the job.

BERNSTEIN

Chapin did contact you then?

SEGRETTI

Sure — off the record.

BERNSTEIN

On orders from Haldeman?

SEGRETTI

I don't know anything about Haldeman, except Dwight's frightened of him — everybody's frightened of him — Christ, I wish I'd never gotten messed around with this — all I wanna do is sit in the sun; sit, swim, see some girls.

BERNSTEIN

It gets interesting if it was Haldeman, because our word is that when Chapin says something he's gotten the OK from Haldeman, and when Haldeman says something, he's gotten the OK from the President.

SEGRETTI

Can't help you.

BERNSTEIN

At USC, you had a word for this — screwing up the opposition you all did it at college and called it ratfucking.
(*SEGRETTI half-smiles, nods*)
Ever wonder if Nixon might turn out to be the biggest ratfucker of them all?

CUT TO

CLOSE UP — *SEGRETTI staring at the girls and the blue water.*

SEGRETTI

What would you have done if you were just getting out of the Army, if you'd been away from the real world for four years, if you weren't sure what kind of law you wanted to practice, and then one day you got a call from an old friend asking you to go to work for the President of the United States...?

HOLD *on the question, then —*

CUT TO

WOODWARD AND BERNSTEIN

back in D.C., walking through the airport.

BERNSTEIN

What would you have done?

WOODWARD

You asking would I have been one of the President's men? (*beat*) I would have been.

As *they continue on —*

CUT TO

WOODWARD

alone in the underground garage. Tense, jumpy. He looks at his watch, paces around. It's all eerie as hell. Then, from the ramps, footsteps.

CUT TO

DEEP THROAT *moving out of the shadows, smoking, as always.*

> **DEEP THROAT**
> My turn to keep you waiting. *(approaches)* What's the topic for tonight?

> **WOODWARD**
> Ratfucking.

> **DEEP THROAT**
> In my day, it was simply called the double cross. I believe the CIA refers to it as Mindfuck. In our context, it simply means infiltration of the Democrats.

> **WOODWARD**
> I know what it means — Segretti wouldn't go on the record, but if he would, we know he'd implicate Chapin. And that would put us inside the White House.

> **DEEP THROAT**
> *(nods)*
> Yes, the little ratfuckers are now running our government.

> **WOODWARD**
> Who? — be specific. How high up?

> **DEEP THROAT**
> You'll have to find that out, won't you.

> **WOODWARD**
> The slush fund at CREEP financed the ratfucking, we've almost got that nailed down, so —

He stops as suddenly DEEP THROAT *dives down behind the nearest car.*

WOODWARD *dropping beside him.*

> **WOODWARD**
> What?

> **DEEP THROAT**
> Did you change cabs?
> *(as* WOODWARD *nods)*
> It didn't work, something moved there —

And as he points

CUT TO

THE SHADOWS BY THE RAMP. *You can't see a goddamn thing. But there is the* SOUND, *faint but distinct, of breathing.*

CUT TO

WOODWARD *standing, staring into the darkness. He is scared, wipes his mouth. He doesn't move for a moment. Then he walks directly into the darkness and as he's gone —*

ZOOM TO

A HORRID FACE IN CLOSE UP, *red-eyed, unshaven, beaten — there are half-formed scabs and cuts. He is leaning against a wall, shivering. He looks, for all the world, like a perpetual drunk.*

CUT TO

WOODWARD *in the shadows, coming closer.*

CUT TO

THE DRUNK. *He blinks slowly, tongue lolling outside his mouth. He watches* WOODWARD *approach.*

CUT TO

WOODWARD *coming still closer.*

CUT TO

THE DRUNK. *He blinks very slowly now. Maybe he isn't even certain* WOODWARD'S *there.*

CUT TO

WOODWARD *stopping in front of the drunk. They look at each other for a long time. Then:*

WOODWARD
Who are you?

CUT TO

THE DRUNK. *Nothing, no reaction.*

CUT TO

WOODWARD *studying the other man.*

CUT TO

THE DRUNK. *And he blinks again, then slowly, shivering, begins sliding down the wall.* WOODWARD *reaches for him, holds him up.*

CUT TO

WOODWARD *managing to get out his wallet, take out some bills. He starts up the ramp with the drunk, and as they disappear up the ramp out of sight, he gives the drunk the money.*

> **WOODWARD**
> Here. *(softly)* Forget your troubles and just be happy.

CUT TO

DEEP THROAT *pacing and smoking. He is visibly upset; scared maybe. He glances over as* WOODWARD *comes back down the ramp alone.*

> **DEEP THROAT**
> *(self-mocking)*
> I hope you noticed how coolly I behaved under the threat of discovery.

> **WOODWARD**
> *(impatiently)*
> Do Justice and the FBI know what we know, and why the hell haven't they done anything about it?

> **DEEP THROAT**
> They know, but they focused on the burglary — if it didn't deal with the break-in, they didn't pursue it.

> **WOODWARD**
> Why didn't they? — who told them not to?

> **DEEP THROAT**
> Someone with authority I'd imagine, wouldn't you? *(coughs)* Don't you know what you're onto? Come *on*.

> **WOODWARD**
> Mitchell knew then.

> **DEEP THROAT**
> Of course — my God, you think something this big just happens? The break-in and the cover-up, of course Mitchell knew, but no more than Ehrlichman.

> **WOODWARD**
> Haldeman too?

> **DEEP THROAT**
> You get nothing from me about Haldeman.

And from his tone, you know HALDEMAN *scares him.*

> **WOODWARD**
> Why did they do all this for Chrissakes? — what were they after?

DEEP THROAT

Total manipulation. I suppose you could say they wanted to subvert the Constitution, but they don't think along philosophical lines.

WOODWARD

Talk about Segretti —

DEEP THROAT

— don't concentrate on Segretti or you'll miss the overall scheme too.

WOODWARD

There were more then.

DEEP THROAT

Follow every lead — every lead goes somewhere —

WOODWARD

— the Canuck letter — was that a White House operation —

DEEP THROAT
(nods, bigger)

— don't you miss the grand scheme too.

WOODWARD

How grand?

DEEP THROAT

Nationwide — my God, they were frightened of Muskie and look who got destroyed — they wanted to run against McGovern, and look who they're running against. They bugged, they followed people, false press leaks, fake letters, they canceled Democratic campaign rallies, they investigated Democratic private lives, they planted spies, stole documents, on and on — don't tell me you think this was all the work of little Don Segretti.

WOODWARD

And Justice and FBI know all this?

DEEP THROAT

Yes, yes, everything. There were over fifty people employed by the White House and CREEP to ratfuck — some of what they did is beyond belief.

WOODWARD
(stunned)
Fifty ratfuckers directed by the White House to destroy the Democrats?

CUT TO

DEEP THROAT

DEEP THROAT
I was being cautious. *(inhales)* You can safely say more than fifty...

Silence in the garage. HOLD... *then —*

CUT TO

THE FIFTH FLOOR OF THE *POST*

and it's noisy. Not as noisy as it's going to get, but there is more tension around just now than there has been previously.

CUT TO

AN ATTRACTIVE WOMAN IN HER MID-30S. On her desk is her name, MARILYN BERGER. She is watching BERNSTEIN who is standing by the water cooler nearby. As she gets up —

CUT TO

BERNSTEIN drinking water.

BERGER
Do you guys know about the Canuck letter?

BERNSTEIN
(nods, drinks)
Um-hmm. *(stops, looks at her)* Why?

BERGER
I just wanted to be sure you knew who wrote it.

As she speaks —

CUT TO

WOODWARD working at his desk, suddenly looking up as a SCREAM comes from the direction of the water cooler and as everyone turns to see, here comes BERNSTEIN dragging BERGER over to WOODWARD's desk.

BERNSTEIN
(hysterical)
Tell him what you just told me.

BERGER
Just that Ken Clawsen — he used to be a reporter here before he went to work for Nixon — I had him over for a drink a few weeks ago and he told me he wrote the Canuck letter. *(she looks from one of them to the other)* You did want to know, didn't you?

And now from her —

CUT TO

WOODWARD AND BERNSTEIN *in a corner of the room, talking low and fast.*

> **BERNSTEIN**
> You think we're being set up? — Christ, Deep Throat tells you last night that the letter came from inside the White House and up traipses Marilyn naming names.

> **WOODWARD**
> It makes a crazy kind of sense — remember that initiation rite they have at the White House? Each new member of the President's staff has to prove his guts by getting an enemy of Nixon.

> **BERNSTEIN**
> You think this was Clawsen's initiation?

> **WOODWARD**
> Could have won him a fraternity paddle with a White House seal. *(beat)* God knows it worked.

CUT TO

A FROZEN SHOT OF MUSKIE IN THE SNOW *in tears, standing on the flat-bed truck. This was in the New Hampshire primary, just after the Canuck letter was published.*

> **WOODWARD** (v.o.)
> You claiming it was all a misunderstanding, Ken?

> **CLAWSEN** (v.o.)
> Absolutely — Marilyn's gotten it totally wrong —

CUT TO

WOODWARD ON THE PHONE.

> **WOODWARD**
> She's an awfully good reporter — I can't remember her getting too much wrong before, can you?

> **CLAWSEN** (v.o.)
> That's a bullshit question, that's a question straight out of Wichita, Kansas.

> **WOODWARD**
> Sorry, Ken; listen, one last thing: where did your talk with Berger happen?

> **CLAWSEN** (v.o.)
> Where? *(beat)* What do you mean, where?

WOODWARD
(casually)
Well, was it in a bar, her apartment, some restaurant—

CLAWSEN (v.o.)
— I've completely forgotten where it was, except I know it wasn't her apartment.

There is the sound of him hanging up the phone. Hard. WOODWARD hangs up quietly, rubs his eyes, calls out to BERGER who is at her desk—

WOODWARD
Non denial-denial, Marilyn—

BERGER is about to answer when her *phone rings. She picks it up, turns to WOODWARD, mouths "it's him" and we*

CUT TO

BERGER ON THE PHONE. Again Clawsen on the other end.

CLAWSEN (v.o.)
For Chrissakes, don't tell them I came to your place.

BERGER
I already told them.

CLAWSEN (v.o.)
Oh, that's terrific, that's just so terrific, I'm thrilled you did that.

BERGER
I have a clear conscience.

CLAWSEN (v.o.)
Marilyn, I have a wife and a family and a cat and a dog.

Now from this—

BRADLEE IN HIS OFFICE GESTURING

and we

CUT TO

WOODWARD AND BERNSTEIN heading toward the office. As they enter—

BRADLEE
I got Clawsen on hold—

WOODWARD
—his dialing finger must be falling off—

BRADLEE

— what do you think? —

WOODWARD

— he went to her apartment and he told her —

BERNSTEIN

— if he did it or just said he did it, God knows.

BRADLEE

I could care less about where it happened; what happened is what counts. *(calling out to his SECRETARY)* Put him on. *(picks up the phone)* Ken, I'm sorry, it was Goddamn Beirut and they were having a crisis, what's up, kid? *(pause)* Slow down, Ken, you sound frazzled. *(pause)* A wife and a family and a cat and a dog, right, Ken. *(pause)* Ken, I would never print that you were in Marilyn's apartment at night — unless, of course, you force me to.

CUT TO

CLOSE UP — BRADLEE. He is genuinely enjoying himself. Now, he puts his hand over the receiver —

BRADLEE

It's like they taught us at Harvard: few things are as gratifying to the soul as having another man's nuts in a vise . . .

Now, as he goes back to talking —

CUT TO

A BIG HEADLINE IN THE *POST* READING: NIXON AIDES SABOTAGED DEMOCRATS.

Now we HOLD on that headline as the three deniers are visible through it in the same places they spoke before.

WHITE HOUSE SPOKESMAN

The story is based entirely on hearsay and —

CREEP P.R. MAN

— we at the Committee are continually amazed at the creativity shown by the *Washington Post* and —

WESTERN SENATOR

— although I am a Republican, I would like to state in a pure bipartisan spirit that I am happy that this latest onslaught against the intelligence of the American people will be wrapping fish tomorrow. I offer my condolences to the fish . . .

And now, the headline fades as we

CUT TO

SIMONS IN ROSENFELD'S OFFICE

WOODWARD and BERNSTEIN hurry in.

> ROSENFELD
>
> Speak.

> BERNSTEIN
>
> We've just been talking to Young —

> SIMONS
>
> — which Young?

> WOODWARD
>
> Larry Young, a California lawyer —

> BERNSTEIN
>
> — he was going to go into law practice with Segretti.

> ROSENFELD
>
> And? —

> WOODWARD
>
> — and he says Chapin hired Segretti —

> SIMONS
>
> — well and good, but when will he say it on the record.

> WOODWARD
>
> He just did.

> BERNSTEIN
>
> He'll give us a sworn statement.

> WOODWARD
>
> We're inside the White House now.

ROSENFELD and SIMONS just look at each other. They should be happy, and maybe they are. But at the moment more than anything else they look scared... HOLD. Then —

THE MONTPELIER ROOM OF THE MADISON HOTEL.

It's a very fancy restaurant and BRADLEE is at a corner table as WOODWARD and BERNSTEIN sit down. They are exhausted.

> BRADLEE
>
> Look, I wanted to talk because things are getting really hairy and there's a couple of things we've got to be careful of because —

A waiter is nearby.

BRADLEE
(continuing)
— either of you want a drink or should I order? —
(They don't.)

— because —

And suddenly he lapses into perfect French with the waiter, ordering lunch and salad and as the waiter nods and goes

BRADLEE
(continuing)
— because our cocks are on the chopping block and you've got to be sure that you're not just dealing with people who hate Richard Nixon and want to get him through us. You see, I don't give a shit who's President — I really don't, it's an adversary situation between them and us and it's always gonna be. I never had a closer friend than Jack Kennedy and *once* I printed something that pissed him off and for seven months I didn't exist.

A wine steward appears, hands BRADLEE the list. As he examines it, a man walks up to the table, stands there ...

MAN
You none of you know who I am, do you?
(they don't)
You screw me up good, you don't even know what I look like.

BRADLEE
OK, you've had your preamble; who the hell are you?

MAN
Glenn Sedam — you wrote about me last week, you said I was one of the guys at the Committee who was sent reports. You were wrong.

BERNSTEIN
Baldwin told the FBI it was you.

SEDAM
Baldwin told the FBI it was someone whose first name sounded like a last name. They showed him a list and he picked me but it wasn't me, it was Gordon Liddy. *(looks at the reporters)* My phone hasn't stopped ringing, my wife's hysterical, my kids think I'm mixed up with the burglary, my friends don't like me around all of a sudden.

CUT TO

CLOSE UP — SEDAM

SEDAM
You fucked around my life, you two. *(starts off)* I just wanted to say thanks.

BRADLEE watching WOODWARD and BERNSTEIN, who are clearly upset.

> **BRADLEE**
> That didn't sound to me like a non-denial denial; could you have been wrong?
>> *(they nod)*
> You had a good source?
>> *(nod)*
> Did he have an ax?
>> *(pause. Then another nod)*

CLOSE UP — BRADLEE

> **BRADLEE**
> All right, you made a mistake maybe, we all have, just don't make another. And watch your personal lives, who you hang around with. Someone once said the price of democracy is a bloodletting every ten years. *(beat)* Make sure it isn't our blood...

Now from BRADLEE —

CUT TO

HUGH SLOAN

holding a broom and dustpan at his front door.

> **SLOAN**
> I really can't talk now —

> **BERNSTEIN**
> — this'll only take one second —

> **SLOAN**
> — my wife just had the baby, my in-laws are arriving, I'm trying to get the house in some kind of shape.

> **WOODWARD**
> A boy or a girl?

> **SLOAN**
> A girl. Melissa.

CUT TO

INSIDE THE HOUSE. WOODWARD and BERNSTEIN are helping SLOAN with the housework. WOODWARD has a dust mop, BERNSTEIN a dust cloth. We are mostly in the living room throughout, and also throughout, the three guys beaver away tidying.

> **WOODWARD**
> *(holding up a cup)*

Where does this go?

SLOAN points to a shelf. WOODWARD moves to put the cup in its proper place.

> **WOODWARD**
> *(continuing)*

— That cash fund that financed the sabotaging of the Democrats — five guys had control —

> **BERNSTEIN**
> *(ticking them off)*

— Mitchell, Stans, Magruder, Kalmbach —

> **WOODWARD**

— we're working on the last guy now and we're going all the way — that fifth man was Haldeman.

> **SLOAN**

— I'm not your source on that —

> **BERNSTEIN**

— *it's gotta be Haldeman* — someone from the White House had to be involved —

> **WOODWARD**

— and it wasn't Ehrlichman or Colson or the President.

> **SLOAN**

No, none of those.

> **BERNSTEIN**

— that leaves Haldeman, period.

> **SLOAN**

I'm not your source on that.

He picks up a dust pan, starts sweeping it full.

> **WOODWARD**
> *(taking the dust pan, helping out)*

— look, when the Watergate grand jury questioned you, did you name names?

> **SLOAN**

Of course — everything they asked —

> **BERNSTEIN**

— if we wrote a story that said Haldeman controlled the fund? —

SLOAN

—let me put it this way: I'd have no problems if you did.

WOODWARD and BERNSTEIN look at each other while SLOAN empties the dust pan into the trash and from there, quickly —

CUT TO

A LONG LONG LONG SHOT OF A COUPLE

walking in a park.

We can't really make them out clearly, we never do in this little sequence. But the guy is wearing a windbreaker and has a crew cut and the woman with him is dressed casually too. He has his arm around her, and they are deep in conversation.

WOODWARD'S VOICE (v.o.)

Hey?

PULL BACK TO REVEAL

WOODWARD and BERNSTEIN sitting on a park bench swilling down a six-pack.

WOODWARD

I think that's him.

BERNSTEIN

Who?

WOODWARD

Haldeman.

CUT TO

THE COUPLE walking along. We just can't quite make them out. But it might be.

CUT TO

WOODWARD AND BERNSTEIN staring after the couple, trying to focus.

BERNSTEIN

Nah. *(squints hard)* Maybe.

WOODWARD

What if I went up and introduced myself — think he'd slug me?

BERNSTEIN

Well, we are trying to ruin his life.

WOODWARD

It's nothing personal, though. *(looks troubled)*

BERNSTEIN

What's the matter?

WOODWARD

Same as with Magruder, I don't like it when they turn out to be human.

BERNSTEIN
(nods)

I wish we were investigating Attila the Hun.

WOODWARD

Maybe we are . . .

CUT TO

THE SLOW-WALKING COUPLE. *They continue on. We still don't see them quite clearly.* HOLD . . . *then* —

CUT TO

A PUDGY LITTLE MAN HALF-HIDDEN BEHIND A MAGAZINE.

PULL BACK TO REVEAL

A DRUGSTORE-TYPE PLACE. WOODWARD *and* BERNSTEIN *are at the adjoining table.*

PUDGY MAN

— Goddamnit, I'm not gonna say it again — you get nothing about Haldeman outta me —

WOODWARD

— we don't need it now, because tomorrow's story is about the FBI —

BERNSTEIN

— about how all you supposed experts really blew the whole investigation —

FBI GUY
(stung)

— we didn't miss so much —

WOODWARD

— you never knew Haldeman had control of the slush fund —

FBI GUY

— it's all in our files —

BERNSTEIN

— not about Haldeman —

FBI GUY

— yeah, Haldeman, John Haldeman.

And he gets up quickly, goes. WOODWARD *and* BERNSTEIN *savor the moment but only briefly as it hits them —*

> ### BERNSTEIN
> —Jesus—

> ### WOODWARD
> — he said John Haldeman, not Bob Haldeman —

And as they take off after the agent —

CUT TO

BRADLEE'S OFFICE.

WOODWARD, BERNSTEIN, BRADLEE, SIMONS, ROSENFELD. *Wild tension. The editors have a long story and they all read and pace, read and pace; the reporters look traumatized with fatigue. All this goes fast.*

> ### BRADLEE
> *(staring at the typed story)*
> — I don't know, I don't know, it feels thin —

> ### SIMONS
> — Christ, I wish I knew if we should print this —

> ### ROSENFELD
> — listen, we didn't make them do these things — once they did, it's our job to report it —

> ### SIMONS
> *(to the reporters)*
> — go over your sources again —

> ### WOODWARD
> — Sloan *told* the Grand Jury — he answered everything they asked him — that means there's a record somewhere —

> ### BERNSTEIN
> — and the FBI confirms — what more do you need? —

> ### ROSENFELD
> *(whirling on* BERNSTEIN*)*
> — listen, I love this country, you think I want to bring it down? — I'm not some goddamn zany, I was a hawk —

> ### SIMONS
> — Harry, weren't you just arguing the opposite way? —

ROSENFELD

—maybe I'm tense—

BRADLEE

—well shit, we oughtta be tense—we're about to accuse Mr. Haldeman who only happens to be the second most important man in America of conducting a criminal conspiracy from inside the White House—*(beat)* —it would be nice if we were right—

SIMONS
(to the reporters)

—you double-checked both sources?—

They nod.

BRADLEE

—Bernstcin, are you *sure* on this story?

BERNSTEIN

Absolutely—

BRADLEE
(to WOODWARD)

—what about you?—

WOODWARD

—I'm sure—

BRADLEE

—I'm *not* sure, it still feels thin—*(looks at SIMONS)*

SIMONS
*(to WOODWARD and
BERNSTEIN, after a pause)*

—get another source.

Now quickly

CUT TO

WOODWARD AND BERNSTEIN huddling outside BRADLEE's office.

BERNSTEIN

How many fucking sources they think we got?—

WOODWARD

—Deep Throat won't confirm—I never thought he was scared of any-one, but he's scared of Haldeman.

BERNSTEIN

I know a guy in the Justice Department who was around the Grand Jury.
(looks at WOODWARD*)*

WOODWARD

— We got twenty minutes to deadline —

And as he speaks

CUT TO

BERNSTEIN *talking softly from a relatively private phone in the newsroom. The voice of the lawyer is also whispered and scared to death.*

LAWYER'S VOICE (o.s.)
(barely audible)
... You shouldn't ever call me like this, Carl...

BERNSTEIN

Will you confirm that Haldeman was mentioned by Sloan to the Grand Jury?

LAWYER'S VOICE (o.s.)
... I won't say anything about Haldeman... not ever...

BERNSTEIN
(desperate)
All right — listen — it's against the law if you talk about the Grand Jury, right? But you don't have to say a thing — I'll count to ten — if the story's wrong, hang up before I get there — if it's OK stay on the line till after, got it?

LAWYER (o.s.)

Hang up, right?

BERNSTEIN

Right, right — OK, counting: one, two — *(he inhales deeply)* — three, four, five, six — *(now he's starting to get excited)* — seven, eight — *(inhales deeply)* — nine, ten, thank you.

LAWYER (o.s.)
You've got it straight now? Everything OK?

BERNSTEIN
(on a note of triumph)
Yeah!

And on that shout

CUT TO

A HEADLINE IN THE *POST*—A PHOTO VISIBLE OF HALDEMAN:

"TESTIMONY TIES TOP NIXON AIDE TO SECRET FUND"

CUT TO

The White House Spokesman

> **WHITE HOUSE SPOKESMAN**
> On the record let me say just this: the story is totally untrue. On background, I'd like to add that Bob Haldeman is one of the greatest public servants this country has ever had and the story is a goddamned lie.

Now fast zoom to

BRADLEE

roaring out of his office doorway.

> **BRADLEE**
> *Woodstein!*

CUT TO

Woodward and Bernstein *tearing into* Bradlee's *office — he stands scowling at the TV set in a corner of the room — outside, it is raining like hell.*

CUT TO

The TV set. Sloan *is walking along toward a large office building, he is flanked by a lawyer. A TV Reporter (it was* Daniel Schorr*) is walking alongside, mike in hand.*

> **SCHORR**
> Mr. Sloan, would you care to comment on your testimony before the Grand Jury.

> **SLOAN**
> My lawyer says —

> **SLOAN'S LAWYER**
> — the answer is an unequivocal *no*. Mr. Sloan did not implicate Mr. Haldeman in that testimony at all.

CUT TO

Woodward and Bernstein. *They look sick. Desperate, tired, stunned, confused; there is nothing to say.*

CUT TO

Bradlee *glaring at them.* HOLD ON Bradlee . . . *then*

CUT TO

THE FEDERAL BUREAU OF INVESTIGATION

in the rain, and

CUT TO

A CORRIDOR IN THE BUILDING AS THE PUDGY FBI MAN retreats down the hall. WOOD-WARD and BERNSTEIN, soaked, chase after him.

> FBI MAN
>
> — I'll deny everything — *everything* — I never talked to you about Halde-man — I never talked to you about anything — I'm not talking to you now —

> BERNSTEIN
>
> — what went wrong? —

> WOODWARD
>
> — for Chrissakes just tell that —

> PUDGY FBI MAN
>
> — fuck you fuck you fuck you —

And he tears into an office, slams the door and as we hear it lock —

CUT TO

THIS IS WHERE THE SOURCE BURNING SCENE WOULD COME BUT I AM NOT WRITING IT FOR THIS VERSION.

My reasons are as follows: (1) it is a complicated long scene to put down; (2) we are terribly late in our story; (3) it would mean, here, two hours into the movie, we are bringing in an entirely new character, the FBI agent's head to whom they go, and I think that is unnecessary and confusing; and (4) most important, I think the characters have been abused enough in this version — we have added the Sedam scene and they are berated more in this version by the CREEP people before things turn. (5) Finally, all this can show in reality is that they are desperate, and I would rather let the actors give that to us. I feel that it would be a genuine error at this time in the flick to go into the convolutions of how it's bad manners for a reporter to burn a source, if we've got anything going by this point, I can't conceive of much an audience will be less interested in than the reporters misbehaving.

However, if the scene is requested next time through, I shall be only too happy to oblige.

What I would like to do is cut from the FBI saying "fuck you fuck you fuck you" and locking his door to the following:

WOODWARD AND BERNSTEIN walking in the rain. It's pouring as they leave FBI Headquarters and they are in anguish.

> BERNSTEIN
> *(after a while)*

Woodward?

> WOODWARD

Hmm?

> BERNSTEIN

What *was* the mistake? Do you think it's been rigged, all along the way, leading us on so they could slip it to us when it mattered? They couldn't have set us up better; after all these months our credibility's gone, you know what that means?

> WOODWARD
> *(nods)*

Only everything...

They are soaked. Nearby is a garbage can, they grab papers, hold them over their heads, start to walk. Now —

CAMERA MOVES UP HIGHER TO REVEAL

The papers they grabbed were the Post *front page. (This happened.) And as they walked, the Haldeman story was on their heads.* HOLD *on the reporters walking miserably through the rain. Now —*

CUT TO

THE *POST.*

A tremendous pall has settled on the city room. People walk by, glancing at WOODWARD *and* BERNSTEIN, *who sit almost immobilized at their desks, wet, whipped; no energy left.*

CUT TO

BRADLEE'S OFFICE. SIMONS *sits across from* BRADLEE *as* ROSENFELD *enters quietly with a bundle of teletype paper.*

> SIMONS
> *(indicating the papers)*

More denunciations?

> ROSENFELD
> *(nods)*

One Senator just gave a speech slurring us 57 times in 20 minutes.

BRADLEE *has started typing something brief. When* ROSENFELD's *done, so is he. He hands it to* SIMONS.

SIMONS

What's this?

BRADLEE

My non-denial denial.

ROSENFELD

We're not printing a retraction?

CUT TO

CLOSE UP — BRADLEE. He is thoughtful for a while. Then, spinning around, staring out towards the newsroom:

BRADLEE

Fuck it, let's stand by the boys.

And he stands, spins out of the room as we

CUT TO

THE FLOWER POT ON WOODWARD'S TERRACE.

The rain has stopped. The apartment is dark. It's late at night. Inside, the phone RINGS and

CUT TO

WOODWARD'S APARTMENT in the dark as he manages to knock the phone off its cradle.

WOODWARD

Hello?

BERNSTEIN'S VOICE (o.s.)

What'd you find?

WOODWARD

Jesus Christ, what time is it?

BERNSTEIN

You overslept?

WOODWARD

Goddamnit! —

He fumbles for the lamp, as it falls with a CRASH —

CUT TO

WOODWARD — MOVING. Hair wild. clothes half-buttoned, he runs through the dark Washington streets as we

CUT TO

TWO WELL-DRESSED MEN in the shadows across the street, going in the same direction and

CUT TO

WOODWARD spotting them, picking up the pace and

CUT TO

THE TWO MEN moving faster too and now

CUT TO

A BUNCH OF CABS. WOODWARD jumps into the first and as it roars off

CUT TO

THE TWO MEN getting into a cab also, roaring off in the same direction and

CUT TO

WOODWARD'S CAB taking a corner fast and as it goes on, HOLD until the second cab takes the same corner, faster, and now

CUT TO

WOODWARD jumping out of his cab, fumbling into his pockets for change as we

CUT TO

THE TWO MEN getting out of their cab, paying, and as their cab drives off

CUT TO

WOODWARD diving back <u>into</u> his cab and in a moment it is roaring again through the night and we

CUT TO

THE TWO WELL-DRESSED MEN standing there on the sidewalk, watching as WOODWARD disappears into the night and then suddenly,

ZOOM TO

DEEP THROAT IN CLOSE UP AND MAD.

>   **DEEP THROAT**
> —you were doing so well and then you got stupid, you went too fast—
> Christ, what a royal screw up—

PULL BACK TO REVEAL

DEEP THROAT AND WOODWARD in the underground garage.

> **WOODWARD**
> —I know, I know, the pressure's off the White House and it's all back on the *Post*—

> **DEEP THROAT**
> —you've done worse than let Haldeman slip away, you've got people feeling sorry for him—I didn't think that was possible. A conspiracy like this— the rope has to tighten slowly around everyone's neck. You build from the outer edges and you go step by step. If you shoot too high and miss, then everybody feels more secure. You've put the investigation back months.

> **WOODWARD**
> We know that—and if we were wrong, we're resigning—*were we wrong?*

> **DEEP THROAT**
> You'll have to find that out, won't you?—

CUT TO

WOODWARD *exploding.*

> **WOODWARD**
> —I'm tired of your chickenshit games—I don't want hints, *I want what you know!*

CUT TO

DEEP THROAT. *He blinks for a moment. Then he begins to whisper.*

> **DEEP THROAT**
> It *was* a Haldeman operation—the whole business—he ran the money, but he was insulated, you'll have to find out how—

WOODWARD *takes a breath, nods.*

> **DEEP THROAT**
> (*continuing*)
> —wait—(*almost a smile*)—there's more . . .

And from his weathered face

CUT TO

WOODWARD

walking up to his apartment house later that night. He sees, and then we see, BERNSTEIN, *asleep at the front door. He comes awake as* WOODWARD *approaches.*

> **WOODWARD**
> We gotta go see Bradlee—I'll fill you in in the car.

CUT TO

BRADLEE IN HIS DOORWAY IN THE MIDDLE OF THE NIGHT.

It's a house with a lawn and from somewhere there is the SOUND of dogs barking.

> BRADLEE
> You couldn't have told me over the phone?

CUT TO

WOODWARD AND BERNSTEIN moving up the walk to BRADLEE.

> WOODWARD
> We can't trust the phones, not anymore. Deep Throat says so.

As WOODWARD beckons for him to move out into the lawn —

> BRADLEE
> We can't talk inside either?

> WOODWARD
> *(headshake)*
> Electronic surveillance.

CUT TO

THE THREE OF THEM MOVING OUT ONTO THE LAWN. It's October now. You can see their breaths as they speak.

> BERNSTEIN
> I finally got through to Sloan — it was all a misunderstanding that we had:
> he *would* have told the Grand Jury about Haldeman, he was ready to, only
> nobody on the Grand Jury asked him the goddamn question.

> WOODWARD
> So I guess you could say that we screwed up, but we weren't wrong.

> BRADLEE
> *(nods)*
> Anything else from Mr. Throat?

> WOODWARD
> Mitchell started the cover-up early, everyone is involved in the cover-up,
> all the way to the top. The whole U.S. intelligence community is mixed
> in with the covert activities. The extent of it is incredible. *(little pause)* And
> people's lives are in danger, maybe including ours.

CUT TO

BRADLEE. He nods again, starts walking the two reporters back toward WOODWARD's car.

> **BRADLEE**
> He's wrong on that last, we're not in the least danger, because nobody gives
> a shit—what was that Gallup Poll result? Half the country's never even
> heard the word Watergate.

CUT TO

THE *RED KARMANN GHIA as the three approach.*

> **BRADLEE**
> Look, you're both probably a little tired, right?
> *(They nod.)*
> You should be, you've been under a lot of pressure. So go home, have a
> nice hot bath, rest up fifteen minutes if you want before you get your asses
> back in gear— *(louder now)*—because *we're* under a lot of pressure, too,
> and *you* put us there—not that I want it to worry you—nothing's riding
> on you except the First Amendment of the Constitution plus the freedom
> of the press plus the reputation of a hundred-year-old paper plus the jobs
> of the two thousand people who work there— *(still building)*—but none of
> that counts as much as this: you fuck up again, *I'm gonna lose my temper.*
> *(pause; softer)* I promise you, you don't want me to lose my temper. *(shooing
> them off)* Move-move-move—what have you done for me tomorrow...?

And as they get back into the car—

CUT TO

THE NEWSROOM—EARLY MORNING

and it's empty pretty much, except at their desks sit WOODWARD *and* BERNSTEIN, *typing
away. They type on and on and as they do, voices are* HEARD, *the same voices we've become
familiar with, the* WESTERN SENATOR, *the* CREEP P.R. MAN *and the* WHITE HOUSE
SPOKESMAN.

> **WESTERN SENATOR** (o.s.)
> Although I'm a Republican, I would like to state in a pure bipartisan spirit
> that the greatest political scandal of this campaign is the brazen manner
> in which, without benefit of clergy, the *Washington Post* has set up house-
> keeping with the McGovern campaign...

> **CREEP P.R. MAN**
> For twenty years, the Eastern liberal press has been trying to smear Dick
> Nixon. Fortunately, the American public is too smart to be fooled by...

> **WHITE HOUSE SPOKESMAN**
> I have been informed reliably by John Dean that no one connected with
> the White House...

WESTERN SENATOR
(coming in, overlapping)

It is only our pathetic *Post* that deliberately tries to infuse the Watergate caper with a seriousness far beyond those shenanigans that have been the stock in trade of political pranksters ever since...

WOODWARD and BERNSTEIN work on. And now, as the voices continue condemning, we see them — all the President's men — as their faces flash on the screen for an instant — only these aren't fashion portraits we're looking at, these are the mug shots of the men taken when they went to jail and they flash on, the mug shots and the name and across each the word <u>convicted</u>. There's VIRGILIO GONZALES — <u>convicted</u>, and EUGENIO MARTINEZ, <u>convicted</u>, and FRANK STURGIS, <u>convicted</u>, and BERNARD BARKER, <u>convicted</u>, and JAMES McCORD, <u>convicted</u>, and HOWARD HUNT, <u>convicted</u>, and GORDON LIDDY, <u>convicted</u>, and DONALD SEGRETTI, <u>convicted</u>, and DWIGHT CHAPIN, <u>convicted</u>, and now the denunciations are louder, shriller, briefer.

WHITE HOUSE SPOKESMAN

An insult to the American public —

CREEP P.R. MAN

— the deplorable tactics employed by the *Washington Post* —

WESTERN SENATOR

— I have been given access to evidence in possession of the White House and that evidence —

WOODWARD and BERNSTEIN type on. Their machines are the only SOUND in the enormous room. And now more mug shots appear —

JEB MAGRUDER, <u>convicted</u>, EGIL KROGH, <u>convicted</u>, JOHN DEAN, <u>convicted</u>, JOHN EHRLICHMAN, <u>convicted</u>, CHARLES COLSON, <u>convicted</u>, HERBERT KALMBACH, <u>convicted</u>, and LARUE and PORTER and MITCHELL and HALDEMAN — all, all the President's men — <u>convicted</u>. Now —

THE CAMERA STARTS TO MOVE toward the pillar, the one that separates the two reporters, and the denunciations are still going on, but not so loud now, not so fierce.

WESTERN SENATOR

Well, if I was wrong, I sure the hell wasn't alone —

CREEP

— the fact remains that except for Watergate, we ran one hell of a great campaign...

The CAMERA is almost at the pillar now.

BERNSTEIN bums a cigarette from a cleaning lady. WOODWARD kicks his typewriter. Then they both go back to work.

Now we're at the pillar. That's all we see. Just that. And all we HEAR is the two reporters working away, on and on until—

FINAL FADE OUT.

THE END

MAGIC

DIRECTOR	RICHARD ATTENBOROUGH
PRODUCERS	JOSEPH E. LEVINE
	RICHARD P. LEVINE
CINEMATOGRAPHER	VICTOR KEMPER
EDITOR	JOHN BLOOM
PRODUCTION DESIGNER	TERENCE MARSH
MUSIC	JERRY GOLDSMITH
SCREENPLAY	WILLIAM GOLDMAN
	(FROM HIS NOVEL)

STORYTELLING ON FILM

I have always been *only* a storyteller.

I was twenty-four when I wrote my first novel, *The Temple of Gold*, and when I entered the playing field, all I brought with me was a sense of story and an ear for dialogue. I did not have the stylistic grace of my beloved Irwin Shaw. I had not the interest or dazzle to try experimental stuff like Joyce. I could not describe like Fitzgerald. I did not have the religious torment of Dostoyevsky or the sweep of Tolstoi or the insanity of Cervantes or the genius of Chekhov and if you think who am I, writing these names down, well, these were the guys that moved me.

I was staggered in the mid-sixties, when it turned out that I seemed to have this facility for storytelling on film. (I had never seen a screenplay til I was in my thirties. Now some guys are has-beens before they even see their thirties.) I never thought of writing movies so when it happened, I tried not to think about it too much, because if I did, well of course, that was dangerous because I don't think all that much or all that well when I work, since for good or ill, I am totally instinctive.

The most frightening moment of my movie career took place on one of my major disasters, *Heat*.

The situation in the story was this: My hero, Nick Escalante, a Las Vegas bodyguard (who refers to himself as a chaperone), is in despair so he does what he always does at such times, he consoles himself by going to the Liberace Museum. The head of the local Mafia, a good acquaintance, comes for him there and says they must go immediately to the head Mafia guy's office for a confrontation with a minor Mafia guy who has accused Escalante of murder. Come along, the head Mafia guy says, I have to find out the truth.

And Escalante asks, "What do you mean, I'm on trial?"

And the reply comes, "For your life, I should think."

And then we cut to the minor Mafia guy waiting at the Head Guy's office, *which is in another part of Vegas.* It looked like this on the page:

ESCALANTE

What do you mean, I'm on trial?

HEAD MAFIA GUY

For your life, I should think.

(and on these words)

CUT TO

THE MINOR MAFIA GUY IN THE HEAD GUY'S OFFICE

MINOR MAFIA GUY
(pointing at ESCALANTE)

Escalante did it, he killed them!

I gave it to one of the amazing number of directors who worked on the flick. (There were six in all, and yes, that is a record, and like DiMaggio's batting streak, one that will never be broken. I am sanguine because it must always be remembered that the big six toiled on what was only a thirty-six day shoot.) Anyway, I knew what I was giving the one guy to read was not Shakespearean. But it was also nothing that deserved particular comment being absolutely ordinary, standard screenwriting. I was simply getting my main guy from one situation into another quickly, moving him from point A to point B.

The director read it and then looked at me, and I remember being surprised, because he was angry, and he said, "This is ridiculous. You can't do it like this."

Can't do what?

"*This.*" He slapped the pages.

Why?

"*It makes no sense for chrissakes! — Don't you know anything about screenwriting?*"

I was getting scared now.

He went on. "*Here's* how you have to do it if you want the audience to understand what in hell's happening. You have to have a shot of the two of them leaving the Liberace Museum. And then a shot of the two of them getting into the head Mafia guy's limo. And then a shot of the limo starting. And then a shot of the limo moving through Vegas. And then a shot of the limo stopping in front of the head guy's office building. And then a shot of the two of them going into the building and getting into the elevator. Then a shot of them coming out of the elevator and entering the head Mafia guy's office. Where his secretary says there's someone waiting inside. *Then* you can go into the office where the minor guy can accuse him of murder. Now go write that down."

I was too scared to write anything then.

It seems so strange looking back on that moment now. The ineptitude of the director. (Will you be shocked if I tell you he hasn't worked a whole lot lately?) But more than that, my own fear. And do you know what I was afraid of?

I was afraid that he was right. And just what would that mean, class?

Only the end of everything for me.

That of course is insanely melodramatic, but not an exaggeration because if what he was demanding was valid, then *storytelling had changed*. And I had not been able to sense what was in the air and change with it. It would have meant that my entire career, as a short story writer and playwright and novelist and now screenwriter — was all of it, now and forever, over.

We can write three kinds of screenplays: originals, adaptations of other writers, and adaptations of our own stuff. I have done all three. *Butch* was an original, but so was *The Year of the Comet*, which did only slightly less well. *All the President's Men* was, of course, Woodward and Bernstein's. *Misery* was imagined by Stephen King.

But six of my novels have been made into movies, and I worked on four of them: *Marathon Man, Magic, The Princess Bride,* and *Heat.* (*Soldier in the Rain* and *No Way to Treat A Lady* complete the half dozen.) And, of course, every screenplay is complicated and difficult. But originals are the worst, obviously, because imagining a coherent story can be, even for the most fortunate of us, a bitch. Interestingly, at least for me, adaptations of other people's work are the least complicated, because I don't care how much the other guy suffered to get things right in the book. I have a movie to put down and I can't worry about him. I would have thought adapting my own would have been the least difficult, since you have the story pretty well down and you've heard the people talking.

But you lose so much.

And you lose stuff that was so hard to write in the novel. In *Marathon Man,* for example, the scene of the Nazi, Szell (Olivier), in the diamond district was pretty straight, just keep it and cut it and shape it for a flick. But I tried so hard in the novel to make it a surprise that Doc (Roy Scheider) was Babe's (Dustin Hoffman) big brother. I set up all kinds of ruses and misdirections so when the reveal came in the book I hoped the reader was legitimately *rocked.*

No surprise at all in the movie. Ho-hum at best.

And the structure of the novel for *Magic* was radically different from the movie. In the novel, a great deal of the first part is a journal written by a character named "Fats." You don't know Fats is the dummy til a hundred pages of the novel have gone by. And when you do find out, in a casual remark made by a secondary character, I wanted the reader to say "holy shit," shocked and surprised. You know on page fifteen of the screenplay. And it's no big deal.

Much of that first part of the novel is sort of a mystery. Corky (Anthony Hopkins) may be a serial murderer of women. At one point, early on in the movie's history, Mike Nichols gave just a brief thought to directing it. Well, if he had, none of what's in the screenplay now would have probably been there because Nichols was interested in the serial killer part, not a word of which is in what follows.

Norman Jewison was the first director and I wrote the first draft for him. He called me from California after he read it and said, with genuine shock, "It's good." (My first drafts better be, since I am one of the world's shittiest rewriters.) I flew out and we worked on improving it and I only mention this — since Norman left soon thereafter following a fight with producer Joseph E. Levine — because a couple of memorable things happened, moments which I still treasure.

1) Norman wanted a major star for what became the Anthony Hopkins part. We were Out There, it was Friday, but we were both due to fly East that afternoon, something we were both looking forward to. Anyway, on this Friday morning we get a phone call. An agent. Telling us a client of his, a Major Star, has read the script, is seriously interested, wants to talk to us about it.

Yesss, as Marv would put it.

Problem: the Major Star is booked up with important meetings and cannot see us until Sunday afternoon. He wants to talk seriously about the script on a non-superficial level. Will we wait the forty-eight hours?

There is only one answer to that question.

Sunday afternoon and we drive to the Major Star's home, park, knock on the door. And wait. We shuffle and squint. I, the more edgy of the duo, trot out to the street to see if we have the right address.

We do.

Eventually the Major Star appears. In a bathing suit. He has been out in the back by the pool and didn't hear.

He is barefoot.

And he is smoking a joint.

He ushers us out to the pool. Where a bunch of his friends are frolicking. The Major Star gets in the shallow end and smokes and screws around and pretty soon it's clear he doesn't want to talk to us about the script on any level, superficial or not. Because he hasn't read it. But he says he's been busy and will absolutely get around to it when he has a chance.

We leave, get back in the car, Norman starts to drive. And he is pissed.

"Because he kept us waiting? Because he hadn't read it?"

"*Because he didn't offer us the joint.* Don't you see? — that other stuff is *agent* bullshit. Agent probably said we were desperate just to be able to tell people we'd met, would the guy do us a big favor and nod in our direction. The joint is what's important."

"Why?"

"Because when he didn't offer it, that's the *star's* bullshit. Make it a glass of red wine. If you came to my house and I met you at the door drinking a glass of red wine and didn't offer you any, I'm saying *fuck you*. And that's what he was saying to us."

2) Norman lived at the beach and we would work all day and then at night, hit someplace for dinner. There was a Polynesian restaurant not far away and one night we stopped there and went in. The maître d' met us at the door and said "you may not want to eat here." A weird start to a meal, yes? We asked why, and then I realized there was a look of surpassing sadness behind his eyes. He answered with these words:

"Our blender is broken."

To this day, I think if Aristotle had been with us, we might have had an entirely different definition today of the true meaning of tragedy.

When I re-read *Magic* just now, I had the altogether terrific experience of flashing back to the movie itself, and Burgess Meredith was perfect and Tony Hopkins I feel is one of the two greatest film actors in the world now (Morgan Freeman is the other) and he was so wonderful here. But running stride for stride with him was Miss Olsson. I think Ann-Margret is the least appreciated emotional actress anywhere. I haven't seen her in twenty years or talked to her in ten but I have had a crush on her since *Pocketful of Miracles* and *State Fair*. And still do.

There. Now you know everything.

CAST LIST

ANTHONY HOPKINS	CORKY / VOICE OF FATS
ANN-MARGRET	PEGGY ANN SNOW
BURGESS MEREDITH	THE POSTMAN (BEN GREENE)
ED LAUTER	DUKE
E. J. ANDRE	MERLIN
JERRY HOUSER	CAB DRIVER
DAVID OGDEN STIERS	TODSON

A WORD ABOUT THE FLASHCUTS:

At various times, throughout what follows, we are using what we call "flash-cuts."

These basically are a way of filling out, fleshing out what Corky is saying. For example, when he speaks of his father, we might see his father — but Corky goes right on talking.

In other words, the flashcuts slow up nothing.

They are also, always, *silent.* So if we flashcut to someone laughing, we see it, but don't hear any sound.

They are, again also, brief. They are almost blinks.

But we hope they will people Corky's life, make it more real, without getting in the way of the story.

The only reason I have put this page in at the front is this: the flashcuts will *read* longer than they *take.* In other words, this version will not move as quickly or more than likely as smoothly as the one before.

But the scenes themselves will play as quickly as if there were no flashcuts at all.

Remember then: they are fast.
                 they are silent.
                 they tell us more than we can learn by dialog.
                 they interrupt nothing: all scenes are continuous.

If anyone is still awake, they may now start the screenplay.

In the darkness, there is the quiet rasping sound of someone having trouble breathing. As the sound goes steadily on —

FADE IN ON

AN ABSOLUTELY SENSATIONAL ROOM,

and the CAMERA *already in a steady panning motion. The room is in a small apartment that is absolutely jam-crammed with magic apparatus.*

The breathing sound continues, getting just a bit louder, as we pan by bookcases filled to bursting with volumes of every size and age, all dealing with one aspect of magic or another. On the floor is box after box piled high with incredible paraphernalia: egg bags and collapsible birdcages and wands and handkerchiefs of every color, and billiard balls, some hollow, some not, and false fingers and thumb tips and dozens of decks of playing cards and make-up — beards and mustaches galore — and top hats and sponge balls and flags and silks and linking rings and tables with secret drawers half pulled out and —

— and the breathing sound is getting a lot louder now, as we're clearly moving in on whoever's breathing.

There are framed posters too — forty years old some of them. And these posters have one thing in common: the name MERLIN JR. *He is playing at every theatre for which there's a poster, and in some, his name is small and at the bottom, in others, large and at the top—and when his name is large we see his picture too, and in these old pictures he's a young man, huge and terribly homely, doing his best to smile for the camera, his large hands holding playing cards or his mouth breathing flames.*

Now at last we see him as he is. Aged and weak, he lies dozing on a sofa in this wild jumble of a place, a thin blanket half covering his body. He is clearly one very sick old man. Now, from MERLIN —

CUT TO

CORKY *quietly entering the apartment, carefully closing the door without a sound. He moves immediately to* MERLIN, *studies the old man briefly.* CORKY *seems distraught, takes a deep breath. He lightly touches* MERLIN'S *forehead with the backs of his fingers, gently pulls the blanket up so that it properly covers the giant.*

CORKY WITHERS *is a sweet young man, bright and shy. He is casually dressed, cardigan sweater, slacks, and shirt open at the throat.*

MERLIN
(eyes still closed)

Did you knock 'em dead, Corky?

CORKY
(turns quickly, goes to refrigerator)

I did everything right.

MERLIN
(eyes open now)
You mean it went perfect? *(shakes his head)* Don't I wish I'd been up to going — your first time ever on your own, and me not there to see.

CORKY
(taking medicine from refrigerator)
Don't you make it more than it was.

MERLIN
And don't you give me that inferiority crap. I'm an old man, I only want
to hear good news. The five lift go OK?

CORKY
(returning with medicine and spoon)
I never did it better.

FLASHCUT TO

CORKY'S HANDS BEAUTIFULLY EXECUTING A CARD MANEUVER.

CUT TO

CORKY and MERLIN as MERLIN balefully eyes the medicine. If this much isn't clear so far,
let's say it here and now: MERLIN adores the young man, and CORKY reveres MERLIN.

MERLIN
When you're famous, don't forget me.

CORKY
I'll never forget you, now open.

MERLIN
(he hates his medicine)
What's the point, I'm ready for the taxidermist anyway.
*(But he takes it. As CORKY
heads back to the refrigerator)*
Not three guys alive can do what you can do with cards. I tell you Kid,
you're as good as the game already, and before you're done, you're gonna
leave 'em all behind.

CORKY
Sure, sure, sure, another Houdini —

MERLIN
— Houdini was a schmuck, I'm talking giants, like Leipzig even. *(settles
back)* Were you scared? I was when I started.

CORKY
I suppose you could say I was reasonably panicked.

FLASHCUT TO

OUTSIDE THE HOLLYWOOD STARDUST, A REASONABLY CRUMMY JOINT OFF SUNSET. TWO SIGNS OF INTEREST IN THE WINDOW. THE FIRST LISTS THE CURRENT ATTRACTION "SECOND AND FINAL WEEK: THE DREAMERS."

THE OTHER SIGN, ABOVE IT, PERMANENT, READS: "EVERY MONDAY 8 P.M.: <u>AMATEUR NIGHT</u>."

CORKY STANDS STARING AT THE AMATEUR NIGHT SIGN. AS HE ENTERS THE CLUB —

FLASHCUT TO

INSIDE THE HOLLYWOOD STARLIGHT. THE MAIN ROOM IS CURTAINED OFF BEYOND. THIS IS THE BAR AREA WHERE THE AMATEUR PERFORMERS WAIT TO GO ON. A DOZEN OR SO MILL AROUND, SMOKING. CORKY STANDS ALONE IN A CORNER, WORKING WITH CARDS, WATCHING THEM DANCE IN HIS HANDS.

CUT TO

MERLIN *and* CORKY *by the sofa.*

> **MERLIN**
> Any other magicians?

> **CORKY**
> *(shakes his head)*
> The men all wanted to be Bob Dylan and the girls did Barbara Walters imitations.

FLASHCUT TO

THE SAME FLASHCUT WE JUST SAW ONLY NOW WE REALIZE, CORKY'S RIGHT. THE MEN DO CARRY GUITARS AND THE GIRLS SOMEHOW MANAGE TO RESEMBLE BARBARA WALTERS. NOW ONE OF THE GIRLS TURNS, FLEES TOWARD THE STREET.

> **CORKY** (over)
> A bunch of them panicked before their time came.

> **MERLIN** (over)
> Not you, though.

CUT TO

CORKY *and* MERLIN *by the sofa.*

> **CORKY**
> *(beat)*
> Not me.

FLASHCUT TO

A BEARDED M.C. TYPE GESTURING AN INTRO AND CORKY CLUMSILY MOUNTING THE LITTLE STAGE. HE'S PERSPIRING, TRIES FOR A SMILE, DOESN'T COME CLOSE.

FLASHCUT TO

THE LIGHTS. BRIGHT AND HOT AND

FLASHCUT TO

THE AUDIENCE. SPARSE, MAYBE HALF FULL. SOME YOUNG, SOME NOT. SOME SOBER, MOST NOT. AND NOT ALL OF THEM PAYING ATTENTION. THERE'S A COUPLE NECKING OFF TO ONE SIDE — THE GIRL'S TRYING TO SEE THE STAGE, THE GUY'S MORE INTERESTED IN HER BODY.

FLASHCUT TO

TWO SCHOOLTEACHER TYPES. ONE OF THEM HAS HICCUPS. SHE DRINKS FROM A GLASS OF WATER, HOLDING HER NOSE.

FLASHCUT TO

THE MAIN TABLE IN THE FRONT, HALF A DOZEN WEALTHY LOOKING PEOPLE, PROBABLY SLUMMING FOR THE NIGHT. ONE WOMAN DOMINATES THIS GROUP — A RICH-BITCH TYPE, MAYBE FORTY, SLEEK AND DARK. EVERYTHING THAT CAN BE LIFTED OR FIXED TO MAKE YOU KEEP YOUR LOOKS HAS BEEN DONE TO HER. ON SIGHT, YOU JUST LOATHE HER.

FLASHCUT TO

CORKY ON STAGE, LOOKING AROUND HALF FROZEN. FINALLY BRINGS OUT A DECK OF OR-DINARY PLAYING CARDS.

CUT TO

CORKY and MERLIN by the sofa.

MERLIN
You start with flourishes?
> (CORKY nods)

Those are the best attention grabbers.

FLASHCUT TO

CORKY, ON STAGE, DOING A SPRING FLOURISH, THE CARDS SEEMING ALMOST TO JUMP FROM ONE HAND TO THE OTHER. THEN A GRACEFUL DROP FLOURISH, ENDING IN KIND OF A BOW. HE STANDS, PERSPIRING WORSE NOW, LOOKS AT THE AUDIENCE.

FLASHCUT TO

THE NECKING COUPLE. HE'S ALMOST GOT HIS HAND ON HER BREAST. SHE SLAPS IT AWAY.

FLASHCUT TO

A GROUP OF YOUNG PEOPLE. THEY KIND OF CLAP.

FLASHCUT TO

THE RICH BITCH. THE GUY NEXT TO HER WHISPERS SOMETHING AND IT BREAKS HER UP. SHE THROWS BACK HER HEAD AND ROARS.

FLASHCUT TO

CORKY, KIND OF FROZEN, SURPRISED AND

FLASHCUT TO

THE RICH BITCH. LAUGHING.

CUT TO

CORKY *and* MERLIN *by the sofa.*

> MERLIN
> And the flourishes were good?

> CORKY
> *(too quickly)*
> Oh, they were great.

CUT TO

MERLIN. *And now for the first time he watches* CORKY *more closely. He is starting not to believe.*

> CORKY
> Then I told this pudgy lady at ringside to please pick any card she wanted as long as it was the ace of spades.

FLASHCUT TO

THE PUDGY LITTLE LADY, HOLDING UP THE ACE OF SPADES, SURPRISED AND EXCITED AND

FLASHCUT TO

CORKY, STANDING PALE IN THE BRIGHT LIGHTS IN THE HALF EMPTY ROOM, LOOKING AROUND AND

FLASHCUT TO

THE SCHOOL TEACHER TYPES. ONE OF THEM STILL HICCUPS. EMBARRASSED, SHE GETS UP, HURRIES OUT AND

FLASHCUT TO

A TABLE OF THREE, LEAVING THE STARDUST AND

FLASHCUT TO

CORKY, *STARING AROUND AND HE IS DRENCHED NOW, EMBARRASSED BUT TRYING TO HANG IN AND*

CUT TO

CORKY *and* MERLIN *by the sofa.*

> **CORKY**
> I forced the ace on her just right and everybody loved that a lot. So when I had 'em I went right into the Rising Aces.

> **MERLIN**
> And the five lift worked great?

> **CORKY**
> *(nods)*
> It really did.

FLASHCUT TO

THE FIVE LIFT IN CLOSE UP. *(WE SAW IT BEFORE. GRACEFUL AND PERFECT.)*

FLASHCUT TO

CORKY, *RUBBING HIS HANDS TOGETHER AND*

FLASHCUT TO

THE RICH BITCH. *LAUGHING ON AND*

FLASHCUT TO

THE ACES, *RISING MIRACULOUSLY OUT OF* CORKY'S *HANDS AND*

FLASHCUT TO

THE RICH BITCH. *AND SHE WILL NOT STOP LAUGHING.*

FLASHCUT TO

CORKY, *SUDDENLY SCREAMING AT THE AUDIENCE, SWEATING AND WILD AND*

CUT TO

CORKY *and* MERLIN *by the sofa.*

> **MERLIN**
> I'm telling you Kid, you're as good as the game.

> **CORKY**
> Thank you. *(shrugs)* Then I took a few bows and got off. *(He makes a smile.)*

CUT TO

MERLIN. CLOSE UP. There is a pause. Finally —

> **MERLIN**
> *(soft and sad)*
>
> Aw Kid, don't bullshit me . . .

CUT TO

CORKY. He hesitates. Quietly —

> **CORKY**
>
> I really did do everything right. *(beat)* Only nobody much cared.

> **MERLIN**
>
> And?
>
> *(CORKY shakes his head.)*
>
> Go on.

> **CORKY**
> *(this is very hard for him)*
>
> I guess I cracked.

FLASHCUT TO

CORKY IN CLOSE UP. SCREAMING AT THE AUDIENCE.

FLASHCUT TO

THE AUDIENCE. STARING UP AT HIM. IT'S ALL WEIRD NOW. NIGHTMARE TIME.

FLASHCUT TO

CORKY IN EXTREME CLOSE UP. GOING ON AND

FLASHCUT TO

THE RICH BITCH, LAUGHING.

CUT TO

CORKY and MERLIN by the sofa.

> **CORKY**
>
> You stupid sons of bitches, I said, don't you know how hard that was, that's a thousand hours of my life you just saw.

> **MERLIN**
>
> They don't care from hard, Kid — they want to be entertained.

                              CORKY
                (stands — he has been deeply humiliated
                and he's not bothering to hide it anymore)
I didn't exactly do you proud, all in all.

                              MERLIN
Did you talk to the people, Corky, did you use your charm, give the good
patter?

                              CORKY
                (goes to far window, stares out at the night)
I can't, you know that.

                              MERLIN
You got to — you think people liked my magic? — they like me — all my
great jokes about how everyone was always mistaking me for Cary Grant.
That's what won 'em over. The magic only kept 'em there.

CUT TO

MERLIN, *tiring badly now. Voice softening.*

                              MERLIN
Corky?
                              (no reply)
You want to be as good as the game, don't you?

                              CORKY
                              (back turned)
You know I do.

                              MERLIN
                              (drifting)
Then you better find yourself some charm, Kid.

CUT TO

CORKY, *turning; deeply moved. Soft —*

                              CORKY
... how ... ?

CUT TO

MERLIN. *Eyes closed as at the start. There is a pause. Then —*

                              MERLIN
... you'll think of something ...

HOLD ON THE OLD GIANT. HOLD. *Then —*

FADE OUT

In the darkness comes the babble of voices. They sound happy and young, men and women maybe in their twenties. Bursts of occasional excited laughter.

FADE IN ON

A LONG LINE OF PEOPLE, mostly young couples and —

PAN ALONG THE LINE TO THE FRONT — we're back at the Hollywood Stardust again. Only there are a few changes. For one, the BEARDED M.C. is at the door, trying to deal with the large crowd. For another, in the window of the place is a large photo of CORKY and beneath that, the printed sign: 28th week.

CUT TO

A BLACK LIMO gliding up, stopping.

A MAN OF FORTY gets out. His name is GEORGE TODSON and he's quite handsome and wearing quite possibly the most expensive hairpiece in the Western World. He touches it surreptitiously as he gets out, walks toward the Stardust, pauses at the picture of CORKY a moment, then goes to the BEARDED M.C. by the door.

> **TODSON**
> I'm George Todson. I'm meeting Mr. Ben Greene.

> **BEARDED M.C.**
> *(impressed)*
> Yessir; he's inside.

He opens the door for TODSON, who enters.

CUT TO

THE LEGENDARY BEN GREENE seated at a back corner table in the club. He's small, bald, probably close to 80, and just maybe the most successful talent agent ever. (He is nicknamed THE POSTMAN and will be called that in the stage directions, but never in actual dialogue.)

> **TODSON**
> *(as they shake)*
> I guess this Withers is your latest sensation.
> *(THE POSTMAN nods)*
> You've booked him into a very classy spot, Ben.

> **POSTMAN**
> I found him here — not easy getting him to move.

> **TODSON**
> *(looking around the dump; it's jammed)*
> He likes this place?

POSTMAN

He bombed here his first time out; didn't give up, worked his ass off, came back a year later, hit it big. *(takes out a cigar)* Never been a magician like him.

TODSON

You dragged me down here for a *magician?* — I'm in the network business, we can't book those guys on kiddie shows anymore —

POSTMAN

— your father got his start working for me, you little fart, don't tell me what bombs — magic is misdirection, that's all it is, and misdirection is getting the people to look in the wrong place at the right time.

TODSON

So?

POSTMAN

Well of course magic's had trouble on the tube — you can't misdirect a goddam camera.
        (As TODSON grunts, sits back glumly —)

CUT TO

The BEARDED M.C. standing on stage.

BEARDED M.C.

Say hello to Corky Withers.

CUT TO

The AUDIENCE, applauding as CORKY wanders on stage, and he's dressed exactly as he was the first time, cardigan sweater and all, and he looks just as insecure. He does the same spring flourish, follows with the drop flourish. There is some applause, not a whole lot.

CORKY
(hard to hear)

Ordinary deck of cards.

CUT TO

TODSON and THE POSTMAN. TODSON is really unhappy.

TODSON
(to THE POSTMAN)

Loaded with stage presence — I can't decide does he remind me more of Errol Flynn or Valentino.

CUT TO

CORKY, fanning the cards for a pretty girl in the front.

> **CORKY**
> Would you pick any card you want as long as it's the ace of spades.
> *(The PRETTY GIRL holds up the card*
> *for the audience — it's the ace of spades.*
> *Applause again, still not much.)*

CUT TO

TODSON and THE POSTMAN

> **TODSON**
> Dynamite opening, Ben. Does he actually get better? Amazing.

> **POSTMAN**
> I guess he's a little tense tonight on account he knows we're here.

CUT TO

CORKY, throat dry, going on.

> **CORKY**
> My teacher was a great man, Merlin Junior —
> *(someone laughs)*
> — truly — and this is his version of the Rising Aces.

CUT TO

ANOTHER ATTRACTIVE GIRL AT RINGSIDE. CORKY hands her the deck, keeping the four aces held out; he shows the aces to the audience.

> **CORKY**
> All right — here are the four aces and we'll put them on top of the deck —
> *(he does — then to the ATTRACTIVE GIRL)* — now would you please pick any
> card you want and cover the aces? —
> *(she does)*
> — thank you — now — *(And suddenly he stops, terribly flustered.)* — omigod
> I'm sorry, I did that wrong, you don't cover the aces in this trick, one sec' —
> *(And as he takes the deck back, reaches to take off the top card — suddenly —)*

> **VOICE FROM THE AUDIENCE**
> *(it's a rough, street-smart voice, whisky-filled)*
> — he's gonna pull a five lift, watch him — *watch him* —
> *(CORKY freezes, stares out*
> *into the audience as we)*

CUT TO

THE POSTMAN and TODSON. TODSON stares around.

TODSON

Goddam drunks—

VOICE FROM THE AUDIENCE

—he's not lifting just the top card, he's gonna grab five—

CUT TO

CORKY, *upset, staring around for the heckler too.*

CORKY

I'm sorry—if you think you can do better, you're welcome to try—

VOICE FROM THE AUDIENCE

—just gimme a hand getting up there, schmucko, and step aside.
*(And as CORKY starts into the audience
everyone begins applauding.)*

CUT TO

TODSON *and* THE POSTMAN *as the applause builds.*

TODSON

What's going on?

THE POSTMAN *shrugs, says nothing.* TODSON *stares across the dark room.*

CORKY

You really think you're good?

VOICE FROM THE AUDIENCE

I'll guaranfuckingtee ya I am.
(And on that—)

CUT TO

CORKY *and* FATS *moving back onto the stage.* FATS *is a large ventriloquist's dummy, dressed like a longshoreman. He is everything* CORKY *isn't. Vulgar, abrasive, you name it.* CORKY *handles him brilliantly.*

CORKY

Well, you've ruined the Rising Aces—

FATS
(soft)

—you see the girl with the jugs? *(He stares at a girl at ringside.)*

CORKY
(quickly)

The young lady in the white sweater, yes, I see her, so what?

FATS

I wonder if she'd like a little roll in the shavings with me.

CORKY

I don't think you're funny —

FATS
(points to the audience)

— well, *they* do —

(And we)

CUT TO

The AUDIENCE *and* TODSON *taking it all in. They do think* FATS *is funny. When he goes for a laugh, he gets it.*

TODSON
(a little interested now)

Nice gimmick, the dummy. What's his name?

POSTMAN

Fats.

TODSON
(watching closely now)

Really a clever *schtick*.

CUT TO

FATS *and* CORKY, *interrupting each other.*

CORKY

I will now change a diamond into —

FATS

— I guess the reason I'm such a great lover is —

CORKY

— I don't want to hear about your sex life —

FATS

— tell us all about yours, then — everybody likes short stories —

CORKY
(as the audience starts to laugh)

— don't encourage him. *(holds a deck of cards to* FATS*)* Pick a diamond and I'll hold it and it'll change into a heart.

FATS
(taking a diamond)

If you're so great, change it while *I'm* holding it.

> CORKY

You won't give it back?

> *(FATS shakes his head "No")*

There's another trick ruined; you're impossible tonight.

> FATS
> *(whispering into CORKY's ear)*

It's on account of our guests.

> CORKY

Right. Folks, I'd like you to meet Mr. George Todson, who runs CBS Television.

> *(TODSON stands, sits, to brief applause)*

And my agent, Mr. Ben Greene.

> *(As he stands up —)*

Stay standing, would you, Ben? I want the people to know what you mean to me and Fats.

CUT TO

FATS, roaring in.

> FATS

Ben only handles the biggies — Vera Hruba Raison, Keefe Braselle — those Faith Domergue retrospectives we all flock to? — those were Ben's idea — he's plotted Garbo's career since she left Metro — and tonight, after a marathon negotiation, he has just booked Miss Vicki to six months in the Superdome!

CUT TO

The AUDIENCE, which has been laughing, breaks into applause now as THE POSTMAN sits down. TODSON has been laughing too.

> TODSON

Kid's good, I'll give you that.

> POSTMAN

Good? I've got maybe the best magician in fifty years matched with the first X-rated dummy on the block — *(glances at TODSON)* — eat your heart out.

CUT TO

FATS and CORKY.

> CORKY

I'd like to try some estimations —

FATS

—you're not gonna change my diamond into a heart— (*suddenly* FATS, *who has been holding the diamond card, looks at* CORKY) —Jesus—

CORKY

—what?—

FATS

—it turned into a heart while *I* was holding it. (*And he holds the card up now* —*it has changed suits.* FATS *shakes his head.*) How'd he *dooooo* that?

CUT TO

TODSON *and* THE POSTMAN *as the audience applauds again.*

TODSON

How *did* he do it?

CUT TO

THE POSTMAN. CLOSE UP. *As the applause builds louder and louder he just smokes very contentedly on his cigar... HOLD a moment. Then—*

CUT TO

THE POSTMAN *and* TODSON *making their way backstage toward the dressing room area.*

TODSON

You say he really bombed here the first time out?

POSTMAN
(*nods*)

Course, he didn't have the dummy then.

TODSON

Dummy helps, no question. (*hurrying to keep up*) Local talent?

POSTMAN
(*head shake*)

Brought up around Grossingers. I think his old man worked at the health club, gave massages, something like that. (*knocking on a door*) Me.

FAT'S VOICE
(*from inside*)

Shit, it's old Gangrene.

TODSON
(*laughs*)

Gangrene—that's funny.

THE POSTMAN *gives him a look, opens the door as we*

CUT TO

CORKY'S DRESSING ROOM. *Small, with the usual debris on the make-up table. Two photos in a leatherette holder. One is of* MERLIN *with a sweet-faced, chubby lady.*

THE OTHER PHOTO *is of a* VERY PRETTY GIRL, *maybe seventeen. It looks like a newspaper shot. She's at the peak of a cheerleading jump and wearing the proper costume.*

CORKY *sits holding a needle and thread, working at fixing a small tear in* FATS' *coat.* FATS *lies across his lap.* CORKY *smiles nervously as* THE POSTMAN *and* TODSON *enter.*

> POSTMAN
>
> Just wanted to make a quick in the flesh intro — Corky, our visitor from New York, George Todson.

> CORKY
> *(as they shake)*
>
> How do you do, sir.

> TODSON
>
> You've got a lot of potential — *(And he stops, suddenly startled as we quickly)*

CUT TO

FATS, *reaching up, grabbing* TODSON *by the arm —*

> FATS
>
> What about me?

> TODSON
>
> You're good too, Fats.

> FATS
> *(sitting up)*
>
> Thanks, Mr. Wigson — *(he is staring at* TODSON'S *hairpiece now, riveted on it)* — I mean Mr. Toupeson —

> CORKY
>
> *Tod*son.

> POSTMAN
> *(laughing)*
>
> That's what *I* call funny.

> FATS
> *(whispering to* CORKY)
>
> Is this *the* George Todson — the guy known throughout televisionland as "Limp Dick" George?

CORKY

He doesn't mean anything.

FATS
(to THE POSTMAN *who is roaring)*
You'll strain your pacemaker.
*(*TODSON *smiles, he's clearly impressed.)*

POSTMAN
(to TODSON*)*
Give us one sec'?

TODSON
(starts out, stops)
How *did* you change the diamond to the heart?

FATS
I'm the misdirection — while we're bullshitting, you could bring an elephant on stage —

POSTMAN
(finishing)
— which is why *this* magician wouldn't bomb on the tube — the camera watches their faces, not Corky's hands.

CUT TO

CORKY, FATS, *and* THE POSTMAN *smiling, nodding, waiting while* TODSON *exits. The second he's gone —*

CORKY
(soft)
You think he liked it?

POSTMAN
Calling him "Limp Dick" George probably didn't advance our cause, but on the whole I would say it was senfuckingsational.

FATS

See? I'm catching.

CORKY

What happens now?

POSTMAN
Now? We reel him in slow — it'll be months before I bring you to New York, not til they're ready to make a deal. Meanwhile, you'll finish here and I'll book you at a small lounge in Vegas, for the experience.

CUT TO

THE POSTMAN, *going on, building, as* CORKY *and* FATS *watch.*

POSTMAN
Same with the talk shows, nice and easy. Kathy Crosby up in Frisco, Dinah Shore down here. Kup in Chicago, Griffin, building to Carson. *(indicating* FATS*)* You keep Motormouth here in line, and it'll be my job to get those droolers at CBS panting for you. Sound OK?

CORKY
Yessir.

POSTMAN
You're a good kid, Corky.

FATS
(his head up to CORKY'S *ear again)*
Hey, you know what I think?

CORKY
What do you think?

FATS
We're gonna be a star...

CUT TO

CORKY. CLOSE UP. *Hard to tell what he's thinking.* HOLD *for a moment. Then from* CORKY *we quick*

CUT TO

FATS AND DINAH SHORE,

and she's laughing really hard as FATS *nuzzles her neck passionately.* CORKY *sits alongside, a deck of cards in his free hand, kind of embarrassed by* FATS' *behavior as we*

PULL BACK TO REVEAL

that we've been watching this through one of those large mobile television cameras. We're in the TV studio and it's filled with the equipment and movement and quiet chaos that goes on backstage.

Now an ASSISTANT *signals that there are 30 seconds left to go, and* DINAH *catches it, straightens her hair, turns to* CORKY.

DINAH
Can you give me half a minute's advice for any young people who might be watching?

FATS
(barging in before CORKY can reply)
Well, Dinah, it's not an easy life, being a dummy—you've got to constantly be working on your facial expressions and you've got to find some schmucko and teach him to talk without moving his lips, and your sex life can be murder unless you're willing to spend a lot of your time around lumberyards—

CUT TO

A young ASSISTANT, waiting in the chaos of cables and moving cameras as DINAH laughs, goes into her sign off, and the show ends. The ASSISTANT moves in as CORKY and DINAH shake hands, and she, suddenly surrounded by assistants starts away.

ASSISTANT
Mr. Withers?
(CORKY turns)
Phone. *(And as he gestures across the stage area—)*

CUT TO

CORKY, lugging FATS, making his careful way in and out of workmen toward a wall phone. CORKY picks it up; it's noisy as he tries to speak.

CORKY
Hello? Yes?

POSTMAN (over)
(on the phone)
This is your modest, humble and legendary agent—you free for lunch tomorrow?

CORKY
'Course—

POSTMAN (over)
—OK, The Four Seasons, one o'clock.

CORKY
(stunned)
You mean in New York? What about? Is it good news or— *(he realizes THE POSTMAN has hung up)*

CUT TO

THE BACKSTAGE AREA as CORKY leaves the phone, moves toward the dressing rooms.

CORKY
(muttering, shaking his head)
Crazy— *(suddenly turns to FATS)*—tell me it was good news.

> FATS
> *(right on cue)*

It was good, it was good.

> CORKY
> *(affirming)*

Has to be good—you don't ask someone to fly 3,000 miles otherwise. Tell
me I'm right.

> FATS

You're absolutely one hundred percent on the money correct.
> *(CORKY closes the dressing room door*
> *on that, and as it clicks shut—)*

CUT TO

A WHITE DOT MOVING TOWARD CAMERA.

*HOLD, as the dot slowly materializes into a dazzling white Corniche, zooming down Park
Avenue, weaving in and out of traffic as we*

CUT TO

*THE POSTMAN at the wheel of his beloved eighty thousand dollar car. Driving like a ma-
niac, he makes a wild left turn from the center lane as we*

CUT TO

*THE DOORMAN OF THE FOUR SEASONS. THE POSTMAN guns his Corniche into the no
parking area in front of the place. As the DOORMAN hurriedly moves in to do his duty—*

PULL BACK TO REVEAL

*CORKY, standing alone and out of sight, watching, hidden in the driveway entrance next to
the restaurant. He is, as always, casually dressed, tieless. And terribly nervous as he watches
THE POSTMAN get out of his car.*

> POSTMAN
> *(nodding politely)*

Franklin, it seems I'm breaking the law— *(he gestures to the "no parking" sign)*
—if only there was some way you might help. *(he does a flourish—money is
now in his right hand)* Hmm—you must have lost these two tens, Franklin;
they look like yours.

> DOORMAN
> *(accepting the money)*

I'll see no one touches it, sir.

POSTMAN

No one must *ever* touch a Rolls but a Rolls man. *(he smiles, enters the restaurant)*

CUT TO

CORKY, still standing as before, uncertain. He starts out, hesitates, moves back to where he was before, alone in shadow. HOLD *for a moment, then —*

CUT TO

The MAITRE D' *of the Four Seasons, standing imperiously by the reservations desk. This is the outer room, lovely and bright. An odd look crosses the* MAITRE D'*'s face as we*

CUT TO

CORKY, hesitantly making his way up the stairs toward the reservations desk. He glances nervously around the elegant room and

CUT TO

All the handsome, well dressed, secure-seeming people, and from them, suddenly —

FLASHCUT TO

THE RICH BITCH — THE ONE WHO WAS LAUGHING ALL THROUGH HIS ACT THAT TERRIBLE FIRST NIGHT AT THE STARDUST — AND CORKY'S BACK IN HIS MIND TO THAT NIGHTMARISH TIME AND SHE WILL NOT STOP HER GODDAM LAUGHING AND

CUT TO

CORKY, frozen in the Four Seasons, his hand going to his open throat as he realizes he's the only man there without a necktie and

CUT TO

The MAITRE D', *watching, not smiling at all and*

CUT TO

CORKY, panicked, beginning to retreat and

CUT TO

The MAITRE D', *staring toward* CORKY —

MAITRE D'

Excuse me — one moment —

CUT TO

CORKY, *half stumbling as the* MAITRE D' *closes in.*

> **MAITRE D'**
> —perhaps I can help you—

> **CORKY**
> *(barely getting it out)*
> —Ben Greene please...?

CUT TO

The MAITRE D', *all smiles now.*

> **MAITRE D'**
> Oh, Mr. Greene. Of course. *(And as he gestures toward the main room —)*

CUT TO

CORKY. CLOSE UP. *Giving one gigantic sign of relief.* HOLD *for only a moment before we*

CUT TO

THE POOL ROOM *of the Four Seasons, which has to be the prettiest restaurant anywhere, and, waiting at the best table,* THE POSTMAN. *He watches as* CORKY *is ushered in.* THE POSTMAN *has an odd look on his face; the eyes betray nothing. There's a bottle of red wine, two glasses, both properly filled.*

> **CORKY**
> *(sits)*
> Hi.
> *(nothing from* THE POSTMAN*)*
> Is everything OK?
> *(still no reply)*
> With the network people, I mean.

> **POSTMAN**
> Have a cigar for later, Corky. *(he hands over an enormous cigar)* Take two, they're big. *(he hands over another)* I *invented* conspicuous consumption; don't you forget that.

> **CORKY**
> Listen, if you're trying to get my attention, you've got it.

> **POSTMAN**
> Do me a favor?
> *(*CORKY *waits)*
> Try not to turn shitheel—that's almost an automatic once a guy makes it big, I'd love to see you beat the odds.

CORKY

Maybe I won't make it big. *(tense, excited)* What is it? — I've just come 3,000 miles, no more games, tell me —

POSTMAN

Two years ago you couldn't get arrested, two years from now you're gonna have it all: CBS wants a pilot special, Cork.

CORKY

A what?

POSTMAN
(sips wine)

A pilot special is what they gave Rich Little awhile back. When they're hot for someone like they are for you, they make a contract that hinges on the first show: if it hits, you're off and running for a bunch more.

CORKY

And it's all set and everything?

POSTMAN

It's set, but it's not set-set. Boiler plate needs slugging out: who'll spend how much for publicity, how much for guest stars, you'll have to take the medical exam, just agent stuff — *(stops)* — what's wrong?

CUT TO

CORKY. Kind of a half smile.

CORKY

I don't think I want to take the medical exam.

CUT TO

CORKY and THE POSTMAN

POSTMAN
(shrugs)

Any special reason?

CORKY

You mean is there anything the matter with me? — no; I haven't got leukemia.

POSTMAN

What then?

CORKY

It's a matter of principle.
(THE POSTMAN waits)

Remember that first night you came backstage at the Stardust and said you wouldn't mind handling me? Remember what I said?

POSTMAN
Goddam right—you said I could *represent* you, but you wouldn't *sign.*

CORKY
That was principle too—because if we're happy with each other, our word should be enough, to hell with signing some piece of paper.

POSTMAN
But why is this with the medical exam "principle"?

CORKY
They're saying there's something wrong with me. (quieter now) Well, I say I'm fine. I'm fine and I don't need any doctors poking around inside, thank you.

POSTMAN
Are you serious about this?
                              (CORKY nods)
I mean, is this a dealbreaker?

CUT TO

CORKY. He nods his head. Softly —

CORKY
I guess it is . . .

                              (Now from here —)

CUT TO

THE POSTMAN, STORMING INTO THE NEW YORK BRANCH OF THE WILLIAM MORRIS AGENCY AND THEN

CUT TO

SADIE, THE POSTMAN's black secretary, seated in his outer office.

THE POSTMAN's VOICE is audible coming down the corridor. SADIE is as old as he is, immaculately dressed.

POSTMAN (over)
Sadie? *Sadie? (he comes in, stops by her desk)* What's the first rule for being an agent?

SADIE
Never forget an actor killed Lincoln.

POSTMAN
Head of the class. *(He turns, goes into his office as we —)*

CUT TO

THE POSTMAN'S OFFICE. *Big, impressive, all kinds of plaques and photos on the walls. He moves to his desk, rubs his eyes. SADIE has moved into the doorway, waiting.*

> **POSTMAN**
> Get me Bernstein in legal.
> > *(SADIE nods)*
> Corky's turned impossible, would you believe that?

> **SADIE**
> *(surprised)*
> Last one I would have guessed. *(She turns, starts for her phone.)*

> **POSTMAN**
> *(eyes to the heavens)*
> I should have been a cesspool digger like my mother wanted. *(He sits there, shaking his head as we)*

CUT TO

CORKY AND FATS. IN HIS HOTEL ROOM ON CENTRAL PARK SOUTH.

They seem a little different. Heads close together, CORKY is staring dead ahead, concentrating.

> **FATS**
> Corky's so cheap he sent his girlfriend out to hustle last night —

> **CORKY**
> — not true, not true, just ignore him —

> **FATS**
> — and when she came back this morning he asked how much she'd gotten and she said, "Sixteen dollars and ten cents" and Corky said, "Ten cents? My God, who gave you ten cents?!" and she said, "Everybody." *(beat)* Dammit.

CUT TO

CORKY *and* FATS, *a different angle, and what we begin to see is that he's staring at a mirror and is rehearsing.*

> **CORKY**
> *(with extreme care — watching his lip line*
> *for the slightest movement. In his own voice)*
> "And she said 'everybody.'" *(again)* Everybody. *(slower, practicing with great care)* Body. Buh. Buh. Body. *(As we've watched, the movement has gone from slight to unnoticeable. Satisfied, he uses his FATS voice now)* "And she said 'everybody.'" *(As he's about to go on the phone rings and he picks it up.)*

POSTMAN (over)

Couldn't budge 'em, Cork.
                    (CORKY *just grips the phone*)
You there?

CORKY

I thought you said they wanted me —

POSTMAN (over)

— they do, but —

CORKY

— didn't you explain about the principle? —

CUT TO

THE POSTMAN IN HIS OFFICE. THREE MEN *in dark suits and ties sit around in chairs.*

POSTMAN

Kid, this is company policy — *legal* company policy — I'm sitting here
with three of our genius lawyers — my God, their I.Q.'s alone must total
up to a hundred — we've called CBS a dozen times and they're not about
to spend half a million and find out on taping day there's some kind of
health problem —

CUT TO

CORKY, *loud.*

CORKY

There's no problem!

POSTMAN (over)

Corky —

CORKY

— you — make — them — understand. (*And as he slams down the phone —*)

CUT TO

THE POSTMAN. *He shakes his head, turns to the lawyers.*

POSTMAN

Shoo for awhile, huh fellas? Lemme deal with this alone.
                    (*As the lawyers start to rise —*)

CUT TO

CORKY IN HIS ROOM. *He stands over the phone, taut, wild. Now he whirls, starts pacing
around aimlessly, caged. He passes the mirror he was practicing in, stops, stares.*

CUT TO

CORKY'S FACE IN THE MIRROR. His left eye is starting to flutter, his face seems pale. Now there is a faint pulsing along his left temple and as he grabs his head, starts to knead it, pressing all he has against the left side of his face —

CUT TO

FATS, watching.

CUT TO

CORKY, discomfort growing, spinning as the phone rings again and as he picks it up, mutters "yes?"

> POSTMAN (over)
> Kid, I don't have to ask what the trouble is because I know what it is.

> CORKY
> I told you before —

CUT TO

THE POSTMAN in his office.

> POSTMAN
> — it's just success, kid — please believe me — that's all you're afraid of, you want it but you're frightened of it, it happens to 'em all at this stage —

> CORKY (over)
> — *principle*, can't you get that?

> POSTMAN
> I'll take the goddam medical with you — Christ, I've had two strokes, my varicose veins are in all the best medical journals, if I'm not afraid of what they'll find —

CORKY, his left eye beating badly now.

> CORKY
> — not afraid —

> POSTMAN (over)
> — just stay right there — I'll be right over, we'll talk it through, we'll —

> CORKY
> — *I'm not afraid!*

> POSTMAN (over)
> Hang tight, Cork, I'm on my way.

> CORKY
> (*huge*)
> *I — won't — be — here. (And as he slams the phone back into its cradle —)*

CUT TO

THE CLOSET *as* CORKY *drags down a couple of suitcases and*

CUT TO

THE DRESSER *as* CORKY *pulls out drawers full of clothes and*

CUT TO

THE BATHROOM *as* CORKY, *frantic, swoops up his toilet articles, throws them into a kit, runs back to the suitcases and*

CUT TO

CORKY, RUNNING ALONG CENTRAL PARK SOUTH,

hailing a cab, starting toward it but it's occupied and now he begins running even faster and the luggage looks heavy but he manages to pick up his pace even more as we

CUT TO

ANOTHER FULL CAB *and*

CUT TO

ANOTHER CAB, *crammed with people and*

CUT TO

CORKY, *wildly running, and across the street he sees an empty cab and without looking one way or the other he charges for it — cars swerve to avoid him, some people yell, some honk horns but he keeps on, keeps on —* HOLD ON THE NOISE AND CONFUSION OF THE CITY AS CORKY CONTINUES TO RUN...

NOW — SILENCE — AND WE'RE LOOKING AT SOMETHING PRETTY BUT WE CAN'T TELL QUITE WHAT, BUT IT'S YELLOW AND LOVELY AND WE

PULL BACK TO REVEAL

Leaves. Thousands and thousands of yellow leaves blowing along a country road — we're in the Catskills now, off the main drag. Some of the trees are already beginning to look barren.

PULL BACK FARTHER TO REVEAL

THE CAB CORKY WAS RUNNING TOWARD. *It's driving along the country road. As it comes to an intersection —*

CUT TO

INSIDE THE CAB. CORKY sits in the back, his suitcases beside him. He holds a deck of cards, does a one-hand cut over and over.

The DRIVER is a kid, 20 at the outside, sharp and slender. He's a chronic bubble gum chewer, too.

KID DRIVER
(glancing at a road sign)
Should hit Grossinger's inside another 20 minutes.

CORKY
(suddenly looking carefully around)
That can wait — *(to the KID DRIVER)* — take your next left, keep going into town.
(As the KID DRIVER nods —)

CUT TO

A SMALL EMPTY HOUSE. It's on a forlorn small-town street.

CUT TO

CORKY in the back seat, staring at the empty place, the cab is motionless, motor running. Now —

FLASHCUT TO

THE SAME HOUSE ONLY WHEN PEOPLE LIVED IN IT. A RUNTY, POWERFUL MAN IN A GROS- SINGER'S SWEATSHIRT IS TOSSING A FOOTBALL WITH A LARGE, POWERFUL TEENAGE BOY.

ON THE FRONT PORCH OF THE HOUSE, IGNORED, A SMALL BOY SITS WATCHING AND WHIT- TLING ALONE. THIS IS CLEARLY CORKY.

FLASHCUT TO

CORKY, CLOSE UP, HE STOPS HIS WHITTLING, LOOKS OUT AT THE OTHER TWO.

FLASHCUT TO

THE FATHER AND OLDER BROTHER. THEY PAY CORKY NO MIND.

FLASHCUT TO

THE FOOTBALL IN MIDAIR.

FLASHCUT TO

THE BIG BROTHER RUNNING, MAKING A GRACEFUL CATCH.

FLASHCUT TO

THE FATHER, FIST CLENCHED AS IN TRIUMPH.

FLASHCUT TO

CORKY, *ALONE, WATCHING THEM MOVE OFF DOWN THE STREET. (DURING THIS, THE FOLLOWING TALK HAS BEEN GOING ON BETWEEN* CORKY *AND THE KID CAB DRIVER.)*

> **KID DRIVER** (over)
>
> Your place?

> **CORKY** (over)
> *(quietly)*
>
> I was born there.

> **KID DRIVER** (over)
>
> You must remember it being a whole lot bigger, huh?

> **CORKY** (over)
>
> No.

> **KID DRIVER** (over)
>
> Wanna get out.

> **CORKY** (over)
>
> No point.

CUT TO

THE TWO OF THEM *in the cab and the empty house beyond.*

> **KID DRIVER**
>
> Family all gone?
> *(*CORKY *nods, gestures to drive on)*
> You're lucky — I live with four brothers — all assholes. *(He blows a bubble, drives on.)*

CUT TO

CORKY, *in the backseat, lost in thought. As the cab moves away —*

FLASHCUT TO

THE HOUSE AND THE TWO MEN PLAYING FOOTBALL. GRADUALLY, THEIR IMAGE FADES: THEY JUST DISAPPEAR AS WE

CUT TO

A SMALL TOWN CEMETERY. *It's on a hill, postcard pretty. The cab is stopped again, motor running.*

CUT TO

CORKY *in the back seat. The windows are fogged, as he turns and looks out —*

FLASHCUT TO

A BURIAL IN PROGRESS. THE OLDER BOY WHO WAS THROWING THE FOOTBALL STANDS BESIDE A WOMAN. THERE IS A MINISTER, JUST A FEW OTHERS. THE LITTLE BOY WHO WAS WHITTLING STANDS A BIT APART. IT'S CORKY AT HIS FATHER'S FUNERAL.

CUT TO

CORKY in the back seat of the cab. As he wipes the fogged up windows with his arm, the image of the funeral fades away, leaving just the plain cemetery and the rows of graves.

> **KID DRIVER**
> I don't wanna come on like some ghoul, but you got people in there?

> **CORKY**
> *(blinks)*
> People? *(quiet)* Just family.

> **KID DRIVER**
> Wanna get out here then?
> > *(CORKY says nothing, just stares at the graves as we)*

CUT TO

ANOTHER COUNTRY ROAD and the KID DRIVER making good time.

> **KID DRIVER**
> You're probably wondering why I'm all the time suggesting you get out —
> > *(CORKY doesn't understand)*
> — most guys would be afraid you'd take off and stiff them for an 80 dollar tab. Reason I'm not afraid is I know you're good for the money. I caught you on the Carson show, you must get a ton for that.

> **CORKY**
> Exposure, mainly.

> **KID DRIVER**
> How'd you luck into it? — I sing great, I know they'd cream over me —

> **CORKY**
> — my agent — William Morris — arranged it —

> **KID DRIVER**
> — is this Morris guy a personal friend of Carson's — that how it works? —

> **CORKY**
> *(half smile now)*
> — William Morris is the name of an agency, not a guy and — *(suddenly all*

attention) — hold it. *(sharper)* Right here.
                                    (As the car slows —)

CUT TO

A SIGN, *flaking but still legible. It reads:*

FINAST CABINS
Your Private Pleasure Dome
On the Shores of Lake Melody.

CUT TO

THE CAR, *stopped, motor running, as* CORKY *gets out, starts across the road and*

CUT TO

THE BUNGALOW COLONY.

There are a lot of these in the Catskills. This one has a large house, halfway down the hill from the road. And below it, scattered on the grounds, a couple of dozen cabins of various sizes. Beyond the cabins, at the bottom of the hill, a deep blue lake, barely big enough for water skiing. The largest and clearly nicest cabins are nearest the water.

Right now, the place looks deserted.

FLASHCUT TO

THE COLONY IN THE OLD DAYS; *THE PLACE FILLED WITH MOTHERS AND KIDS AND PEO-PLE FISHING AND*

FLASHCUT TO

A GIRL, BLONDE, WE DON'T QUITE GET A SOLID LOOK AT HER, PROBABLY IN HER TEENS, BUT SHE'S LEADING A BUNCH OF LITTLE KIDS IN A GAME AND THERE ARE SHRIEKS OF LAUGHTER AND

CUT TO

CORKY *and the deserted colony as he continues toward the main house.*

CUT TO

THE HOUSE *as* CORKY *knocks on the door. He knocks again, rings the bell. It's chilly. He throws his arms across his body for warmth.*

                              CORKY
Hey? *(no answer)* Anybody?

                    FEMALE VOICE (over)
                         (from inside)
What do you want?

> **CORKY**

Cabin?

> **FEMALE VOICE** (over)

We're kind of closed.

> **CORKY**
> *(looks around the place)*

Something by the lake is what I'm after. This is just the kind of place I'm looking for, I won't be disturbed here.

> **FEMALE VOICE** (over)

That's for sure.

CUT TO

THE SECOND FLOOR WINDOW *and the* FEMALE *peering down — can't see her clearly; sun off the glass.*

> **FEMALE**

But like I said, we're kind of closed.

CUT TO

CORKY, *looking up, taking out his wallet.*

> **CORKY**

Fifty bucks a night — in advance.

> **FEMALE**

We just reopened.
> *(Now on that —)*

CUT TO

THE CAB, *motor running, the* KID DRIVER *standing alongside as* CORKY *gets out his suitcases.*

> **KID DRIVER**

You don't want me waiting? How you gonna get to Grossinger's?

> **CORKY**

I'll call a local cab when I need one. *(looks at the* KID*)* Eighty, you said, right?

> **KID DRIVER**
> *(quickly)*

Not counting tip.

> **CORKY**
> *(the money in his hands)*

One hundred for the driving —

(the KID DRIVER *is pleased*)
— another hundred for a favor. (*He holds it out.*)

                              KID DRIVER
Name it.

                                CORKY
You didn't bring me here.

The KID DRIVER'S *face breaks into an understanding smile — he grabs the dough, then* CORKY'S *hand, shakes it up and down, really excited and as he keeps on shaking —*

CUT TO

THE LARGEST CABIN NEAREST THE LAKE.

THE FEMALE *from the house unlocks the front door, opens it, leads* CORKY *in.*

CUT TO

INSIDE THE PLACE. CORKY *looks around. She breaks the silence.*

                                FEMALE
What you see is what you get. (*gesturing*) Bedroom's back there — (*pointing*) — kitchenette, bathroom across. Here's your key.

                                CORKY
Fine. (*Takes it, hands her some money.*)

CUT TO

The FEMALE. *She glances at* CORKY, *takes the money, goes, closing the door behind her.*

CUT TO

CORKY. *He hesitates, then goes quietly to the window facing up the hill. The* FEMALE *walks into view, moving up the path toward the main house. She doesn't once glance back.* CORKY *stares.*

CUT TO

CORKY. CLOSE UP. *On his face now, a dreadful look of sadness. Then —*

                              FATS (over)
                      (*his voice muffled and distant*)
Helllllppp — hellllllpp — calling all schmucko's — *save* me —
                        (As CORKY *turns —*)

CUT TO

FATS' SUITCASE *as* CORKY *opens it, takes* FATS *out, goes back to the window with* FATS, *stares up at the retreating figure of the girl. CORKY watches her steadily while FATS glances all around the place, getting used to his surroundings.*

FATS

I hate the country already, it's full of leaves. All you hear is crunch, crunch, crunch. *(taking in the cabin)* This is Grossinger's? *(staring at CORKY)* You think I'm some palooka from Palookaville? You book us into this dump for a coroners' convention?

(CORKY says nothing)

Why the silent act? *(Now he turns his head, follows CORKY's glance, sees the distant girl.)* I wonder if her ass is on ball bearings —

CORKY

— shut up —

FATS

— oooh — hooo — sounds like I stepped on a corn.

CORKY
(soft)

No, it's just... *(that terrible sadness is still with him)* ... I carried her picture all these years and she didn't remember me.

(FATS looks at CORKY —)

CUT TO

CORKY. CLOSE UP. *Quiet.* HOLD. *Then —*

CUT TO

A PICTURE OF ELVIS PRESLEY.

Only after we look at it a moment, we realize it isn't Elvis, just somebody who looked a lot like him when the photo was taken. Now —

PULL BACK TO REVEAL

PEGGY ANN SNOW, looking at the picture a moment, then taking a large book from a bottom shelf — we're in the living room of the main house — and as she flips the book open —

CUT TO

THE BOOK. It's her Normandy High Yearbook and she turns pages until she comes to a young lovely cheerleader caught at the peak of her jump. The caption reads — "PeggyAnn Snow Scores One for Our Side."

CUT TO

PEG, studying herself. She takes the book a few steps, in front of a mirror. Now she can see herself and the picture at the same time. She shakes her head, closes the book, turns and we

CUT TO

THE KITCHEN. *A* CAT *is eating out of its bowl.* PEG *moves up behind it, lifts the animal, holds it very close.*

> **PEG**
> *(soft)*

He didn't remember me.

HOLD ON PEG. *That same terrible look of sadness is in her eyes too . . . From there —*

CUT TO

THE MAIN HOUSE

PEG *is cleaning out a large closet. She turns as there comes a knock on the door.*

> **CORKY'S VOICE** (over)

I'm sorry.

> **PEG**

What?

> **CORKY'S VOICE** (over)

No soap.

> **PEG**
> *(going to the door)*

I didn't think you'd like it. You leaving now?

> **CORKY'S VOICE** (over)
> *(laughing)*

I didn't mean "no soap" that way — I meant there wasn't any; or towels for that matter.

> **PEG**

C'mon in; you can grab what you want and — *(she opens the door — shrieking)* — omigod, you brought Fats!

CUT TO

CORKY *and* FATS *standing in the doorway.*

> **FATS**
> *(turning to* CORKY*)*

And you thought Peg didn't remember.

> **PEG**
> *(to* CORKY *now)*

You knew who I was too?

> *(*CORKY *nods)*

> FATS
> *(as he and CORKY move inside)*
> Well why didn't you two at least grunt at each other? —

> CORKY
> *(flustered)*
> — she was upstairs and I couldn't tell for sure — the sun was reflecting —
> *(shrugs)* — by the time I was sure, I figured she'd have said something but
> she didn't so I just shut up.

> FATS
> *(turning to PEG now)*
> What's your story?

> PEG
> Well, it's been so long and I watch you on the TV but when he didn't say
> anything, I didn't want to embarrass anybody —

> FATS
> *(shaking his head)*
> — we're all so goddam sensitive I could whoopse.

CUT TO

PEG, *laughing now, looking at* FATS.

> PEG
> He's just as cute as on the tube —

> FATS
> *(outraged)*
> — *cute?* Virile, yes; sexy, yes; Ronald Reagan is cute.

CUT TO

FATS, *watching* PEG, *then* CORKY, *as they stare at each other a moment inside the front
door.* FATS *just turns his head from one to the other.*

> PEG
> *(really excited, to CORKY)*
> Could I hold him just once?
> *(FATS starts panting excitedly)*
> I'll be careful.
> *(CORKY hesitates, hands FATS over)*
> He's heavy —

> FATS
> *(outraged again)*
> *Husky*, you bimbo.

PEG
(to CORKY*)*

His lips didn't move.

FATS
(very Bogart)
That's 'cause you're not stroking my levers, sweetheart.

CORKY
(pointing to the slit in the back of FATS' *outfit)*
Right in there.

CUT TO

PEG, *slowly sliding her fingers into the slit and before she's ready —*

FATS
(big)

She goosed me!
*(*PEG *pulls her hand out fast, surprised.)*

CORKY

Ignore him. Go right ahead.

PEG *puts her hand in the slit again, touches a lever.* FATS' *eyes cross. She touches another, his ears wiggle. She moves her hand farther up and* FATS *begins making sexual groans.* PEG *breaks out laughing.*

CORKY
(smiling)

Don't encourage him.
(Now from that —)

CUT TO

THE FRONT DOOR, OPEN, PEG *on the steps,* CORKY *and* FATS *just below.* CORKY *carries towels, washrags, soap, etc.*

PEG
So if you need anything else —
*(From down below in the woods
now, a cat's cry.* FATS *jerks around)*
— that's just my big old cat, probably found a dead bird.

FATS
Probably *made* a dead bird —

PEG
(as CORKY *starts away)*
— hey? You wouldn't want any wine or anything?

CORKY
(*quick nod*)

Terrific—lemme just get my stuff down to the cabin and maybe clean up a little and—

FATS

—wait a minute, what *stuff*? There's mostly *me* and I wanna stick around.
(CORKY *waves, starts down the hill,*
PEG *closes the door as we*—)

CUT TO

FATS *and* CORKY, *walking slowly through the night.*

FATS

She hugged me to her bosom.
(CORKY *nods*)
I suspect she found me irresistible.

CORKY

Don't we all.

FATS

How late you gonna stay up there?

CORKY
(*shrugs*)

I don't know, why?

FATS

If you stayed late, that might mean you were getting hugged to her bosom too.

CUT TO

FATS. CLOSE UP IN THE NIGHT. *His eyes seem almost blazing.*

FATS

Which might just make old Fats jealous— (*beat*)—and we wouldn't want that— (*longer one*)—would we now...
(HOLD ON FATS' STARING
EYES AWHILE. *Then*—)

CUT TO

A HALF EMPTY JUG OF GALLO HEARTY BURGUNDY.

Behind it, a fireplace. We're in the living room of the house. PEG *and* CORKY *sit on opposite couches, drinking.*

                                    PEG

You never really told why you were here.

                                   CORKY

Hiding.
                            (she looks at him)
Got to get my head on straight. My agent—he looks like the Ancient
Mariner in that poem we hated in high school—
                                (she nods)
—he's negotiating for a shot for me to maybe make it big—we argued—
I thought it was just principle. *(drinks)* The truth is probably I'm scared
of success, that's all.

CUT TO

THE FIRE, as PEG crosses to it, begins shifting the logs with a poker.

                                    PEG

You always were this weirdly timid person, Corky, that's for sure.

                                   CORKY
                            (nods, watches her)
Folks still run this place?

                                    PEG

Nah; they took a condo near Launderdale, said it was mine but I couldn't
make a go.

                                   CORKY

You miss em?

                                    PEG
                    (shoves at the logs a moment; sparks fly)
No more'n they miss me. Don't tell me you miss yours.

FLASHCUT TO

*A WOMAN—WE SAW HER BRIEFLY AT THE FUNERAL SCENE—ONLY NOW WE'RE IN THE
KITCHEN OF THE HOUSE CORKY GREW UP IN. HE'S SEATED AT THE KITCHEN TABLE, WHIT-
TLING, WATCHING AS SHE POURS A GLASS OF MILK INTO A GLASS. SHE'S HAVING TROU-
BLE—HER HANDS AREN'T STEADY—AND THE MILK SPILLS TO THE FLOOR. SHE BEGINS
TO CURSE AND*

FLASHCUT TO

*CORKY, LIKE A SHOT, GRABBING A RAG, CLEANING UP THE MESS. HIS MOTHER WATCHES,
TAKES A HALF STEP, THEN LEANS AGAINST THE SINK AND WE REALIZE SHE'S NOT EX-
ACTLY SOBER.*

During this, PEG and CORKY go on talking.

               CORKY (over)
Course I do. Every kid cares about his parents.

               PEG (over)
Where is that written, for chrissakes? Your old man never once gave squat
for you and your ma just took off, didn't she?

CUT TO

*THE TWO OF THEM in the living room, PEG by the fire, CORKY watching her; the back
light is very flattering to her.*

               CORKY
Well, I don't guess they were very happy, either of 'em. *(looks around)* Too
bad you can't make this place work.

               PEG
The Catskills are dying, and that's the truth. Me and Duke are looking to sell.

               CORKY
          (he means this next, and it's true)
God, you're beautiful.

               PEG
              (smiles)
Don't I wish.

FLASHCUT TO

*PEG AS A HIGH SCHOOL CHEERLEADER AND WE'RE IN SLOW MOTION AND IT'S LATE AF-
TERNOON AND SHE'S MOVING SLOWLY TOWARD THE CAMERA AND IT'S ALL FILLED WITH
THE HAZE OF MEMORY AND SHE CONTINUES TO MOVE FORWARD, NOW SHE'S RUNNING
GRACEFULLY, AND IT'S ON A FOOTBALL FIELD AND THE BACKGROUND'S DEEP GREEN AND
SHE REALLY IS A GLORY. (They continue talking over.)*

               CORKY (over)
I had such a crush on you.

               PEG (over)
Well, no one ever accused you of having good taste, Corky.

               CORKY (over)
When I moved away, I whittled you a present. A wooden heart.

FLASHCUT TO

*CORKY. LATE AFTERNOON OUTSIDE THE GYM OF HIGH SCHOOL. HE STANDS SHIVERING,
STARING UP AT THE LIT GYM.*

FLASHCUT TO

PEG, COMING OUT OF THE GYM AND

FLASHCUT TO

CORKY, STARTING TOWARD HER, A GOOD DISTANCE AWAY, THEN SUDDENLY TURNING, HURRYING OFF AND

FLASHCUT TO

CORKY, OPENING HIS FIST, STARING AT THE WOODEN HEART. IT'S REALLY LOVELY. NOW, AS HE DRAWS BACK HIS ARM —

FLASHCUT TO

THE WOODEN HEART, THROWN THROUGH THE AIR TOWARD SOME WOODS. IT ARCS SLOWLY THROUGH THE SKY, AND IS GONE. (As always, the talking has continued.)

> **PEG** (over)
> You never gave it to me though.

> **CORKY** (over)
> I lost it before I got it finished. Anyway, what if you didn't like it? I mean, what if you laughed?

CUT TO

PEG, in the present, getting up from the fire, starting back to the chair.

> **PEG**
> As has already been stated, weirdly timid. But I knew you had a crush. I was always pretty for you.

> **CORKY**
> I didn't say pretty.

> **PEG**
> You didn't pick up on my "Duke" mention either. He is, after all, my consort, my spouse — *(messing with the logs still)* — I'm very big on enlarging my vocabulary.

> **CORKY**
> Are you very big on Duke?

> **PEG**
> We separate what seems like every full moon — it hasn't been your everyday Debbie Reynolds marriage.

CUT TO

CORKY, refilling his glass and hers as she returns to the couch. There's a lot of sadness in the room just now. The fire is blazing.

CORKY

Where is he?

PEG

Quick business trip. *(looks at her watch)* More specifically, at this hour I would guess he'd be seducing some barmaid.

CORKY

Sorry.

PEG
(shrugs)

Whatever.

CORKY
(quickly)

Does he still look so much like Elvis Presley?

CUT TO

PEG, *starting to answer, but then with no warning, she is crying, her face buried in the cushions of the couch.*

CUT TO

CORKY, *quickly taking her wine glass, bringing it to her.*

CORKY

Here — hearty burgundy, very medicinal.

PEG
*(fighting to get control,
embarrassed, wiping her eyes)*

Admit it — *now* I'm beautiful...
(HOLD ON PEG. Then —)

CUT TO

FATS IN THE CABIN, SEATED IN A CHAIR.

CORKY *comes in and FATS is talking before he's through the door.*

FATS
(grumpily)

How was the orgy?
(CORKY says nothing, unbuttons his shirt)
Did you score?

CORKY

The high point of the evening was when I reduced her to tears.

> ### FATS
> Hey schmucko, attaway —
>> (CORKY *moves toward the bathroom*)
> — when are we moving?

> ### CORKY
>> (*shrugs*)
> Tomorrow, day after; soon.

CUT TO

THE BATHROOM AS CORKY *enters, quietly shuts the door, leans his head against the wall, closes his eyes, whispers: "Peggy Ann Snow, Peggy Ann Snow, Please let me follow wherever you go."*

> ### FATS (over)
>> (*muffled*)
> What'd you close the door for?

> ### CORKY
> I'm contemplating taking a piss, you mind?

> ### FATS (over)
> Ohhh — dainty, ain't he? (*muffled still, but louder*) Stick your head out one sec'.
>> (*As* CORKY *opens the door —*)

CUT TO

FATS. CLOSE UP. *Angry —*

> ### FATS
> *Were you thinking of her?*
>> (CORKY, *shocked, says nothing.*
>> FATS *continues to stare.* HOLD *on the*
>> *unblinking eyes . . . Now —*)

CUT TO

A BEAUTIFUL STRETCH OF WOODS, FLOODED WITH SUNLIGHT.

We're around the lake from the cabins, PEG *and* CORKY *are walking close together. We hear them talking, but it's not realistic in the sense that they're close enough for us to see clearly. It's as if their sounds were drifting to us on autumn winds.*

> ### PEG
> So how long did you work with this Merlin guy?

> ### CORKY
> I worked *for* him —

FLASHCUT TO

CORKY LOADING UP A MAGIC SUIT—A TUXEDO JACKET—AND THE LINING IS FILLED WITH PULLS AND HOOKS AND TINY POCKETS. CORKY IS TAKING SILVER DOLLARS AND PUTTING THEM IN GROUPS OF FOUR IN VARIOUS HOLDERS ON THE INSIDE.

> **CORKY** (over)
> *—years.* He taught me everything, but I never performed or like that; never on my own.

CUT TO

THE BEAUTIFUL STRETCH OF WOODS as before.

> **PEG**
> Why not?

> **CORKY**
> Probably afraid I'd fail.

> **PEG**
> Dope.

> **CORKY**
> It wasn't til the week he took really sick that I got the guts to try—an amateur show in L.A.
> *(As they continue to move—)*

CUT TO

AN ABSOLUTELY GLORIOUS GIANT OAK. They sit beneath it, close together.

> **PEG**
> You bring any tricks up with you?

> **CORKY**
> I don't do tricks—
> *(she looks at him funny)*
> —tricks means something set up beforehand, a box with a fake lid, a stacked deck of cards; I don't do that.

> **PEG**
> You just use whatever's available?
> *(CORKY nods)*
> Here—amaze me. *(And she tosses him an acorn.)*

> **CORKY**
> *(catching it)*
> An *acorn?* Come on, willya.

> **PEG**

That was available.

> **CORKY**
> *(sighs)*

What the hell, I'll try, give me an acorn.

CUT TO

CORKY. He shows her his hands, they're empty, the acorn's gone.

> **PEG**
> *(a little excited)*

Do that again. *(She hands him another acorn.)*

> **CORKY**

Do what again?

CUT TO

PEG. She looks at his hand—it's empty again.

> **PEG**

You bastard— *(And she starts to laugh.)* —I really love magic.

> **CORKY**

Not magic. Just skill. All explainable.

> **PEG**

I don't think I want to believe that. Can you explain everything?

> **CORKY**

Pretty much.

> **PEG**

What can't you explain?

> **CORKY**

Look—I don't want to get into this—magic's just to entertain, you're not supposed to take it seriously.

> **PEG**
> *(pushing it)*

What can't you explain?

FLASHCUT TO

OUTSIDE A HOSPITAL WARD. CORKY SITS ON A BENCH ALONE NEAR THE MAIN DOOR. HE WORKS WITH A DECK OF CARDS ALMOST UNCONSCIOUSLY. EVERY SO OFTEN HE GLANCES INTO THE WARD ITSELF.

MERLIN SITS INSIDE ALONGSIDE A BED. HIS CHUBBY WIFE IS IN THE BED. THEY ARE CLOSE TO EACH OTHER.

CORKY SITS AND WAITS, THE CARDS MOVING IN HIS HANDS WITHOUT HIS PAYING ANY ATTENTION AS HE CONCENTRATES ON MERLIN AND THE SICK WOMAN.

> **CORKY** (over)
> Merlin — his wife was his assistant before me — they were close, they really cared and those last days in the hospital with her ... *(pause)*

CUT TO

CORKY and PEG as before under the tree.

> **CORKY**
> *(quietly)*
> ... those last days he claimed he could read her mind ...

> **PEG**
> You believe that, don't you?

> **CORKY**
> I don't know; I want to, I guess. See, in their act, they used to do a lot of phony telepathy crap with mostly cards. *(beat)* But those last days, they both wanted it enough, wanted to touch each other enough, was how he put it.

> **PEG**
> Do you know the exact procedures they did and everything —

> **CORKY**
> Course but — *(looks at her)* — please; let's not get into this.

> **PEG**
> It'll be fun.

> **CORKY**
> *I'd fail.*

> **PEG**
> So what?

FLASHCUT TO

THE RICH BITCH FROM THE HOLLYWOOD STARDUST. LAUGHING. ALWAYS LAUGHING.

> **CORKY** (over)
> I don't want you thinking bad of me, let's say.

CUT TO

CORKY and PEG as before.

PEG

Forget the whole thing — *(And she rises abruptly, starts walking off —)*

CORKY
(calling after)

I'm trying to get *away* from pressure — please —

CUT TO

PEG. *Stops, glances back.*

PEG

Who's putting you under pressure? Not me! I just thought it might be a kick — *(turning again)* — but it's forgotten.

CUT TO

CORKY. *After a moment he jumps up, hurries after her as we*

CUT TO

TWO DECKS OF PLAYING CARDS ON A TABLE, ONE BLACK, ONE RED.

PULL BACK TO REVEAL

THE LIBRARY OF THE MAIN HOUSE. *PEG and CORKY sit across a coffee table from each other, the cards in between. PEG is excited and pleased, CORKY very tense, hesitant. The room is half lit; there's something eerie about the whole place. You get the feeling something not necessarily pleasant is about to happen.*

CORKY

OK, you've shuffled both decks, right?
(PEG nods)
Take either deck then.
*(She picks the one farthest
from her, the black.)*
Pick one card from your deck and look at it.
(She glances at the ten of hearts.)

PEG

Now what?

CORKY

You must really look at it.

PEG
(surprised at his tone)

I'm looking, I'm looking, don't get mad.

CORKY
(quiet again)
Put it back and cut the cards as much as you want.
(she cuts twice)
Now take my pack and find your card and take it out.

CUT TO

PEG, *as she takes the ten of hearts from the red deck.*

CORKY
OK; just keep that one card.

PEG
(as she puts his deck down)
What happens now?

CORKY
What happened with Merlin was she put the card next to her heart while
he went through her deck kind of like this. *(He picks up the black deck, riffles through.)*

PEG
What's my card?

CORKY
I don't know — you've got to think hard.

PEG
(closes her eyes)
OK, I'm thinking really hard. *(opens her eyes)*

CORKY
(embarrassed)
Sorry. *(starts to put her deck down)*

PEG
Just a damn minute — *you've* got to think hard too — I want this and you're
so goofed up with doing it wrong you won't even try. Well, I'm concentrating my ass off.

CUT TO

CORKY. *Nothing. He riffles through the cards faster and you can sense a building desperation —*

CUT TO

PEG, *watching him.*

PEG

Close your eyes and *think*.

CUT TO

CORKY. *He closes his eyes, holds the pack tight.*

CORKY

I'm sorry, I told you, I asked you please — *(And now his eyes open wide.)* — omigod, it's red isn't it?

PEG
(her excitement building too)
I don't know, maybe it is, maybe it isn't, I give away nothing... *(but she's practically squeezing the ten of hearts now and as she starts to close her eyes again —)*

CUT TO

CORKY. CLOSE UP. *And there's light perspiration forming now and he's deep into something, his body rigid and now he's beginning to breathe harder and*

CUT TO

PEG, *caught up in it too, and she takes the hand that isn't holding the card, puts the knuckles in her mouth, bites down hard and*

CUT TO

CORKY, *frantically going through her deck, taking one card out and*

CUT TO

PEG. *Christ she wants this and*

CUT TO

CORKY. *He does too, his hands are trembling.*

CORKY
(whispered)
...turn...

CUT TO

THE CARDS. *She turns over the ten of hearts. He turns over — the deuce of diamonds.*

CUT TO

PEG, *staring at it, and for a moment she's stunned, but then she's got it all under control.*

PEG

Listen, we came close, what the hell we had fun, that's the name of the game anyway — *(And as she starts to stand —)*

CUT TO

CORKY. *Pale.*

CORKY

Sit down, Peg —

(she hesitates)

— get back down!

CUT TO

PEG, *sitting quickly, and for the first time now, she's starting maybe to get afraid.*

CUT TO

CORKY, *and maybe she's got reason to be, because he looks terrible, pale and taut and now, as we watch, his left eye starts to flutter and he rubs it as he talks, rubs it hard, but it keeps on blinking.*

CORKY

That was your fault — you started out fine, I got the red fine, but then you let me drift, you humiliated me Peg, and I want to know why.

PEG

Corky, Jesus, forget —

CORKY

— I was in bad shape in New York, Peg — *(rubbing his temple now)* — I had to run and where do you go when there's no place to go, you go home, except there was nothing but empty houses and old cemeteries and then I figured I'd stop by here and ask your folks about you, where were you living, what city, how many kids — I never expected to find you — I've loved you all my goddam life and I needed a piece of good news about Peggy Ann Snow — and now you humiliate me. *(gesturing sharply)* Shuffle the goddam cards *fast.*

CUT TO

PEG, *a little more frightened and as she starts quickly to shuffle,* CORKY *stares at her, the vein beat in his temple visible now.*

CORKY

We're going to do it right this time — *(his voice is getting strange)* — I just know we will because we both want it enough.

PEG

But...what if it...I mean, how upset will you be if you miss?

CORKY

Very. *(beat)* But that's not going to happen, is it, Peg; are you done shuffling?
(she nods)
Then take your card and look at it and put it back, and cut them.

CUT TO

PEG, *following orders; this time her card is the three of clubs. She puts it back, cuts the deck in the silence, conscious always of* CORKY'S *eyes. Then she goes through his deck, takes out his club three.*

CUT TO

CORKY, *taking her deck, holding it in his hands.*

CORKY

Look at me, Peg —
(she does)
— we're not going to close our eyes this time, we're going to watch each other just like Merlin and his wife, only you're not dying, are you, Peg —

PEG

— should I think now?

CORKY

Yes. Very hard.

PEG

I am.

CORKY

No, I can tell by your eyes you're not.

PEG

I'm frightened is why —

CORKY

— nothing to be afraid of —

CUT TO

PEG'S *EYES.*

PEG

But if it goes bad —

CUT TO

CORKY'S *EYES.*

CORKY

— I'm calm. It won't go bad — not if two people want something as much as we want this —

CUT TO

PEG. CLOSE UP. *Staring.*

CUT TO

CORKY. CLOSE UP. *God knows what he's thinking but his eyes are boring in on her relentlessly and*

CUT TO

PEG, *suddenly damn near shocked out of her skin as her cat brushes her legs and as she yells —*

CUT TO

CORKY, *unruffled, still staring at her —*

CORKY

— it doesn't matter — nothing in this world matters except what we're doing, do-you-believe-that?

PEG

I would like . . . to believe that, yes.

CUT TO

CORKY'S EYES.

CORKY

. . . there must be nothing in your mind but your card . . . nothing in your mind but what . . . ?

CUT TO

PEG'S EYES.

PEG

. . . my card . . .

CUT TO

CORKY'S EYES. *Dead silence now.*

CUT TO

PEG'S EYES. *The silence goes on. They are staring at each other, nothing else exists, not in this or any world and*

CUT TO

CORKY'S EYES. *He's like some great hypnotist from some other time, staring, staring and*

CUT TO

PEG, *clutching her three of clubs, staring as the silence seems about to break around her and*

CUT TO

CORKY, *and suddenly his eyes are filled with tears.*

> **CORKY**
> *(numb)*
> ...is it...?...please...the...three of clubs...

CUT TO

PEG, *managing to nod, turning over her card. She looks like she might cry too. Now —*

CUT TO

CORKY, *sagging back in the chair, closing his eyes.*

> **CORKY**
> ...see...?...see...?...I didn't fail...

CUT TO

PEG. *She sits there, watching him; she is terribly moved. As she slowly gets up, just begins to cross to* CORKY —

FLASHCUT TO

PEG IN SLOW MOTION AND YOUNG, HAIR FLYING, RUNNING TOWARD THE CAMERA AS BE-FORE AND

CUT TO

PEG *in the living room of her house, starting to take a step toward* CORKY *in the chair and*

FLASHCUT TO

PEG IN SLOW MOTION AND YOUNG, GLORIOUS, RUNNING CLOSER AND

CUT TO

PEG *in the living room, another step closer and*

FLASHCUT TO

PEG IN MEMORY, ANOTHER STEP CLOSER AND

Now we cross cut — the girl in the present, the girl from the past, both of them moving closer

and closer and the crosscutting continues until the girl in the past is almost at the camera and at that moment she launches into the most graceful leap and right then —

CUT TO

CORKY AND PEG ROLLING OVER IN BED, THEY'RE IN CORKY'S CABIN BY THE LAKE, NAKED, MAKING LOVE.

The blinds are down, it's dark, even though outside there are still slants of late afternoon sun trying to get through. We are nearing the end of their time now, we see it mostly in shadow and silhouette, and as their bodies rhythmically rise and fall and rise we

CUT TO

FATS, in the next room, listening, listening, and the breathing from the bedroom is getting louder and FATS just sits there and now we start a series of quick cuts, back and forth, from the dark bedroom to the living room and each time we go to CORKY and PEG they are more abandoned, building, and each time we return to FATS it's more of a CLOSE UP *AND MORE AND MORE until when they climax we*

CUT TO

FATS' eyes. Extreme *CLOSE UP. From the angle we're watching it looks like he's thinking. God knows what. HOLD ON FATS. Now —*

CUT TO

THE BED. CORKY and PEG lie in each other's arms. It's the inevitable "later."

> PEG
> I'll bet they don't give service like *that* at Grossinger's.
> *(CORKY says nothing)*
> Drop in again in fifteen years.

> CORKY
> Why the jokes?

> PEG
> I'm kind of feeling my way along, I never fooled around before. *(looks at CORKY)* True. I guess sex wasn't that big a deal in my life.

> CORKY
> What about Duke?

> PEG
> Mainly he blew in my ear a lot.
> *(CORKY can't help laughing)*
> True. I deceived him into thinking it drives me mad. He tongues away at me and I moan a lot but secretly I'm making grocery lists. *(kisses CORKY)* I can be a very crappy lady when I put my mind to it.

> CORKY

I'll take you just like you are.
> *(she rumples his hair)*

Well?

> PEG

Huh?

> CORKY

I meant that about taking you. Will you come or not?

> PEG

What are you talking —

> CORKY

— I'm serious — I got lots of money with me — let's you and me take off.
Just us.

> PEG

I dump Duke and you'd leave Fats, that your offer?

> CORKY

It's not crazy goddamit — you don't care for Duke and you know it —

CUT TO

PEG. *Gently.*

> PEG

— I'm sorry, Baby, but it's just impossible.
> *(CORKY kisses her. As they break —)*

Well, improbable, maybe.
> *(And now he starts to hold her,*
> *stroke her body, kiss her eyes —)*

Unlikely then; let's put it that way ... *(As she holds him —)*

CUT TO

**THE MAIN HOUSE AS THE TWO OF THEM APPROACH. GETTING
DEEPER INTO DUSK.**

> PEG

Thanks for walkin' me home, mister.

> CORKY

Peg?
> *(she studies him)*

Just say the word and we'll go.

                              PEG

A man appears after fifteen years and says "Run away with me," a girl ought
to at least be able to take a bubble bath and think a little.
                        (CORKY *nods*)
After that I'll get dinner started.

CORKY *holds up his index finger, kisses it, then places it gently on each of her nipples.*

                              CORKY

I saw that in a French movie once.

                              PEG

Why the hell were you so shy all those years ago . . .

She goes inside and CORKY *stands still a moment. Then he breaks into a wild jubilant run,
tearing down the hill, veering in and out like a drunken driver, leaping for tree branches
and we've never seen him like this before, never nearly this happy. Now* —

CUT TO

FATS *as* CORKY *steams in.*

                              CORKY

What d'ya say, Sports Fans.
                        (FATS *grunts*)
Getting your period?

                              FATS

Kind of blue is all.
                  (CORKY *grabs a deck of cards,
                     does a dazzling flourish.*)
That don't help.
                  (CORKY *shrugs, drops the cards back.*)
Everybody's passing me by, Laddie, and I'm just sitting here like some lump.
(sighs) I miss the city bad.

                              CORKY

The country grows on you —

                              FATS

— so does fungus —

                              CORKY

— I told you once already we'd leave —

                              FATS

— *when?* —

                              CORKY

— when *I* want to, now drop it —

> FATS

—what's so great here? — *tell me that* —

> CORKY

—simmer down!

CUT TO

FATS, watching CORKY. Little pause. When FATS talks next, things are quiet again, quiet and reasonable.

> FATS

OK. How's this for a solution? You stay around and turn hayseed, I'll head on back to Manhattan where there's action.

CUT TO

CORKY. No reply.

> FATS

I take it the silence means "no"?

> CORKY
> *(shrugs)*

Discussion's over, that's all.

> FATS
> *(suddenly big)*

I — want — out — of — here.

> CORKY
> *(big right back)*

Simmer — the — hell — down!

> FATS
> *(And they're into it now —)*

Just because —

> CORKY

—watch it mister —

> FATS

—just because —

> CORKY

—you been warned —

> FATS
> *(bursting out)*

—just because some sagging bitch of an ingenue drops her pants for you —

CORKY

— that's it! —

FATS
(imitating PEG)
— oh Corky, you do it so good, oh my God, Corky, you're even better than the garbage man —

CUT TO

CORKY, grabbing FATS roughly, and the second he does —

CUT TO

FATS, CLOSE UP. Screaming in sudden surprise as we

CUT TO

THE POSTMAN. He stands mute in the cabin doorway, staring, ashen and pale, and from his old face

CUT TO

CORKY, really pleased to see the old man.

CORKY

How do you like it? — I think it's gonna be terrific —

THE POSTMAN says nothing, just looks at them.

FATS

— what's with Gangrene? — Blue Cross repossess your tongue?

CORKY

Come on in, Ben — I'll do the whole routine — *(stops)* — how the hell did you ever find me, you're amazing —

FATS

— I'll bet it was that kid cab driver — he must have called the office and found you —

CORKY

— is that it? — that's right, I told him I was with William Morris — *(shaking his head)* — he looked like a hustler so I gave him a hundred to shut him up — how much did you give him to talk?

POSTMAN

Doesn't matter.

CORKY

Right, right, you're here, that's the main thing, so grab yourself a seat and

watch, but remember I haven't got this anywhere near performance level
yet —

> **POSTMAN**
> *(cutting in)*
> — how long you been like this, kid?

> **CORKY**
> Like what? *(starts laughing)* Omigod, you don't think that was for real, how
> do you think I rehearse?

> **POSTMAN**
> No good.

> **CORKY**
> It's for the *act* — for chrissakes, watch now — *(to an imaginary audience)* —
> Ladies and Gentlemen, for your viewing pleasure, my version of The
> Miser's Dream —

> **FATS**
> — was it a wet dream? —

> **CORKY**
> — shut up — *(to the audience again)* — imagine if you will —

> **FATS**
> *(cutting in on cue)*
> — when I have a wet dream, all that happens is I wake up covered with saw-
> dust.

> **CORKY**
> If you don't stop interrupting, I'm going to put out a contract on you with
> a Mafia woodpecker —

> **FATS**
> *(sighing)*
> — what I wouldn't give for a wood pecker —

> **CORKY**
> *(to the audience)*
> — don't encourage him, ladies and gentlemen. *(now he looks at* THE POST-
> MAN*)* Merely great beginning, wouldn't you say?

> **POSTMAN**
> *(soft)*
> Is this why you wouldn't take the medical exam? Figured someone would
> find out?

> **CORKY**
>
> Bullshit, I'll take the stupid exam, I was afraid of success, like you said, I needed to get my head on straight. I'll take the exam, do the show, whatever you want.

> **POSTMAN**
>
> What I want, kid, is for you to see somebody.

> **CORKY**
> *(beat)*
>
> Who ... who would I see?

> **POSTMAN**
> *(big)*
>
> *Quit with the games.*

> **FATS**
> *(bigger)*
>
> *Quit with the yelling!*

> **CORKY**
>
> Shut up.

> **FATS**
>
> He should show a little gratifuckingtude — you been slaving, coming up with great new stuff— *(to THE POSTMAN)* — that was blockbuster material, mister — when I come back with wanting a wood pecker, they'll *plotz* in Vegas, that's *funny.*

> **POSTMAN**
>
> Nothing's funny. Not any more. *(And he starts for the door.)*

> **CORKY**
>
> What're you gonna do?

> **POSTMAN**
>
> Make a few phone calls.

> **CORKY**
>
> Tell people, you mean?

> **POSTMAN**
>
> *Corky, you're not in control.*

CUT TO

CORKY. He just stares across the quiet cabin. Then —

> **CORKY**
>
> Ben? You owe me a listen, don't you think?

CUT TO

THE POSTMAN. *He stops, nods.* CORKY *gestures toward the single sofa.* THE POSTMAN *moves to it, sits, as* CORKY *starts talking.*

> **CORKY**
> I *was* kind of out of control — nothing loony tunes or like that, but back in the city, I could feel myself starting to slip down the iceberg.

> **POSTMAN**
> So you took off.
> *(CORKY nods)*
> And now you're fine?

> **CORKY**
> *(nods again, quietly)*
> On account of Peg.

> **FATS**
> She's the local town pump, terrific knockers —

> **CORKY**
> — shut up. *(back to* THE POSTMAN*)* I've known her since high school. I never figured I'd have a chance with her, only now everything's changed, she *believes* in me, and if you went around telling lies, if she stopped believing… *(there is a pause)* … I don't think I'd like that.

> **POSTMAN**
> Girls are for down the line, kid, right now, you've gotta let me help, I know a lot of people, great doctors —

> **FATS**
> — he means headshrinkers —

> **CORKY**
> — shut *up* —

> **FATS**
> — he thinks you're a fruitcake —

> **CORKY**
> — he doesn't — he never said that — he's on our side —

CUT TO

FATS. *Big.*

> **FATS**
> — he's the fucking villain, don't forget that — *never forget that* —

CUT TO

THE POSTMAN, *looking at them.*

> **POSTMAN**
> —kid, you're not, as we sit here, responsible and I can prove it.

> **CORKY**
> How?

> **POSTMAN**
> Easy. I'll ask you to do a little something—something anyone ought to be able to do—and if you do it, we'll forget the whole thing, and if you can't, we'll think about getting you to see somebody fast, is it a deal?

> **CORKY**
> *(smiles)*
> Name it.

> **POSTMAN**
> *(there is a pause; then—)*
> Make Fats shut up for five minutes.

CUT TO

CORKY, *starting to laugh.*

> **CORKY**
> Five *minutes?* I can make him shut up for five years.

> **POSTMAN**
> Wonderful. *(He points to the chair across from him.)*

> **CORKY**
> *(smiling as he sits)*
> I feel like the village idiot if you want to know the truth.

CUT TO

THE POSTMAN. *He says nothing.*

CUT TO

CORKY, *watching him.*

> **CORKY**
> Can *we* talk, or has it gotta be strictly semaphore.
> *(THE POSTMAN shrugs.)*

CUT TO

THE POSTMAN. *He reaches into his inside coat pocket, brings out an Individuale. Carefully, he bites off the end, lights it, blows smoke.*

CUT TO

CORKY, *still with half smile.*

> **CORKY**
>
> How long so far?

> **POSTMAN**
> *(checking his watch)*
>
> Thirty seconds.

> **CORKY**
>
> Gosh — that leaves four and a half minutes to go, think I'll make it?
> *(THE POSTMAN inhales deeply, blows smoke.)*
> You don't happen to have another of those.
> *(THE POSTMAN reaches into his
> coat pocket, hands a cigar to CORKY.)*
> Take two, they're big — remember when you said that?

> **POSTMAN**
>
> A pro never forgets his good lines, kid.

> **CORKY**
>
> How long now?

> **POSTMAN**
> *(looks at his watch again)*
>
> Coming up to a minute.

CUT TO

CORKY. *He nods, concentrates in the silence on the cigar. He sticks it in his mouth, gets it lit. Then —*

> **CORKY**
> *(looking dead at THE POSTMAN)*
>
> Think we'll laugh about this someday?

> **POSTMAN**
>
> Might.
> *(CORKY nods, drums his
> fingers on the chair arm.)*

> **CORKY**
>
> It'd be a terrific scene if you ever write your autobiography — *(excited suddenly)* — hey, I know what you should call it: *Failing Upwards, or How to*

Succeed in Show Business by Outliving Everybody.
                    (THE POSTMAN *makes a smile*)
Two minutes yet?

                    POSTMAN
                    (*head shake*)
Minute forty-five.

CUT TO

CORKY. *He leans back, closes his eyes.*

CUT TO

THE POSTMAN. *He sits, impassive, staring, smoking his cigar. He reaches over for an ashtray, flicks his ashes neatly. The silence is the longest so far.*

CUT TO

CORKY. *Eyes still closed, he starts talking.*

                    CORKY
This is very cruel of you, you know that.

CUT TO

THE POSTMAN, *looking at* CORKY. *Quietly* —

                    POSTMAN
I don't mean it to be.

                    CORKY
                    (*eyes open now*)
I don't know if I'll ever be able to forgive you.

                    POSTMAN
That would be sad.

                    CORKY
Time?

                    POSTMAN
                    (*glances at his watch*)
Two and a half minutes to go.

CUT TO

CORKY. *Long pause. Then, almost imperceptibly, his head begins to shake.*

                    CORKY
... I can't make it ...

CUT TO

THE POSTMAN. *Answering back just as softly.*

> **POSTMAN**
> ...I didn't think you could...
>> *(And on that—)*

ZOOM TO

FATS. <u>HUGE</u> CLOSE UP. *Belting it out—*

> **FATS**
> Hello, everybody, this is Mrs. Norman Maine—my mother thanks you, my father thanks you, my sister thanks you and I thank you—you have nothing to fear but fear itself, nothing to give but blood, sweat, and tears, nothing to lose but your chains— *(building)*—here he is, boys— *(louder)* —here he is, world— *(roaring)*—here's *Fats*!

CUT TO

THE POSTMAN, *standing slowly as* CORKY *watches.*

> **FATS**
>> *(looking up at* CORKY*)*
> You're not letting him out of here?

> **CORKY**
> I think you better sit down.

> **POSTMAN**
>> *(slowly for the door now)*
> Kid, I lived through Tallulah Bankhead and the death of vaudeville, I don't scare easy.

> **CORKY**
>> *(rising)*
> I need my *chance*—

> **POSTMAN**
> —your only chance is to get help fast and that's what I'm gonna see happens— *(And he's almost to the door as we—)*

CUT TO

CORKY, *running at the old man, grabbing him, trying to spin him around but* THE POSTMAN *twists free and then for the first time, he's yelling—*

> **POSTMAN**
> —don't—you—ever—raise—a—hand—to—me—*again!* (His anger is almost biblical now.)

> **CORKY**
>
> You're taking my one chance —

> **POSTMAN**
>
> — *I'm* your one chance. *(And he's moving slowly out the door and gone.)*

CUT TO

CORKY, staring for a moment at the departing figure disappearing in the heavy dusk — then he turns, begins to pace the cabin —

> **FATS**
>
> He's right — the Postman's right, you are crazy.

> **CORKY**
>
> I tried to stop him, didn't I?

> **FATS**
>
> Tried? — *tried?* — you *failed.*
>> *(CORKY continues his frantic pacing.)*
> Goddamit, look at me!
>> *(CORKY stops, stares.)*
> You know it's the hatch for you.

> **CORKY**
>
> But there's nothing wrong with me —

> **FATS**
>
> — I know that and you know that, but all those pissant drones who run the world, they hate us because we're special — they'll put you somewhere deep and lonely —

> **CORKY**
>
> — don't . . . *(And for an instant, his left eye starts blinking.)* . . . talk that way —

> **FATS**
>
> — cut the migraine shit, schmucko —
>> *(CORKY's hands start massaging his temples.)*
> — don't you care about anything? — Christ, don't you even care about the girl? —

> **CORKY**
>
> — Peg? — I love Peg —

> **FATS**
>
> — I hope she loves you too — so on visiting day she can bring crayolas and the two of you can color together —
>> *(And on that —)*

CUT TO

Fats and Corky, and it's gone fast up til now but that's slow compared to this next and it builds in pace and volume —

CORKY

—what do you *want* from me?—

FATS

—you know goddam well what—

CORKY

—I don't—

FATS

—liar—

CORKY

—tell me—

FATS

—weakling—

CORKY

—I'm not, I'm not—

FATS

—stop The Postman —

CORKY

—I can't—

FATS

—gutless fuck—

CORKY

—I can't —

FATS

—stop the Postman!—

CORKY

—how?—how?—with what?—

FATS
—MEE—MEE—MEE—MEE—MEEEEE!
(And now suddenly—)

CUT TO

THE POSTMAN, CLOSE UP

as the first blow stuns him and he does a half turn, grunts, blinks in the twilight as we

CUT TO

FATS, *being swung through the air again,* CORKY *holding tight to his feet so that he's like an ax flying, and we're in the woods, not far above the lit cabin and*

CUT TO

THE POSTMAN *as the second blow lands, and his hands were raised to ward off the attack but* FATS *breaks through and as he smashes home, there is that hollow sound of wood against skull and* THE POSTMAN *starts to stagger now as we*

CUT TO

FATS, *flying through the air and this time as he hits he gives a cry of pain —* <u>ANHHH</u> — *as if he were the one in anguish, not the old man and*

CUT TO

THE POSTMAN, *slipping to his knees, blood coming from his nose now, and*

CUT TO

FATS, *attacking again, and again there is the hollow sound as he strikes home, and right after,* FATS' *answering cry of pain, and now* THE POSTMAN *is crawling, or trying to, but* FATS *is relentless, again he strikes, again and*

CUT TO

PEG'S CAT, *moving through the woods. There is a hollow sound. The cat stops. Another hollow sound. The cat looks. Pause. Finally, one last time there is the hollow sound. Silence in the woods then. Except for the awareness now of heavy breathing, of someone having been through a terrible exertion. And as that breathing continues and the* CAT *moves off —*

CUT TO

CORKY. DRAINED. *He leans against a tree, the body of* THE POSTMAN *visible behind him.* CORKY *is panting. There is blood on his shirt. And as a sudden look of surprise hits his face —*

CUT TO

THE HOUSE UP ON THE HILL *and* PEG *in the front doorway.*

CUT TO

CORKY, *staring up at her, wild now, glancing around at the body, back toward* PEG, *then back to the body again as we*

CUT TO

PEG, *moving away from the house — a long distance off but obviously on her way down and*

CUT TO

CORKY, *trying to control his breathing, suddenly shouting out —*

CORKY

— what is it? — what's up? —

CUT TO

PEG, *stopping, staring down. From her position, he is hard to see.*

PEG

Oh. I meant to ask, did you want me to unthaw the asparagus tips or the french cut green beans?

CUT TO

CORKY; *he blinks at the question. From behind him now, there is the beginning of moaning.*

CORKY

Either.

PEG
(moving down again)

No fair — you're the man, you've got to make the decisions —

CORKY

— Asparagus tips —

PEG
(stops)

— and do you like your steak rare?

CORKY

Any way you — *(stops)* — yes — rare —

(The moaning sound is louder
now in the following silence.)

PEG

— hey? How come you're in the woods?

CORKY

Walking. Thinking.

PEG

About me? You changing your mind about me?

CORKY

Jesus, no —

PEG

— you better not, you bastard — *(She half waves, half smiles, turns and as she moves back to the house —)*

CUT TO

A PAN SHOT OF THE WOODS AS THE MOANING SOUND INCREASES. *Now we pass the body of* THE POSTMAN, *still as before, face down. The sound of pain clearly doesn't come from him and as the* CAMERA *moves on —*

> FATS' VOICE (over)
>
> ... Laddie ... Laddie ...

> CORKY (over)
>
> What ... ?

> FATS
>
> ... my head ... you broke it ...

And now the CAMERA *is on* FATS *who lies sprawled out, eyes wide, and what he says is true: his skull is starting to splinter. Now —*

CUT TO

CORKY, *kneeling beside* FATS *who continues to moan in deep anguish.*

> CORKY
>
> What'll I do ... ?

> FATS
>
> ... can't think ... help me ...

> CORKY
>
> I will, don't you worry, I'll take care ... (*And as he reaches down, starts to lift* FATS —)

CUT TO

FATS, CLOSE UP, *and the instant that* CORKY *starts to move him, a terrible cry of pain bursts out and on that —*

CUT TO

FATS' SUITCASE LYING OPEN ON THE COUCH.

We're back in the cabin and the suitcase is filled with tape and all kinds of hats and shoes and changes of clothes and we

PULL BACK TO REVEAL

CORKY, *winding tight shoe lace-like pieces of tape around* FATS' *skull. As he pulls it tight, making* FATS *look all right again —*

> CORKY
>
> This should do it — (*one final adjustment*) — better?

FATS

I guess. *(beat)* Does it show?

CORKY
*(getting a wig out of the case — FATS
is bald at the moment, the old
wig, bloody, is lying on the floor)*
I'll put this on and slip you into your overall outfit with the cap — no
one'll be able to tell a thing.

CUT TO

*FATS, as CORKY adjusts the new wig, pulls the cap down tight, next sets to work changing
FATS' clothes. During this —*

CORKY
I've been doing some thinking — What would you say if I called the police and told?

FATS

Get serious —

CORKY

— he's *dead* —

FATS

— he was giving senility a bad name — he wouldda died next week, next
year at the outside — all you did was edge God out a little, nothing wrong
with that.

CORKY

I still say —

FATS
(cutting him off)
— you're not being logical, look — Gangrene was taken care of because
he was going to have you put away and if you tell the cops *they'll* have you
put away —

CUT TO

CORKY, working quickly. FATS is starting to look terrific again.

CORKY
— but what would we do with him?

FATS
Go bring me any identification from Gangrene — everything in his pockets.

CORKY

Why?

FATS

Time for a little dip—get yourself some stones, put them in his pockets—

CORKY
(stops working on FATS, shakes his head)

—I'm not that strong a swimmer.

FATS

Just dog paddle out to the middle and drop him down—

CORKY

—I know this lake—there's snapping turtles out there, everybody said that, and once there was a water moccasin scare—

FATS

—I don't much care if the Loch Ness Monster's out there and *ravenous*—

And now, in the distance, the sound of PEG's voice going "Corkeeee"...

CUT TO

The window that faces up the house. PEG is visible, back lit, standing in the doorway.

CORKY goes to the window, calls out.

CORKY

Yes?

PEG
(barely audible)

...steak's going in...

CORKY

Yes.

PEG

...see ya when ya get here... *(As she closes the door—)*

CUT TO

FATS, staring.

CUT TO

CORKY, hesitating, crossing the cabin, staring out at the water in the early evening moonlight.

FATS
(soft)

...do it beautifully...

(And on that —)

CUT TO

THE SHORE OF LAKE MELODY. NIGHT.

We're not far from the cabin. HOLD. *Sounds from the wood nearby. Now a bird sound. Then wind. It's cold. The water looks uninviting. And now without any warning or noise, a large turtle moves into view. God knows if it's a snapper or not but you don't want to mess with the thing as it plods toward the water, starts to swim out, disappears, and once it's gone—*

CUT TO

THE CABIN WINDOW THAT FACES THE WATER. FATS has been propped up so that he's looking out. He sits there, motionless, eyes wide as we

CUT TO

THE SHORE AGAIN and CORKY dragging THE POSTMAN down toward the chill water. He's in his shorts and he holds THE POSTMAN under both arms. As he gets closer to the water, the ground gets wetter, and his feet sink slightly into the shore as he pulls them out, there is a suction sound.

CORKY is cold already, his body covered with goosebumps, and he is not relishing what he's doing. At the water's edge he changes his grip slightly he's beginning now to shiver. He glances far up the hill toward the main house and

FLASHCUT TO

PEG, AS CORKY REACHES OUT, QUICKLY TOUCHES HER NIPPLES AND

FLASHCUT TO

PEG, STOKING THE FIRE IN THE LIVING ROOM, SMILING AT HIM AND

FLASHCUT TO

PEG, HER ARMS AROUND HIM AS THEY MOVE TOGETHER IN BED AND

FLASHCUT TO

PEG, CLOSE UP. SMILING, REACHING OUT, GENTLY TOUCHING HIS FACE AND IN HER EYES YOU CAN SEE IT — SHE CARES. NOW —

CUT TO

CORKY, gathering courage by the water's edge and

CUT TO

FATS in the window, watching. Eyes wide.

CUT TO

CORKY and the OLD MAN, as he glances one last time up toward where PEG is. Then, a quick deep breath and he begins backing into the water. The lake stays shallow for a while and CORKY continues moving through the chill water quickly, THE POSTMAN less of a burden now that the lake is taking most of the old man's weight, and when it's chest high, CORKY shifts grips, releases the old man's armpits, goes into a lifesaving position, his left arm around THE POSTMAN's chest, and when that's secure, CORKY pushes off, sidestroking out into deeper water and as he does

CUT TO

The lake, the surface dark, not easy to see, even with the moonlight and

CUT TO

CORKY, very cold now, swimming along, and

CUT TO

FATS in his window from CORKY's point of view, starting to get smaller as CORKY continues his journey and

CUT TO

SOMETHING on the lake surface near CORKY, and it looks like a stick, it must be a stick, except now it goes down under the water and there's a small ripple where it used to be and maybe it was the mouth and face of a snapper, maybe not, we don't really see enough to know for sure as we

CUT TO

CORKY, beginning to labor now, swimming on, frightened, keeping at it, cold, keeping at it, and

CUT TO

THE FACE OF THE POSTMAN, being carried through the deepening lake and

CUT TO

CORKY, swimming slower, breathing more heavily and as he glances in toward shore

CUT TO

THE CABIN and FATS and we're a good ways off now, forty yards, more maybe and

CUT TO

CORKY, swimming again, teeth chattering, both from fear and freezing and he takes an-

other stroke, another and as a sound of something else in the water makes him give a lit-
tle cry as he spins around

CUT TO

A WIDENING RIPPLE—*maybe a fish jumped, we don't linger long enough to see as we*

CUT TO

CORKY, *really getting frightened now, it's all over his face, the fear and from that—*

CUT TO

—THE POSTMAN, *as slowly his eyes start to open.*

CUT TO

CORKY, *swimming alone, laboring badly, and* THE POSTMAN's *face is away from him so*
he doesn't know and as he takes another stroke—

CUT TO

THE POSTMAN, CLOSE UP, *blinking slowly and*

CUT TO

CORKY, *swimming and*

CUT TO

THE POSTMAN *starting to raise his hands and*

CUT TO

CORKY, *watching as the hands move out of the water, the body begins to turn and as he screams*

CUT TO

THE LONG BONY FINGERS OF THE POSTMAN *as they clutch at* CORKY's *throat, dig into his*
flesh and

CUT TO

CORKY *and* THE POSTMAN *and* CORKY *tries to break the old man's grip but the fingers*
are digging deeper and tighter into his neck and as they flail and sink

CUT TO

FATS *watching from the window, and he almost seems to be leaning forward more against*
the screen, trying to see across the lake's surface until we

CUT TO

THE LAKE as CORKY and THE POSTMAN burst out and CORKY gasps, tries for air, but THE POSTMAN will not let go no matter how much CORKY pounds and pounds and as they start to sink a final time —

FLASHCUT TO

A WHOLE SERIES OF WHAT YOU MIGHT CALL "DROWNING MAN" IMAGES — JUMBLED AND INCOHERENT, WITHOUT ORDER, AND THEY COME FAST, REALLY LIKE BLINKS, AS WE SEE PEG AND THE RICH BITCH WOMAN LAUGHING AT THE CLUB AND CORKY FROZEN OUTSIDE THE FOUR SEASONS, AFRAID TO GO IN AND CORKY IN HIS NEW YORK HOTEL ROOM, SLAMMING DOWN THE PHONE AND CORKY PACKING, THROWING THE CLOTHES WILDLY INTO HIS SUITCASE AND HIS FATHER IS THROWING A FOOTBALL AND HIS MOTHER IS UNABLE TO WALK STEADILY AND HIS BROTHER IS BEING BURIED AND

CUT TO

THE SURFACE OF THE LAKE. The water is rippling. But no one is in sight. HOLD as the ripples widen in the night. KEEP HOLDING. Yellow moonlight butters the water. It's really lovely . . . Now —

CUT TO

BRIGHT MORNING SUNSHINE

AND PEG standing a little distance above CORKY's cabin. Her back is to the main house up the hill.

> **PEG**
> Water's on to boil for your instant.

CUT TO

CORKY, yawning, coming out the doorway, looking up at her, but before he can say a word —

> **PEG**
> Careful. *(beat)* Duke got home late last night — way after dinner — he didn't much like the notion of me being here alone with a man. He's watching us.

CUT TO

THE MAIN HOUSE from CORKY's point of view. The first floor living room window more precisely. It's hard to tell for sure, but maybe someone's standing staring out, motionless.

CUT TO

CORKY and PEG

> **CORKY**
> You think it's smart for me to come up there?

                                           PEG
I think he wants to watch us together.

                                          CORKY
Give me five minutes. *(he turns to the cabin, stops, turns back to* PEG*)* Has he
got a telescope?
                          *(*PEG *looks at him, confused)*
Because if he doesn't I'd like to say that going to bed with you was maybe
the three best things that ever happened to me and I'd love some instant,
and I adore you, and I take it with cream and sugar, and your breasts belong in the Louvre which is a museum in Paris that I plan on visiting with
you once you get wise and decide to leave the old ear-blower.

CUT TO

PEG, *looking down at* CORKY, *not the least unhappy.*

                                           PEG
Are you ever something.

                                          FATS
                           (his voice from the cabin)
He means Parris Island where the marines take basic training, not Paris,
France —

                                          CORKY
                             (as PEG *smiles —)*
Don't encourage him . . .
                              (And now —)

CUT TO

DUKE, SIPPING COFFEE AT THE SMALL KITCHEN TABLE,

*and he doesn't look like Presley, not any more. He's balding and has a paunch and bags un-
der the eyes from too much boozing. He still seems powerful, an ex-jock gone badly to seed.
As he glances up —*

PULL BACK TO REVEAL

PEG *at the stove as* FATS *and* CORKY *enter.*

                                          CORKY
                               (excited)
My God, Duke, how are you?

                                          DUKE
                             (as they shake)
Doin' OK.

                              PEG
You take your coffee —
                    (DUKE watches her — with only a brief beat)
—how?

                             CORKY
                    (sitting across from DUKE)
Everything.

                             DUKE
Sorry I wasn't here to greet you, help with the entertaining and all.
                    (On the word "entertaining" he glances
                    at PEG who is readying CORKY's coffee.
                    Sexual tension is clearly in the room.)
But somebody's got to earn a living.

                             CORKY
You're still in real estate, right?

                             DUKE
Gave that up. Dull. What I really love is the out of doors, fishing, hunting; *that* probably seems dull to someone like you.

                             CORKY
No, not at all —
                    (as PEG puts down his coffee)
— perfect.

                             DUKE
Doing a little selling nowadays — sundries, like that. Surprised Peg here
didn't bring you up to date.

                             CORKY
She may have — the truth is, once I start drinking wine, you can forget
about me.

CUT TO

FATS, starting to talk.

                             FATS
Corky can get drunk on water —
                    (DUKE looks at FATS)
— 'course he can also get drunk on land.

                             CORKY
You can do better than that.

FATS

What's the point? — you're too stupid to understand the punch lines.

CORKY

That's not true.

FATS

Not true? You were eleven before you could learn to wave goodbye. In a battle of wits, you're unarmed. *(whispers to DUKE)* The only way Corky'll be able to broaden his mind is to put it under a train.

CUT TO

DUKE, *intrigued, studying* FATS, *then looking at* CORKY.

DUKE

Clever. It really is.

FATS
(hurt)

Don't tell him that, tell me that, *I'm* the talent.

DUKE

My mistake.

FATS

Listen, that stuff you sell? — you don't happen to have a penis do you, my last one caught Dutch Elm disease, it's murder getting an erection.
(And on that —)

CUT TO

DUKE, *really starting to laugh and*

CUT TO

CORKY, *clamping his hand over* FATS' *mouth, but* FATS *starts going "mmmm mmmm mmm."*

CORKY
(during this — to DUKE)

You travel a lot in your work?

DUKE
(shaking his head)

My God, how do you do that? It's terrific, I'm really glad you're here for me to see.

CORKY

Thank you. *(looks down at FATS who is still going "mmmm")* Will you be good now?

> *(FATS nods "yes")*

I mean it, promise?

> *(FATS' head bobs up and down, "yes, yes, yes")*

FATS
*(to CORKY, softly, as
CORKY takes his hand away)*

Ask him if he's glad I'm here too.

CUT TO

DUKE. *He's got a decent smile. Now he nods.*

DUKE

The both of you.

> *(HOLD on DUKE a moment, then —)*

CUT TO

PEG *in the kitchen doorway as* DUKE, *lumberjack shirt on now, leaves.*

PEG

How long you gonna be?

DUKE

As long as it takes to board up the far cabins.

CUT TO

CORKY *and* FATS *at the table;* CORKY *is finishing his coffee, blowing on it, watching the steam rise.*

PEG
(as she holds the door half open)

Don't get all overheated and catch cold now. *(She closes the door.)*

CORKY
(staring at the steam)

How'd I do?

PEG
(staring after DUKE)

Just unbelievable.

FATS
(miffed)

Too bad Fats wasn't here — he might have been a little help, gotten a few laughs —

> PEG
> *(looking at FATS)*

—you're *always* unbelievable.

> FATS
> *(whispering to CORKY)*

Brains as well as boobs.

PEG smiles, glances out the back door, crosses to the table, sits. She looks at CORKY, slides her lovely hand into his palm. It's a quiet moment, gentle, relaxed. The tension that began the scene has ended. HOLD ON PEG and CORKY. Then—

CUT TO

DUKE, SEEN THROUGH LEAVES, WALKING ALONG.

He holds a hammer and a tool box. As he walks along

PULL BACK TO REVEAL

THE WINGED VICTORY. No, that isn't a typo, and this isn't the statue in France. It's small and metal and it's a very famous emblem and now

PULL BACK A LITTLE FARTHER TO REVEAL

A WHITE CORNICHE. It stands stuck in mud in a rutty path that leads down the back of the property to the lake.

DUKE is still walking as before. He hasn't seen the car yet, he's going at right angles to it—

—only now he does see it and he just stops dead. For an instant, he stands there. Then slowly he moves toward the machine. When he reaches it he looks at it, touches the Winged Victory on the hood with the tip of his finger.

Now he moves around to the driver's door, opens it, closes it, stands there, confused.

Then he takes off for the house as we

CUT TO

CORKY, carrying a few pieces of firewood to his cabin. He stops as DUKE calls to him from up the hill, PEG stands in the background.

> DUKE

You drive a Rolls?

> CORKY
> *(half smile)*

Don't I wish. *(Clutching the wood tighter, he strolls on again.)*

> DUKE

Well, it's somebody's white Rolls parked out there—

CORKY
(stops again)

—was it a Corniche?

DUKE

A what?—

CORKY

—did the top come down?
(DUKE *nods;* CORKY *throws the wood*
aside, starts to run as we)

CUT TO

THE CORNICHE *stuck in the mud as* CORKY *and* DUKE *circle it,* PEG *watching them both.*

CORKY

That's gotta be Gangrene's—*(shaking his head)*—why would he leave it though?

DUKE

Whose is it?

CORKY

My agent's—*(glances through the window)*—keys in and everything—he's rich as hell, but still, you just don't leave an 80 thousand dollar car and walk away. *(puzzling it out)* He must have come looking for me.

DUKE

Looking for you?

CUT TO

CORKY; *he hesitates, studying* DUKE.

CORKY

If I level with you will you not nose it around?
(DUKE *nods)*
I'm in hiding; I've got a lot of career problems and I haven't been behaving all that normal.

DUKE

Can you find out what's happened?

CORKY
(nods)

I can sure as hell try.
(As they all three start away,
CORKY *turns to* DUKE.)
Would you mind trying to get it unstuck?

CUT TO

DUKE, *smiling.*

> **DUKE**
> Me driving an 80 thousand dollar car? I'd mind that a lot. *(And as he turns back —)*

CUT TO

CORKY. CLOSE UP. ON THE LIVING ROOM PHONE.

> **CORKY**
> *(into receiver)*
> Sadie? It's me, is he in? *(little beat)* Thanks.

CUT TO

PEG, *in the kitchen doorway, watching.*

> **CORKY**
> *(covering the phone, talking soft to her)*
> Could I have maybe two minutes worth of privacy? This may get kind of raunchy.

PEG *nods, moves out of* CORKY's *view into the kitchen. But not so far as to be out of earshot, because when he starts talking, she hesitates, then stops, quietly listening.*

CUT TO

CORKY. *CLOSE UP.*

> **CORKY**
> *(into phone)*
> Don't yell at me, goddamit— *(pause, softer)* —of course I appreciate that you're worried about me, but— *(pause, louder suddenly)* —I'm sick of hearing about my erratic behavior, mister, at least I'm not senile, at least I'm not leaving my car in the woods— *(quick beat)* —huh?— *(shaking his head)* —boy, am I smart—here I call up to find how *you* are and I end up telling where *I* am. How'd you ever find me? *(beat)* And I *schtupped* that bastard cabbie a hundred bucks not to tell. *(beat)* You came up and parked and then what, snuck around like an old pervert? *(beat)* We were on a long walk is why you didn't find anybody— *(quickly)* —never mind who "we" is, finish about the car.

PEG. *Listening.* CORKY *is starting to laugh now.*

> **CORKY** (over)
> I'd love to have seen that, a rich old fart like you trying to hitchhike a ride to Grossinger's. When you got there, why didn't you have them come unstick your car?

CUT TO

CORKY, *CLOSE UP.*

> **CORKY**
> *(holding the phone away
> from his ear a moment)*
> Quit yelling, all right, all right, nobody touches your Rolls but a Rolls man,
> forgive me. One sec'. *(covers receiver)* Peg—

CUT TO

PEG, *hurrying to the doorway.*

> **PEG**
> Huh?

> **CORKY**
> Quick go tell Duke to leave the car just where it was.

PEG *nods, turns and we*

CUT TO

THE BACK DOOR *as she approaches, starts out, stops as we*

CUT TO

DUKE, *walking toward the back door.*

CUT TO

PEG, *hurrying across the kitchen to the living room doorway again. As she does—*

> **CORKY** (over)
> *(his voice laughing again)*
> —so you're paying for *two* Rolls guys to come up and take care of your car?

> **PEG**
> *(gesturing as she whispers to* CORKY*)*
> Duke's already on his way.

CUT TO

CORKY. *He nods, circles his thumb and forefinger.*

> **CORKY**
> *(into the phone)*
> Yessir, that was the "we."

CUT TO

PEG, *listening again, only just behind the doorway now.*

> **CORKY** (over)
> *(whispering now)*
> Yessir, a lot. *(beat — then louder)* It's not ridiculous, I've known her always —

CUT TO

CORKY. CLOSE UP.

> **CORKY**
> — yes, very, but that's not why I love her, I'm not some moonstruck kid —
> *(beat)* — yes, she's married *(interrupting himself)* but it's about to break up
> anyway, I'm no homewrecker, believe me —

CUT TO

PEG. *Listening, she turns as* DUKE *comes in the back door —*

CUT TO

CORKY, *as the sound of the door closing comes to him.*

> **CORKY**
> — and I'm not talking about puppylove, Ben — *(CORKY's eyes are closed now)*
> — the subject is salvation... *(HOLD on CORKY. He is, at this moment, moved.*
> *Now from his face —)*

CUT TO

DUKE.

*He holds a water glass of scotch in one hand, the half empty quart bottle in the other and he's
pacing across the upstairs bedroom. He looks angry, brooding, by now a little drunk.*

PEG *moves from the bathroom, clad in a slip. She opens a closet door, takes out an ironed
skirt, begins dressing.*

> **DUKE**
> Some fish. *(stops by the window, glares down at the lake and CORKY's cabin)*
> Some fish he takes me for. *(glance at PEG)* Your old pal I'm talking about.

> **PEG**
> I suspected.

> **DUKE**
> That story is so fulla holes —

> **PEG**
> — why do you keep repeating that, so a car's here, who cares?

PEG *sits at a small vanity, begins applying a small amount of make up.*

CUT TO

DUKE, *watching her. He finishes his glass, pours some more scotch.*

> **DUKE**
> People just don't leave Rolls' in the woods, goddamit.

> **PEG**
> Corky agrees with you — it's a crazy story but there it is.

> **DUKE**
> Some happy coincidence — guy drives ninety miles and you and Corky *just happen* to be off in the woods while he's snooping. *(whispering)* You put out for him in the woods, did you?

> **PEG**
> I love it when you're drinking —

> **DUKE**
> — well, why didn't you tell me about this goddam legendary walk before?

CUT TO

PEG. *Working on her eyelashes now.*

> **PEG**
> No comment.

> **DUKE**
> Listen to me — I *know* his story's bullshit because I got the car out of the mud and it was nothing — now if I can do it, anybody can —

> **PEG**
> — maybe he tried, maybe he couldn't, he was old —

> **DUKE**
> *(quickly)*
> — Corky never said he was old —

> **PEG**
> — he must have to me —

> **DUKE**
> *(quickly)*
> — when? —

> **PEG**
> — we were having dinner probably —

DUKE
(quickly)
— unh-uh — he got squiffed fast and flaked out, that's what he said earlier —

PEG gets up from the vanity, goes back to the closet, grabs a scarf, as we

CUT TO

DUKE, spinning her around.

DUKE
— how did you know he was old, did you see him? — *(grabbing her now)* — *answer that* —

PEG

— no, I never saw him —

DUKE
— why not, he must have rung the bell — a man drives ninety miles, he's gotta ring the goddam doorbell, wouldn't you agree? —

PEG
— I didn't answer any bell, now quit this!

CUT TO

DUKE, rougher and rougher now.

DUKE
Why not? What were you doing that was so imp — *(And now he stops.)* — did he ring while you were screwing? Is that it? *(bigger)* That is it, isn't it?

PEG

It *isn't* —

DUKE
— why didn't you invite him in to watch? —

PEG

— *shut your dirty mouth* —

DUKE

— did you screw Corky?

PEG

No!

CUT TO

PEG as DUKE hits her in the mouth, backhands her hard and —

                    DUKE
— I'll pound you, you keep lying —

                     PEG
— I'm — not — lying —

CUT TO

DUKE, *as he backhands her again, harder, and there are quick tears of anger in her eyes now and*

CUT TO

PEG, *trying to break loose but he's strong and*

CUT TO

DUKE — *out of control now —*

                    DUKE
— I got all day —

CUT TO

PEG, *as the third blow hits, sends her spinning back into the door and he grabs her again and*

CUT TO

DUKE, *and Jesus, it's like he's enjoying this and again his hand is ready and*

                    DUKE
— the truth — the goddam truth — *(all he's got)* — *did you fuck him?* —

CUT TO

PEG. CLOSE UP. *Screaming —*

                     PEG
No. — *no!* — I didn't — *(beat — then huge)* — BUT I WANTED TO.
                (And on that —)

CUT TO

DUKE. *He blinks, stunned.*

CUT TO

PEG, *ripping her arms free.*

CUT TO

PEG *and* DUKE, *standing close, staring at each other. No sound but their breathing.* HOLD *on their anger. They look like two club fighters who have pounded each other til they're arm weary.* HOLD . . . *Then —*

CUT TO

DUKE. IT'S A LITTLE LATER.

He stands by a rowboat moored in front of CORKY's *cabin. Fishing equipment is already put in.* CORKY *is in the open doorway.*

> DUKE
>
> C'mon, it'll be fun. If you don't like fishing, I'll let you row.
> *(CORKY hesitates)*
> I just had a good talk with Peg, now I'd like one with you.

> CORKY
> *(disappearing inside)*
> I'll grab a jacket. *(his voice now calling)* Where is Peg?

> DUKE
> *(going to the boat)*
> In town. "Making a decision" she said.

CUT TO

CORKY, *a windbreaker on now, exiting the cabin, closing the door.*

> CORKY
>
> You seem upset.

CUT TO

DUKE, *watching* CORKY.

> DUKE
>
> Should I be?
> *(CORKY says nothing, locks the cabin door.)*
> Why you doing that?

> CORKY
> *(shrug)*
> Habit.

> DUKE
>
> I mean, we trust each other, don't we?

> CORKY
> *(to the boat)*
> 'Course.
> *(DUKE gestures for CORKY to get in as we)*

CUT TO

DUKE, *pushing off powerfully and as the boat drifts out into the lake,* DUKE *seats himself in the middle, takes the oars, strokes with evident skill.*

CUT TO

CORKY, *staring at the water. They are going in the direction he took* THE POSTMAN *the night before.*

CUT TO

THE WATER. *You can see a good way down.*

CUT TO

CORKY, *concentrating on the water. Then he looks at* DUKE.

> **CORKY**
> *(brightly)*
> You're the one wants to fish, let's try over there — *(he points in another direction)* — I'll do the rowing.

> **DUKE**
> I know the best holes — when I get us there, you can take over.

CUT TO

THE WATER AGAIN.

CUT TO

DUKE *as* CORKY *nervously stares down at the lake.*

> **DUKE**
> What are you looking for?

> **CORKY**
> *(quickly watching* DUKE*)*
> Nothing at all.

> **DUKE**
> You were sure examining things.

> **CORKY**
> *(shrugs)*
> Pretty.

CUT TO

CORKY, *watching as* DUKE *brings in the oars, reaches for a bottle of scotch, takes a swallow. Then he holds the bottle out to* CORKY.

                              CORKY
        I'm not much of a drinker, told you that.

                              DUKE
        You told me a lot of things. *(another swallow, puts the bottle down)*

                              CORKY
        What's that supposed to mean?

CUT TO

DUKE. CORKY is very tense now. DUKE reaches for his bait casting rod, the plug is already in place. He casts.

CUT TO

THE PLUG landing with a soft splash. We're very close to where THE POSTMAN was taken. Maybe over it.

CUT TO

DUKE, reeling in.

CUT TO

THE BOAT AND THE TWO MEN. The silence is getting hard for CORKY now. DUKE finishes reeling in, casts again.

                              DUKE
        Peggy said you screwed her last night.

                              CORKY
                      (breaks out laughing)
        Damn. And I told her to keep it a secret.

                              DUKE
        Think it's funny, do you?

                              CORKY
        I shouldn't laugh, it was all kinda sweet — I put on my rubber suit and Peg
        got out her whips and chains — it was sort of your standard for-old-times-
        sake-orgy.

DUKE says nothing, just reels slowly in.

                              CORKY
        Is that why —

                              DUKE
        — shit — snagged on something —

CORKY

—is that why you brought me out here? Try and get me to admit to something that never happened? If it is, I'd like to go back in now.

DUKE
(pulling at the rod)

Heavy—

CORKY

—I'd like to go back in now, Duke.

CUT TO

THE PLUG, *as* DUKE *pulls it free, reels quickly in.*

CUT TO

DUKE, *casting again. As he does, quietly*—

DUKE

What she said was she wanted to go to bed with you. *(beat)* I'm losing her, Corky, and I don't know what to do.

CORKY

All she does is talk about you, Duke—you're not losing anybody.

DUKE

When I said before I quit the real estate business? There wasn't any business left to quit.

CORKY

Tomorrow you're gonna regret you talked like this, so let's bag it for now, all right?

DUKE

See, Peg came in when I was on top and she's stuck with me all the way down and— *(big)*—god*damn*it.

CUT TO

THE PLUG. *Or where it would be. But it's underwater now.*

CUT TO

THE BOAT *and* DUKE *trying to get free.*

DUKE

Feels like a whale.

CORKY

I'm cold, let's get the hell in.

> DUKE

I can't get it loose —

CUT TO

THE OARS as CORKY grabs them, tries to row away —

> DUKE

— you're breaking my pole —

> CORKY

— trying to help —

> DUKE

— well don't help, the whole thing's coming now. (*And as he puts the pole down, begins pulling the strong line in hand over hand —*)

CUT TO

CORKY, *frozen and*

CUT TO

THE WATER *and*

CUT TO

DUKE, *pulling and pulling and*

CUT TO

THE WATER *and something's starting to get visible down there, coming closer and closer and*

CUT TO

CORKY, *gripping one oar like a baseball bat and*

CUT TO

DUKE, *leaning over, pulling at whatever the hell is down there and*

CUT TO

THE WATER AND HERE IT COMES AND IT'S BIG *and*

CUT TO

CORKY, *exhaling sharply as the log breaks the surface, and* DUKE *unhooks his plug, drops it back.*

> CORKY
> *(very quietly)*

Any of that scotch left?

> *(DUKE hands it over; CORKY
> takes a huge swallow.)*

> DUKE

Thought you weren't much on booze.

> CORKY

Freezing my nuts off is all.

CUT TO

DUKE, *who nods, takes the bottle back, starts to drink, suddenly stops dead, mouth slack as we*

CUT TO

THE NEAR SHORE AND THE BODY OF THE POSTMAN, *lying motionless, half in and half out of the water . . .*

CUT TO

DUKE, *and as he grabs the oars, starts rowing like hell —*

CUT TO

THE POSTMAN *as* DUKE *and* CORKY *scramble out of the boat, run to him, kneel by the body.*

> CORKY
> *(looking at THE POSTMAN)*

I wonder who he is?

> DUKE

I was thinking it might be your Rolls guy.

> CORKY

You kidding? — Gangrene's only about six foot three — *(indicating a pocket)* — see what his wallet says.

> DUKE
> *(touching THE POSTMAN's trouser pocket)*

Nothing. *(a frisk of other pockets)* Stripped clean.

> CORKY
> *(confused)*

That doesn't make sense — there must be some identification — are you sure there —

CUT TO

DUKE, *interrupting, excited.*

> **DUKE**
> —Jesus Christ, he might be still alive—

CUT TO

CORKY, *excited too.*

> **CORKY**
> —fantastic—

CUT TO

THE POSTMAN *as* DUKE *gestures to* CORKY—

> **DUKE**
> —I'll do the kiss of life—run up to the house—call Normandy Hospital
> —tell them to get over—

> **CORKY**
> *(taking off running like hell from the lake)*
> —right—

> **DUKE**
> *(shouting after* CORKY*)*
> —and stay at the house til they get there so you can direct 'em straight here—

> **CORKY**
> *(shouting back, over his shoulder)*
> —gotcha—

CUT TO

DUKE, *straightening out* THE POSTMAN's *body. He tilts the old man's head back, opens his mouth, reaches in, checks to see that the tongue has not been swallowed. Then he pulls briefly at* THE POSTMAN's *teeth to see that they're not false. Now he hesitates a moment, glances up as we*

CUT TO

CORKY, *flying through the woods, heading for the main house. Now—*

CUT TO

DUKE AGAIN. *He hesitates, then, with his left hand, pinches* THE POSTMAN's *nose shut. Finally he tilts* THE POSTMAN's *head way back to the proper angle, puts his own mouth over the old man's and blows once, very hard.*

No reaction. DUKE *lifts his head, gets another deep breath of air, again puts his mouth over* THE POSTMAN's, *again, blows hard into the other mouth.*

CUT TO

THE POSTMAN. *His chest cavity is starting to swell ever so slightly.*

CUT TO

DUKE, *swallowing air, getting ready for a third try. He does the kiss another time, blowing very hard, pinching* THE POSTMAN'S *nostrils tightly shut as he does so.*

CUT TO

THE POSTMAN, *his chest cavity swelling still more. Now —*

CUT TO

DUKE, *bending now, pressing his ear tight against* THE POSTMAN'S *heart. There are still some clothes in the way so he rips at the shirt, getting it open enough so that he can put his ear directly to the flesh above the heart.*

CUT TO

DUKE. CLOSE UP. *You can see it on his face: nothing, no heartbeat.*

CUT TO

THE POSTMAN *as* DUKE *kneels over him, straddling his body, and now he's done blowing, instead he presses sharply down on the old man's rib cage, damn near hard enough to crack it.*

CUT TO

DUKE, *relaxing the pressure a second, then applying it again, then relaxing it, then pressure again. He sets up a quick rhythm, applying and relieving the pressure maybe close to a dozen times. Now —*

CUT TO

THE POSTMAN, *lying there and*

CUT TO

DUKE, *bending over again, pressing his ear hard into the bare skin above the old man's heart.* DUKE *stays like that a moment.*

Then he shakes his head a little, stares down at the body, closes THE POSTMAN'S *eyes. As he starts to lift the body —*

CUT TO

THE ROWBOAT, *sliding silently in toward shore by* CORKY'S *cabin.* THE POSTMAN *lies sprawled and dead across one seat.* DUKE *gets out, stares at the cabin a moment, then glances at the corpse. He hesitates, then takes a key from his pocket and as he does —*

CUT TO

THE FRONT DOOR OF THE CABIN

as DUKE *hurriedly inserts the master key, unlocks the door, slips inside and as he step from sight —*

CUT TO

THE CABIN. *It's dark, empty, totally silent. The blinds are drawn. Slender stripes of sun slant in here and there.*

CUT TO

DUKE, *closing the door silently. He pockets the key, turns, looks around.*

CUT TO

The cabin. DUKE'S *standing by the door near the living room closet. Beyond the living room is the bedroom, the bath and kitchenette in between and*

CUT TO

DUKE, *starting to take a silent step forward, then suddenly giving a startled cry as we*

CUT TO

FATS, *watching* DUKE. *He's seated on a stool by the kitchenette which has the curtain drawn across it.*

CUT TO

DUKE, *a little flustered by having the dummy scare him. He shakes his head, moves to the desk, starts to open and shut the empty drawers as quietly as he can.*

CUT TO

THE LIVING ROOM CLOSET *as* DUKE *feels around inside, finds nothing of interest. The suitcases are in the back and he takes them out, quickly opens the first and it's* CORKY'S, *empty.* DUKE *opens the second case, looks inside and*

CUT TO

FATS' CASE. *All the stuff we've seen before, tape and canvas strips and changes of clothes and —*

CUT TO

DUKE, *taking out* FATS' *wig. He studies it carefully, touches the hair — there are bits of dried red stuff matted here and there.* DUKE *looks at the wig a moment more. Slowly he puts it back, closes the case.*

CUT TO

THE LIVING ROOM as DUKE glances around it one last time, then heads for the bedroom in the back, passing the narrow area between the kitchenette and bath where FATS still sits, staring as before at the door. As DUKE moves past —

CUT TO

THE BEDROOM as DUKE enters, goes straight to the closet, and as he opens it —

CUT TO

THE CLOSET as DUKE begins a quick search but there's nothing much, a few of CORKY's clothes on hangers, period.

CUT TO

DUKE, the silence broken only by the sound of his footsteps as he crosses from the closet, starts to look at the bedroom dresser.

CUT TO

THE TOP DRAWER as DUKE opens it. Nothing. Underwear and socks and that's it.

CUT TO

THE SECOND DRAWER. Even emptier. A pair of pajamas, a couple of shirts, that's all.

CUT TO

DUKE, frustrated, slamming the second drawer, then quickly glancing around because it made a louder noise than he means. He reaches down for the third drawer and as he does —

CUT TO

DIRTY LAUNDRY. The shirt and stuff we saw CORKY wearing on the cab ride up, all rumpled and stuffed inside.

CUT TO

DUKE hesitates, then, not all that happily, he puts his hand into the dirty laundry and shoves it aside and we

CUT TO

THE DRAWER. A Patek Philippe watch is there. It looks, and is, incredibly expensive.

CUT TO

DUKE, examining the watch. Then he goes back into the drawer, pulls out a wallet, examines it.

CUT TO

A BUNCH OF CREDIT CARDS. *All of them made out to a Ben Greene.*

DUKE
(muttering)

Ben Greene? Greene? *(now he's got it)* Gangrene, son of a bitch — *(And as he takes out some photos from the wallet —)*

CUT TO

THE POSTMAN *with a lot of famous faces: Berle, Sinatra, Jack Benny, George Burns, Bing Crosby.*

CUT TO

DUKE, *staring at all the photos.*

DUKE

It *is* the Rolls guy — *(And as he folds up the wallet —)*

CUT TO

THE BEDROOM *as* DUKE *stuffs the wallet and watch into his pocket, closes the door, starts quickly out and*

CUT TO

FATS *staring into the bedroom as* DUKE *starts to exit — he's still sitting as before in front of the kitchenette curtain but his head has turned around and*

CUT TO

DUKE, *stopping dead in front of* FATS, *staring at the dummy and as the realization hits home —*

CUT TO

DUKE, *starting to scream as we*

CUT TO

FATS *raising his right arm high — he holds a knife and as he slashes out*

CUT TO

DUKE, *frozen, trying to protect himself but too late as we*

CUT TO

FATS, *driving the right hand home, sliding it under* DUKE's *rib cage and as the blood begins*

CUT TO

DUKE, *gasping, half turning, and*

CUT TO

FATS and now his left arm strikes, and it has another knife and it jams in harder and

CUT TO

DUKE, crying out as the right hand knife strikes again and

CUT TO

FATS, and it's like he's beating a bass drum as one arm curves out, then the other, then the first and

CUT TO

DUKE, staggering back against the near wall, just across, starting to slide down and

CUT TO

FATS, and he's relentless, and as DUKE's body sinks FATS keeps on hitting, only now it's higher than the rib cage, now it's the chest and now it's the shoulder and

CUT TO

DUKE as FATS slashes his neck and he's on his knees now, DUKE's trying to crawl away but

CUT TO

FATS AND HE WON'T LET HIM, he's swinging away, right arm, left arm, right arm, left and

CUT TO

DUKE, with the floor swimming in blood and his face is bloody, his mouth is bloody, there's blood in his eyes, he's blind from it and

CUT TO

FATS, arms raised, staring down. He hesitates and we

CUT TO

DUKE. Dead.

FATS, as he drops the knives they skip along the floor.

CUT TO

DUKE. Lying there as we

PULL BACK TO REVEAL

CORKY, CLOSE UP, stunned, staring down at DUKE from the kitchenette area.

CORKY

Jesus, Jesus —

FATS

— don't panic —

CORKY

— what have you done? — (He runs to the door of the cabin, locks it frantically.)

FATS

— I said don't panic! —

CORKY

— what am I gonna do — omigod —

CUT TO

FATS, staring at the door and CORKY —

FATS

— you're gonna listen and — *(interrupting himself — huge) — and—listen —
to — me!*

CUT TO

CORKY, numb, upset, he manages to look at FATS.

CUT TO

FATS.

FATS
(rattling it out)
You're gonna zoom to my suitcase and whip out one of those nice long
pieces of canvas and you're gonna wrap part of it around Duke here and part
around Gangrene and you're gonna get a big rock and wrap the rest around
it and row out and drop the bundle over the side — *(beat)* — and if you do it
right I'll be able to say, "Good going schmucko, two birds with one stone.'

CORKY

Quit with the goddam jokes —

FATS

— and after they're dumped you hustle in here and clean up good and unless you're a bigger nincomfuckingpoop than I think, inside of twenty
minutes you'll be taking a nice hot shower.
(And on that last word —)

CUT TO

THE BATHROOM SHOWER ON FULL BLAST

and CORKY *finishing up.*

He runs the water down on his face a moment more, then turns off the spigots and

CUT TO

A TOWEL *as* CORKY *reaches for it, begins drying himself thoroughly as we*

CUT TO

THE LIVING ROOM OF THE CABIN *as* CORKY, *half dressed now, emerges. He passes the window, glances out, stops and we*

CUT TO

THE ROWBOAT OUTSIDE THE CABIN

Alone and forlorn-looking, PEG *sits in the boat, gently rocking, staring off. It's getting cold now, as late afternoon sets in.* PEG *doesn't seem to notice.*

CUT TO

CORKY, *coming out of the cabin, putting on a sweater.*

> **CORKY**
> You've had quite a day I guess.

> **PEG**
> *(shrugs)*
> Whatever. *(looks at* CORKY*)* Where's Duke?

> **CORKY**
> We had a bad scene — he tried to get me to admit I'd bedded down with you, and when he couldn't, he said he was going hunting and didn't much want me around when he got back.
> *(*PEG *nods)*
> Are *you* going to be around when he gets back?

> **PEG**
> That's what I'm here to tell you.
> *(Gestures for him to sit, he nods,*
> *steps into the rowboat as we)*

CUT TO

PEG. CLOSE UP.

> **PEG**
> I drank enough crummy coffee today in enough rotten luncheonettes to qualify for the Guinness Book of Records —

CUT TO

CORKY, *breaking in.*

CORKY
— who wins — me or Duke? — just tell me that first —

CUT TO

PEG, *looking at him. She reaches out, takes his hand, holds it.*

PEG
— I will, promise, but see, I'm not much good at thinking and I've spent all afternoon trying to learn how, so you're gonna have to bear with me.
(CORKY nods)
OK. Duke never hit me til today and I think — don't laugh — that means he still cares —

CORKY
— if he'd kicked you, would that have meant true love?

PEG
Dammit —
(CORKY signals he's sorry)
— OK. You. God knows *you* care — it's not just that our thoughts touched like with Merlin and his wife when she was dying — that was just icing on the cake. If there's one thing I know, it's that you care. *But what if it stops?*

CORKY
It won't —

PEG
— people change when they get famous — so what if I left and you dumped me and Duke wouldn't take me back — *(big)* — and that was when it hit me.

CORKY
What?

CUT TO PEG.

PEG
So what if you dump me? I'm not *coming* back anyway, there's nothing here for me, not anymore.

CUT TO

CORKY. *Trying to keep control, making sure.*

CORKY
Are you saying —

(she nods)

— my God, you mean I win?

PEG

If I'm a prize, then you're a winner.

CUT TO

PEG, *going into an awkward embrace, eyes closed, holding* CORKY *as tight as she can.*

PEG
(continued)

And as soon as Duke gets home and I explain all this to him in person, we can take off.

CUT TO

CORKY. *A long pause. Then, kind of a sweet smile.*

CORKY

Gee, do you think you ought to put yourself through all that?

PEG

Yeah, I do.

CORKY

You're tired — why let yourself in for a bloodbath?

PEG

Bloodbath?

CORKY
(quickly)

An emotional scene —

PEG

— I got to leave Duke with his pride. He's got to understand *he* didn't fail — *we failed together.*

CUT TO

PEG, *rising now, starting out to shore.* CORKY *precedes her, steadies her.*

PEG

Let's go get packed — he'll be home soon — *(gesturing toward the darkening sky)* — you can't hunt a lot when it's nighttime . . .

CUT TO

CORKY, *as she gives him a quick kiss, starts away.* CORKY *just stands there. Now he half turns, looks not at her but the cabin.* HOLD *on* CORKY.

CUT TO

FATS INSIDE THE CABIN,

watching as CORKY *gets out a suitcase, opens it. He looks at* FATS, *smiles.*

FATS

Omigod — she's leaving Duke for you.

CORKY

On the money.

FATS
(really excited)

Infuckingcredibly fanfucktastic!

CORKY
(little bow)

Thank you, sports fans.

FATS

So where are we off to?

CORKY

Don't get emotional about this —

FATS
(cutting in)

— about what, about what? —

CUT TO

CORKY. CLOSE UP. *There is a pause.*

CORKY

— I think maybe there's just gonna be two of us on the honeymoon.

CUT TO

FATS. *Staring.*

FATS

What's the punch line?
(CORKY *says nothing; continues packing.*)
You don't mean you'd leave me behind even for a little? C'mon Laddie, quit the kidding.

CORKY

My head's on straight now — I want to get to know her, that's all. I want to take her places, show her things, Paris, maybe, like that.

> **FATS**
>
> Schmucko, you never been to Paris yourself, what is this "show her" routine?

CORKY doesn't answer, concentrates on his packing. FATS watches. The silence goes on until finally —

CUT TO

FATS, CLOSE UP, and there's never been such pleading in his voice.

> **FATS**
> (*pleading*)
>
> ...I'll be good...I promise I'll be so good, you'll see...

CUT TO

CORKY. He's terribly upset, keeps on packing.

CUT TO

FATS.

> **FATS**
>
> All I wanna do is tag along.
>   (*CORKY keeps on silently packing*)
> I wanna see Paris too...
>   (*no reply*)
> ...you want me to come crawling, you want me to beg, OK, all right, this is me, Fats, *and I'm begging —*

CUT TO

CORKY, still working, back turned to FATS.

> **CORKY**
>
> — it's not easy for me either —

> **FATS**
> (*big*)
>
> — it is — it is easy — *you won't be alone.*

CORKY concentrates all he has on what he's doing.

CUT TO

FATS, and he stares at CORKY a moment more. Then, in a whisper —

> **FATS**
>
> ...I'll tell...
>   (*And on that, CORKY whirls.*)

CORKY

What'll you tell?

FATS
(still whispering)

...Everything... *(building now)*...I will, I swear...in the middle of the act one night when you don't expect it I'll scream, *"There's bodies in Lake Melody!"*

CORKY
(beat)

I don't see that happening.

FATS

What makes you so sure?

CUT TO

CORKY. CLOSE UP.

CORKY

You're not working with me, not any more. I'm doing a single now...
(HOLD ON CORKY. Then —)

CUT TO

PEG'S SUITCASE. OPEN AND FULL.

PULL BACK TO REVEAL

PEG. *Tense. Taut. She stands in her bedroom a moment until she hears a sound — house creak? door opening? — something. Then she calls out —*

PEG

Duke? *(to the doorway)* That you?

CUT TO

THE STAIRS *by the bedroom door leading down. The place is empty. No more sound. PEG glances at her watch. Almost six. She shakes her head, goes back to the suitcase as we*

CUT TO

THE LAKE. *Darkening. Silent. The water murky and cold.*

CUT TO

CORKY *in his cabin, staring out at the water. He turns, sits, begins doing one handed cuts with the cards.*

CUT TO

FATS. *Watching. The silence is heavy now; just the faint click of the cards is all.*

CUT TO

CORKY, *working with the cards; click, click. His hands are moving as if they had a life of their own.*

CUT TO

PEG'S *VANITY. She is stuffing cosmetics into a traveling bag. The bag is full. She zips it shut, mutters "god<u>damn</u>it," drops the makeup case beside her other packed cases.*

CUT TO

CORKY, *waiting down in the cabin, looking idly as his hands keep moving, faster. He is tenser than before.*

CUT TO

PEG *pouring herself a glass of whisky. Not full or anything, but a decent shot. She pours in some ice cubes, some water, takes a tentative sip. She's tenser than before too. Now she drinks again, a long swallow. She jumps as the grandfather's clock in the corner begins striking.*

CUT TO

OUTSIDE THE MAIN HOUSE *as the clock strikes on. Four. Five. Six. Seven.*

CUT TO

PEG, *finishing her drink. She puts the glass down, picks up the scotch bottle, starts to pour a refill, hesitates. She waits a moment more. The ticking of the clock is audible now. Abruptly, she reaches for another glass and as she pours whisky into them both —*

CUT TO

CORKY IN THE CABIN AND PEG ENTERS WITH TWO DRINKS.

> CORKY
> *(quickly)*
> — how'd it go? Duke understand? —

> PEG
> — we haven't talked yet —

> CORKY
> *(upset)*
> — you mean he isn't back? — Christ, Peg —

> PEG
> — it got kind of scary up there waiting — *(handing the drink over)* — I wanted a drink but I didn't much want to drink alone —

CORKY

—let's get the hell out—send him a goddam telegram later—

PEG

—let's not go through that, my mind's made up—*(drinks)*—besides, he *can't* be much longer—

CORKY

—you don't *know* that—he was drinking heavy when he left here—

PEG

—he take a flashlight with him, did you notice?

CORKY

All I noticed was that huge goddam elephant gun he was carrying when he hinted I vacate the premises—it's stupid waiting around—

PEG

—then I'm stupid—

CORKY
(little louder)
—I didn't say *you* were stupid, I said *waiting* was—

PEG
(little louder still)
—I'm *aware* of your opinion on the subject—

CORKY

—then try agreeing with me for once instead of being stubborn—

PEG
(big)
—*give it a rest, Corky!*

(And on that—)

ZOOM TO

FATS, seated on his suitcase, belting it out—

FATS

"AHHHHHHHHHHH sweet mystery of life at last I've found you." *(imitating Bette Davis)* Fasten your seat belts everybody, it's going to be a bumpy night.

(CORKY gets FATS, brings him over)

PEG
(looking at FATS)
Who were you imitating?

> ### FATS
> That sound you heard was my ego breaking. That was Annette Funicello, my dear.

> ### CORKY
> *(as PEG starts to laugh)*
> Don't encourage him.

> ### FATS
> I'm here to save you two from yourselves— *(to PEG)* Gimme yer palm, keed, I'll read your fortune.
> *(PEG puts her hand in FATS',*
> *raises it so FATS can see better)*
> You've just had your first fight with this drooler you've gotten involved with —

> ### CORKY
> —you've got no talent whatsoever—

> ### FATS
> —let's see you do better—dazzle us with the cards—

> ### CORKY
> —not in the mood.

> ### FATS
> All right, *I'll* do the dazzling.

> ### PEG
> *You* do magic too?

CUT TO

FATS.

> ### FATS
> Corky does magic, I only do tricks— *(excited)*—I know what—get me a couple decks of cards, Peg, and I'll read your mind.

CUT TO

PEG, staring at FATS now.

> ### PEG
> What do you mean?

> ### FATS
> I'll pull the same card from your deck that you've pulled from mine—

> ### PEG
> —that's not a trick—you can't do that—

CUT TO

FATS. CLOSE UP.

FATS

— sure, you just peek at the bottom card after shuffling and it's easy apple pie — Corky makes a big deal production number out of it sometimes, like when he's got some Polock stewardess he wants to screw — he makes them think their minds have touched — never fails —
(As he goes on —)

CUT TO

PEG. CLOSE UP. Numb and horrified and —

FATS' VOICE (over)
— you'll never know how many people want to believe in magic...

PEG
*(Fights for control, really
tries to hang in. Softly —)*
...aw shit... *(And then her face falls apart, her grief has control and she whirls
out of the chair for the cabin door and)*

CUT TO

*Outside the cabin as PEG tears the door open, starts into the night but she only gets a few
steps before CORKY's got her, tries to hold her, tries to calm her —*

CUT TO

*PEG and CORKY and she's smashing out at him and he gets one arm pinioned, then the other,
but not for long, she's crying and humiliated and when she gets an arm free she pounds and
pounds and —*

CORKY
— please! —

PEG
— were you laughing every second? —

CORKY
— please, I said! —

PEG
— WAS I FUNNY, YOU BASTARD SON OF A BITCH — *(And with that
she gives one final twist, breaks wildly free and runs all she has for the house as we)*

CUT TO

FATS, in his chair, waiting.

CUT TO

CORKY, *slamming in but before he can say a word,* FATS *starts talking.*

> **FATS**
> —listen to me—you gotta please just listen—

> **CORKY**
> —make it fast— *(He's standing over* FATS, *hands tense—)*

> **FATS**
> —I will, I will, but—

> **CORKY**
> —no "buts" and no jokes, just get going—

> **FATS**
> *(softer)*
> —OK. Just answer me one question: why do you think I blew the whistle?

> **CORKY**
> To cause pain, because I was leaving, because you were jealous.

> **FATS**
> Wrong, wrong, wrong.

CUT TO

FATS. *CLOSE UP.*

> **FATS**
> I did it because I could.

CUT TO

CORKY. *He says nothing, studies* FATS.

> **FATS**
> And why didn't you stop me? Answer? *You didn't because you couldn't.* Get it? *(And now he breaks out laughing.)* Look at him—he still doesn't understand.

> **CORKY**
> You got your rocks off now?

CUT TO

FATS, *his eyes angled toward* CORKY'S.

> **FATS**
> Better sit down, keed, while I hit you with an explanation—take a load off.
> *(*CORKY *sits on the sofa.)*

Ever since we got together, I laid low — it was best for the act, I let you share the limelight, if there's one thing about me, I'm big —

CORKY

— save us —

FATS

— but then earlier today, when I *begged* you, *pleaded* not to be left behind — when I mortifuckingfied myself, and you pissed ice water all over me, well, schmucko, that tore it. *(tone change now)* If I'm boring you, walking around, I don't care.

(As CORKY begins to pace nervously —)

Fats don't sit quiet while some round-assed hunk steals my glory — you couldn't even make it at an amateur night before I came to the rescue — it was me — I took a failure with the charm of Tricky Dick Nixon and made a *skyrocket*. So it's not gonna be you and her. It's gonna stay you and me, except from now on, even that's changed — henceforth, it's *me* and you.

CUT TO

CORKY.

CORKY

You done? I got a weak stomach.

FATS

You look tired.

CORKY

I'm not.

FATS

Then what're ya yawning for?

CORKY

Yawning? I'm not... *(but now he stretches, yawns.)*

FATS

Gotta wake you up — crawl around a little, that should help.

CORKY

Ya think? *(he starts to crawl across the floor)* Hey, it does help.

FATS

Up and at 'em.

(CORKY jumps to his feet)

Thank me for making you wake up.

CORKY

Thanks, Fats.

FATS
With feeling — like I'd do it —

CORKY
(imitating FATS)
— I'm filled with gratifuckingtude!

FATS
(delighted)
Hey, you got talent after all — let's see what else you can do —
(And now —)

CUT TO

FATS. CLOSE UP. Tight. We only see FATS, but we hear CORKY.

FATS
— Fats says smile, Fats says frown, Fats says touch the ceiling, Fats says
jump up, Fats says jump down spinaround fetch a bail of cotton — little
joke I thought I'd throw in — Fats says get a knife —

CUT TO

CORKY, frozen as the word "knife" hits.

FATS
Come on; from the kitchenette.

CUT TO

THE KITCHENETTE as CORKY takes a knife FATS used on DUKE, brings it out.

FATS
Gee, I wonder what might be fun to do with it?

CORKY
(quickly)
I could whittle something — you know I'm good at that — fast too — just
name it —

FATS
— naw, I'm looking for something with a little more pizazz.

CORKY
(a burst)
Don't do it!

FATS
You really love old Peg, don't you, goddam it's touching.

CORKY

Please don't kill her.

FATS

Hey, schmucko, easy — I would never even dream of depriving *you* of that pleasure.

CORKY

I can't do it.

FATS

There's that old bugaboo of yours again, lack of confidence.

CORKY

I — won't. And — you — can't — make — me!

CUT TO

FATS, watching CORKY.

FATS

OK, OK, wow, I really stepped on a corn that time. If I can't make you, I can't make you, how's your head, Cork?

CORKY

Fine.

FATS

Good. Thought for a sec' there you might be getting a migraine.

CORKY

Nope.

FATS

Just show how wrong you can be.
(And now —)

CUT TO

CORKY, and we're into the longest CLOSE UP *of the picture, and just as before, when we saw* FATS *and heard* CORKY, *now the reverse is true. For awhile,* FATS *is just a voice.* CORKY *stands very straight, holding the knife. Nothing shows at all. He looks just like* CORKY.

HOLD.

The silence goes on. CORKY *stands very straight.*

KEEP HOLDING

Slowly, almost imperceptibly at first, CORKY's *left eye begins to flutter. You can practically see the pulse beating in the temple. He shuts his eyes, opens them again. The fluttering is worse. He's beginning to perspire now.*

STAY WITH CORKY.

The fluttering of the eyelid begins going out of control. CORKY *is clearly getting worse and worse and now we begin a series of flashcuts, some of which we've seen before, some not but we start with a*

FLASHCUT TO

A BUNCH OF DUMMIES IN A MAGIC SHOP. ONE OF THEM IS FATS AND AS CORKY REACHES TOWARD A DIFFERENT DUMMY, IT'S ALMOST AS IF FATS SOMEHOW MOVES, FALLS FORWARD, DRAWS ATTENTION AS WE

FLASHCUT TO

CORKY IN A TINY ROOM HOLDING FATS. BUT AWKWARDLY. HE LOOKS IN A MIRROR. HIS LIPS ARE MOVING MUCH TOO MUCH.

FLASHCUT TO

FATS' HEAD TURNING. CORKY IS BETTER NOW. HIS LIPS DON'T MOVE AS MUCH AT ALL AND

FLASHCUT TO

CORKY STANDING IN FRONT OF THE HOLLYWOOD STARDUST ONLY THIS TIME HE HAS FATS IN HIS ARMS AND

FLASHCUT TO

THE AUDIENCE IN THE STARDUST LAUGHING AND DEEP IN ONE CORNER, WATCHING IT CLOSELY, IS THE POSTMAN AND

FLASHCUT TO

FATS AND DINAH SHORE AND

FLASHCUT TO

THE POSTMAN HANDING OVER CIGARS IN THE FOUR SEASONS AND

FLASHCUT TO

THE POSTMAN AS FATS CRASHES DOWN AGAIN AND AGAIN AND AS THE POSTMAN FALLS

FLASHCUT TO

DUKE AS FATS KNIFES HIM AND

FLASHCUT TO

FATS DOING THE CARD TRICK FOR PEG AND AS SHE RUNS OUT IN TEARS

CUT TO

CORKY, standing there, the flashcuts of FATS' growing power are over. CORKY brings his hands up, presses his palms hard against his eyes which are fluttering worse than we've ever seen them and as CORKY grinds in to try to relieve pressure —

> **FATS' VOICE** (over)

Drop your hands!

>> *(CORKY's hands go back to his*
>> *sides. But his eyes stay shut.)*

Open those baby blues.

>> *(CORKY's eyes are staring*
>> *again, the fluttering wild now.)*

Looks to me like one of those gut wrenchers.

>> *(CORKY manages a nod.)*

Hey, Cork, it's getting bad fast, you're losing color.

>> *(CORKY nods again, pale and sweating now.)*

> **CORKY**
> *(whispering)*

...please...

> **FATS**

Drilling right into the brain, is it?

> **CORKY**

...yes...*Yes*...

CUT TO

FATS, cheery as can be.

> **FATS**

Surprise.

CUT TO

CORKY, standing as before, still in pain, but as we watch, the fluttering begins to slow.

CUT TO

FATS, watching CORKY.

> **FATS**

It came fast, it can go fast, yes? Not so deep anymore?

> **CORKY**

...not...so deep...

> **FATS**

It'll be all gone soon.

CORKY

... thank you ...

FATS
(suddenly roaring)
Want it back a hundred times worse and a hundred days long?

CUT TO

CORKY. *He can only shake his head in silence.*

CUT TO

FATS. *Pleased and contented.*

FATS

Then take the knife on up the hill, lover. *(beat)* And kiss the girl goodbye ...
(HOLD ON FATS a moment.)

CUT TO

PEG LYING ON HER BED, DRAINED.

The tears are gone, she's staring off. Her suitcases, packed and ready, are in a corner of the room. Now there is a sound and as she half sits —

CUT TO

THE DOORKNOB. *It turns. There is a pressure on the thick door from the outside.*

CUT TO

PEG.

PEG
Duke?

FATS (over)
I left schmucko down at the cabin — open up, huh? You and me have
gotta have a quick palaver.

PEG
Corky, there's nothing to say.

FATS (over)
I told you, he's at the cabin — you and me are the only ones can straighten
this out.

PEG
Go 'way, Corky.

>   FATS (over)
Fats.

>   PEG
All right, go 'way, Fats.

>   FATS (over)
That's better — at least we know who we are now. *(softer)* I've got a present that'll make you smile, promise it will.

PEG *lies back, shuts her eyes, says nothing.*

>   FATS (over)
He made it for you. For you to remember him by. He's leaving, Peg, but he wants you to have this.

>   PEG
Have what?

>   FATS (over)
A wooden heart.

CUT TO

PEG, *lying there. She blinks. Probably she's touched a little. She looks at the door again.*

>   FATS (over)
>   *(hurrying on)*
He whittled it for you before he sent me up — he's quick with his hands, say you'll keep it.

>   PEG
Leave it outside the door.

>   FATS (over)
The reason what happened down in the cabin was that he was so humiliated, Peg — see, he never dreamed you'd ever care for him but when you did, and he'd lied to you, it just killed him. He's loved you so long and he couldn't go off with you when there was a lie at the center. Please take his heart, Peg — so he'll know you don't feel contempt for him.

>   PEG
>   *(sitting now)*
Oh, I never felt that.

>   FATS (over)
At least that's something. I'll leave it by the door, Peg. 'Bye.

There is the sound of something being put on the wooden floor outside.

PEG waits a moment, then gets off the bed, takes a step toward the door, reaches for the locked knob with her hand, abruptly pulls her hand back.

                              PEG
Wait a minute, you didn't walk away.

                         FATS (over)
                          (laughing)
Brains as well as boobs.

In spite of herself, PEG half smiles.

                         FATS (over)
             (the sound of steps growing softer now)
Anytime you feel like playing with my levers, you'll call?

                              PEG
Sure, sure.

                         FATS (over)
                           (soft)
...Peggy Ann Snow...
...Peggy Ann Snow...
(softer)...please let me follow...
(a whisper now)...wherever you go...

CUT TO

PEG. CLOSE UP. And the little poem reaches her a little. She stands there, confused, lost in thought.

CUT TO

THE BEDROOM with PEG frozen near the door. It's dark out. Far far beyond is the lake. CORKY's cabin is visible, the one with the lights on.

PEG turns a moment, looks out at the cabin and the lovely lake in the moonlight.

Then she turns, reaches for the door a second time and as she does —

CUT TO

THE HALL OUTSIDE. A quickly cut wooden heart is alone on the floor. Now —

PULL BACK TO REVEAL

More and more of the hall, the CAMERA keeps retreating from the sweet little heart. From the door comes the sound of a lock starting to turn.

KEEP PULLING BACK.

We come to a corner and around it, CORKY waits. Or more precisely, his feet, because that's where we start —

CAMERA MOVES UP ALONG HIS BODY.

The hand holds the knife tight and ready.

CAMERA KEEPS MOVING.

CORKY's chest is moving, he's breathing fast and deeply, in out, in out and now

CAMERA *hits his face and it's a shocker — his eyes are glazed and staring, his mouth has that expression we've seen before but not on him — the bottom line is just this —* CORKY LOOKS LIKE FATS NOW. *Quickly —*

CUT TO

THE DOOR TO PEG'S ROOM, *slowly opening. She peeks out, looks around, sees no one. Then —*

CUT TO

THE WOODEN HEART *as* PEG *reaches down, takes it, holds it close, studies it. She looks both sweet and sad.* HOLD ON PEG'S LOVELY FACE *a moment more, then —*

CUT TO

A SHADOW — CORKY'S SILHOUETTE. *Slowly the knife hand raises, reaches the top of its arc, and as it slashes down*

ZOOM TO

FATS *in his chair in the cabin as* CORKY *drops the knife, the blade covered with blood, on the chair beside* FATS.

FATS
How are things in Glocca Morra, keed?

CUT TO

CORKY. *He moves to the sofa, his back to us, lies down, can't help it, starts to cry.*

CUT TO

FATS. *Watching.*

CUT TO

CORKY, *just sobbing, but trying to get control. When he finally does —*

CUT TO

FATS, *watching him.*

                          FATS
                        (quietly)
It's all right, you've had a big day, let it all out.

CORKY lies there, his back still to us, he nods. The emotional outburst is passing over.

                          FATS
I'll try and keep the yocks under control til you're yourself again.
              (CORKY makes another nod.)
And I promise I won't pull the migraine routine right away either, but I had
to then, you understand that—to get you moving. You're all the time thinking you can't do things you really can, you need prodding, y'know? You got
a terrible inferiority complex, we'll have to work on that.

                         CORKY
                        (soft)
She liked...the heart.

                          FATS
You're a great whittler, she damn well should have.

                         CORKY
She smiled when she picked it up—I saw—she looked so pleased and
everything. I made her happy...me...no tricks or anything.

                          FATS
There's that damn inferiority thing of yours again—I don't want to hear you
running yourself down anymore, you got that...? *(He stops talking suddenly.)*

                         CORKY
What's wrong?

CUT TO

FATS. CLOSE UP.

                          FATS
I don't know how to say this since I haven't got a stomach, but my stomach hurts.

                         CORKY
Bad?

                          FATS
                        (weaker)
Getting...bad.

CUT TO

CORKY, as his arm slips to the floor.

FATS

...getting...real bad now...

CORKY

...goodbye...

FATS

...what's going on...?

CORKY

...we're dying I think is what it is...

He rolls onto his back on the couch. His entire shirt front is red with blood.

FATS

...dying...?

CORKY

...I...I put the knife deep in me...

FATS

...Christ, Laddie, it's spreading...

CORKY
(softer)

...I know...

FATS

...don't leave me here alone...

CORKY

...don't...worry...

FATS

...can you get over...?

CUT TO

CORKY. *He manages to roll off the sofa, lands hard, gasps for breath, pushes up with his arms, crawls slowly to* FATS' *chair.*

CORKY

...what...?

FATS

...put me flat...?

CUT TO

FATS *as* CORKY *takes him, gently places him stretched out on the soft sofa cushion.*

CORKY
(starting to die now)
...Fats...? *(beat)*...she really liked my heart...

FATS
...why didn't you just leave...? Go with her when you had the chance...?

CORKY
...aw...she'd have never gone with me...I couldn't face failure again...
she'd have...turned me down...I couldn't even make her open the door
by myself...it was never me...always us...

FATS
...schmucko...us was you...

CORKY
...huh?...

FATS
...it was you all the time...

CORKY
(there is a pause)
...I wish I'd known that sooner...

CUT TO

FATS. CLOSE UP. Long pause. Then—barely audible.

FATS
...I hope I don't die first is all...

CUT TO

CORKY. CLOSE UP. Another pause, longer.

CORKY
...I think we'll go together, chances are...

HOLD *for a moment on* CORKY. *Then the* CAMERA *starts to pull away in that standard move
that indicates the end of the picture except the second we've established that it's over—*

CUT TO

PEG, *and it isn't over, as she walks out of the main house, holding her suitcases. She puts
them down, looks down at the lit cabin by the water.* PEG *has put on makeup, changed
clothes; she's never looked as soft and lovely.*

PEG
(calling down)
Hey it's me, I changed my mind, let's give it a whack, see how it goes.

(No answer from the cabin. She
takes something out of her purse now,
looks at it — it's the wooden heart)

What do you say?

(no answer)

I'm warning you, Cork, don't play hard to get, I'm a woman, I can always change my mind again. *(And now, for the first time, she imitates FATS.)* You may not have this opporfuckingtunity tomorrow. *(She stands there, half smiling. Now she begins to toss the heart up in the air, catches it, tosses it again and starts walking down to the cabin.)*

HOLD ON PEG.

She keeps walking, holding the heart. Now she kind of breaks into a little run. As she finally reaches the cabin —

FINAL FADE OUT

MAVERICK
A Western

DIRECTOR	RICHARD DONNER
PRODUCERS	RICHARD DONNER
	BRUCE DAVEY
CINEMATOGRAPHER	VILMOS ZSIGMOND
EDITORS	STUART BAIRD
	MIKE KELLY
PRODUCTION DESIGN	TOM SANDERS
MUSIC	RANDY NEWMAN
SCREENPLAY	WILLIAM GOLDMAN

THE LINDA HUNT PART

Linda Hunt was wonderful as The Magician in *Maverick*. Crazy and weird and tough and different and if you wonder what it is that I am smoking as I write this because you saw the movie and don't remember Linda Hunt being in it, well, we are both right. She was in it. She was wonderful. She was cut out of the finished film.

Shit happens.

Sometimes movies are amazingly difficult and time-consuming to get going. *Maverick* couldn't have been easier. It went like this: I met Mel Gibson and his partner Bruce Davey, they said they had the rights to the character and would I like to write the screenplay and I said "sure." Truly as seemingly simple as that.

But I have secrets.

I think all writers do. There are very few projects that I have been offered that I would always say "yes" to. My interests change, needs change, confidence ebbs and flows. A year earlier I might not have done *Maverick*. I said yes for four small reasons and one big one. Here are the four: 1) I loved the old TV show with James Garner. 2) I felt the material was in my wheelhouse. 3) I had never met Gibson but after five minutes I knew he could play the hell out of the part. 4) I had not written a Western in maybe twenty-some years, was glad for the opportunity to try again. And the one big reason? Shamefacedly, here it is:

I knew it would be easy.

That is actually the main reason I came aboard so fast. Because I had been writing originals and them are hard. The last thing in life I wanted was to try another original. But this adaptation had to be a breeze — all I needed to do was pick one of the old TV shows which had too much plot, expand it, and there would be a movie.

One of the shocks of my life happened in my living room where I spent many hours looking at old "Maverick" shows I'd been sent. Because, and this was a crusher — *television storytelling has changed.* These old shows had shitloads of charm, most of it supplied by Garner. But not only was the Garner character generally passive, there was almost no plot at all. *Nothing for me to steal.* I had to essentially write, sob, another original. It was going to be easy money at the brick factory again. (As it always is.)

I set to work trying to figure a story.

All I really had was that wonderful main character. A con man and a gambler. Now if you are given the job of writing a movie about an Olympic gymnast, you know that movie has to climax with her going for the gold. *Rocky* has to end with The Big Fight.

So Maverick had to end with a poker game.

For some reason, the first visual I got was of Gibson sitting on a horse, hands tied, about to be hanged. Rattlesnakes are thrown to scare the horse. As he is about to die, he says, "It had just been a shitty week for me from the beginning." I liked that because I hadn't seen it before and it also told us a lot about the feel of the movie and about the man. He wasn't going to die, it said that much. He was hopefully humorous, it said that too. For me, it set the style of everything that followed.

So Maverick *would begin with him getting hanged.*

To fill in the rest I made this assumption: Maverick *would be a movie about a guy who needed money.*

Why the assumption? Well, this is a movie that has to stand alone, not as one of a thirty-nine episode (they were in those days) TV season. So the poker game climax couldn't be just *any* game, it had to be the most important game of his life. (Had it been just one of thirty-nine episodes, the game would not have needed a particular weight.) Now, if the game is important, it must require important money to enter. And if he already has it, what's the big deal? He would just have to lose it and spend the bulk of the movie getting it back. I didn't like the feel of that. He would be tracking, avenging, and the essence of the character is that he is acted *on.* I decided he needed the money, so he could meet various people and have adventures, all building to The Big Game. My problem was to making getting there be half the fun.

There is no mathematical logic to any of this, it's just how I decided what the narrative might be against what you might decide. No right or wrong storytelling answer exists. *Ever.* I went with my answer for many reasons but chiefly this: it gave me my spine for the movie. And until I have that, I am essentially helpless. Once I have it, I have the confidence to start to write.

In the first draft Maverick meets a banker friend who gives him some money and an Indian friend who gives him the rest. Then I figured a change had to happen — you couldn't just have him going from success to success, this is a movie hero, he has to win but he should sweat a little along the way.

So I had him robbed by the bad guy.

By solving that problem, I presented myself with another: Maverick needed money to get in the game and I didn't have a lot of time for anything elaborate. I needed something oddball and had no idea what, when I got this idea: what if somebody owned those rattlesnakes that are tossed from a sack at the start to scare his horse. Who, though? It had to be someone with a lot of money, obviously, because they would give a lot to my guy. But it also had to be somebody who lived in a desolate place because that's where the hanging took place.

I decided on a nut hermit. (Think of Elisha Cook Jr.) It seemed logical in a lunatic way. A hermit *might* live in this terrible area and since they are strange, he *might* also have pots of money to give to a wandering movie hero in a pickle. Following is the meeting scene between Maverick and The Magician. This might give you a sense of what I was after. OK. Mel Gibson is hanging in space. He struggles. He can't make it. His body hangs motionless. His eyes start to close. This is what happened:

CUT TO

AN ARROW, slicing through the air —

— it hits the rope —

— splits the rope —

— MAVERICK crashes to earth amidst the rattlesnakes.

They hiss at his body, begin to curl.

It's impossible to tell which one of them will strike first. Now —

CUT TO

A GNARLED HAND. That's all we see at first, just the hand. Or rather, TWO GNARLED HANDS. One of them grabs the burlap sack, the other starts scooping up the rattlers, putting them back inside. No fear of consequences. One-two-three-four-five-six, and the rattlers are gone from view. And once they are —

PULL BACK TO REVEAL

THE MAGICIAN, for that, we will learn, is the name of the man we are looking at.

LITTLE OLD MAN, more precisely.

WEIRD LOOKING LITTLE OLD MAN, more precisely still. He is dressed in clothing that neither fits nor matches. One more thing —

— when he talks, HE TALKS VERY LOUDLY. Clearly, he doesn't get a lot of company.

Now he takes a foot, pushes MAVERICK over so he's on his back.

Next he takes an arrow from his quill, puts it in his bow, pulls it back to fire, aiming at MAVERICK'S heart. [Maverick, it might be noted here, is wearing a shirt that is many sizes too small.]

> **THE MAGICIAN**
> I'm a gonna kill you.

CUT TO

MAVERICK. Barely able to speak. Still, this piece of news is not so much depressing as it is strange.

> **MAVERICK**
> *(whispered)*
> ... If you're going to kill me ... why didn't you just let me hang ... ?

CUT TO

THE MAGICIAN, coming closer.

> **THE MAGICIAN**
> 'Cuz then you wouldn't have know'd your crime.

> **MAVERICK**
> *(Blinking up)*
> ... Who are you? and what's my crime ... ?

> **THE MAGICIAN**
> I'm The Magician — and your crime — *(bigger)* — the crime you're gonna die for —

(huge) — the crime that's gonna condemn you to hell is this: *(roaring)* YOU STOLE MY RATTLESNAKES.

CUT TO

MAVERICK. *He's just in terrible shape but he didn't think he was going mad.*

> MAVERICK
>
> ...Do I look like a rattlesnake thief?

> THE MAGICIAN
> *(studies MAVERICK a long while, the arrow still ready. Finally he nods)*
>
> That's exactly what you look like.

> MAVERICK
>
> You're wrong — I play cards.

> THE MAGICIAN
> *(shakes his head)*
>
> A gambler? Not in that shirt.

CUT TO

MAVERICK. *He closes his eyes, tries to laugh —*

— but he can't. Not just because he hasn't the strength but because he is far beyond exhaustion. His body begins to shake, as if with fever. HOLD ON MAVERICK.

Now we're back into the story which is where I needed The Magician to give Maverick the money to enter the game. Why would he have money in the first place? I figured he'd been out there forever, it wasn't illogical to have found valuables from people over the decades who had died on this rough ground.

Why would he give it though? Couldn't be sympathy. Maverick had to earn it. The hermit didn't have a name then. I decided to call him The Magician because I decided he wanted some magic in his life. Not totally illogical — he's a weird old guy coming to the end, clearly his life hasn't had a lot of ups. O.K. He wants magic. I sold the notion to myself.

Problem: Maverick is a gambler, what can he do that's magical?

The great John Scarne did something that I read about once that almost cost him his life. Scarne, after thousands of hours of practice, had taught himself to cut the ace of spades *at will.* He pretended it was a trick but all he did was riffle the cards, spot where the spade ace was, and instantly count how many cards into the deck it was and then cut to it.

Just writing that seems amazing. Scarne almost got killed when he pissed off a major prohibition gangster when he saw Scarne cut the ace and wanted to know the trick. He wanted to be able to do it too. And he thought Scarne was putting him on, claiming it wasn't. So he was going to kill Scarne. Fortunately for one and all, the gangster was finally convinced.

I decided Maverick could also cut the ace of spades at will. He has built into his character marvelous skill with cards. The magician says he wants to see magic before he dies and if Maverick can do something magical, he will let him go and give him the money for the entrance fee. Maverick begins his con, comes up with a story, told sincerely, that he once had magic, the day his mother died he had it, and The Magician says you can do it again and Maverick is reluctant, saying he's convinced he will fail. The magician forces him to try and of course, he cuts the ace of spades, gets the money and goes off to the poker game. Now this was all done straight, the audience did not know it was a trick and at the end of the movie, in the first draft, Maverick is about to tell how he did it and then he changes his mind, saying that life's a little better when there's just a touch of mystery in the air. In other words, he has told us it was magic, not a con.

O.K., exposition's over.

The first draft is accepted, Dick Donner comes on to direct and we start the first of endless months of revisions. Donner likes The Magician, and what he likes about it is the magical aspect, the sense of something strange. He likes it so much he wants more of it.

And I never told him what I just told you: that it was a con.

He did not know the Scarne story. (I've used this material twice so far, as any of you who saw *Magic* know.)

I never told him for this reason: *because he never asked.*

In the second draft it's the same set up, only everything else is different. Maverick cannot cut the ace of spades at will and he really did have the magic the day his mother died. And this time Maverick cuts what we think at first glance is the ace of spades but it turns out to be the ace of clubs — in other words, he fails. But The Magician gives him the money anyway because Maverick has come close and given The Magician hope that the next guy he finds actually will be able to do it. "Hermits need hope," The Magician says, one of the truer lines I've written in my life.

The third draft stays the same with just the amount of money changing. I must explain that I am willing and happy to do any changes here because I am not challenged by anything that's happening — nothing is altering the spine of the movie. It is still about a guy needing money. I get very crazy if you mess with the spine. Otherwise I am totally supportive.

And I think one of the reasons I never told Donner about the Scarne story was because: a) Writers need secrets just as much as hermits need hope. b) I was afraid if I told him the truth Donner would hate it. And want other changes that *would* alter the spine.

Marion Dougherty who is fabulous, is casting the movie and it is Marion who gets this notion: *make The Magician a woman.* She felt it would add a new dynamic. Donner went for it, and as I said, I didn't mind, I was just trying to service the director, and the spine was safe. And once Marion's notion was taken, there was nobody else really who would have been as good for the part as Linda Hunt.

In the fourth draft, the dynamic shifts again: now she gets into his life to give him back confidence, to send him on his way knowing he has a chance to win. She says he came close and next time he'll come closer, all of which leads, of course, to the big card game when the Ace of Spades *is* cut and wins the game for Maverick. Donner liked that because he wanted to get the encounter as mystical as possible — by that time Tom Sanders, our production designer, had come up with some startling and beautiful notions of what the hermit's home might look like.

The fifth draft is essentially the same as the fourth except now The Magician is convinced Maverick has the magic inside him. He cuts the ace of clubs again, but this time the *next card* is the ace of spades. It was hopefully a stranger version and intended to be both different and emotional. This is how the concluding moments read in rehearsal, starting with the reveal of the spade ace as the next card. Henry, it should be noted, is The Magician's pet rattlesnake who has been watching the sequence with great interest.

CUT TO:

MAVERICK *and* THE MAGICIAN

THE MAGICIAN

Next time you'll get it right — maybe the time after the next time. But you got magic inside you — knew it all along — that's what makes me a great hermit. *(beat)* I know things. *(throwing more money at Maverick)* Buy yourselves some clothes that fit — thank me I'll kill you — *(she grabs up Henry)* — now get outta my life. *(sweetly, to Henry)* Yes... there's a good baby... yes...

We leave her there. And that's where I left the sequence after rehearsal. Linda Hunt and Gibson were terrific. No question it was different from anything else in the movie. Donner still liked the notion, still wasn't happy with the scene, but he couldn't verbalize what more he wanted. And frankly, I was tired. I had delivered the first draft in March, it was now August, and after that kind of time with this many changes, you lose not only your zest but your objectivity.

I was out of the loop for the next many months. Donner brought in Gary Ross, who wrote the excellent *Dave*, for another whack at The Magician. I wasn't remotely upset — I didn't have it in me for another go.

It was, apparently, a happy shoot. Which has nothing whatsoever to do with the quality of the film. We don't like to believe it but it's true. I was called out to see the first showing of the film. It wasn't a true sneak — there was an audience of a couple of hundred people but it wasn't in a large neutral theatre somewhere in Pasadena but rather in a place without air conditioning — without *working* air conditioning on the Warners' lot on a hot afternoon.

There was a lot of tension — there always is at such a moment — there should be — my God, if you're not tense then, get out of the picture business — but the time pressure *Maverick* was under made it unendurable. I delivered the first draft on March 12, 1993. That week Gibson said he liked it so we were a "go" project.

And that same week I was told that the movie would open — would *definitely* open on the weekend before Memorial Day, May 20, 1994. Ready or not. I have never been around a flick that went so fast. Thirteen months from first draft without director to being in 2000 plus theatres. This is a terrible gamble to take — movies are slow — there was no time for mistakes.

We all saw the movie on March 13. The picture had to be totally locked and ready to go to the lab for printing by early May. This was not, obviously, a low budget art film. There was no time for tinkering. The picture had to work.

It did and it didn't.

The audience loved Jodie Foster, loved loved Gibson, more importantly, loved *them*. Great affection for James Garner too. Not to mention the crucial ending card sequence. (What always gives you hope at such a time is if the ending holds. If that's happening, even if you're in rough shape, you have a solid chance.)

The Linda Hunt scene was a train wreck.

Sure, it was a rough cut, two and a half hours long. Yes, the air conditioning malfunction was a factor. And Linda Hunt was wonderful.

It still stopped the picture dead.

Gibson was fine too. And it was sure gorgeous to look upon. But it was dead wrong. I don't know why. A different style, maybe. Maybe what was once a simple con to get money had become too convoluted. We'll never know. It just did not work. The audience was confused at first, then, more dangerously, they began to lose interest. When you have a sag like that it can cripple everything that follows.

We met afterwards. The early thoughts were of how to save it but soon we all knew the entire sequence had to be jettisoned. This was a major chunk of film we were eliminating — I would guess ten minutes, maybe twelve — and opening day could not be delayed. Reshoots were scheduled for the next weekend. Instead of The Magician blasting Maverick from a hanging tree — from the second draft on, the original bow and arrow had become sort of an elephant gun — a providential blast of lightning saves him.

But without someone to give him money, guess what? He couldn't be robbed. So the moments when the bad guy robs him are edited out, and Graham Greene as the Indian friend had to be brought back to set up that Maverick's money was in his boot. And then after he is saved you see Gibson hobbling along after his horse showing us the money is safe.

I think we sort of kind of got away with it. It was a loosely plotted movie anyway, so no one noticed. And Donner was able to get the movie down from two and a half hours to two hours ten. I think he could've gotten it down to under two hours, had he been given the time. Maybe it would have worked better. We'll never know. It pleased a lot of people just as it was in the summer of '94. Which is all it was ever meant to do. Let's leave it at that.

One of the great truths of the movie business is that movies are *fragile*. And even the most successful are only a step from disaster. Every step of the way...

CAST LIST

MEL GIBSON	BRET MAVERICK
JODIE FOSTER	ANNABELLE BRANSFORD
JAMES GARNER	ZANE COOPER
GRAHAM GREENE	JOSEPH
ALFRED MOLINA	ANGEL
JAMES COBURN	COMMODORE
DUB TAYLOR	ROOM CLERK
GEOFFREY LEWIS	MATTHEW WICKER
PAUL L. SMITH	ARCHDUKE
DAN HEDAYA	TWITCHY
DENNIS FIMPLE	STUTTERING
DENVER PYLE	OLD GAMBLER
CLINT BLACK	SWEET-FACED GAMBLER
MAX PERLICH	JOHNNY HARDIN

Credits come quickly.

No flourish, just names.

And what do we hear?

This song: the theme from the television series.

Who is the tall dark stranger there?
Maverick is the name.
Riding the trail to who knows where.
Luck is his companion.
Gambling is his game.
Smooth as the handle of a gun,
Maverick is the name.
Wild as the wind in Oregon.
Flowing up a canyon, easier to tame.
Riverboat ring your bell.
Faretheewell, Annabelle,
Lucky is the lady that he loves the best.
Natchez to New Orleans
Livin' on jacks and queens,
Maverick is a legend of the West.

As the song finishes —

— credits come to an end.

And the movie begins . . .

FADE IN ON

A DESOLATE WESTERN LANDSCAPE

Rocks. Cactus. The occasional tree.

Not a place you'd like to spend your summer vacation.

Now there are sounds: A whipping wind begins to get louder. And in the distance, but growing: thunder.

CAMERA STARTS TO MOVE

Slowly, inexorably across this dead place —

— suddenly it stops.

We are in a Sergio Leone tight closeup of just a HIDEOUS LOOKING MAN. *One eye looks straight ahead. The other wanders.*

CAMERA MOVES AGAIN.

The wind is really kicking up —

— suddenly, another stop.

Another Leone closeup.

A SECOND MAN. *This guy makes the first one look handsome. Both his eyes work, which is an improvement. But his face has been horribly burned.*

CAMERA IS MOVING AGAIN.

Louder thunder. A storm is coming fast.

CAMERA STOPS.

We are looking at the least appetizing of the three. Not that he's scarred, not that all his parts aren't in proper working order — it's just that he's so damn <u>frightening</u>.

Not to mention <u>huge</u>.

This is THE ANGEL *and like the other two, he is seated on a horse. And he is staring intently at something. From* THE ANGEL *—*

CUT TO

BRET MAVERICK, *for this is who the trio is looking at.*

MAVERICK'*s thirty, give or take. Enormously appealing. Whether that's because of his considerable physical skills or his sunny personality, who knows. It might be his quiet wit. In any case, we are looking at a handsome young man that everybody likes —*

— oops —

— make that <u>almost</u> everybody.

Because just now he is seated on a horse beneath a tree and a thick rope has been tied around his neck, the rope thrown over a branch. His hands have been tied behind his back. We are about to watch a hanging. His.

> **THE ANGEL**
> (*riding closer*)
> I almost got hung once myself, didn't much care for it, how about you?
> (MAVERICK *says nothing*)
> We're gonna leave you now — not that I wouldn't want to enjoy the fun, but
> I also wouldn't want for someone to come along and see me here. They might
> somehow get the crazy notion I was connected with your accidental death.
> (MAVERICK *just stares at him, makes no reply*)

CUT TO

THE ANGEL. *He gestures for the* OTHER TWO *to ride, and they take off.*

THE ANGEL

On the other hand, I don't think it's too good a thing for a man to be alone out here. Your mind can do cruel things.

And now he takes a burlap sack, tosses it toward MAVERICK. *It lands nearby.*

THE ANGEL

Enjoy the company.

He spurs his horse, rides away.

CUT TO

MAVERICK, *managing to turn his head in the direction* THE ANGEL *took.*

CUT TO

THE ANGEL AND THE OTHER TWO, *disappearing over a nearby hill.*

CUT TO

THE SKY. STORM CLOUDS *convene.*

CUT TO

MAVERICK. *He takes a deep breath, tries to wriggle free of the knotted rope around his neck.*

No luck.

Make that bad *luck.*

The horse has been surprised by his movement, takes a half step.

CUT TO

MAVERICK. *Freezing.*

CUT TO

THE HORSE. *It relaxes, settles down.*

CUT TO

THE SKY AND A THUNDERCLAP.

CUT TO

MAVERICK, *staring at his horse. The noise was* loud.

Either the horse is deaf or it likes thunder. Doesn't budge an inch.

MAVERICK *starts to try and work his neck free again.*

This time the horse doesn't move at all.

MAVERICK sighs with relief, glances around.

CUT TO

THE BURLAP SACK. It is starting to wriggle.

CUT TO

MAVERICK. He holds his breath.

CUT TO

THE HORSE. It hasn't spotted the sack yet.

CUT TO

THE SACK. Wriggling more. Pretty soon it's going to be hard not to spot it.

CUT TO

MAVERICK, caution to the winds now, trying desperately to somehow get free of the noose — — and miraculously, he's starting to make a little headway.

CUT TO

THE HORSE. Calm. Nothing flusters this animal.

CUT TO

MAVERICK, even more headway — he's in pain but he ignores it.

CUT TO

THE SKY. Rain begins.

CUT TO

THE HORSE. It likes the rain.

CUT TO

THE SKY. Opening. Sheets now.

CUT TO

THE HORSE. It could be a statue.

CUT TO

MAVERICK, one eye on the sack as he continues to work to free his neck. Now —

CUT TO

THE SACK AS A RATTLESNAKE PEEKS OUT.

CUT TO

MAVERICK. *Jesus*.

CUT TO

THE HORSE. *Oblivious*.

CUT TO

THE SACK. *Half a dozen rattlers are moving out of the sack now. Close by. Some of them are big, some of them are <u>very</u> big. All of them have fangs.*

CUT TO

MAVERICK, *struggling harder than ever, and he's actually making more headway. It's exhausting labor. As he continues his fight for life —*

> MAVERICK'S VOICE (over)
> It had been just a shitty week for me from the beginning.
> *(Now, from that —)*

CUT TO

A WOODEN SIGN THAT READS: *"ENTERING CRYSTAL CITY."*

> MAVERICK'S VOICE (over)
> I was heading for Crystal City to take some money from the bank. The poker game of my lifetime was starting in St. Louis in just ten days, and I was still short three thousand for the entrance fee.

CUT TO

CRYSTAL CITY, *A CATTLE TOWN. Not much of a place. Dusty. One main street — and almost every storefront indicates that it is either a saloon or a gambling hall.*

(These western towns, it should be noted, were, in their own way, fraudulent. Most of the storefronts were nothing but pieces of wood bigger than the actual establishment they were masking. Stage sets, if you will.)

Just now, a cattle drive is entering the main street. Nothing gigantic, but a lot of noise and dust — and a bunch of dirty, rough looking cowboys. As the dust rises —

CUT TO

MAVERICK, *riding into town from the other direction, as the dust practically makes him disappear. He's wearing different clothes than in the hanging scene.*

CUT TO

THE BANK, *as MAVERICK rides toward it, pauses. A sign in the front indicates it will open the following morning. He moves on.*

CUT TO

The biggest establishment in town. THE FRONTIER. This place actually has a second floor and advertises rooms as well as vices.

CUT TO

INSIDE.

It's darker than we're used to. (All saloons were darker than movies made them.)

MAVERICK is signing the register, paying for the room.

> ROOM CLERK
> *(amazingly pale — he seems*
> *never to have seen the sun)*

Just the one night?

> MAVERICK
> *(nods)*

Taking the St. Louis stage tomorrow.

> ROOM CLERK

Rich Chinaman stopped day before yesterday, took the same stage. Goin' to the poker game. You too?

> MAVERICK
> *(shrugs)*

Hadn't planned on it.

> ROOM CLERK

One night'll be a nickel.

> MAVERICK
> *(grabs his key)*

Bathtub still in the whorehouse?

> ROOM CLERK
> *(points)*

Through the back door. A penny.

> MAVERICK
> *(giving some change)*

Tub clean?

> ROOM CLERK

Not since I been here. *(cackles suddenly)* I love that joke.

CUT TO

THE STAIRS as MAVERICK heads toward them. He slows by the poker table.

> ### ROOM CLERK
> A little advice? Skip tonight. The Angel's playing.

> ### MAVERICK
> So?

> ### ROOM CLERK
> Well, he's mean, practically eats leather. Doesn't like to lose but worse than that, he hates losing to strangers. Violent. Likes pain.

> ### MAVERICK
> Anything else? — I can be charming if I set my mind to it.

> ### ROOM CLERK
> Well, he's mean —

> ### MAVERICK
> — you said that already —

> ### ROOM CLERK
> — did I also say he was six and a half feet tall?

CUT TO

MAVERICK. *For a moment he considers this. Then —*

> ### MAVERICK
> Maybe you better direct me to the nearest quilting bee... *(Now, as he heads on up —)*

CUT TO

THE FRONTIER. EVENING.

The place is busy enough, the bar doing a brisk business.

A POKER GAME is in session. Half a dozen play. A CATTLEHAND, a PREACHER, a SMALL-TIME LOCAL BUSINESSMAN. But it's the other three we pay most attention to.

FIRST IS A VERY YOUNG MAN. Late teens, looks less. Thin. Small. A hundred and thirty pounds after a big meal. This is THE KID. Seems ordinary.

Next to him sits, of all things, a WOMAN. But not ordinary, certainly not in these surroundings. She's elegantly dressed, close to being beautiful. She's married, has a deep southern accent, and hasn't been poor for a long time. Maybe she's thirty. She seems a rotten poker player, but a wonderful flirt. This is ANNABELLE BRANSFORD.

Next to her sits THE ANGEL. We met him already — he tossed the burlap bag of rattlesnakes at MAVERICK just before the hanging. Huge, powerful, not much makes him smile, except winning at cards.

There is an empty seat at the table.

CUT TO

THE STAIRCASE *as* MAVERICK *descends. If before he was grimy from travel, he isn't any-more. He wears a black hat, a black jacket, a black string tie —*

— and just the most beautiful white lace shirt you ever saw.

CUT TO

THE POKER GAME *as* MAVERICK *approaches.*

                    MAVERICK
            (indicating the empty chair)
Taken?

                    ANNABELLE
            (lilting southern accent)
It is now. *(smiles at him)* My name is Annabelle Bransford. And what do people call you?

                    MAVERICK
Bret Maverick, ma'am. *(And as he starts to sit —)*

CUT TO

THE ANGEL, *glaring at* MAVERICK. (<u>We</u> *know that within a week, he'll hang* MAVERICK. *But they haven't met before.)*

                    THE ANGEL
I like the game the way it is.

                    MAVERICK
I bring all kinds of plusses to the table. I hardly ever bluff and I never ever cheat.

                    THE ANGEL
I don't believe it.

                    MAVERICK
Neither do I.

                    THE ANGEL
            (voice rising, not in pitch, but intensity)
I like the game *just* the way it is.

                    MAVERICK
Bet I can change your mind. *(beat)* I promise to lose for at least an hour.

THE ANGEL
(without a pause)
We're playing five card draw.
(As MAVERICK sits —)

CUT TO

MAVERICK, losing a hand to THE ANGEL. THE ANGEL smiles —

— but so does MAVERICK.

CUT TO

MAVERICK losing again, this time to ANNABELLE. She's happy —

— but again, so is MAVERICK.

And now we begin a series of very quick cuts.

Of THE KID, holding his cards. Tightly.

Of THE CATTLEMAN casually making a bet. Very casually.

Of MAVERICK, who doesn't seem to be paying much attention.

He loses again, smiles.

Now THE PREACHER is staring at his cards before betting. For a long beat.

And THE CATTLEMAN is fiddling with his chips.

The chips in front of THE ANGEL are sloppy.

The chips in front of ANNABELLE are neatly stacked. She flicks her fingernails against her front teeth, makes a bet.

THE BUSINESSMAN is toying with his necktie.

THE ANGEL is holding his cards, moving the top to the bottom, then repeating, the top to the bottom.

And MAVERICK loses again, smiles again, just happy to be there.

ANNABELLE is suddenly helpless, giggling, staring at what she's been dealt.

THE ANGEL is smiling happily. He rakes in a pot.

THE BUSINESSMAN's fingers are tapping on the table.

THE KID's hand covers his mouth.

THE ANGEL is bored, looking neither at the other players nor the pot.

ANNABELLE bets big and wins — maybe she's not such a rotten poker player after all.

*MAVERICK tosses in his cards. Another loss. He smiles, glances at the clock on the wall —
an hour and a half have gone by.*

CUT TO

*THE TABLE. MAVERICK and THE KID are the last two in the game. THE KID turns his
cards over. Two pair, aces over queens. MAVERICK has three sixes. He looks at his winning
hand almost in surprise. It's a good sized pot he's won. As he reaches for it —*

> **THE KID**
> *(mumbling something)*
> Don't think ... *(the rest is unintelligible)*

> **MAVERICK**
> Didn't get you.

> **THE KID**
> I said I don't think that hand should count.

> **MAVERICK**
> You got any logical reasons going for you?

> **THE KID**
> My mind wasn't on the game. *(his voice is always soft)*

CUT TO

*THE KID. CLOSE UP. He stares at MAVERICK and something is suddenly clear: His eyes are
deadly.*

CUT TO

MAVERICK. Hesitating now.

> **MAVERICK**
> What's your name, son?

> **THE KID**
> Johnny Hardin.

> **MAVERICK**
> And what do you do for a living?

> **THE KID**
> Oh, mostly I kill people. I'm a gunfighter.

> **MAVERICK**
> Since you're alive, I have to assume you're good at it.

> **THE KID**
> So far nobody's proved otherwise.

> **MAVERICK**
> *(a beat — then)*
> This hand definitely does not count. *(indicating chips)* Take whatever you think's yours, I'll be content with the leavings.
> *(As THE KID does —)*

CUT TO

ANNABELLE. *A quick look of disappointment crosses her face.*

CUT TO

THE ANGEL. *A look of contempt crosses his.*

> **THE ANGEL**
> You always been gutless?

> **MAVERICK**
> *(thinks a minute — then nods)*
> I think so. At least for as long as I can remember. My pappy always said, "He who fights and runs away, can run away another day." *(now he stands — like every other man in the room, he wears a six gun)* Here's the truth — I don't see what's so great about being brave. *(Pulls back his black jacket, clearing his gun)*

CUT TO

THE KID. *Watching. His hand begins to move to his gun.*

CUT TO

ANNABELLE. *This is not a nice place.*

CUT TO

THE TABLE. *All watching MAVERICK now.*

> **MAVERICK**
> *(chatting idly away)*
> See, you're a gunfighter and I'm not, I like to play cards, so the fact is, if I'd faced you down, what chance would I have had? Answer? Zero.
> *(And on that word —)*

CUT TO

MAVERICK, *as suddenly he draws —*

— and it's lightning — you never saw anyone so fast.

CUT TO

THE KID. *Stunned.*

CUT TO

MAVERICK. His voice casual.

MAVERICK

No chance whatsoever.

And now he expertly twirls his gun back into its holster.

CUT TO

ANNABELLE. Leaning toward THE KID.

ANNABELLE

Was that fast?

(*THE KID manages a nod*)

I thought it was fast.

CUT TO

MAVERICK, sitting back down at the table again. This has all gone quickly and quietly. Now he looks at THE KID.

MAVERICK

May I suggest that from now on you keep your mind on the game?

THE KID

Yes. Yessir.

MAVERICK

Then why don't we all get back to poker?

CUT TO

THE ANGEL. Not remotely afraid of MAVERICK.

THE ANGEL

You say you like to play cards.

MAVERICK

Passionately.

THE ANGEL

How come, when you lose all the time?

MAVERICK

Oh, I don't lose *all* the time — just the first hour or so. I like for people to be happy.

THE ANGEL

What happens after that?

                        MAVERICK
Probably I'll win all your money.

                        THE ANGEL
Aren't you a little overconfident?

                        MAVERICK
No. I've just been here before.
                        (And on that —)

CUT TO

THE POKER GAME BEGINNING AGAIN.

And again, we see a series of very quick cuts.

In fact, we see many of the same cuts we saw before — only this time MAVERICK *doesn't lose, he wins.*

THE KID *holds his cards tightly. Too tightly. He makes a bet.* MAVERICK *doubles it.* THE KID *folds. He was bluffing.*

THE CATTLEMAN *casually makes a bet. Very casually.* MAVERICK *doubles it. Another bluff.* MAVERICK *wins again.*

ANNABELLE *is suddenly helpless, giggling.*

MAVERICK *folds. The others bet.* ANNABELLE *wins — she wasn't bluffing.*

THE ANGEL *is guarding his cards with both huge hands. He makes a big bet.* MAVERICK *makes a bigger one.* THE ANGEL *folds. Angrily. He was bluffing.*

THE BUSINESSMAN *is playing with his tie. He bets.* MAVERICK *makes a big raise.* THE BUSINESSMAN *calls. They both have good hands. But* MAVERICK'S *is better.*

THE ANGEL *is bored, makes a bet looking at neither the other players nor the pot.* MAVERICK *makes a big bet.* THE ANGEL *throws his cards down, his anger building as he was caught in another bluff.*

CUT TO

THE CLOCK. *Time is passing.*

CUT TO

THE POKER GAME. MAVERICK *has cleaned out everybody but* THE ANGEL.

THE ANGEL *hesitates, moving the top card to the bottom, does it again, moves the top card to the bottom —*

— now he makes a bet.

Now MAVERICK *makes a bet. A <u>huge</u> bet.*

CUT TO

THE ANGEL *scowling, staring.*

CUT TO

MAVERICK. *Nothing shows on his face. He just waits. Then —*

CUT TO

THE ANGEL. *He wants to bet but you can tell it in his eyes — he's scared he's not strong enough.*

CUT TO

MAVERICK. *The others are watching.* ANNABELLE *smiles at him. He politely touches the rim of his hat.*

CUT TO

THE ANGEL. *He hurls his cards to the table.* MAVERICK *wins.*

CUT TO

MAVERICK, *putting his cards face down, starting to collect the pot.*

CUT TO

THE ANGEL, *suddenly reaching out, grabbing* MAVERICK's *cards, turning them over and as he does —*

CUT TO

MAVERICK's *cards. He has shit. Not even a pair. This time <u>he</u> was bluffing.*

CUT TO

THE ANGEL, *on his feet with a roar —*

> **THE ANGEL**
> *You said you never bluffed!*

> **MAVERICK**
> *(very calm, collecting the pot)*
> No, I said I never *cheated,* and I don't. I also said I *hardly* ever bluffed. This was one of the "hardly's."

> **THE ANGEL**
> You cheated the whole goddam game.

> MAVERICK

What do you think I was doing that first hour? Learning your "tells,"
that's all. Once I could read your hands, once I could read your eyes —
(shrugs) — things just kind of worked out.

> THE ANGEL

I just called you a "cheat."

> MAVERICK

You also called me gutless. I figured you were teasing —
> *(On that —)*

CUT TO

THE ANGEL, blind mad, he reaches his huge arms across, starts to grab MAVERICK when we

CUT TO

FOUR UNSHAVEN BIG MEN bursting through the front door of the place, THE LEAD GUY has his gun drawn —

> LEAD GUY
> *(to THE ANGEL)*

Get away from him — we get him first —

CUT TO

MAVERICK and he's not so casual now. His eyes flick around, looking for a place to move.

CUT TO

THE FOUR UNSHAVEN BIG MEN, THREE of them fanning out behind the LEAD GUY, block-ing anyplace MAVERICK might go.

> LEAD GUY

I spotted ya through the window and it made me believe in the Almighty.

> MAVERICK

You fellas were drinking, you played bad, whose fault is that?

> LEAD GUY

Yours, bastard — everything is your fault. *(beat)* But it's our time come
now. *(And as they advance —)*

CUT TO

MAVERICK, suddenly vaulting the card table, heading for the swinging front doors —

CUT TO

THE FOUR GUYS, and for just a moment they're surprised and

CUT TO

MAVERICK, taking advantage of the moment, sprinting away and

CUT TO

THE FOUR, realizing now, turning, starting after him and

CUT TO

MAVERICK, blasting through the swinging doors and outside and

CUT TO

THE ANGEL AND ANNABELLE AND THE KID AND THE OTHER PLAYERS, moving to a nearby window, staring out into the semi-dark street and

CUT TO

THE FOUR GUYS bolting from the bar and as they leave —

CUT TO

MAVERICK, outside, racing away —

— and then he does a surprising thing: He stops.

CUT TO

THE ANGEL AND ANNABELLE AND THE OTHERS, riveted and

CUT TO

THE FOUR GUYS outside — they stop too.

CUT TO

MAVERICK. He turns now, turns to face them.

CUT TO

THE ANGEL AND THE OTHERS, watching as THE FOUR GUYS stare at MAVERICK, wary, ready for anything.

CUT TO

MAVERICK. And now he does something else surprising. He takes off his gun belt. Drops it.

CUT TO

THE FOUR GUYS. THREE of them look to the LEAD GUY. He hesitates, drops his gun belt too.

CUT TO

THE ANGEL, *watching, as* THE OTHER THREE *follow suit. All of them have taken off their gun belts now.*

And now the FOUR MEN *begin to move slowly toward* MAVERICK.

CUT TO

MAVERICK. *Four of them and all of them dangerous, four of them coming closer in the night.*

And now he does the most surprising thing of all:

He *charges* them.

CUT TO

THE FOUR GUYS, *surprised and then*

CUT TO

MAVERICK, *as he just* explodes —

— because if he was fast when he drew his gun, he's faster in a fight — faster and fearless and as he wades in —

CUT TO

ANNABELLE, *watching. Eyes bright.*

CUT TO

THE ANGEL, *watching, stunned at what he's seeing out there in the night, and*

CUT TO

MAVERICK, *spinning, throwing an elbow into the gut of the nearest* BIG MAN, *the blow connects perfectly and the guy starts to double over, his knees weak, and as he falls*

CUT TO

THE SECOND BIG MAN, *swinging viciously and he knows how to use his fists —*

— but he's slow, too slow as we

CUT TO

MAVERICK, *ducking the blow, coming up with a punch of his own that lands on the side of the jaw and the guy staggers back and down —*

CUT TO

THE KID, *watching and probably he's never seen anything like this, one guy attacking four and*

CUT TO

THE ANGEL, *and for just a moment now, as he stares out almost in disbelief, there's something new behind his eyes: fear.*

CUT TO

MAVERICK *leaving his feet, kicking out with both legs at the* THIRD GUY, *crunching him in the chest, sending him careening back, cartwheeling to earth and*

CUT TO

THE LEAD GUY, *diving at* MAVERICK *from behind, and for a moment he's got him, his arms tight around* MAVERICK *and*

CUT TO

MAVERICK *and the instant this happens, he lets his body go totally limp so the* LEAD GUY *is left having to hold him up, and he hadn't expected this and as* MAVERICK *sags—*

CUT TO

THE LEAD GUY *stunned as suddenly* MAVERICK *stiffens, tosses the* LEAD GUY *over his head and through the air where he lands, hard, and*

CUT TO

MAVERICK *moving back on the* FIRST GUY, *the one he creamed the air out of and as he approaches, the* FIRST GUY *turns, runs and*

CUT TO

THE LEAD GUY *on his feet, gesturing to the others to do the same and*

CUT TO

MAVERICK, *watching as* ALL FOUR *take off into the night.* MAVERICK *picks up his gun belt, straps it on as he heads back toward* THE FRONTIER.

CUT TO

INSIDE *as he enters. He seems remarkably calm, considering what he's just done. Breathing heavily, sure, a little dusty, absolutely, but no more.*

ANNABELLE *hurries to him.*

ANNABELLE

That was the most amazing thing.

MAVERICK
(shrugs)

Sometimes you get lucky is all. *(And as he walks forward—)*

CUT TO

A MIRROR as he passes.

CUT TO

MAVERICK, a glance —

— and then he stops dead —

— now he moves forward —

— he touches his beautiful ruffled lace shirt —

— no question about it, it's dirty from the fight.

CUT TO

MAVERICK. CLOSE UP. A look of blind fury is there.

CUT TO

THE ANGEL, watching, as MAVERICK storms toward him.

>   MAVERICK
> All right — my shirt's damaged, what the hell else bad can happen? — *(pointing to THE ANGEL) — you —* right now — just you and me —

>   THE ANGEL
>   *(pacifying)*
> — what have you got against me? —

>   MAVERICK
> — you tried to stop me from playing, you called me a gutless cheat —

>   THE ANGEL
>   *(scared)*
> — like you said, I was teasing —

>   MAVERICK
>   *(grabbing THE ANGEL by the shirt,*
>   *yanking him forward)*
> — you were like hell —

>   THE ANGEL
>   *(raises his left hand)*
> — my right hand to God —

>   MAVERICK
> — *switch hands!* —
>   *(THE ANGEL obeys — whispered)*
> — who's gutless?

(THE ANGEL hesitates — louder now)

Who?

CUT TO

THE ANGEL. He's never been in this situation before; he's the one used to doing the terrorizing. But he's never met anyone like MAVERICK before.

THE ANGEL
(soft)

I am.

(And the moment that's spoken —)

CUT TO

MAVERICK, sitting amiably back in his chair — ANNABELLE cannot take her eyes off him.

MAVERICK
(as if nothing had happened)

My deal? . . .

(Now, from downstairs —)

CUT TO

MAVERICK IN HIS ROOM, STILL IN HIS GAMBLING ATTIRE.

He is finishing counting his considerable cash winnings as a knock comes on his door. He folds the cash into his jacket pocket, moves to the door.

MAVERICK

Who is it?

ANNABELLE (over)

Annabelle.

CUT TO

THE DOOR as he opens it and there she is, stunning as ever, standing in the hallway. She looks up at him nervously. You can almost feel her southern heart pounding.

ANNABELLE

I . . . I shouldn't be doing this.

MAVERICK

You're just standing in the hallway, Mrs. Bransford — I think that's still legal in this state.

CUT TO

ANNABELLE, moving quickly into his room. She closes the door.

ANNABELLE
If only I weren't married —
> *(and with that she goes into his arms, kisses*
> *him passionately — as they break)*
— I had to do that. My very being cried out for me to hold you.

MAVERICK
Stop by anytime.

CUT TO

ANNABELLE. CLOSE UP. Eyes so bright.

ANNABELLE
We'll likely never see each other again so it's safe for me to tell you — you're the most blindingly attractive man on the face of the earth. *(her cheek brushes his)* And now good-bye. *(She takes a step toward the door)*

CUT TO

MAVERICK. He is a healthy young man and this is a woman of passion and beauty. He reaches out, gently takes her hand, speaks soft, his voice husky.

MAVERICK
. . . Annabelle . . . ?

CUT TO

ANNABELLE, all but trembling. There is a long pause. Then —

CUT TO

MAVERICK. He kisses her forehead.

MAVERICK
(barely a whisper)
. . . if you don't give me back my money, I'll have your ass thrown in jail.

CUT TO

ANNABELLE. Shocked. Hurt.

CUT TO

MAVERICK. He snaps his fingers sharply. He isn't kidding around.

CUT TO

ANNABELLE, as she realizes this.

ANNABELLE
Damn.

And with that, she takes the wad of money she's heisted from his coat, slaps it angrily into his hand. He puts it back into his pocket.

> MAVERICK

Don't get mad at me — I can't help it you're a bad thief.

> ANNABELLE

I'm a good thief, mister — I'm just having a stretch of bad luck.

> MAVERICK

I know about those — *(studies her)* — where you from? Your accent could use a little work too.

> ANNABELLE
> *(her natural Irish accent now)*

Bahston —

> MAVERICK

— and there isn't a Mister Bransford.

> ANNABELLE

And never will be, thank you very much. *(But now her mood shifts. This is grateful)* Most men would have turned me in. I'll do something for you someday. *(she starts for the door)* I'm a liar and I steal so just file this next under "garbage." *(her back still to him)* Men have never been that hard for me —

> MAVERICK

— I believe that.

> ANNABELLE
> *(turning)*

Probably because I never cared. *(Beat — she's sincere here and she isn't used to it. Sincere and embarrassed)* But I did want you. I want you now. But you're too dangerous.

> MAVERICK
> *(shakes his head)*

Pussycat.

CUT TO

ANNABELLE. Hard for her to say.

> ANNABELLE

If we were together , every night when you went off to gamble, I'd go crazy wondering who was after you.

CUT TO

MAVERICK, as she comes into his arms. Gently. A kiss on the cheek.

> ANNABELLE

I couldn't take that.

> *(They separate. She goes to the*
> *door, can't hide her emotions)*

I wish we'd never met; goodbye.

CUT TO

ANNABELLE, *opening the door and gone —*

— but not before one quick glance back. Tears are in her eyes.

CUT TO

MAVERICK. *Touched.*

> MAVERICK

Goodbye, Mrs. Bransford.

Alone now, he starts to take off his jacket. As he reaches into his pocket for his money, it isn't there —

— she's robbed him again —

— he breaks out laughing —

CUT TO

ANNABELLE, IN HER ROOM, HURRIEDLY FINISHING PACKING.

She takes her suitcase, goes to the window, opens it, steps out onto the fire escape. It's clumsy going.

> MAVERICK (over)

Can I be of help?

CUT TO

THE FIRE ESCAPE *and* MAVERICK, *dressed as before, waiting.*

> ANNABELLE
> *(sighs, hands him his money back)*

You've got to admit, I was better the second time. *(Now she starts climbing back in)*

CUT TO

THE TWO OF THEM, *entering her room via the window.*

> MAVERICK

Not just better — good.

> ANNABELLE
> *(a shrug)*

There's hope for me.

> MAVERICK

Now it's time for you to do something *I* want.

He takes off his jacket, tosses it on the bed.

> ANNABELLE
> *(looking at the bed, then at him)*

You're not getting that.

> MAVERICK

Lady — I don't want to go to bed with you, I'd be too frightened — what if I dozed off? God knows what parts of me you'd steal. *(indicating his smudged shirt)* But obviously I can't clean this, and obviously you must know how to. *(beat)* I don't like too much starch.

> ANNABELLE
> *(smiles as he takes off his shirt,*
> *her southern accent back again)*

If I can't touch you, I can touch your shirt... and daydream. *(she takes the shirt, holds it close.)*

MAVERICK picks up his jacket, goes to the door, opens it.

> ANNABELLE

Sleep well... *(pause)*... Bert.

> MAVERICK
> *(he hates that — correcting promptly)*

Bret. *(And as he goes —)*

CUT TO

THE MAIN STREET THE NEXT DAY,

as MAVERICK, dressed for traveling, heads toward the bank.

CUT TO

THE BANK. Quiet and small. A couple of horses tied outside.

CUT TO

MAVERICK. In a good mood, why not, it's a gorgeous day. Now —

CUT TO

THE BANK AND AN EXPLOSION OF GUNFIRE —

— THEN TWO MASKED MEN RACE OUT, CARRYING GUNS AND MONEY BAGS, JUMP ONTO THE HORSES TIED OUTSIDE, AND TEAR THE HELL OUT OF TOWN.

CUT TO

MAVERICK. As suddenly he races forward toward the building —

CUT TO

INSIDE THE SMALL BANK. CHAOS. TWO TELLERS, still trembling from the previous events and ONE GUARD who is groaning on the floor where he has been knocked down.

CUT TO

MAVERICK, to the nearest TELLER.

> **MAVERICK**
>
Where's Wicker?
> *(As the TELLER points off —)*

CUT TO

AN EMPTY SAFE — well, maybe a few coins are left — and a distraught Bank President, MATTHEW WICKER. He is an elderly man and a splendid one. As he sees MAVERICK —

> **WICKER**
>
Bret — you're a day late and a dollar short.

> **MAVERICK**
>
The money you owed me was in there?
> *(WICKER nods)*
>
The whole thousand?

> **WICKER**
>
Don't worry — posse'll catch 'em.
> *(And on the word "posse" —)*

CUT TO

THREE ELDERLY OVERWEIGHT MEN ON OVERWEIGHT HORSES. One of them wears a badge. This is the posse.

PULL BACK TO REVEAL

WE ARE IN WICKER'S OFFICE — a sign on his desk announces his name and job — and he and MAVERICK are staring out the window as the THREE ELDERLY MEN ride by.

> **MAVERICK**
> *(stunned)*
>
That's what you call "law enforcement"?

> **WICKER**
>
> We can't get the best — job's too dangerous. *(pointing to POSSE)* They're a dogged bunch, they'll track 'em down eventually.

CUT TO

MAVERICK, *slumping into a chair across from WICKER's desk.*

> **MAVERICK**
>
> I haven't got "eventually," not with St. Louis staring at me. *(shakes his head)* And I don't like the way my luck's been running — your thousand's gone and a couple days back I stopped by Porkchop Slim's for his thousand — and he *died* — widow used the money for the funeral. Half the town got drunk on *my* earnings.

> **WICKER**
> *(distraught)*
> Soon as I heard about the All Rivers Championship I knew you'd be collecting your debts. What is it, twenty-five thousand just to enter?
> *(MAVERICK nods)*
> Was I going to put you over?

> **MAVERICK**
>
> Between you and Porkchop and what Joseph owes me, I'd be there. *(beat)* I'm going to have to play a lot of extra poker these next days and my luck better be good.

> **WICKER**
>
> You don't need luck — I've been playing half a century, nobody's better than you. *(beat)* Have you ever thought not having the entrance fee might be the luckiest break of all?

> **MAVERICK**
> *(gives WICKER a look)*
> Not even once.

> **WICKER**
>
> Bret — do you know why people like you? It's because you're *happy*. You may be the only happy man left alive, ever wonder why?

> **MAVERICK**
>
> Stupidity's got to rank right up there.

CUT TO

WICKER. CLOSE UP.

> **WICKER**
>
> It's because you're so totally and completely irresponsible. You drift, you're

a nomad without a desert, you play, you win and if you don't, it doesn't bother you. Mortgage payments? Getting a raise? Never crosses your mind. But if you take the All Rivers, you'll be rich. Money brings responsibilities along. Poor people won't go near you 'cause they'll be intimidated. Rich people won't associate with you 'cause of how you got there. You'll be all by yourself, stuck in the middle. Your life will be over. *(beat)* Think about it.

CUT TO

MAVERICK. *He is.* HOLD *on* MAVERICK. *Then —*

CUT TO

MAVERICK, AS HE EXITS THE BANK,

still lost in thought. He walks along. There is an alley beside the bank and he moves into it, not looking around. The alley is empty —

— or rather, <u>was</u>.

Because now, THE FOUR LARGE MEN *he beat up the night before enter the alley too.*

MAVERICK, *with his thoughts, is unaware.*

THE FOUR LARGE MEN *look even more menacing in the daytime. Now — they close in around* MAVERICK.

MAVERICK
(still not turning)

Anybody see you?

LEAD GUY

Not a soul.

MAVERICK *turns, reaches into his pocket for the money he won the night before.*

MAVERICK

You guys come in any later last night, that monster would have eaten me alive.

LEAD GUY

Anyone suspect anything?

MAVERICK
(shakes his head)

You were great — couldn't have gone better.

LEAD GUY

Truth is, we enjoyed it.

MAVERICK
(starting to pay them)
Thanks for letting me hire you for the night.

LEAD GUY
Thank *you* for going so easy on us.

CUT TO

MAVERICK. He shakes his head.

MAVERICK
Easy? Damn. *(finishing paying)* Those were my best shots.
(From this —)

CUT TO

THE FRONTIER

as MAVERICK enters. The ROOM CLERK calls to him.

CLERK
Mister Maverick? *(he holds up a carefully wrapped package)* Mrs. Bransford
left this for you.

CUT TO

*THE PACKAGE. It's the laundered shirt, neatly folded, with tissue paper covering it. Inside,
you can see the outline of a note.*

CUT TO

MAVERICK. Touched. As he turns to go upstairs —

CUT TO

MAVERICK, IN HIS ROOM, FINISHING PACKING.

The wrapped shirt is on his bed. He picks it up gently, takes the tissue off.

CUT TO

THE SHIRT. Gorgeous. The note is in an envelope. MAVERICK opens it.

CUT TO

THE NOTE: "Mister Maverick,
I'll never forget you.
Wish me luck.
A woman's gotta do what a woman's gotta do."
A.

CUT TO

MAVERICK as he puts the note down, picks the shirt up. It has never been as beautiful. A look crosses his face. He starts to unbutton the shirt and we

CUT TO

THE MIRROR IN HIS ROOM. He stands in front of it with the shirt on —

— barely on would be more accurate —

— she has shrunk the shit out of it —

— it's almost like he's wearing something from Toys R Us.

Steaming, he whirls out of the room as we

CUT TO

THE ROOM CLERK AS MAVERICK TEARS UP.

> MAVERICK
>
> Where's Mrs. Bransford?
> > *(As the CLERK shakes his head —)*

CUT TO

THE MAIN STREET

as MAVERICK explodes out the door, looks around.

CUT TO

THE END OF THE STREET. The stage has arrived. ANNABELLE is standing nearby. MAVERICK takes off in her direction and

CUT TO

ANNABELLE, watching as MAVERICK reaches her. This goes snappily.

> MAVERICK
>
> You did this on purpose!

> ANNABELLE
>
> You bet.

> MAVERICK
>
> This was my lucky shirt.

> ANNABELLE
>
> Do your own laundry.

> MAVERICK

Good thing you're a woman.

> ANNABELLE
> *(turning away)*

Quit making a spectacle of yourself — just go buy yourself another one —

> MAVERICK
> *(spinning her around, holding her shoulders)*

— my underwear comes from New York, where the hell you think that shirt was made? Paris, France, lady — you think they sell them in the dry goods store?

> ANNABELLE

No harm looking — try the kiddies' department —
> *(And now comes a new*
> *male voice, deep and powerful)*

> MAN (over)

I think the polite thing would be to remove your hands from that lovely lady.
> *(As MAVERICK turns —)*

CUT TO

JUST AN INCREDIBLE LOOKING MAN — we'll find out soon enough his name is ZANE COOPER.

He is raw-boned, blue-eyed, muscle and sinew; rugged as they come. There is also something about him we don't know yet but we will: COOP is so <u>good</u>, so fucking honorable, he seems like someone out of another era —

— which in point of fact, he is. COOP is the western hero who dominated movies for most of this century. In other words, we are looking at John Wayne or Gary Cooper. Not only has he never done anything bad, the <u>thought</u> of doing any thing bad has never crossed his mind.

> ANNABELLE
> *(very thick southern — as MAVERICK*
> *takes his hands from her shoulders)*

Sometimes when you least expect it, a hero arrives.
> *(COOP is embarrassed)*

It's true — Mister . . .

> COOP

Zane Cooper. Folks call me "Coop" which sits just fine.

> MAVERICK
> *(COOP ticks him off on general principles)*

Coop.

ANNABELLE
(indicating MAVERICK)
This silly looking creature is named Maverick. *(a step closer to COOP)* And
I'm Annabelle Bransford. I'm taking this stage, once it's ready.

COOP
*(his hat has been off since
she began speaking to him)*
So am I.

CUT TO

MAVERICK. Death.

MAVERICK
That's my stage, too. *(beat)* Oh, this is just gonna be a helluva lot of fun.

ANNABELLE
(to COOP)
I'll bet you've protected women before.

COOP
At every opportunity, ma'am.

ANNABELLE
Well, I believe you were sent to protect helpless me. *(a glance at MAVERICK)*
I don't know what this ruffian would have done to me if it had just been
the two of us alone on the stage.

COOP
I hope you can relax and enjoy the journey now. *(Looking at her)* Here's
my feeling — if there weren't any women, we'd all be dead. So it's my job
to see no harm comes to 'em.

MAVERICK
What kind of sense does that make? If there weren't any men, who'd be
around?

CUT TO

COOP. He studies MAVERICK a moment. Then — very flat —

COOP
Were you mocking me?

MAVERICK
Before I answer, does it bother you?

COOP
I can get ruffled.

> MAVERICK

Why don't we just say I was totally agreeing with you in an unusual way.

> COOP

I know your problem — somebody found you charming once, and it went to your head.
>> *(As they study each other —)*

CUT TO

THE STAGECOACH AS BEFORE. BUT IT'S A LITTLE WHILE LATER.

MAVERICK stands outside; he's changed shirts. His saddlebag is slung over a shoulder.

COOP is finishing tying his luggage and ANNABELLE's to the roof of the vehicle. He jumps gracefully down.

> ANNABELLE
>> *(peeking a lovely head out — a smile to*
>> *COOP, her deepest southern drawl)*

Wherever would the world be without true gentlemen?

As COOP, shy, gets into the stage —

CUT TO

THE NEAREST BAR AS A CORPSE WALKS OUT. Obviously, not an actual corpse, just the most sickly looking man you ever saw. He heads for the stage.

MAVERICK opens the door for him.

> SICKLY LOOKING MAN
>> *(pointing up to the front)*

I'm the driver.

> MAVERICK

You OK?

> SICKLY LOOKING MAN

Why are people always asking me that? *(holding out a shaky hand —)* Help me up, son, or we'll never get a move on.

MAVERICK jumps nimbly up to the seat, starts to pull the DRIVER up — it isn't easy, but the old guy gets there.

CUT TO

THE DRIVER, in his seat now, the reins in his hands. MAVERICK gets down, enters the coach.

THE DRIVER shouts "TIMBERRRRRR!" and the two horses start to move as we

CUT TO

THE STAGE, *leaving town.* HOLD *briefly, then —*

CUT TO

A DECK OF CARDS.

It is being manipulated dazzlingly with one hand. Then the deck is put in the other hand. The manipulation is just as skilled.

Outside, the terrain is going bumpily by as the stage moves ahead.

CUT TO

ANNABELLE AND COOP, *inside the stage.*

> ANNABELLE
> Bert here has aspirations toward someday being a card player.

CUT TO

MAVERICK, *sitting across. Makes no reply. Just continues with the cards. One thing might be noted: As he does this, his eyes are closed.*

CUT TO

THE THREE OF THEM.

> COOP
> I'm not totally ignorant of cards. Can't be in my line of work.

> ANNABELLE
> And pray what might that be?

> COOP
> Lawman. Same as my pa. Same as his pa too.

> ANNABELLE
> *(looking up at him, in awe)*
> I'll bet you're the best there is. I can tell things about a man.

> MAVERICK
> *(eyes still closed)*
> I can't quite place your accent, Mrs. Bransford. What part of the South you from?

> ANNABELLE
> Ever been to Mobile?

> MAVERICK
> No.

> ### ANNABELLE
> Well, I'm from Mobile.

CUT TO

MAVERICK. His eyes open now.

> ### MAVERICK
> Oh, you mean Mobile, Ala*bama* — I been there — betcha we know lots of the same people, you start.

> ### ANNABELLE
> *(suddenly near tears — buries*
> *her head in COOP's shoulder)*
> I've tried so hard to forget that place — *(now she looks up longingly at him)*
> — I endured such personal tragedy there.

MAVERICK gets out a handkerchief, dabs at his eyes, mutters "bravo."

> ### COOP
> A woman's suffering's not a funny thing. *(beat)* Bertie.

HE AND MAVERICK stare at one another. You get the feeling they're not going off on vacations together. HOLD. Then —

CUT TO

THE STAGE.

Moving along over the continual rough terrain. It's later in the day.

CUT TO

INSIDE. ANNABELLE has been flirting, drawing COOP out in conversation. MAVERICK, still playing unconsciously with the cards, can't help but listen.

> ### ANNABELLE
> *(gasping — caught up in the story)*
> But how could you face them down, Coop? I mean, even you. Against eight men, all of them outlaws; eight men, all of them armed.

> ### COOP
> *(might be his credo)*
> A man gives his word to do his job, he's got no choice but to do it.

> ### ANNABELLE
> But you must have been afraid.

> ### COOP
> Course I was, Miss Annabelle — but I'll tell you what I truly believe — fear

is a glorious thing because when it's gone, you realize how wonderful life can be.

> MAVERICK
> That is the purest bullshit—that's like saying what a friend we have in pain, because when it's gone, we feel better. Fear stinks, you're welcome to mine.

> ANNABELLE
> Mr. Maverick doesn't believe in bravery.

> MAVERICK
> Now Mrs. Bransford, all I said was I think it's overrated.

CUT TO

COOP. *He smiles. He has, by the way, a wonderful smile.*

> COOP
> I just realized something.

> MAVERICK
> What's that?

> COOP
> You're everything I detest.

> MAVERICK
> *(imitating* COOP—*he does it well)*
> "A man gives his word to do a job, he's got no choice but to do it." *(himself again)* A man's got a million choices—starting with going back on his word.

> ANNABELLE
> Where would the world be if everybody was like you?

> MAVERICK
> World would be OK—have a lot more poker tables, a lot less violence. When I went into the War, my pappy said, "Son, if you dare to come back with a medal, I'll kill you with my bare hands." *(beat)* Brought me up to be obedient.

> COOP
> How long were you in?

> MAVERICK
> The whole way.

> ANNABELLE
> With the famous Ulysses S. Grant's poker playing battalion, I'm sure.

CUT TO

MAVERICK, *playing with the cards, staring out.*

> MAVERICK

No, I was captured early, prisoner for awhile, sent out here rather than go crazy in jail, scouted, did what I could to help with the Indians, brought in Geronimo once, helped him get free once, he belonged free.

CUT TO

ANNABELLE, looking at him.

> ANNABELLE

I don't believe it.

> MAVERICK
> *(looks at her — quietly)*

Neither do I... *(As he stares out again —)*

COOP brings ANNABELLE close, whispers to her — but MAVERICK, again, can't help but hear.

> COOP

Something tells me that inside that buffoon, there's a real human being trying to get out.

> ANNABELLE

You think it's possible?

> COOP
> *(beat)*

God moves in mysterious ways...
> *(HOLD briefly, then —)*

CUT TO

THE ANGEL,

in a foul mood, walking into the dimly lit Frontier. It's evening. He goes to the bar. THE BARTENDER immediately pours three shots of whisky into a water glass —

—and THE ANGEL downs it in a gulp. (That, by the way, is how people drank in the West. Visitors were astounded by the speed of drinking there.)

As he puts the glass down, indicates a refill —

—there is the sound of nearby laughter. He glances up —

CUT TO

THE FOUR COWBOYS MAVERICK clobbered in the fight. They are down the bar from THE ANGEL. And they are the ones laughing. Clearly, at him. As they whisper and their laughter builds,

CUT TO

THE ANGEL. He takes his second drink which is now poured, drops it down the hatch, and walks over to the cowboys.

                              THE ANGEL
                              (dead sober)
One question — are you, by any chance, laughing at me?

                              LEAD COWBOY
                              (feigning fear)
Heavens to Betsy, no.
                         (Now they all four laugh again)

                              THE ANGEL
I want to know the joke.

                              LEAD COWBOY
You, asshole.

                              THE ANGEL
Explain that!

                              LEAD COWBOY
Not unless you pay us one helluva lot more than Maverick did.
                    (And on that bit of information —)

CUT TO

THE ANGEL IN CLOSE UP. He's not taking this well.

                              THE ANGEL
                              (hard to talk)
He paid you to fall down.

CUT TO

THE FOUR LARGE GUYS, nodding.

                              LEAD GUY
Paid us good, too.

CUT TO

THE ANGEL as he slowly rips off a piece of the bar and starts swinging it, catching them off guard — it goes like a streak this next —

— but what he does is cream each of them in the face, and as they bleed, groan, fall to the floor —

                              THE ANGEL
                              (not even breathing hard)
I'll let you fall down for free. *(he looks down at the stunned quartet)* Maverick

was mine anyway . . . *(beat)* . . . 'cept now it's personal . . .
             (HOLD on THE ANGEL. Now —)

CUT TO

INSIDE THE STAGE.

It's next afternoon. Both men doze.

                        ANNABELLE
              (shaking them — a bit alarmed)
         Do you think he's found a shortcut?

CUT TO

OUTSIDE. *Clearly, whatever dusty road they were following, they have left it —*

— they are going like hell across very rough country. The rocking inside is bad and getting worse as we —

CUT TO

MAVERICK AND COOP, *both sticking their heads out the window, shouting at the driver.*

CUT TO

THE DRIVER. *Slumped in his seat. Limp. Eyes closed.*

CUT TO

INSIDE THE COACH. COOP *is getting ready for action.*

                          COOP
                      (to MAVERICK)
         Go on up there and stop the stage —

                        MAVERICK
         — I'm not sure I want to do that —

                          COOP
         — the wheels are coming loose! — if they fall off, we're all of us dead —
         I'll climb out and secure the wheels, you handle the driver — let's *go* —

CUT TO

MAVERICK. *He nods, reaches out for the nearest door, shoves it open and*

CUT TO

MAVERICK, *moving out the door — and this is the beginning of a really hairy journey.*

CUT TO

THE TERRAIN flying by. Bumpy and dusty and

CUT TO

*MAVERICK, holding on to the side of the stage. It's not a matter here of him falling off —
he's too powerful and athletic for that — but he's blinded by the dust and is trying like hell
to get his bearings. Plus, this is not anyone's idea of comfort.*

CUT TO

THE TERRAIN. A huge rut —

CUT TO

*MAVERICK flying half off the stage, managing to hold on, pull himself back to where he
was and now, coughing and still unable to see a lot, he begins his climb.*

CUT TO

The railing around the roof as he grabs hold, first with one hand, then with the other and

CUT TO

THE HORSES pounding along — as they hit another huge rut —

CUT TO

*MAVERICK, being flipped up and onto the roof, where he lands hard, but still manages to
keep hold of the railing.*

CUT TO

*INSIDE OF THE STAGE. COOP sits comfortably, listening to the sounds of MAVERICK's ef-
forts above. ANNABELLE doesn't understand.*

> **ANNABELLE**
> You said we'd die if the wheels came off.

> **COOP**
> Rest easy, Miss Annabelle, wheels are just fine. *(It's very bumpy — he reaches
> out, takes her into his arms)* For protection, you understand.
> *(she nods)*

Now she looks up as more sounds come from the roof.

> **ANNABELLE**
> *(indicating the roof)*
> You don't think he'll kill you?

> **COOP**
> *(nah)*
> In the long run, he'll thank me in his prayers ...

*(As he continues to hold the
frightened* ANNABELLE *—)*

CUT TO

THE ROOF AND MAVERICK. *The terrain is bumpier than ever —*

— and this is where it starts to get tricky — he inches forward across the luggage toward where the driver is —

— except there's a difference in level. THE DRIVER *is several feet below and getting down has to be timed just right because if you hit a bump when you're trying to get off the roof — not a good thing.*

CUT TO

THE DRIVER. *He lies sprawled and motionless on the seat. The reins are still in his hands — but loose — he has no control over the animals.*

CUT TO

MAVERICK, *getting ready to lower himself down and*

CUT TO

THE HORSES, *picking up speed and*

CUT TO

THE TERRAIN, *flashing by and*

CUT TO

MAVERICK, *making his move and*

CUT TO

A GIGANTIC RUT *and*

CUT TO

MAVERICK, *thrown wildly off balance as he tries to get to the driver's seat and as he is about to fall off the entire rampaging stage —*

CUT TO

COOP, *peering out the window toward the front where* MAVERICK *is. He starts to chuckle.*

COOP
(Going back to ANNABELLE. *A sweet memory)*
How well I remember my first runaway stage — broke both legs before I got her under control. *(to* ANNABELLE*)* There's a knack to doing it. *(beat)* I

feel this young man's going to be just fine. *(he holds her again)* Like I said, protection.

CUT TO

MAVERICK, *managing to grab* THE DRIVER, *who doesn't look any worse than when we first met him except now he* is *dead. Plus, being dead, he's not grabbing hold of anything that's of any use to* MAVERICK, *so his body begins sliding along the seat and*

CUT TO

MAVERICK, *off the stage now and getting, he realizes, very close to shit creek —*

— he makes a desperate lunge, just manages to grab hold of the railing that circles the driver's seat as we

CUT TO

THE DEAD DRIVER, *sliding along, still holding the reins, his body coming closer and closer to* MAVERICK *and*

CUT TO

MAVERICK, *letting go of the* DEAD DRIVER, *grabbing the rail with both hands, forcing himself up to the seat just as the* DEAD DRIVER *starts to fall off it —*

— but not before MAVERICK *can grab him, pull him back on so now they're both on the driver's seat,* MAVERICK *reaching for the reins, which brings* THE DEAD DRIVER'S ARMS *around his neck.*

CUT TO

MAVERICK, *doing his best to ignore the corpse and take control of the reins —*

— which at last, thank God, he does —

— and laying the corpse onto the seat he takes the reins, one in each of his powerful hands —

                                MAVERICK
                                  (roaring)
        Just whoa, goddamit! (And as soon as he utters his mighty command —)

CUT TO

THE HORSES *as they start to go* _faster_ —

— they are zooming along now and

CUT TO

MAVERICK, *as their sudden burst almost pulls him out of the seat, catapulting him forward and*

CUT TO

COOP AND ANNABELLE, *getting bounced all the hell around.*

ANNABELLE
You don't think it might be nice to go out there and help him?

COOP
I *could* do that, absolutely—but after he's worked so hard, I think he might resent it. *(beat)* This is a confidence builder for the lad—I'm filling him with pride. You'll see.
(From them—)

CUT TO

THE CORPSE, *lying on the seat, bumping up and down and*

CUT TO

MAVERICK, *steaming mad now—he takes the reins again, really pulls on them with everything he's got. This time he shouts*

MAVERICK
Timberrr!

CUT TO

MAVERICK. CLOSE UP. *Stunned—my God, it worked.*

CUT TO

THE HORSES, *at last slowing and, exhausted, as they come to a halt—*

CUT TO

MAVERICK, *wiped out, taking a deep breath as he sits for a moment on the driver's seat. Then—*

CUT TO

THE GROUND *as he vaults down, opens the stage door.*

COOP *and* ANNABELLE *sit there.* COOP *smiles, claps his hands in applause.*

COOP
Most excellent.

MAVERICK
(still hasn't got his breath back)
What's with the wheels?

COOP

All rock solid.

MAVERICK
(beat)
You fixed four wheels that were falling off in just the time it took me to stop
the stage?

COOP

Turns out I was wrong — wheels were fine all along.

ANNABELLE

He was doing you a favor — don't you feel a whole lot better about yourself now that you've done something brave?

CUT TO

MAVERICK. There is a pause. Then, smiling amiably back at COOP —

MAVERICK

Oh, I get it, this was for *my* benefit. Build character. So I could handle life's
highways and byways.

COOP

Exactly.

MAVERICK
(shakes his head)
Funny, you'd think I'd be mad.

COOP
(to ANNABELLE)
Look at him — bursting with pride.

MAVERICK

One thing though?
(COOP looks at him — as MAVERICK does
his lightning draw, cocks his pistol, aims it
at COOP's head — he could almost shoot)
Try not to help me again!
(From that —)

CUT TO

A FRESHLY COVERED OVER GRAVE.

MAVERICK AND COOP *are covered with sweat from the digging.* ANNABELLE *is with them.*

It's later in the afternoon now.

COOP

I suppose somebody ought to say something nice about the deceased.

ANNABELLE

How do we know he was nice? We don't know anything about him. All
he had in his wallet was the names of some whorehouses.
> *(And now, offscreen, the sound of
> MAVERICK'S VOICE in song—)*

CUT TO

MAVERICK, who has started into "Amazing Grace"—

*—and the shocker is this: Not that the song is gorgeous, it's one of the most beautiful songs
ever written—no, the stunner is that MAVERICK can really sing. A strong, firm voice echo-
ing out over the rough land.*

MAVERICK

"Amazing Grace
How sweet the sound..."

*—and now, surprisingly, COOP joins in. And here's something else you didn't expect: he
can sing, too.*

COOP AND MAVERICK
(in harmony)

"...that saved a wretch like me..."

And now ANNABELLE, touched by what's happening, joins them, her voice high and lovely.

ANNABELLE AND COOP AND MAVERICK

"...I once was lost
But now am found..."

*And now, as they come to the end of the first verse, ANNABELLE sings different words from
the men. She realizes her mistake, stops, and listens to them.*

COOP AND MAVERICK

"...was bound..."

ANNABELLE

"...was blind..."

Here she stops, lets them sing in harmony the last line.

COOP AND MAVERICK

"...but now I'm free..."

She looks at them, mutters she's sorry, and they all sing the last verse beautifully.

ALL THREE

"Through many dangers,
    toils and snares,
I have already come.
But Grace has led me
    safe thus far.
And Grace
    will lead me home..."

(They all stand close together as the
echo of the song dies. Then—)

CUT TO

A SMALL TELEGRAPH OFFICE.

THE ANGEL storms in. ONE OLD GUY works there.

THE ANGEL

Wire come yet?

(The OLD GUY hands him a piece of paper)

CUT TO

THE ANGEL. CLOSE UP. Reading it, crumpling it. Almost a smile now—

THE ANGEL

It'll be a pleasure.

(And as he leaves—)

CUT TO

THE STAGECOACH, LATER IN THE AFTERNOON.

Shadows getting longer.

ALL THREE are seated outside up front now. COOP holds the reins.

COOP

We should start looking for a place to hole up for the night— *(to ANNA-BELLE)*—you can sleep in the coach, we'll sleep on the ground.

MAVERICK

I think we should throw fingers to see who sleeps inside.

ANNABELLE
(to MAVERICK)

Think how humiliated you'd be if I let you sleep inside while I froze.

COOP

I wouldn't bet him on that, Miss Annabelle.

> MAVERICK
> *(ignoring this last — to* COOP)
>
> Listen, I need to find some folks who owe me, and I'm in a hurry, so tomorrow, let's make up the time the gravedigging cost us.

> COOP
>
> Just here to serve you, Bertie.

> MAVERICK
>
> Thanks. *(beat)* Oh, and one more little thing. My name is not Bertie, it's not Bert, and in case you were wondering, Bertram isn't it either. *(building)* It is *Bret.* Now, since neither of you are what anyone might call smart, I'll throw in a few memory hints. It rhymes with *bet.* If you enjoy the classics, try Romeo and Juli*et.* Or think of this: *Bret* is dead-*set* against being in *debt yet.* *(suddenly pleased)* Hey, I liked that one.
> *(As the stagecoach moves slowly on —)*

CUT TO

THE SKY. Dusk won't be long now.

CUT TO

THE STAGECOACH, moving as before, when —

— there is the sudden sound of high-pitched sobbing —

— as the stagecoach takes a turn in the road —

CUT TO

JUST THE MOST PATHETIC SIGHT ANYONE EVER SAW:

A COUPLE OF COVERED WAGONS filled with nuns, widows, and crying children. Several wounded men.

CUT TO

COOP pulling the stage to a halt, vaulting to the ground, hurrying to the wagons. As he goes —

CUT TO

MAVERICK AND ANNABELLE watching. She gets out a flask, takes a pull of whiskey, offers him some.

> MAVERICK
> *(shakes his head)*
>
> Never have, but thanks.

> ANNABELLE
>
> More for me. *(As she takes another swig —)*

CUT TO

COOP, *returning to the stage with a* TALL RAWBONED WOMAN.

COOP

Sneak attack —

TALL RAWBONED WOMAN

— they wounded our husbands but we managed to protect our savings. So they'll be back for sure.

COOP

I promised we'd take them safe where they were headed — *(to* MAVERICK*)* — it's back to Crystal City and don't tell me, I know it's out of your way. *(to the* RAWBONED WOMAN*)* I'll get some fires going.

ANNABELLE
(to the RAWBONED WOMAN)

Who did it?

RAWBONED WOMAN

Indians.

CUT TO

MAVERICK, *in the gathering darkness.*

MAVERICK

Ma'am, it wasn't.

RAWBONED WOMAN
(angry)

I seen half a dozen men in war paint. That's good enough for me.

MAVERICK

Doesn't matter what you saw — there isn't a hostile even close to here.
(And the <u>instant</u> he says that —)

CUT TO

THE HILLS. *Indian war drums have suddenly started. Loud and frightening.*

CUT TO

THE WOMEN AND CHILDREN AND WOUNDED, *whirling, staring up into the hills, scared.*

CUT TO

COOP AND ANNABELLE. COOP *reaches for his gun, wary. She looks at* MAVERICK.

> ANNABELLE

Right again.

CUT TO

THE HILLS *as the drums grow more threatening.*

CUT TO

MAVERICK, *watching, listening. God knows what's going on behind his eyes.* HOLD ON
MAVERICK . . . *Now —*

CUT TO

THE NEXT MORNING.

Not all that early. ANNABELLE *and* COOP *are busy helping the wagon train get ready to
move. Now* MAVERICK *appears. He leads a large horse.*

CUT TO

ANNABELLE, *sees him, can't believe it.*

> ANNABELLE

You're *leaving?*

> MAVERICK

I told you I was in a hurry — people owe me, I got to collect.

> ANNABELLE
> *(still shocked at this behavior)*

You're just running out?

> MAVERICK
> *(pointing to the* RAWBONED WOMAN*)*

Bought the beast from her for a dollar, so at least I'm not a horsethief, feel
better? Be out of your life in ten minutes.

> ANNABELLE

I can't believe anyone would abandon a bunch of women and wounded and
nuns and children.

> MAVERICK

It's like anything else — once you set your mind to it, it's not hard.
> *(As she gives him a look of contempt —)*

CUT TO

MAVERICK, *as he leaves his horse and belongings, goes to talk to the* RAWBONED WOMAN.
ANNABELLE *watches, then turns away.*

CUT TO

COOP, ANNABELLE *with him, a few minutes later, as* MAVERICK *rides off, leaving the wagon train.* COOP *just shakes his head.*

CUT TO

MAVERICK. *He seems kind of cheery about it all.*

CUT TO

A hill just ahead —

— MAVERICK *races up the hill, reaches the crest, is gone.* HOLD.

CUT TO

MAVERICK, RIDING ALONG AND FAST, AS BEFORE.

He is in fact, exactly as before —

— but a hair less cheery.

CUT TO

SOME FLAT TERRAIN.

MAVERICK *rides into view. And not only is the cheery look gone, he is going at a slower pace.*

CUT TO

THE SUN, HIGHER IN THE SKY.

CUT TO

MAVERICK, *riding along, but slowly. He reins in, sits there motionless a moment. Then he turns his face upward and shouts out loud.*

MAVERICK

I HATE MY CONSCIENCE.

And now, muttering to himself, he turns his horse, starts riding in a totally different direction. HOLD. *Then —*

CUT TO

THE SUN. STILL HIGHER.

CUT TO

A PIECE OF ROCKY GROUND. *It shows nothing of interest.*

PULL BACK TO REVEAL

MAVERICK on his haunches, studying the rocky ground

—for a long moment, he just stares, doesn't move —

CUT TO

MAVERICK. CLOSE UP. *There is nothing on the ground of value or interest. Absolutely nothing —*

— except to MAVERICK — because he's seen something there.

CUT TO

MAVERICK, standing, getting back on his horse. He clucks at it. It starts to move —

— but slowly. Very slowly.

CUT TO

MAVERICK. Eyes on the ground.

CUT TO

A PATCH OF SAND.

Undisturbed by anything except the wind. The sun's not so high in the sky now.

PULL BACK TO REVEAL

MAVERICK, on his haunches again, studying, studying.

CUT TO

THE SAND. That's all it is, just sand.

CUT TO

MAVERICK still watching it. Then he rises, whistles for his horse, gracefully mounts.

And rides very slowly forward.

If it isn't clear by now, it should be: MAVERICK's following something.

Who knows? Maybe he was an Indian scout after all. In any case, this much is clear: the man has instincts other people don't have.

CUT TO

THE SKY. GETTING TOWARD SUNSET.

CUT TO

MAVERICK, riding along, watching the terrain. No sound but the wind —

— he stops —

— listens —

— no question, he's hearing something.

We can't. But he is.

He urges his horse forward, <u>verry</u> slowly.

CUT TO

THE TERRAIN *they're going over. Rocky again. The* HORSE'S *hooves make sounds.*

CUT TO

MAVERICK. *Quickly he reins in. Dismounts. He ties the horse to a small tree, puts his finger to his lips.*

> **MAVERICK**
> *(as if the horse were human)*

Shhhh.

CUT TO

THE HORSE. *It nods as if it understands.*

CUT TO

MAVERICK.

> **MAVERICK**
> *(pats the horse's head, whispers)*

If you're smarter than I am, keep it to yourself.

CUT TO

THE HORSE. *It nods again.*

CUT TO

MAVERICK, *moving slowly away.*

CUT TO

MAVERICK'S SHADOW. *Hardly visible — it's dusk now.*

CUT TO

MAVERICK, *moving slowly forward. He might be a shadow, too — he makes no sound.*

CUT TO

THE GROWING DARKNESS. You can't see him, but MAVERICK is moving by.

CUT TO

HIS SHADOW. Just barely visible. It moves silently forward. Slowly, without any sound —
— then it freezes.

CUT TO

MAVERICK. CLOSE UP. Staring ahead. Now —

CUT TO

A CAMPFIRE. HALF A DOZEN MEN sit around, drinking. They are all six of them white. And a couple still have paint on their faces and bodies. HOLD. Then —

CUT TO

THE WAGON TRAIN. NIGHT. LIT BY THE MOON.

MAVERICK comes riding up. Then —

> COOP (over)
> Bring it to a halt.

CUT TO

COOP. He lies against a rock. ANNABELLE lies close alongside. MAVERICK dismounts, moves to them.

> MAVERICK
> Found 'em. Six men. Snow white. Some of them still had paint on.
> *(COOP looks dubious)*
> Come with me — it's not that long a ride, now that I know where they are.
> I need someone to vouch for what I'm saying.

> ANNABELLE
> What's with you and Indians?

CUT TO

MAVERICK. CLOSE UP.

> MAVERICK
> Not a thing. I just figure they've eaten enough shit for one lifetime, don't
> you?

CUT TO

ALL THREE. COOP considers this, nods.

> COOP

Man's got a point.

> MAVERICK

Let's go — these guys were drinking heavy, they're not up to anything tonight.

> ANNABELLE
> *(rising along with COOP)*

This could be exciting.

> COOP

Could be dangerous, too.

CUT TO

ANNABELLE *staring up at* COOP.

> ANNABELLE

Couldn't be as dangerous as being a married woman and lying in the moonlight next to the most blindingly attractive man on the face of the earth.

COOP, *embarrassed, turns away.*

ANNABELLE's *eyes flash at* MAVERICK. *He sticks his finger in his mouth as if to upchuck. Now from that —*

CUT TO

THE THREE OF THEM RIDING IN SILENCE. *Still nighttime. As they go across a small but fast stream,* both MAVERICK *and* COOP *lead her horse along.*

CUT TO

THE THREE OF THEM, *out of the stream now, riding through the night. There is a lot of eye-play between them in what follows.*

> ANNABELLE
> *(to* MAVERICK*)*

Could you teach me to be a great card player?

> MAVERICK

Not if I lived to be even as old as Coop.

> ANNABELLE
> *(she's stung by* MAVERICK's *rejoinder.* COOP
> *isn't all that thrilled about it either)*

Could you teach me to be a *better* card player?

MAVERICK

You tend to giggle when you get a good hand. I'd work on that some. Poker's about bluffing and giggles tend to give things away.

ANNABELLE

It's just so much fun beating men — *(to COOP)* — not you, Zane. *(to MAVERICK)* What else?

MAVERICK

When you bluff, you've got two dead giveaways — first one is you touch your thumb to your little finger.

COOP
(looking at her)
Annie? The last thing you need is to pick up "wisdom" from a money-grubbing failure. A real man's enough to see you through.

MAVERICK
(to ANNABELLE)
It's a shame you're married. You and Coop would sure have the most beautiful babies. *(beat — to COOP)* Of course, you wouldn't be able to lift them. *(back to her)* Besides, you're pretty for a poker player, most men won't notice anything but that, forget about improving.

ANNABELLE

Not pretty for a woman, just for a poker player, that it?

MAVERICK
(amazed)
My Lordy, she is female after all . . .

COOP
(beat — to MAVERICK)
You have any doubts on that subject, I'll vouch for her . . .

MAVERICK

What does *that* mean?

CUT TO

COOP. *No reply. But he seems very happy with himself.*

CUT TO

ANNABELLE, *between the two men, looking first at one, then the other, as we —*

CUT TO

THEIR HORSES. *Tied up in the same place* MAVERICK *tied his before.*

CUT TO

THE THREE *walking in dead silence.*

CUT TO

ANNABELLE *as her boot brushes a small stone, sending it skittering.*

CUT TO

MAVERICK AND COOP, *both of them whirling, glaring at her.*

CUT TO

ANNABELLE. *She mouths "Sorry." They move on in silence again. Now —*

CUT TO

THE SIX MEN WE SAW BEFORE. *Under blankets, some snoring, some not. Whiskey bottles on the ground. Their six horses tied nearby.*

There is the remains of a fire. It's not as high as it was, but it's still burning, giving off, along with the moon, the only light.

PULL BACK TO REVEAL —

MAVERICK, COOP, AND ANNABELLE, *on their haunches.* MAVERICK *and* COOP *have pulled back bushes, giving them room to see. This next is whispered and fast.*

> **MAVERICK**
> *(to* COOP*)*
> See the paint on a couple of faces?
> *(*COOP *nods)*
> OK, you'll vouch for that, that's all the proof I need.

> **COOP**
> Might be a bunch of drunken cowpokes fooling around.

> **MAVERICK**
> I'm telling you, they're it.

> **ANNABELLE**
> Proof is identification. If anyone from the wagon train recognizes them, you're home free.

> **COOP**
> Right now, what you got is nothing.

CUT TO

MAVERICK. CLOSE UP. *They're right. He glances at the* SIX MEN.

MAVERICK

Fug. *(to* COOP*)* We can bring 'em in easy, we can surprise them.

COOP

What's this strange new word that's entered your vocabulary? — "we?" — this is your show.

MAVERICK
(stunned)

You'd let me face down six men?

COOP

But of course.

ANNABELLE
(her voice louder than before)

Don't worry — they're probably drunk and Coop brought in eight dead sober.

CUT TO

MAVERICK AND COOP, *both of them clapping a hand on her mouth as we*

CUT TO

THE SIX MEN. One of them has heard something — he goes up on one elbow, looks around. He reaches under his blanket for a moment, brings it back out — he holds a gun.

CUT TO

THE GUY WITH GUN. He stands — he's wearing long underwear — stares around.

CUT TO

MAVERICK AND COOP *AND* ANNABELLE. *No one moves.*

CUT TO

THE GUY WITH GUN. He takes a step in their direction, then another, another —

CUT TO

ANNABELLE whose eyes are widening. Then —

CUT TO

THE GUY WITH GUN, suddenly stopping, reaching down, grabbing a whisky bottle which is what he was after all the time, drinking from it as he returns to his blanket, gets under it. He drinks a little more, eyes closed, then puts the bottle down.

CUT TO

THE THREE. *Whispering soft again.*

>   ANNABELLE
> See? Drunk—it'll be easy.
>   *(He glares at her)*
> I'm just trying to up your spirits.

>   MAVERICK
> The one thing would do that is if *you* went out there. *(to COOP)* What if
> there's trouble?

>   COOP
>   *(dead serious now)*
> That's a different story.

>   MAVERICK
> If I whistle, you'll come running?

>   COOP
> Right by your side.

>   MAVERICK
> And none of this "wheels are coming off" shit?

>   COOP
>   *(the great lawman now)*
> That was about broken bones—this is about dying.

>   MAVERICK
>   *(He takes a breath. COOP's words have
>   impact. He turns to ANNABELLE)*
> Give me your gun.

>   ANNABELLE
>   *(surprised)*
> Why? It's just a little bitty thing and you're the fastest draw anyone's ever
> seen. What in the world do you want my gun for?

>   MAVERICK
>   *(hesitant)*
> I admit it, I am fast—*(this bursts out)*—but I also can't hit much when there's
> real people I'm aiming at, now give me your gun, I need all the bullets I can
> get.

CUT TO

ANNABELLE. *She hands over a small pistol. He tucks it into his belt behind his back.*

>   ANNABELLE
> I never know whether to believe you.

                             MAVERICK

Neither do I.

              (And as COOP *gives him a look*
                 of encouragement —)

CUT TO

THE SIX MEN *sleeping by the fire.*

                  MAVERICK (over)

Hi, everybody.

              (As they blink their eyes open —)

CUT TO

MAVERICK *sauntering toward them alone, his gun in his holster.*

                  MAVERICK

I'm Bret Maverick. *(He makes a nice smile)*

CUT TO

THE SIX GUYS. *Staring around at each other. What the hell is* <u>this</u>?

CUT TO

MAVERICK. *He moves closer, stops. Just the flickering fire light with help from the moon. The terrain is flat, dusty.*

                  MAVERICK

You're probably wondering why I'm here and it's just to give you one little piece of information — *(beat)* — right now, right at this very second — *(beat — quietly)* — guns are aimed at each and every one of your pretty little heads.

CUT TO

THE SIX GUYS. *Blinking. They've all had too much to drink, sure, but this is news you don't forget in a hurry. Now they stare at the area around them.*

CUT TO

MAVERICK. *Going on calmly, without a care in the world.*

                  MAVERICK

Now, you've got a perfect right to know who's out there and why.

CUT TO

COOP AND ANNABELLE *crouched, hidden, watching.* COOP *misses nothing.*

CUT TO

MAVERICK pointing to the nearest of the SIX.

> ### MAVERICK
> The man who'll blow your brains out is Marshal Zane Cooper. *(to the NEXT GUY)* Johnny Hardin's out for you. You probably know him, unbeaten as a gunfighter.

CUT TO

THE SECOND GUY. The start of genuine fear among the SIX.

CUT TO

ANNABELLE breath held, watching as before. COOP is ready for anything.

> ### MAVERICK
> *(to THIRD GUY)*
> You belong to Ugly Annie Bransford — clocks have been known to beg for mercy when Ugly Annie comes near —
> > *(ANNABELLE is steaming)*

> ### COOP
> *(whispered)*
> Admit it, that was funny.

CUT TO

MAVERICK, chatting amiably on.

> ### MAVERICK
> Why this fuss? 'Cause some Indians killed some whites attacking a wagon train. I believe that, but some of the women, you know how hysterical they can get, think it might have been whites masquerading. Silliest thing I ever heard of. Besides, no fool of a woman could recognize a man in war paint on horseback anyway. So all this is going to cost you is a few hours of beauty sleep.

CUT TO

THE SIX. Scared worse than before; scared of all kinds of things now. He's getting them, no question.

CUT TO

MAVERICK. Convincing as hell.

> ### MAVERICK
> The reason I'm the one out here is, well, some people think I can talk pretty good — not that I'm exactly helpless with a gun —

CUT TO

MAVERICK. CLOSE UP — *and again he does what we saw back in the saloon — the phenomenal fast draw. In this light, it's blinding.*

CUT TO

THE SIX MEN. *Their fear is palpable.*

CUT TO

ANNABELLE. *Watching. Transfixed. COOP's eyes scan for possible trouble.*

CUT TO

MAVERICK *expertly spinning the gun back into its holster.*

CUT TO

COOP. CLOSE UP. *Taut, sensitive to every nuance, every possible danger.*

CUT TO

MAVERICK. *He's got them and he knows it.*

> **MAVERICK**
> So all you've got to do is stand up in your cute long underwear and put your hands on top of your heads.

CUT TO

THE SIX. *A hesitation. Then —*

CUT TO

THE NEAREST GUY. *He scrambles to his feet, puts his hands on his head.*

CUT TO

THE SECOND GUY. *He scrambles up too, his fingers locking together on the top of his head.*

CUT TO

THE THIRD GUY, *jumping up —*

— but with a gun in his hand and —

CUT TO

THE FOURTH GUY, *on his knees, but his gun's ready too and —*

CUT TO

MAVERICK —

—he sticks two fingers into his mouth and <u>whistles</u> loud and clear and the instant that happens—

CUT TO

THE SIX HORSES *moving forward immediately, going as far as their ties will allow them, and from them—*

CUT TO

COOP, *with* ANNABELLE*—and he hasn't moved at all. Just stands there as the sound of gunfire begins—*

> ANNABELLE
> *(turning to* COOP*—surprised)*

He whistled—

> COOP
> *(nods)*

—and very well, too.

> ANNABELLE

Aren't you going out there?

> COOP
> *(aghast)*

A man could get killed doing that.

> ANNABELLE

What if *he* dies?—

> COOP

—I'll feel really bad for days—
> *(Now, from them—)*

CUT TO

MAVERICK

—only he isn't there—

—because from here on until it's over, he's in constant movement, and we've known he could draw and we've known he could play cards but we didn't know 'til now how quick he was—

—plus one more thing—

—every time he fires, he hits what he's aiming at—

—and he's in mid-dive now, as the bullets land where he was, and he comes out of the dive into a roll, and as he comes up out of the roll firing—

CUT TO

THE FOURTH GUY, *the one on his knees, as* MAVERICK'S *bullet hits his forearm and he screams, drops the gun, scrambles after it with his good hand and*

CUT TO

MAVERICK, *risking one more shot and he squeezes it off, goes into a sideways roll as we*

CUT TO

THE THIRD GUY, *the one who began the firing, as* MAVERICK'S *shot crushes his shoulder and he screams too, but the pain has him and he drops his gun and falls and*

CUT TO

COOP *watching the action unfold, not a muscle moving, and*

CUT TO

THE FIFTH AND SIXTH GUYS *blasting away and*

CUT TO

MAVERICK, *the roll over but still on the ground as he fires off two shots and as he starts to get to his feet —*

CUT TO

THE FIFTH AND SIXTH GUYS, *one hit on the hand, the other on the knee, and the knee guy is done, crying out in pain but the hand guy, it isn't over for him and*

CUT TO

THE FIRST AND SECOND GUYS, *the ones with their hands on the tops of their heads and by now they've managed to drop to earth, reach around, find their weapons and*

CUT TO

MAVERICK *diving again, rolling up —*

— but this time he doesn't fire, instead goes into a <u>second</u> dive, and we hadn't expected it and neither did anybody else as we

CUT TO

THE FIRST AND SECOND GUYS, *doing their best to shift their aim and*

CUT TO

MAVERICK, *coming up to one knee, concentrating on the* FIRST GUY *and*

CUT TO

THE SECOND GUY, *moving away and for just a moment he's got* MAVERICK *dead in his sights and*

CUT TO

MAVERICK, *blasting the* FIRST GUY, *hitting him in the thigh and as he starts to fold*

CUT TO

THE SECOND GUY, *about to squeeze off a deadly shot when we*

CUT TO

ANNABELLE, *terrified and then something amazing happens —*

— COOP *draws. And if* MAVERICK *is fast, well,* COOP *is too, and two shots come almost at once and*

CUT TO

THE SECOND GUY *as the first shot from* COOP *takes the gun from his hand, the next shot crunches into his shoulder and he cries out, begins to spin to earth and*

CUT TO

COOP, *the gun already back in its holster and*

CUT TO

ANNABELLE *— did she just see what she thought she saw?* COOP *just stares out as before as if nothing had taken place.*

CUT TO

MAVERICK, *looking at the* SECOND GUY *— watching him hit the ground and for just a moment he's not quite sure what happened but there isn't time to think as we*

CUT TO

THE FOURTH GUY *who was hit in the forearm and now he's got his gun in the other hand and as he does his best to aim —*

CUT TO

MAVERICK, *firing another perfect shot —*

— ooops —

— his gun makes a clicking sound — no more bullets —

> **MAVERICK**
> *(cursing himself)*
> Learn to count, asshole— *(And as he drops his pistol, reaches around for ANNA-*
> *BELLE's—)*

CUT TO

COOP *watching idly,* ANNABELLE *alongside.*

> **COOP**
> The lad definitely has potential—

> **ANNABELLE**
> *(she really isn't sure)*
> —did you just help him?—

> **COOP**
> *(shakes his head)*
> —like I said, it's his show.

CUT TO

ANNABELLE, *studying* COOP *a brief moment, as we*

CUT TO

ANNABELLE'S PISTOL, *in* MAVERICK's *hand now*—

—it really is small—

—and now he does a move he hasn't tried before—

—he jumps <u>backwards</u>, goes into a fast somersault, comes up with the tiny pistol almost disappearing in his hand and

CUT TO

THE FOURTH GUY, *firing, but wild and*

CUT TO

MAVERICK, *firing*—

—dead solid perfect—

—he's nailed him in the shoulder and as this guy cries out, drops the gun—

CUT TO

MAVERICK, *staring at the little gun*—

>   **MAVERICK**
>   *(to himself)*
>
> Damn thing actually works —

CUT TO

THE FIFTH GUY, *who was shot in the hand and he's trying to use both his hands now but no chance as we*

CUT TO

MAVERICK, *spinning, firing, one two three times and*

CUT TO

THE FIFTH GUY, *and he's hit in the hand, the leg, the knee and as he screams and falls —*

CUT TO

MAVERICK. *The only one standing. All around him now, the* SIX GUYS *writhe —*

— and the sound of gunfire, which was so deafening just a minute ago, well, that's gone . . .

CUT TO

MAVERICK. CLOSE UP. *Exhausted by what he's just been through.*

CUT TO

COOP, *moving out from where he had been standing.* ANNABELLE, *stunned by what she's just seen* MAVERICK *do, follows.*

>   **MAVERICK**
>   *(staring at* COOP*)*
>
> Do you ever tell the truth?

>   **COOP**
>
> I don't know what it is, but I just love lying to you.

>   **ANNABELLE**
>
> Are you all right?

>   **MAVERICK**
>   *(a bit confused)*
>
> I don't know how the hell I got that second guy?

>   **COOP**
>
> I saw that, it was great — you caught him on a ricochet.

>   **MAVERICK**
>
> I did? *(shakes his head)* Damn, I just hope I didn't use up all my luck tonight,

gotta save some for the poker tables. *(to* COOP*)* And you're lucky I'm not dead — if I was, I swear to God I'd kill you . . .
> *(HOLD on the* THREE *of them — then —)*

CUT TO

COOP AND MAVERICK, DAYLIGHT,

leading the SIX WOUNDED MEN *who are bound on their horses. An attempt has been made to help them with their wounds.* ANNABELLE *rides a little ahead, occasionally glancing back at the* TWO OF THEM. HOLD. *Then —*

CUT TO

LATE AFTERNOON.

THE WAGON TRAIN *has moved to a different location, stopped for the night.*

MAVERICK *is building a fire for cooking for himself and* COOP *and* ANNABELLE. ANNABELLE *comes over.*

> ANNABELLE

You the chef?

> MAVERICK

Somebody's gotta do it, Coop's busy with the prisoners and you'd more than likely shrink the food.

> ANNABELLE
> *(stung)*

I can cook.

> MAVERICK

All those famous Mobile delicacies? *(rubs his stomach)* Yum.

> COOP *(over)*

Maverick?

CUT TO

COOP, *approaching. This is prettier country now. The hills are bigger, their colors more bright.*

> COOP
> *(gesturing back to the wagon train)*
> — I just spent a long time with the wagon train people and your six — they were definitely the ones. Positive identification.

> MAVERICK

Like I told you, no hostiles around here.
> *(*COOP *seems bothered)*

What?

COOP

Those war drums—you heard 'em, I heard 'em, we didn't make it up. Who was banging 'em? I can't figure it.

ANNABELLE (over)

Coop?

CUT TO

ANNABELLE. CLOSE UP. Scared out of her mind.

ANNABELLE

Maybe it was them?

(And on that—)

CUT TO

THE HILLS SURROUNDING THEM.

And maybe <u>FIFTY</u> <u>INDIANS</u>, *maybe more. All mounted and armed.*

All in war paint.

CUT TO

MAVERICK getting to his feet. Carefully. COOP makes no move.

CUT TO

THE WOMEN AND KIDS. Frozen.

CUT TO

THE SIX GUYS MAVERICK FOUGHT. Handcuffed to one of the wagon trains. Pale with terror.

CUT TO

THE INDIANS. A series of blood-curdling cries.

CUT TO

ANNABELLE, moving between MAVERICK and COOP. Neither of them is particularly over-joyed at this moment either.

CUT TO

THE SKY. DUSK. The Indians have the dying light behind them.

CUT TO

A LONG SHOT OF THE ENTIRE TABLEAU. The wagon train with its helpless wounded and women and children. MAVERICK and COOP standing on either side of ANNABELLE.

And surrounding them, above them, silent and deadly, the war-painted Indians.

For a long moment, no one moves —

— then —

— the sound of someone on horseback from behind the Indians. A few of them separate, making room —

— and there he is —

CUT TO

THE INDIAN OF EVERY WHITE MAN'S NIGHTMARES.

A massive figure, rippling with brutal power. There is a terrifying cruelty behind his eyes.

He sits on a magnificent white horse.

He wears a long headdress.

And war paint that makes him seem, if that's possible, even more frightening.

He reins in at the top of the hill, glares down at the intruders.

CUT TO

THE WOMEN AND CHILDREN. *No one breathes.*

CUT TO

THE NIGHTMARE INDIAN, *as suddenly, in a deep, guttural voice, he speaks.*

> **NIGHTMARE CHIEF**
> (*his words are subtitled*)
> Hello, Bret, you've come for the money I owe you?

CUT TO

MAVERICK, *glancing around at the others.*

> **MAVERICK**
> Anybody get all that?
> > (*No one does*)

> **ANNABELLE**
> (*to* MAVERICK)
> You know about Indians, can you speak to him?

> **MAVERICK**
> I'll do the best I can.

*Now he takes a step forward and when he speaks, it's in Indian too. (*THROUGHOUT THIS, HE AND JOSEPH, FOR THAT IS THE CHIEF'S NAME, SPEAK INDIAN — AND THEY ARE THE ONLY ONES WHO UNDERSTAND THE LANGUAGE.*)*

> MAVERICK
> *(subtitled)*
> Joseph, you've got to do me a favor — go with me on this — I'll explain later.

> JOSEPH
> *(subtitled)*
> How long will it take — I'm getting cold.

> MAVERICK
> *(subtitled)*
> I'll make it quick — scream at me now.

CUT TO

JOSEPH, letting loose a blood-curdling sound.

CUT TO

Panic among those down below. COOP *turns to* MAVERICK.

> COOP
> What's he saying?

> MAVERICK
> *(nervous)*
> We've committed a terrible sin — this is sacred ground.

> ANNABELLE
> We didn't know it was sacred — tell him we're just here for the night.

> MAVERICK
> *(he nods, speaks up to*
> JOSEPH *in Indian — subtitled)*
> Shake your head and fire your rifle in the air — look really mad — lots of words.

CUT TO

JOSEPH, doing as told. Even though you know he's obeying orders, it's very impressive.

CUT TO

ANNABELLE, edging closer to MAVERICK *and* COOP.

> ANNABELLE
> Did he understand we didn't know?

> MAVERICK
> *(nods — upset)*
> But he still says his gods demand a sacrifice.

> COOP
> What kind of sacrifice?

> MAVERICK
> *(long pause — then, whispered)*
> Human. *(up to JOSEPH in Indian — subtitled)* You're doing great — point your finger around at everybody and speak angry.

CUT TO

JOSEPH, *his long finger taking in everyone down below. Fury comes from his throat.*

CUT TO

MAVERICK. *Really worried now.*

> MAVERICK
> If someone passes the Indian Bravery Test, he won't kill the rest of us. *(beat)* But one of us has to go with him.

> COOP
> What's the Indian Bravery Test?

> MAVERICK
> He says he cuts off both hands — if you don't make a sound, you pass.

CUT TO

COOP

> COOP
> Hell, I couldn't do that — nobody could do that —

CUT TO

MAVERICK, *up to JOSEPH.*

> MAVERICK
> *(subtitled)*
> Hold up one finger and holler some.

CUT TO

JOSEPH. *It's getting darker. As he does what he's told, he seems like a figure out of myth.*

CUT TO

ANNABELLE *and* COOP, *staring at MAVERICK, waiting.*

MAVERICK
One person has to go with him right now — *(pause)* — or he'll slaughter us all.

CUT TO

JOSEPH, *as suddenly he starts laughing and talking.*

JOSEPH
(subtitled)
I never did anything like this before — it's fun.

CUT TO

MAVERICK, *quickly explaining* —

MAVERICK
He's laughing about the pain to come — he loves to see suffering —

ANNABELLE
(glancing up)
— you can tell that just by looking at him —

CUT TO

JOSEPH, *firing his weapon at the skies again, shrieking louder than ever.*

CUT TO

MAVERICK.

MAVERICK
(to COOP and ANNABELLE)
He wants blood *now (up to JOSEPH, subtitled)* — don't overdo it.

CUT TO

COOP and ANNABELLE, *looking toward MAVERICK.*

MAVERICK
Can't let him have a woman.
(COOP nods)
That leaves us plus the wounded. *(beat)* I don't think he'd be satisfied with someone already damaged. Besides, they've got to be brought to justice legal like.

CUT TO

COOP. *He nods again. There is a long silence. Then he starts to talk* —

COOP
You've got a lifetime ahead of you yet. I'll go. Besides, it's my turn — I almost got you killed twice already.

CUT TO

MAVERICK. CLOSE UP. *He shakes his head.*

> **MAVERICK**
> I can't do the things you can. Someone needs to run the wagon train right—
> you're the one for that. Save the women and nuns, see the kids are OK, give
> the hurt men settlers courage. You gotta be the one. But it's OK—third time
> lucky.

CUT TO

ANNABELLE, *staring at* MAVERICK. *The bravest words she ever heard have just been spoken.*

> **ANNABELLE**
> Bret—

> **MAVERICK**
> *(raises his hand)*
> —a man's gotta do what a man's gotta do. *(to* JOSEPH—*subtitled)* One more
> minute and I'm coming.
> *(And on that—)*

CUT TO

A WAGON AND MAVERICK *moving out from behind it. It's just a minute or two later—*
he carries his saddlebag—

—and he's changed clothes—

—the shrunken lucky shirt is back on.

CUT TO

COOP, *as* MAVERICK *goes to him.* COOP *gives him a manly embrace.*

> **MAVERICK**
> You were right, Coop—I never in my life felt better than I do right now—
> *(Now from* COOP—*)*

CUT TO

ANNABELLE. *And it's clear in her eyes—she doesn't want him to go.*

> **MAVERICK**
> *(soft; brave)*
> I liked it just now when you called me Bret.

CUT TO

MAVERICK, *as* ANNABELLE, *moved, throws herself into his arms.*

MAVERICK
Listen to me now.

ANNABELLE
What? What, dear Bret?

MAVERICK
When you're going to bluff, don't flick your fingernails against your front teeth. That's the second giveaway you've got to work on.

ANNABELLE
(coming apart)
Even at a moment like this, you're thinking of others.

MAVERICK
Goodbye, my lady.
> *(They kiss — briefly — passionately —*
> *then they break —)*

CUT TO

THE TWO OF THEM *as he looks up the hill toward JOSEPH. Now he looks back at her.*

MAVERICK
(incredible courage in the face of danger)
See, now when they cut my hands off, my lucky shirt'll fit again... *(And he mounts his horse, rides up toward his fate as we —)*

CUT TO

COOP, *moving to ANNABELLE, folding her into his arms. She clings to him desperately.*

CUT TO

A LONG SHOT OF THE ENTIRE WAGON TRAIN WATCHING MAVERICK GO. *Each and every one of them desperately moved.* HOLD...

CUT TO

JOSEPH, *as MAVERICK reaches him.*

JOSEPH
(in English now, he speaks well)
What was all that?

MAVERICK
(riding away with JOSEPH)
Tell you later. *(beat)* I could die happy right now...
> *(From that —)*

CUT TO

MAVERICK AND JOSEPH IN A LARGE TEEPEE.

JOSEPH is clearly the leader of his tribe and his teepee reflects this. Gorgeous skins as rugs, gorgeous feather headdresses hanging from the walls.

At the moment, the two of them are giggling like schoolchildren as they pass a pipe back and forth. God knows what they're smoking, but it isn't Camel Filters.

Now, very suddenly, here they come again —

— the wardrums.

JOSEPH doesn't pay attention. MAVERICK makes his way to the tent flaps, throws them open, looks out.

CUT TO

A LOVELY INDIAN VILLAGE. Neat, well tended, and in the center —

— a bunch of Indians wearily beat war drums.

CUT TO

JOSEPH, as MAVERICK drops the flap.

> MAVERICK
>
> Why the drums?

> JOSEPH
>
> We had a rotten harvest so when this Russian Archduke came along and wanted to see the "real West" — *(shrugs)* — I said OK. He pays well. We go whooping around in war paint like idiots and beat those stupid drums. *(shakes his head)* He likes me to speak like we're supposed to in books. *(the cliché Indian now)* "How, White Man." *(beat)* You people are such assholes. *(and now he lapses into silence. Not a happy man)*

> MAVERICK
>
> Don't get so down — it's not like you're married to him.

> JOSEPH
> *(miserable)*
>
> That's not it — Bret, I don't have the thousand I owe you — I don't have five cents except in wampum.

CUT TO

MAVERICK, really upset.

> MAVERICK
>
> I was wrong — it's third time *unlucky*. *(shaking his head)* Now I've got to win *three* thousand in the next couple of days just to be able to enter.

> JOSEPH
> I'll make it up to you someday, I swear.

> MAVERICK
> No point in both of us being down, you did your best.

During this he has reached for his saddleback, rooted around inside, pulled out a leather drawstring bag.

> MAVERICK
> Let me check again — cross your fingers — maybe I'm closer than I think.

He hefts the bag —

— then he opens it —

— after which he goes in shock — the bag is filled with rolled up Sears Catalog paper.

> MAVERICK
> That rotten Annabelle — *(big)* — how could she rob me when I was going to face my doom? *(He drops the now empty bag — deep gloom has descended)* I'll bet she's taken off with it, too — I'm a dead man.

CUT TO

JOSEPH. And now the thing you least expect: a smile.

> JOSEPH
> What a good idea . . .
> > *(As MAVERICK looks at him*
> > *as if he were crazy —)*

CUT TO

JOSEPH.

The next afternoon, riding his magnificent horse at full gallop. As he begins to slow —

PULL BACK TO REVEAL

A large number of tents, all of them surrounding something we hadn't expected to see: A LARGE RAILROAD CAR.

It rests on a siding of track.

CUT TO

INSIDE THE CAR AS *JOSEPH ENTERS. It is ornate, filled with artwork of all kinds, clearly Russian in origin.*

Seated in the middle of a thick sofa is THE ARCHDUKE *himself.*

He's the kind of guy if he wasn't so rich and powerful, you'd want to clobber. Spoiled beyond belief, the product of decades of inbreeding, he is reminiscent of Peter Ustinov in Quo Vadis *when he played Nero.*

> JOSEPH
> *(speaking in flawless French — subtitled)*

Good afternoon. I hope His Majesty has had a happy day.

> ARCHDUKE
> *(in flawless French too — subtitled)*

I know you were taught by missionaries but I hate it when you speak that way — it simply isn't authentic. Now do it right.

> JOSEPH
> *(raising his right hand)*

How, White Man.

> ARCHDUKE
> *(English now)*

Hello, Noble Savage — I've had a terrible day. I've killed every animal in sight and it's boring me.

> JOSEPH

Mighty one from across seas has not had greatest Injun thrill.

> ARCHDUKE

And what might that be?

> JOSEPH

Kill Injun.

CUT TO

THE ARCHDUKE. *Staggered.*

> ARCHDUKE

Is that legal here?

> JOSEPH

If no one find out, very legal. *(beat)* Much wampum needed.

> ARCHDUKE
> *(He's into it now)*

I've never shot anyone before. How much?

> JOSEPH

Thousand dollars.

> ARCHDUKE

Would we have to tie him up? That doesn't seem sporting.

> **JOSEPH**
> Him loose. But easy hit. Dying anyway.
>   *(Now, as THE ARCHDUKE*
>   *starts to get excited —)*

CUT TO

A DESERTED ROCKY CANYON. LATER IN THE AFTERNOON.

MAVERICK, magnificently painted to look like an Indian, stands alone. From a distance, in point of fact, he actually looks like an Indian. Now, at the sound of horses, he bends over, groaning, his hands across his stomach as we

CUT TO

JOSEPH and THE ARCHDUKE, riding up, dismounting. JOSEPH holds his giant bow and arrow, THE ARCHDUKE his hunting rifle.

> **JOSEPH**
> Me go give him courage.
>   *(THE ARCHDUKE starts with him)*
> No — Indian law say death be private.
>   *(THE ARCHDUKE nods, stops as we)*

CUT TO

MAVERICK, in terrible pain as JOSEPH approaches. This next is subtitled, in Indian.

> **MAVERICK**
> Did you fix his gun?

> **JOSEPH**
> Couldn't — he never let it out of his hands.

> **MAVERICK**
> Then I have one question for you — what's in it for me if I die?

> **JOSEPH**
> I got him up to five hundred dollars.

> **MAVERICK**
> Worth the risk.

> **JOSEPH**
> I thought you'd see it that way.

CUT TO

THE ARCHDUKE, rifle aimed.

ARCHDUKE

Tell him to start running.

JOSEPH
(moving into the line of fire — shouting)

No — no — no — wrong —

ARCHDUKE
(as JOSEPH runs up)

— *what's* wrong? — *(gesturing toward the sky)* I don't want to lose the light.

JOSEPH

Injun shot by white man's weapon never reach happy hunting ground. *(handing over his bow and arrow)* Injun must die Injun way.

ARCHDUKE
(grumpily exchanges weapons)

I've never used one of these.

JOSEPH

Easy.

ARCHDUKE

Tell him to start running.

JOSEPH
(to MAVERICK — subtitled)

Don't go too fast — I told him you were dying.

CUT TO

MAVERICK, sort of limping along.

CUT TO

THE ARCHDUKE. Aiming the bow and arrow.

CUT TO

MAVERICK, limping on, groaning brilliantly.

CUT TO

THE ARCHDUKE. MAVERICK dead in his sights now —

— and he <u>fires</u> —

— and he <u>misses</u> —

— and he stings his hand like hell. He cries out, shakes his hand.

ARCHDUKE
(throwing the bow down, taking his rifle)
No wonder you people were so easy to conquer — your hands must have
hurt all the time.

JOSEPH
(moving in front of the rifle)
Two thousand.

ARCHDUKE
You don't think he'll mind missing Heaven?

JOSEPH
Not if you shoot fast —

        (And on that —)

CUT TO

MAVERICK, *seeing the rifle aimed at him, he's stunned, but before he can move —*

CUT TO

THE ARCHDUKE. *One shot rings out and*

CUT TO

MAVERICK *screaming in pain, his hands go to his heart, blood is all over. He staggers once,
falls on his face, motionless.*

CUT TO

JOSEPH *and* THE ARCHDUKE

JOSEPH
*(mounting up quickly, gesturing
for THE ARCHDUKE to follow)*
Come.

ARCHDUKE
(thrilled)
Can we do this again tomorrow?

JOSEPH
(shakes his head)
Only one each tribe.

ARCHDUKE
(on his horse now)
You're just going to leave him for the vultures?

CUT TO

JOSEPH. He considers this. Then nods.

>   JOSEPH
> Never liked him much anyway.
>   *(And as they ride off—)*

CUT TO

THE INDIAN VILLAGE.

MAVERICK is finishing removing his paint as JOSEPH rides up. Evening now. Fires all over.

>   MAVERICK
> He could have killed me.

>   JOSEPH
>   *(handing bow and arrow)*
> Fire.
>   *(MAVERICK does — same as with*
>   *THE ARCHDUKE; it hurts)*
> An amateur can't hit anything after he's used my bow. *(smiles)* Don't be
> mad—I got him up to a thousand. I can pay you what I owe you now.

>   MAVERICK
>   *(touched)*
> I appreciate that.

>   JOSEPH
>   *(an arm around MAVERICK)*
> What are friends for...?
>   *(Now, from the two of them—)*

CUT TO

THE NEXT DAY

and *MAVERICK, dressed as he was when he went off with JOSEPH, riding along a trail go-ing the opposite direction as when he left.*

CUT TO

A TURNING IN THE TRAIL, ROCKS ON EITHER SIDE.

As he takes it—

CUT TO

A RIDERLESS HORSE. THE RIDER, face down, lies moaning in deep pain. His body is at a funny angle — legs could be broken.

CUT TO

MAVERICK, reining in, dismounting.

MAVERICK

Hang on.

CUT TO

THE GUY ON GROUND. *The groaning is louder.*

CUT TO

MAVERICK, kneeling, gently turning the guy over.

CUT TO

THE GUY. CLOSE UP. *He's the first person we saw in the movie, the guy with the wandering eye who witnessed the hanging.*

CUT TO

MAVERICK. *Has no idea who the guy is.*

CUT TO

WANDERING EYE. *He whispers. As* MAVERICK *bends close —*

CUT TO

THE ANGEL AND THE GUY WITH THE BURNED FACE, *appearing behind him and while he is unaware,* BURNED FACE *grabs his gun from its holster while* THE ANGEL *delivers a vicious kick to the back of the head.*

CUT TO

MAVERICK, falling to the ground, stunned, in sudden pain. He starts to rise —

— but too late —

— THE ANGEL *delivers another terrible kick — this one flush in the stomach.* MAVERICK *gasps.*

CUT TO

THE ANGEL. *Another kick into the stomach. This one harder.* MAVERICK *is beginning to go pale. Impossible to breathe now.*

THE ANGEL

Should have paid your cowhands more, Maverick. *(And now he kicks* MAVERICK *brutally in the neck —)* Lucky for you I'm not the kind who minds being made a fool of. *(As he gestures for others to join him in beating the hell out of* MAVERICK *—)* I never would have let you make the poker game — but before you done what you done, I might have let you live.

CUT TO

MAVERICK, *trying to retaliate as best as he can —*

— but the attack was too sudden, too vicious —

— and as the beating continues —

CUT TO

THE SKY. THUNDER AND TORRENTIAL RAIN —

— WE ARE BACK AT THE SHOT THAT ENDED THE OPENING SEQUENCE —

— MAVERICK'S HANGING.

The rattlers are moving out of the burlap sack.

They wriggle closer to MAVERICK on his horse.

His horse is a rock.

MAVERICK struggles to free himself harder than ever, all he's got and more and

THE RATTLERS will not stop — will — not — stop —

— THE HORSE sees the rattlers now —

— and doesn't budge.

MAVERICK in desperation increases his efforts.

Thunderclaps.

Lightning.

THE RATTLERS start to curl.

Totally without warning, MAVERICK's horse bolts.

MAVERICK's body drops into space.

He hangs helpless in mid-air.

THE RATTLERS continue to curl.

MAVERICK fights somehow to free his neck from the noose —

— trying somehow to find a way to survive.

No good.

Not enough breath.

His body's struggling becomes more feeble.

Then more feeble still.

He is a strong and powerful man but in the last hours he has been in gunfights, been beaten half to death —

— his energy is going.

Going.

Almost gone now.

His body hangs motionless in space.

Nothing left.

As his eyes start to close —

— the loudest thunderclap of all. Deafening —

— and the whole goddamned branch MAVERICK is hanging from is ripped from the tree, and as it falls hard to the ground, MAVERICK with it —

— the rattlers are all around him. He's landed, stunned, in their midst.

It's impossible to tell which one of them will strike first. Now —

CUT TO

TWO GNARLED HANDS. That's all we see at first, just the hands. One of them grabs the burlap sack, the other starts scooping up the rattlers, putting them back inside.

No fear of consequences. One-two-three-four-five-six, and the rattlers are gone from view. And once they are —

PULL BACK TO REVEAL

THE MAGICIAN, for that, we will learn, is the name of the man we are looking at.

LITTLE OLD MAN, more precisely.

WEIRD LOOKING LITTLE OLD MAN, more precisely still. He is dressed in clothing that neither fits nor matches.

When he talks, HE TALKS VERY LOUDLY. Clearly, he doesn't get a lot of company. Right now he isn't talking at all, just staring at MAVERICK's still body.

He also is carrying the biggest shotgun anyone ever saw. It is what blasted the tree branch to the ground.

Now he takes a foot, pushes MAVERICK over so he's on his back.

Next he aims the huge weapon at MAVERICK's heart.

THE MAGICIAN
I'm a gonna kill you.

CUT TO

MAVERICK. Barely able to speak. Still, this latest piece of news is not so much upsetting as it is strange.

MAVERICK
(whispered)
... If you're going to do that ... why didn't you just let me hang ...?

CUT TO

THE MAGICIAN, coming closer.

THE MAGICIAN
'Cuz then you wouldn't have know'd your crime.

MAVERICK
(blinking up)
... Who are you? ... and what's my crime ...?

THE MAGICIAN
I'm The Magician — and your crime — *(bigger)* — the crime you're gonna die for — *(huge)* — the crime that's gonna condemn you to hell is this: *(roaring)* YOU STOLE MY RATTLESNAKES.

CUT TO

MAVERICK. He's just in terrible shape but he didn't think he was going mad.

MAVERICK
... Do I look like a rattlesnake thief?

THE MAGICIAN
(studies MAVERICK a long while, the huge gun still aimed. Finally he nods)
That's exactly what you look like.

MAVERICK
You're wrong — I play cards.

THE MAGICIAN
(shakes his head)
A gambler? Not in that shirt.

CUT TO

MAVERICK. He closes his eyes, tries to laugh —

—but he can't. Not just because he hasn't the strength but because he is far beyond ex-haustion. His body begins to shake, as if with fever. HOLD ON MAVERICK. *Now —*

CUT TO

A BIG RATTLESNAKE IN CLOSE UP.

PULL BACK TO REVEAL

THE MAGICIAN'S CABIN. MAVERICK *lies on a cot. Clearly, he has been ill.*

THE RATTLER *begins to slither up a leg of the cot on which he lies.*

CUT TO

THE MAGICIAN, *sitting across the room in a rocking chair.*

> **THE MAGICIAN**
> *(as if to a dog)*
> Henry, you get offa there this minute!

CUT TO

THE RATTLER. *It knows who's boss. It slithers down the leg of the cot, scoots across the room.*

CUT TO

THE ROOM. *Just as strangely furnished as* THE MAGICIAN *is strangely dressed.*

It's not a small room at all. And on the walls are some beautiful oil paintings. Some gorgeous handmade quilts.

On the floor — a large and obviously expensive oriental rug.

In the corner — several huge bags.

Plus one more thing: The whole room is filled with rattlesnakes of varying shapes and sizes.

CUT TO

MAVERICK, *eyes slowly opening. He manages to lift his head, take in his surroundings.*

> **MAVERICK**
> . . . This hell . . . ?

> **THE MAGICIAN**
> No, ya fool, it's my home — I decided you was too dumb to steal my babies.

> **MAVERICK**
> w long I been sick?

> **THE MAGICIAN**
> st track of what year it was years ago. Couple days, maybe more'n

a couple. *(gets up, comes over, looks down at* MAVERICK*)* Color's coming back. I think being hung is what got you off your feed. Rest a little more, you'll be fine.

MAVERICK*'s eyes are closed again before the sentence is finished. Now —*

CUT TO

THE MAGICIAN COOKING AT THE STOVE IN ANOTHER CORNER OF HIS HOME.

CUT TO

MAVERICK. *He sits in a chair at a small wooden table with two chairs. A thick blanket is thrown across his shoulders.*

THE MAGICIAN *brings him a plate of food. Or at least a plate of* <u>something</u>. MAVERICK *looks at it suspiciously.*

> MAVERICK
>
> What do you call this?

> THE MAGICIAN
>
> I don't think it pays to ask too many questions.

CUT TO

THE PLATE. *At least nothing looks alive.*

CUT TO

MAVERICK. *He takes a bite; that's enough.*

> THE MAGICIAN
>
> You'll wanna get your strength back.
> *(*MAVERICK *says nothing)*

CUT TO

THE MAGICIAN. *He studies* MAVERICK *in silence.*

CUT TO

MAVERICK. *And this is the first time we've ever seen him like this: He's down.*

> MAVERICK
>
> Right now, I don't know what I need it for. See, there's gonna be a poker championship — twenty-five thousand entrance fee. Poker's what I've done all my life and I wanted to know how good I was. Once and for all. *(beat)* Got robbed. What I had's probably been spent. Game may have started already for all I know.

> **THE MAGICIAN**
> Lemme tell you something true—money ain't worth shit.

CUT TO

MAVERICK. CLOSE UP. Long pause. Then—

> **MAVERICK**
> It wasn't the money...it was the knowing.
> *(HOLD ON MAVERICK. Then—)*

CUT TO

OUTSIDE THE CABIN. DAY.

There's a strange feel to it. It's sunny but there's thunder. Huge clouds scud across the horizon.

TWO CHAIRS set up alongside a large tree stump. MAVERICK sits in one of them, staring at the sky.

The ground around him is filled with rattlers, taking in the sunshine.

CUT TO

THE MAGICIAN carrying a couple of the large bags we saw in a corner. They're heavy, causing a problem for him. He has a large pistol tucked into his belt. MAVERICK is unarmed.

MAVERICK is starting to look like himself again. His problem is the rattlers. He eyes them suspiciously as THE MAGICIAN walks toward him.

> **THE MAGICIAN**
> *(spotting the look)*
> Oh, don't worry none. They're sweet as pie—*(beat)*—lest, of course, I tell them to bite.

> **MAVERICK**
> But you wouldn't do that.

> **THE MAGICIAN**
> *(he means this)*
> Do it in a fingersnap if people rile me.

CUT TO

THE GROUND as he puts the bags down—

—a few rattlers hiss, slither out of the way.

THE MAGICIAN sits in the other chair.

THE MAGICIAN

Been thinking about your finances. *(pointing to a bag)* Guess what's in here? *(big)* The answer to your troubles.

CUT TO

THE BAG *as he opens it, pours out its contents.*

It's shit — worthless — tin plates, cups, ladles.

THE MAGICIAN

Some of them's real old — *(He pronounces this next "anti-cues")* — antiques.

MAVERICK
(tactfully)

I don't think the tournament will accept — *(beat)* — even genuine anti-cues.

THE MAGICIAN

Figgered. *(And now as he rips open the other bag —)*

MAVERICK

Oh, good. More plates.

CUT TO

MAVERICK. *Shocked. And we find out why as we*

CUT TO

THE MAGICIAN *holding the other bag wide — and it's* <u>stuffed</u> *with cash.* THE MAGICIAN *grabs a handful, holds it out. It's tied up in a bundle.*

THE MAGICIAN

I got twenty-five times twenty-five thousand in here. *(he slaps the bundle of money down on the tree trunk)* There's more'n your entrance fee right there. Counted it out last night.

CUT TO

THE TWO OF THEM, THE MONEY, AND TREE STUMP *between them. And of course, the snakes hissing contentedly on the ground.*

MAVERICK

Incredible.

THE MAGICIAN
(shrugs)

Nah — I been a hermit here forty years — this is rough country, lot of people die. When I find 'em I keep what looks valuable. *(he picks up the bundle of money, holds it out)* Want it? No loan or nothing, I'd just give it to you. I'd like that.

MAVERICK reaches for the money —

— THE MAGICIAN pulls it back.

> THE MAGICIAN
> *(roaring)*
> *Now I ain't no fool —* I want something in return —

> MAVERICK
> — what?

CUT TO

THE MAGICIAN. CLOSE UP. One word.

> THE MAGICIAN
> Magic.

CUT TO

MAVERICK. Nothing makes sense.

CUT TO

THE MAGICIAN. Tossing the money back and forth as he speaks.

> THE MAGICIAN
> See, all my life people thought I was magical because of my way with animals, but I knew I wasn't, they just liked me. *(beat)* Before I die, just once, I want to see real magic. You do that, this here's yours. You don't do that, well, I'll just send you on your way on foot. Or shoot you, if you'd prefer. *(indicates his pistol)*

> MAVERICK
> You'd just kill me?

> THE MAGICIAN
> Why not? — you'd be dead a dozen times over already, not for me.

CUT TO

MAVERICK. He nods.

> MAVERICK
> *(soft; reflective)*
> I had magic in my hands, once. Real magic ... *(shakes his head)* But those were special circumstances — no way I can do it again.

> THE MAGICIAN
> Why was they special?

MAVERICK
(*moved*)
My mother was dying and I wanted to please her before she left.

THE MAGICIAN
Try now.

MAVERICK
I'd fail.

CUT TO

THE MAGICIAN as suddenly he makes a sound we haven't heard from him before and

CUT TO

THE RATTLERS, starting to go wild and

CUT TO

MAVERICK, frozen.

MAVERICK
— I'll try, I'll try — I promise — OK?

THE MAGICIAN makes another strange sound. The snakes calm down.

THE MAGICIAN
Figured you might change your mind.
(*Now, from that —*)

CUT TO

A DECK OF CARDS resting on the tree stump.

PULL BACK TO REVEAL

MAVERICK AND THE MAGICIAN, seated across from each other. The rattlers have gathered round too.

CUT TO

MAVERICK, eyeing the snakes. He's nervous. But it's not just the reptiles — he knows what failure means and it's very clear behind his eyes: He doesn't think it can work. And if it doesn't, he's going to die.

CUT TO

THE MAGICIAN, excited. He places the huge wad of money on the trunk near the cards.

THE MAGICIAN
Let's get the magic going.

MAVERICK

Give me a horse — let me have a chance to get out of here alive.

THE MAGICIAN

Let's get the magic going.

MAVERICK
(deep breath)

Your cards?

(THE MAGICIAN nods)

I ever see them, touch them?

(THE MAGICIAN shakes his head)

CUT TO

MAVERICK. He breathing more deeply now. It's almost as if he's trying to enter a different state. He stares up —

CUT TO

THE GIANT CLOUDS, moved by the wind.

CUT TO

THE MAGICIAN, waiting.

CUT TO

THE RATTLESNAKES, waiting.

CUT TO

MAVERICK. Voice almost in a reverie.

MAVERICK

I loved my mother a whole lot . . . she was everything you could want —

THE MAGICIAN

— you stalling?

MAVERICK

I guess.

THE MAGICIAN

Don't.

MAVERICK
(quickly —)

Think of a card, *fast* —

(THE MAGICIAN nods)

CUT TO

MAVERICK. *Firm now.*

> **MAVERICK**
> Ace of spades

CUT TO

THE MAGICIAN. *Now he's shocked. Finally he nods.*

> **THE MAGICIAN**
> Amazing.

> **MAVERICK**
> Naw, that's nothing, there's no magic there, it's just like you with your animals — most people think of the ace of spades.

CUT TO

MAVERICK. CLOSE UP. *Voice low, now. The firmness gone. This is not a man brimming with confidence.*

> **MAVERICK**
> No, the magic part would be if I could cut to the ace of spades — *(beat)* — cut right to it — *(beat)* — with my eyes closed.

CUT TO

THE MAGICIAN, *studying him.*

> **THE MAGICIAN**
> You can make a thing like that happen?

> **MAVERICK**
> *(shaking his head)*
> I don't think so. But like I told you, it happened once. See, if my eyes were open, you might think it was a trick. But if I'm blind, and God picks that moment to smile, that's magic, right?

> **THE MAGICIAN**
> I want that — I want to believe you can do that.

> **MAVERICK**
> Shuffle the cards.

CUT TO

THE CARDS *as* THE MAGICIAN *takes them, begins shuffling.*

CUT TO

THE CLOUDS. *The wind is getting stronger.*

CUT TO

MAVERICK, *staring up. He pays no attention whatsoever to the cards.*

CUT TO

THE RATTLESNAKES. *Little movement. They wait.*

CUT TO

THE MAGICIAN, *shuffling and shuffling until, satisfied, he slaps the cards messily down in a clump.*

CUT TO

MAVERICK, *reaching quickly out, never lifting the cards or anything like that. He just straightens them into a neat pile, riffles them once and then —*

CUT TO

MAVERICK. CLOSE UP. *He takes his hands away from the cards, puts them in his lap.*

It's as if he's trying to go into a deep trance now.

He's breathing deeply. And now something strange: the wind turns into music. A gorgeous theme. It plays on.

CUT TO

THE MAGICIAN, *caught up in it, watching. Getting really excited.*

CUT TO

MAVERICK. *And now he closes his eyes. His breathing is getting very deep now. The wind music is louder, more beautiful.*

He drops his hands into his lap.

HIS HEAD *lolls back — and suddenly the music is gone —*

— his eyes open, he shakes his head.

MAVERICK

I was trying to go somewhere in my mind. Couldn't.

THE MAGICIAN

I believe in you — I was watching — you were getting into a trance — you were almost there.

> MAVERICK
> *(dubious)*
You just want it to happen, that's all — nothing felt right.

> THE MAGICIAN
You got to work at this — if magic was easy, everyone would do it. You did it for your mother, you can do it for me.

CUT TO

THE MAGICIAN. Very loud.

> THE MAGICIAN
I want some real magic in my life before I die — now do it!

CUT TO

MAVERICK. Nervous. He sits back in the chair again, closes his eyes, breathes deep, deeper. The wind music is back.

His hands are limp in his lap. The music is glorious.

CUT TO

THE MAGICIAN. Watching, hoping. He picks up a rattler, strokes it for luck, puts it back. He wants this desperately.

CUT TO

MAVERICK. His voice strange. The music continues through this.

> MAVERICK
... right hand ...

> THE MAGICIAN
What about it?

> MAVERICK
Take it. Lift it.
> *(THE MAGICIAN obeys)*
Now put it on the cards.
> *(THE MAGICIAN obeys)*

CUT TO

THE CARDS ON THE TREE STUMP, MAVERICK's hand, still limp, resting on them —

— then the hand gains tension —

— the fingers move —

— move up and down the deck.

CUT TO

MAVERICK. God knows where he is now but he's a long way from here. The breathing deep, regular; the eyes shut. The wind music has never been as fine.

CUT TO

THE MAGICIAN, thrilled, watching MAVERICK's hand; it moves as if it had a life of its own.

CUT TO

MAVERICK'S HAND. It stops.

CUT TO

MAVERICK. Voice stranger than before.

> **MAVERICK**
> ...right hand...

> **THE MAGICIAN**
> What about it?

> **MAVERICK**
> ...lift it...
>   *(THE MAGICIAN obeys)*
> ...turn it...
>   *(THE MAGICIAN obeys)*
> ...look...
>   *(THE MAGICIAN stares)*

CUT TO

THE CARD. For a moment we think he's done it, cut the ace of spades —

— but on second glance we can see he missed. The ace of clubs is the card.

CUT TO

MAVERICK. Eyes open now, sees he's failed again. The wind music is dead, gone. MAVERICK leans exhausted back in his chair for a moment. Then he starts to rise.

> **MAVERICK**
> I'll be leaving you now.

CUT TO

THE MAGICIAN. And he's never looked happy. He grabs the money, shoves it at MAVERICK.

> **THE MAGICIAN**
> I'll give you one of my horses, too.

MAVERICK
Why? I failed.

THE MAGICIAN
You come close, don't you see? Ya fool, that means it's possible. Maybe the next guy will do it. You gimme hope. Hermits need hope — *(grabbing some more bills, tosses them to MAVERICK)* Buy yourself some decent clothes like mine — thank me, I'll kill you — *(beat)* — now get outta my life...

CUT TO

MAVERICK, watching as THE MAGICIAN picks up a couple of little rattlers, pets them, closes his eyes. We leave him like this. Happy. HOLD briefly. Then, from this desolate place —

CUT TO

AN EXPLOSION OF PEOPLE AND NOISE. A MOB BY A RIVERBOAT.

We're in St. Louis on a gorgeous afternoon.

By the gangplank, a brass band blasts away; behind them is a sign reading: "The First Annual All River's Poker Championship."

PULL BACK TO REVEAL

MAVERICK, making his way through the crowd. He looks terrific again, wears new clothes —

— not to mention a new shirt. This one fits. As he moves toward the boat —

WOMAN'S VOICE (over)
Oh, how I prayed for your survival.
                    (And on that —)

CUT TO

ANNABELLE, for it was her voice, as she goes to him. She's thrilled he's there, holds him, kisses his cheek.

ANNABELLE
My very own hero, alive and well.
                    (He untangles himself from her)
Have I said something to upset you?

MAVERICK
Mrs. Bransford, I like to think I enjoy a prank as much as the next man, but have you no memory of robbing me blind as I went off to face death with the Indians?

ANNABELLE
(hurt)
If you ever believed anything I told you, believe this — I did not do it...

(*MAVERICK isn't buying it —*
he just stares her down)
...then. *(beat)* It happened when I thought you were ditching the wagon train. And I felt just horrible about it.

MAVERICK
Not so horrible that when I came back you returned it.

ANNABELLE
(fiddle-de-dee)
I hope nothing ever makes me feel *that* horrible.

CUT TO

THE CROWD AROUND THEM. MAVERICK *spots someone but* THE GUY *turns away so that we're not totally sure who it was.*

CUT TO

MAVERICK *and* ANNABELLE. *She's looking around too.*

ANNABELLE
Oh Bret, my beautiful perfect male, I don't want to seem ungrateful but why were you three thousand short? *(looking around again)* I was hoping to find a wealthy inebriate I could pick-pocket the remaining money from — I've only been able to break even these last days at the poker tables.

MAVERICK
You mean you can't enter?

ANNABELLE
(she can't)
And my poor pure heart was so set on it.

CUT TO

MAVERICK. *Without hesitation, he reaches into his pocket, pulls out money.*

MAVERICK
This is my twenty-five exactly — *(counting out some bills)* — take three thousand.

CUT TO

ANNABELLE. *Delighted. Grabs it.*

ANNABELLE
Is there no end to your goodness?

MAVERICK
I've always been a sucker for a pretty face with a sad story.

ANNABELLE
Heaven will welcome you for this. *(puts it in her purse)* Now tell me how you escaped.

MAVERICK
Got 'em all drunk and slipped out in the confusion.

ANNABELLE
How could I not adore you?

MAVERICK
You're irresistible —

ANNABELLE
(nods)
— how true.

MAVERICK
(leaving her)
Make me proud.
(As he goes —)

CUT TO

MAVERICK, *moving through the crowd. Now —*

CUT TO

THE MAN WE DIDN'T QUITE SEE BEFORE *as* MAVERICK *grabs him roughly by the shoulder, spins him around —*

— it's THE ARCHDUKE, *very surprised at being treated this way.*

ARCHDUKE
Do you have the least notion who I am?

MAVERICK
I know who *I* am and that's what matters — *(beat)* — Maverick, Indian Affairs.

CUT TO

THE ARCHDUKE. *He starts to say something, stops when the last words are spoken.* MAVERICK *roughly drags him along.*

MAVERICK
It's over for you, Dukey — Joseph talked.

ARCHDUKE
I don't know anyone by that name.

MAVERICK

That's what he said about you when I started investigating the murder. Once I jailed him, he sang. Once I get you behind bars, guess what, you will too.

ARCHDUKE

But I am not American.

MAVERICK

If you was, you'd get twenty years. *(shakes his head)* Now it's just three years in the pokey and a three thousand dollar fine.

ARCHDUKE
(desperate)

I have three thousand dollars right here. *(takes out a wallet)*

MAVERICK

You know the penalty for bribing someone in Indian Affairs?

ARCHDUKE
(panicked)

I was going home anyway. *(practically throwing three thousand at MAVERICK)* This way I pay my dues and save you the cost of the trial.

MAVERICK
(hesitant)

Court is overworked, I admit it. *(beat)* Give you a break — *(taking the money, gestures for THE ARCHDUKE to go)*

CUT TO

THE ARCHDUKE; *he starts off, stops, looks closely at* MAVERICK's *face.*

ARCHDUKE

Why do I think I've seen you before? *(Now he turns again, hurries away we)*

CUT TO

THE GANGPLANK *and the crowd is bigger.* MAVERICK *moves up alongside* ANNABELLE.

MAVERICK

Guess what? I'm entering too — miscounted. *(As he takes her arm —)*

CUT TO

ANOTHER GAMBLER, *coming towards them. Handsome, tall, trim, he's got a smile that might melt the world.*

MAVERICK
(they're friends)

Thought you'd be here. *(introducing)* Mrs. Bransford, this is Mr. Smith. *(they nod politely)*

STUTTERING GAMBLER
(said perfectly)
Peter Piper picked a peck of pickled peppers.

MAVERICK
(delighted)
That's wonderful.

STUTTERING

(It turns out he has a speech problem.
Explaining to ANNABELLE)
Duh-doesn't come up much in cuh-conversation, an' it's all I can say right.
(Now, from that —)

CUT TO

THE BRASS BAND *in all its glory. As MAVERICK and others move up the gangplank —*

CUT TO

MAVERICK, *being shown into a stateroom by a uniformed steward. He tips the guy who leaves. He seems casual and confident.*

MAVERICK *takes out his money, stares at it.*

MAVERICK. CLOSE UP. *Holding the money. For the first time now we can see he's edgy. He tilts his head, as if listening for something —*

— and now, very faint, the wind music is back —

— but only for an instant. Silence in the room again.

MAVERICK's *edginess increases as we*

CUT TO

A ROOM THAT IS DEFINITELY *NOT* SILENT.

We are in the main cabin of the Grand Republic, for that is the name of the steamer.

It's got chandeliers, ornate woodwork, high ceilings —

— it is also over 100 feet long.

With lots of people.

They mill around, expectantly. Bars on both walls with busy bartenders.

Tables with leather armchairs have been set up in the center of the room.

People are already drinking heavily.

CUT TO

THE MOB. *Noisier now.* MAVERICK, *in a corner, watches it all.* ANNABELLE *joins him.*

> **ANNABELLE**
> *(quickly)*
> I'm getting nervous—I remembered both giveaways you taught me and I won't touch my fingers together and I won't flick my teeth—but if I'm going to win, I need more tells—

> **MAVERICK**
> —you have zero chance of winning—the only reason I gave you the three was in hope of personally ruining you.

> **ANNABELLE**
> *(stung)*
> I could get lucky, Mister Man.

> **MAVERICK**
> *(what she said is true)*
> OK, you're right—when someone's hand is shaking as he makes a big bet, don't go against him, hard to fake nerves—when a guy asks for a rule clarification before he bets, run and hide, he knows the rules and is trying to sucker you— *(Now, as the music starts, he looks around as we)*

CUT TO

FOUR MUSICIANS. *They <u>never</u> stop playing. The group consists of a fiddler, a cornet player, a fifer, and the fourth has an upright piano.*

Their repertoire is stuff like "Sweet Betsy From Pike," "Lily Dale," "The Yellow Rose of Texas," many lovely sentimental love songs of the 1870s.

They only add to the excitement and hubbub.

CUT TO

ANNABELLE, *eyes half-closed, muttering to herself, trying to remember it all. Now, suddenly—*

CUT TO

THE ANGEL. *Better dressed than when we last saw him. Still the kind of presence that could scare children, but at least now he's clean. He stares at* MAVERICK, *shocked.*

> **THE ANGEL**
> How the hell did you get here?

> **MAVERICK**
> I'd move away, Angel.

> THE ANGEL
> *(still in disbelief)*

Answer me.

> MAVERICK

No, bastard, answer me — what did you mean when you said you never would have let me make this game? Who was trying to stop me?

> THE ANGEL
> *(back in control)*

Ask me no questions. *(beat)* Gonna be a real pleasure playing you again — sorry my partners can't be here to see, but they both died sudden of the croup. *(he laughs, starts to go —)* I hope we can be close friends — after all, what happened between us was just in fun... *(as he goes —)*

> MAVERICK
> *(shakes his head in bewilderment)*

Any others of the gang around? It's like old home week.

> ANNABELLE
> *(speaking to someone unseen)*

He got them all drunk on fire water and escaped in the confusion.
> *(And on that —)*

CUT TO

COOP. *He never looked braver or tougher. He wears a Marshal's badge. He embraces MAV-ERICK fervently.*

> COOP

I knew you couldn't die — God had to spare the bravest man in the West.

CUT TO

MAVERICK. *He can't help it, he's blushing.*

> ANNABELLE
> *(pointing — sweet)*

Lookit, so embarrassed.

> COOP
> *(to ANNABELLE — soft)*

Modesty goes hand in hand with courage.

> MAVERICK
> *(in agony)*

Isn't this card game *ever* going to start?
> *(And the <u>instant</u> that's spoken —)*

CUT TO

A GIGANTIC GONG BEING STRUCK.

CUT TO

THE GONG. It is being struck by a powerful ship's steward.

CUT TO

THE ROOM. Quieting. Bursts of tension laughter. Even the musicians, for once, quiet.

CUT TO

MAVERICK. No doubt about it, he's anxious.

CUT TO

A MIDDLE-AGED, IMPRESSIVE MAN moving up beside the gong. This is COMMODORE DEVOL, who owns the ship. He addresses the enormous room without the need of any artificial help — the man has a set of lungs.

> ### COMMODORE DEVOL
> Welcome to my ship and the First Ever Annual Championship. The only reason it exists is because I want to win it. *(looking around)* I'll be quick and the rules are simple. We play 'til we drop. Winner takes all. Dealer can call one break of one half hour. Soon as you're busted, you're gone. Twenty of us are entered which means I plan on winning half a million dollars by morning.

CUT TO

THE CROWD. Half a million is a fortune and this registers.

CUT TO

MAVERICK. The noise from the crowd is enormous. A RICH CHINAMAN nods to him. MAVERICK smiles.

> ### MAVERICK
> *(in greeting)*
> Twitchy. *(to ANNABELLE)* Never try reading him.

ANNABELLE nods, clicks her teeth with her fingernail, then remembers that's a no-no, slaps her own hand, folds her arms.

CUT TO

THE COMMODORE. Asking for quiet.

> ### THE COMMODORE
> Gamblers — every spectator has paid a hundred dollars to be here — so let's make it a great contest. *(beat)* An *honest* great contest — and for that reason,

I have imported one of the remarkable lawmen in the West to run things. Marshal Zane Cooper, come here.

CUT TO

COOP. He moves up alongside THE COMMODORE.

> **COOP**
> Thank you, Commodore Devol. *(beat)* Anyone caught cheating forfeits his entrance fee and is banned. *(raises his gun)* See this? It's the only one allowed in this room. Anyone breaking that law will risk me breaking their bones. *(He's done)*

> **THE COMMODORE**
> Contestants step forward — and *bring your money.*

CUT TO

MAVERICK, as he makes his way forward through the crowd.

CUT TO

A BUNCH OF OTHERS — we recognize ANNABELLE and THE ANGEL — doing the same.

CUT TO

COOP.

He holds a large satchel —

— it is crammed with hundred-dollar bills.

PULL BACK TO REVEAL...

THAT THE SATCHEL is resting on one of the four poker tables. Coop is finishing counting.

Behind him, in the midst of the tables, is a decent-sized safe.

> **COOP**
> *(to THE COMMODORE)*
> Half a million. *(He locks the satchel, pockets the key. To the assembled)* I bought this satchel myself yesterday — I have the only key.

CUT TO

THE SAFE. He deposits the SATCHEL inside. Slams it shut, spins the dial.

> **COOP**
> This safe was made for this contest — I selected the combination — no one else aboard knows it. *(to THE COMMODORE)* The money's as protected as I know how to make it.

CUT TO

THE GAMBLERS, *looking at the safe. Not without a certain amount of lust.*

CUT TO

THE TABLES. *Each has an immaculately dressed dealer ready. One of them is older than the others, rougher, more experienced.*

> **COOP**
> *(to the assembled)*
> A moment of silence. *(He bows his head)* When the great ship Constitution exploded and eleven died, here is how the papers reported the event. "Among the dead was a gambler, who was buried separately." *(beat)* Lord, may we bury no gamblers today.

> **THE GAMBLERS**
> *(All together)*
> Amen.
> *(Now, the formalities over, we)*

CUT TO

THE PLAYERS *fanning out, taking seats, as the dealers open decks, begin shuffling cards and*

CUT TO

A LARGE GRANDFATHER CLOCK. *It reads six o'clock.*

CUT TO

THE CROWD, *deep around the tables. Many of them hold liquor glasses.*

CUT TO

THE FIRST TABLE. *Five players.* MAVERICK *sits;* STUTTERING *is alongside him.*

CUT TO

ANOTHER TABLE. *Five more.* ANNABELLE *sits;* TWITCHY, *the rich Chinaman, sits across from her.*

CUT TO

ANOTHER TABLE. *Five men.* THE COMMODORE *and* THE ANGEL *are here.*

CUT TO

A FOURTH TABLE *and five players we don't know. Cards are dealt.*

CUT TO

MAVERICK, starting to pick up his cards until he looks around —

— several people are bending over behind him, trying to spot what he has. He manages to avoid their glances, looks at his hand, tosses it in.

CUT TO

STUTTERING. He gives MAVERICK a questioning glance.

> **MAVERICK**
> My pleasure.
>> (STUTTERING *indicates*
>> *his cards, shakes his head*)
> Stuttering checks.
>> (*As the others bet —*)

CUT TO

ANNABELLE, betting. Now she glances across the table toward TWITCHY.

CUT TO

TWITCHY. And now we see what MAVERICK meant and why the nickname — the guy is <u>all</u> tics. He blinks, mutters, fidgets, you name it he does it and it's impossible to tell what's conscious and what isn't. Plus, being Chinese, he wasn't all that easy to begin with.

CUT TO

THE ANGEL and THE COMMODORE. THE ANGEL can't stop smiling as he pulls in a pot.

CUT TO

ANNABELLE, winning a pot. Playing very professionally.

CUT TO

MAVERICK, having folded again. STUTTERING makes a gesture to him.

> **MAVERICK**
> Stuttering raises two hundred.
>> (STUTTERING *cackles as we —*)

CUT TO

A LONG BAR. CUSTOMERS ARE ORDERING DRINKS LIKE CRAZY.

CUT TO

THE GRANDFATHER'S CLOCK. AFTER SEVEN.

CUT TO

MAVERICK —

*—and now a series of flash cuts fly by, like we saw when he first played, only much quicker—
we know what he's doing now, clocking the enemy.*

CUT TO

A SWEET FACED GAMBLER ACROSS FROM MAVERICK. *Well-dressed, a lovely shirt with
beautifully ironed, very wide cuffs.*

CUT TO

MAVERICK, *folding again, standing, stretching, walking briefly away from the table.*

CUT TO

COOP *as* MAVERICK *approaches, speaks to him briefly.* COOP *nods.*

CUT TO

MAVERICK, *sitting back down.*

CUT TO

THE MUSICIANS, *playing away.*

CUT TO

THE SWEET FACED GAMBLER, *winning a big pot. As he rakes in his chips—*

CUT TO

COOP, *whispering in his ear.*

CUT TO

THE SWEET FACED GAMBLER. *Totally shocked. He mouths the word "me?" as he points to
himself.*

CUT TO

COOP, *escorting the guy away from the table to a corner of the room—*

—and then ripping at his jacket, the wide-sleeved shirt.

THE SWEET-FACED GUY *has been playing with a metal sleeve holdout—a bunch of cards
are held in place, hidden by the shirt.*

COOP *grabs the guy, pulls him the hell out of the room and*

CUT TO

MAVERICK. *And now he wins a big pot, looks up.*

CUT TO

COOP, standing across from him, mouths the word "Thanks." MAVERICK nods.

> **COOP**
> *(indicating the empty chair)*
> Sudden illness, gentleman. *(taking the guy's chips)* Divide these among your-
> selves. House rules.

> **STUTTERING**
> Hot shit.

(As they start to divide the chips —)

CUT TO

THE GRANDFATHER'S CLOCK. IT'S TEN IN THE EVENING NOW.

CUT TO

THE ROOM. The first of the ticket holders are beginning to fade.

CUT TO

COOP, never stops moving, watching everything going on.

CUT TO

THE BAND. Getting tired.

CUT TO

THE GAMBLERS. One of the tables is gone — only three are left, fifteen players.

CUT TO

OUTSIDE. The ship sails up the river in the night. Tranquil. Total peace.

CUT TO

THE SECOND POKER TABLE. ANNABELLE has never been through anything like this and she tries to relax her body, takes a very deep breath, rubs her eyes.

(In truth, these marathon poker games were brutal for the participants. The physical strain never stopped growing. Their backs ached from slouching in the chairs for long hours, their arms ached from leaning against the arms of the chairs; their skin got soggy, their eyes got so it was just damn hard to keep them open, much less concentrate. We're not at this stage yet —

— but we will be)

CUT TO

ONE OF THE BARS. NOT MANY PEOPLE AND THOSE THAT REMAIN ARE DRUNK.

CUT TO

THE GRANDFATHER'S CLOCK. TWO IN THE MORNING.

CUT TO

COOP, as before, in constant motion, no sign of fatigue.

CUT TO

THE TABLES. Only two left, only ten players.

CUT TO

THE MUSICIANS. Not very peppy.

CUT TO

MAVERICK. He now plays with four others, STUTTERING and TWITCHY being the ones we know.

CUT TO

ANNABELLE'S TABLE. THE ANGEL and THE COMMODORE and two others.

CUT TO

AN OLD GUY sits across from MAVERICK. He's exhausted.

> **OLD GUY**
> Sorry, I'm wiped out, can't remember my own name anymore. *(pointing to the pot)* It's three thousand to me — I can bet ten thousand, right?

CUT TO

THE TOUGH EXPERIENCED DEALER. Nothing surprises this guy. Along with COOP, he seems in better shape than anybody.

> **TOUGH DEALER**
> Up to you.

> **OLD GUY**
> Why don't I just do that then. *(As he puts out ten thousand in chips —)*

CUTS TO

COOP watching the OLD GUY.

CUT TO

THE OLD GUY, raking in the chips as the others fold. Now, as COOP approaches, grabs him —

CUT TO

A CORNER OF THE ROOM. COOP AND THE OLD GUY. COOP rips open his shirt revealing a breastplate holdout. It conceals an entire hand of cards. As COOP carts him toward the door —

CUT TO

THE PLAYERS AT THE TABLES. All of them showing the strain now. They rub their arms, their eyes, anything to stay sharp.

CUT TO

THE GRANDFATHER'S CLOCK. QUARTER OF FOUR.

CUT TO

THE CHIPS AT ANNABELLE's table. She's doing well. But not as well as THE ANGEL or THE COMMODORE.

CUT TO

THE CHIPS AT MAVERICK'S TABLE. MAVERICK has more than any of the others.

CUT TO

THE MUSICIANS. "Sweet Betsy From Pike" was never played slower.

CUT TO

THE TOUGH DEALER.

TOUGH DEALER
Break at four. Anyone not back in half hour forfeits everything.

CUT TO

THE CLOCK. AS IT STARTS TO CHIME —

CUT TO

THE GAMBLERS, rising, staggering away with fatigue. COOP, made of steel, waits by the safe. After a moment, he signals for a steward as we —

CUT TO

MAVERICK'S ROOM.

The sounds of wild sex — MAVERICK groaning with pleasure, the bed springs in constant motion. (We can't see the bed yet; we're looking at a porthole which has the curtains closed.)

MAVERICK (over)
Oh you are good — yes, so good, the best, don't stop, please, I'll die if you stop —

                                    ANNABELLE (over)
— how much am I worth?

                                    MAVERICK (over)
Five hundred. No. A thousand — *(The loudest cry of pleasure yet as we —)*

PULL BACK TO REVEAL

We have been hearing a massage. Both are dressed as before. He lies face down on the mattress. She straddles him, her fingers moving up to his back, his shoulders, his neck. As she stops —

                                    ANNABELLE
Your turn to do me.

                                    MAVERICK
I'll give you two thousand if you'll keep at it.

                                    ANNABELLE
No good, I've got two thousand. *(now she swats him)*

CUT TO

MAVERICK, sitting as she flops face down. He begins massaging her.

                                    MAVERICK
                                    (irritated)
I think you're in better shape than I am.

                                    ANNABELLE
It's ironing shirts gives me strength
                                    (Now from them —)

CUT TO

THE DECK, AND THE ANGEL IN THE DARKNESS.

He is talking to someone but we can't tell who. Finished, he turns, walks quickly away.

HOLD.

Now another figure moves out of the darkness. It's the one THE ANGEL was talking to, THE TOUGH DEALER.

HOLD.

KEEP HOLDING.

Unnoticed 'til now, a THIRD FIGURE becomes visible from deeper darkness. It's COOP. And as he hurries off —

CUT TO

MAVERICK, MASSAGING ANNABELLE AS BEFORE.

A pounding on the door.

> MAVERICK

Open.

CUT TO

COOP, *moving in.*

> COOP

I was getting tired so I took some air.

> MAVERICK

You? Tired? That's a first.

> COOP
> *(urgent)*

Listen to me — I was leaning against the rail and these two guys started talking — didn't see me — The Angel and the dealer that always seems so fresh? *(beat)* They got something going — couldn't get what, but it's going to be very big, Bret, and you can't win. I heard The Angel say to make sure of that.

CUT TO

MAVERICK. *Amazingly, no reaction.*

> MAVERICK

I'd like a few minutes alone, Annabelle — maybe catch a nap.

> COOP

You just gonna let 'em cheat you? You can beat 'em all.

> MAVERICK

And then what, Coop? After I've bought a nice house and settled down. And then what?

> ANNABELLE
> *(taking COOP's arm)*

Escort me to my room, Zane — I want to change clothes.
> *(As they go)*
And don't fuss — I'm winning anyway.

CUT TO

THE GRANDFATHER'S CLOCK. HALF PAST FIVE.

CUT TO

THE GAMBLERS — only one table left. And six players. MAVERICK, ANNABELLE, THE COM-MODORE, THE ANGEL, STUTTERING, and TWITCHY. THE FIVE MEN all look weary.

ANNABELLE has done her best to disguise any fatigue. Fresh make-up, a lovely new suit, a beautiful blouse.

As the TOUGH DEALER flicks out the cards —

CUT TO

THE BAND. A fourth wind.

CUT TO

THE WINDOWS. MORNING LIGHT STARTS STREAMING IN — COMING UP DAWN.

CUT TO

THE ROOM. A few people enter. Hung over, wiped out.

CUT TO

THE PLAYERS. They all drink coffee now. It tastes like mud but they sip it and let the steam massage their eyes.

CUT TO

THE CHIPS. MAVERICK has stacks in front of him. So does THE ANGEL. THE COMMODORE and TWITCHY are doing OK. But STUTTERING and ANNABELLE are in trouble.

CUT TO

COOP. As fresh as ever, watching it all. The man is clearly without flaw.

CUT TO

MAVERICK AND ANNABELLE, the last two left in a hand. ANNABELLE's pile has shrunk.

> **ANNABELLE**
> *(tossing her head, she turns to THE DEALER)*
> I can bet all I have left, can't I?
> *(THE TOUGH DEALER nods)*
> Then why don't I just do that. *(beat)* Five thousand, Mister Maverick.

CUT TO

MAVERICK. Stares glumly.

> **MAVERICK**
> Silly for me to match that.

CUT TO

ANNABELLE, *says nothing. She gives away none of the tells she had earlier that* MAVERICK *told her about. Just sits there blankly, waiting.*

CUT TO

MAVERICK, *folds his hand, gets set to toss it into the pile.*

CUT TO

ANNABELLE, *couldn't be more disinterested.*

CUT TO

MAVERICK, *at the last second, pulling his hand back.*

>   **MAVERICK**
> I guess I feel like being silly. *(pushes chips into the pot)* Beat two pair and it's yours. *(He shows her his cards — tens and threes —)*

CUT TO

ANNABELLE. CLOSE UP. *She stares across at him now with fury.*

>   **ANNABELLE**
> Bastard. *(And with that, she flings her cards down — she's been bluffing)*

CUT TO

MAVERICK, *gathering in the pot.*

>   **ANNABELLE**
> I'm out of the game.
>   *(MAVERICK says nothing — louder)*
> You just put me out of the game.
>   *(MAVERICK stacks the chips*
>   *silently. Still louder)*
> I didn't do either of my two giveaways — I never touched my thumb with my little finger and I never once flicked my teeth —

>   **MAVERICK**
> — you have three — you always toss your head when you bluff —

>   **ANNABELLE**
>   *(exploding)*
> You didn't tell me that one!

>   **MAVERICK**
> You never want to give everything away, Mrs. Bransford.

ANNABELLE

Have you no sense of shame?

MAVERICK

Considering how hard you slaved for your entrance fee, I may never re-
cover.

CUT TO

ANNABELLE. *She takes a deep breath, gets herself back in control. Then, a lady again, she smiles graciously at* THE COMMODORE, *stands up, moves to* COOP. *As she distracts people,* THE ANGEL *and* THE TOUGH DEALER *exchange a glance.*

COOP *catches it.*

CUT TO

MAVERICK. *It's as if he hadn't seen the glance.*

CUT TO

COOP, *moving closer to the table, circling, checking.*

CUT TO

THE TOUGH DEALER, *casually dealing away.*

CUT TO

MAVERICK, *casually watching him.*

CUT TO

THE DEALER — *only now we see him through* MAVERICK'S *eyes — and what he's doing, and doing brilliantly, is manipulating the cards. Sometimes he deals from the top, some-times the bottom, sometimes the second card, sometimes the third, and sometimes from the middle of the deck which is brutally hard.*

CUT TO

THE TABLE, *back in regular motion as* THE DEALER *finishes.*

Here is how the players are sitting: To the left of THE DEALER, *the first one to bet is* STUT-
TERING. *Then* TWITCHY. *After him,* THE COMMODORE; *next,* THE ANGEL. *Last,* MAV-
ERICK.

CUT TO

STUTTERING, *as he looks at his cards —*

— he's been dealt a straight — two, three, four, five, six — of different suits. A sensational hand. Nothing shows on his face as he gestures to MAVERICK.

> MAVERICK
Stuttering opens with two-fifty.

CUT TO

THE OTHERS. It's a considerable opener.

CUT TO

TWITCHY, looking at his hand —

— he's got a flush — five hearts. More sensational.

> TWITCHY
> *(all parts of his face moving)*
Too early to fold. *(He puts in two-fifty more)*

CUT TO

THE COMMODORE. He's got two tens and three nines. A full house. The best yet.

> THE COMMODORE
Call me a fool, but I think I'll raise a thousand.

CUT TO

THE ANGEL. We don't see his hand yet.

> THE ANGEL
Raise ten thousand.

CUT TO

MAVERICK, as we see his hand. The ten, jack, queen, king of spades —

— plus the two of diamonds.

In other words, not shit, but the odds against hitting what he needs — the nine or ace of spades — are phenomenal. Still, he has to stay. He pushes chips into the center.

So do the other three.

CUT TO

THE POT. A lot of chips — over fifty thousand dollars' worth.

CUT TO

THE TOUGH DEALER. To STUTTERING.

> TOUGH DEALER
How many cards?
> *(STUTTERING smiles)*

MAVERICK

He stands.
                              (TWITCHY nods)

THE COMMODORE

Sounds good.

THE ANGEL

One.
                    (He gets it from THE DEALER,
                     looks at it, seems concerned)

TOUGH DEALER
                        (to MAVERICK)

You?

CUT TO

MAVERICK. Quietly —

MAVERICK

Same — (Then his hand suddenly covers THE TOUGH DEALER's) — but I don't
want it from you.

THE COMMODORE

What're you pulling, son?

MAVERICK

I want a new dealer — and I want a new shuffle — and I want a new cut.
                    (THE COMMODORE looks to COOP)

COOP

Within his rights. I'll shuffle —

THE COMMODORE

— I'll cut.

MAVERICK
                        (shakes his head)
No. (indicating THE ANGEL) Him. He cuts.

CUT TO

THE ANGEL. Smiles.

THE ANGEL

I kind of like that. Shows trust.
                    (COOP shuffles the cards quickly,
                     hands them over)

CUT TO

MAVERICK. Throat dry. He sits back in his chair. The wind music starts.

CUT TO

THE ANGEL. His huge hand slowly cuts the cards.

CUT TO

MAVERICK, watching.

CUT TO

COOP, ANNABELLE beside him. Watching, as THE ANGEL finishes the cut.

CUT TO

MAVERICK. And now he closes his eyes. He seems, at this tense moment, remarkably at peace. The wind music is louder still. He listens a moment more, then opens his eyes.

CUT TO

THE DECK as now THE ANGEL takes a single finger, pushes the top card across the table to MAVERICK.

Who does an amazing thing —

— he doesn't look at it.

Just leaves it face down on the table.

CUT TO

THE PLAYERS who look to STUTTERING to begin the betting. STUTTERING holds up two fingers, wide apart.

MAVERICK
Two thousand.

>   *(STUTTERING puts two thousand in
>   the pot — TWITCHY watches it)*

THE COMMODORE
Raise five thousand.
>   *(As the chips go into the growing pot —)*

CUT TO

THE ANGEL. He looks about to fold — then he suddenly smiles at MAVERICK.

THE ANGEL
I liked it when you did that to the lady. *(chips in)* Raise twenty thousand.

CUT TO

MAVERICK'S LAST CARD. *Still face down.* MAVERICK *hesitates.*

> **THE COMMODORE**
> I'd look at it, son.

> **MAVERICK**
> No need. *(chips into pot)* Raise twenty-five.

CUT TO

THE ANGEL, *exploding.*

> **THE ANGEL**
> What kind of act you pulling? — *look at your card.*
> *(*MAVERICK *says not a word)*

CUT TO

STUTTERING. *He pushes in all the chips he has left.*

> **MAVERICK**
> Stuttering calls.

> **TWITCHY**
> *(to* STUTTERING — *apologetically)*
> Solly. *(pushes more chips in than* STUTTERING *had)*

> **THE COMMODORE**
> We're saying good-bye to the boys now. *(As all his chips go in)* Fifty thousand more.

CUT TO

THE ANGEL. *Studying his hand.*

And for the first time we see it —

—five, six, seven, eight, nine. All of diamonds.

A straight flush.

> **THE ANGEL**
> *(to* MAVERICK*)*
> Want to see me, it'll cost you everything you got. *(pushes in all his chips too, a huge amount)* Hundred and fifty thousand. Half a million in the pot if you match it.

MAVERICK. *Still doesn't look at his last card. Just pushes all his chips in silently.*

HALF A MILLION *in the pot. It's gigantic.*

CUT TO

THE ANGEL. *Turning over his cards.*

CUT TO

THE CROWD AROUND THE TABLE. *Stunned. It's a phenomenal hand.*

CUT TO

MAVERICK. *Silently turns over the cards we've seen.*

Ten of spades.

Jack of spades.

Queen of spades.

King of spades.

CUT TO

THE LAST CARD. *The one he hasn't looked at. Now he slides it toward him, starts to take a quick glance —*

— but first he closes his eyes again and there it is, the wind music —

— only now, without warning, it goes sour. Then it dies.

CUT TO

MAVERICK, *eyes open fast and now you can see it, his confidence isn't there. He grabs the card, looks at it.*

CUT TO

MAVERICK. CLOSE UP. *Stunned.*

> **MAVERICK**
> *(hardly able to talk)*
> ...I...just don't believe it.

CUT TO

THE TABLE. THE ANGEL *reaches for the pot.*

> **THE ANGEL**
> Strange things happen at the poker table.

> **MAVERICK**
> *(hard to hear him)*
> ...I know... *(beat)* ...but... *(beat)* ...who ever dreamed of two straight

flushes in the same hand — lucky for me mine's higher.
             (And on that —)

CUT TO

THE CARD *as he flips it up into the air.*

It spins down.

The ace of spades.

CUT TO

THE ANGEL. *Dead pale as a wild fury begins and*

CUT TO

THE CROWD, *exploding and*

CUT TO

MAVERICK, *standing and*

CUT TO

ANNABELLE, *running into his arms, hugging him and —*

                          ANNABELLE
      Now that you're rich, I forgive you.

CUT TO

THE ANGEL, *screaming — getting out of control —*

                          THE ANGEL
      Miserable cheating son of a bitch — *(And as he starts to rise —)*

— we go into slow motion and

— THE ANGEL'S CHAIR topples over backwards and

— THE ANGEL'S RIGHT HAND goes into his shirt and

— ANNABELLE is watching but

— MAVERICK's back is to the other man and

— now THE ANGEL is bringing out a tiny gun and

— ANNABELLE's mouth goes wide —

— and MAVERICK starts to turn, but too slow, way too slow —

— and THE ANGEL points his gun, starts to fire —

— MAVERICK sees it all now, but he's helpless as we

CUT TO

THE ANGEL, *blood suddenly spurting from his body and the power is such he's all but being yanked backwards and more blood coming and his eyes start to close and*

CUT TO

COOP. *His gun is in his hands, watching as* THE ANGEL *dies.* COOP *grabs the dead man's gun, pockets it.*

CUT TO

MAVERICK *— we're back into regular motion now. He nods thanks to* COOP, *sinks into his chair.*

CUT TO

COOP. *Twirls his own gun back into its holster.*

> **COOP**
> (going to the safe)
> Sorry about that, but this is Bret Maverick's moment, and nothing's going to spoil it.

CUT TO

THE SATCHEL, *with the money inside.*

PULL BACK TO REVEAL

COOP, *pulling it out of the safe, standing —*

> **COOP**
> Sorry, Bret, wish your moment could have lasted a little longer, but there it is —

— and his gun is back in his hand as he moves toward an open window.

CUT TO

MAVERICK. CLOSE UP. *He hadn't expected this — ever.*

CUT TO

COOP, *his gun ready.*

> **COOP**
> I feel real bad about this but I saw all that money and, well, shit, I just wanted it —
> (And on that —)

CUT TO

THE WINDOW — *he vaults gracefully out and*

CUT TO

THE SHIP. *It has docked. A* POWERFUL HORSE *waits at the end of the gangplank —*

— COOP *races to it, leaps on, rides like hell away as we*

CUT TO

INSIDE THE SALON — *this has all gone like a streak and what we have here now is confusion and chaos.*

> **THE COMMODORE**
> *(to some* STEWARDS*)*
> Get some horses — get out there — *get after him —*

> **MAVERICK**
> *(soft)*
> Let him go.
> *(*THE COMMODORE *stares at* MAVERICK;
> *so does* ANNABELLE*)*

CUT TO

MAVERICK. CLOSE UP.

> **MAVERICK**
> *(addressing the crowd, quieting it)*
> The man saved my life. I can always win more money. *(beat)* Besides, I found out what I came for anyway.

CUT TO

THE COMMODORE, *raising his hands. He controls the room.*

> **THE COMMODORE**
> *(to* MAVERICK*)*
> That's a half a million dollars, son. Do I have to remind you of that?

> **MAVERICK**
> Do I have to remind you it's *my* half million? *(He means this)* Coop probably never had a dishonest thought 'til this happened. He's going to be haunted whatever we do. And that's punishment enough for a man. I won't swear out a warrant against him.
> *(*ANNABELLE, *touched,*
> *takes* MAVERICK's *hand)*

THE COMMODORE
(to the crowd — unexpectedly moved)
I know a little something about money — made a lot in my lifetime, gonna make a lot more. But this young man has more wisdom now about what's really valuable than I'll ever have. I had two wives leave me on account of my obsession with making money. *(almost in tears — to* MAVERICK*)* Don't you ever change. *(now, raising an imaginary glass — toasting)* To a champion.
(All in the room echo
THE COMMODORE*'s toast)*

MAVERICK. *Doing his best to keep his emotions in check — but no question about it, at this moment, he is a proud young man. Now, from that —*

CUT TO

ANNABELLE, HER EYES CLOSED.

She's in MAVERICK*'s room and he is taking off her suit coat. He lays it over a chair. She stands as before, in skirt and expensive blouse.*

ANNABELLE
When can I open my eyes? — what is this gift I'm getting?

MAVERICK
(soft)
Just one minute more —
(And on that —)

CUT TO

MAVERICK *as he suddenly grabs her lovely blouse and rips it wide open —*

— ANNABELLE*, shocked, cries out, opens her eyes, her hands trying to cover her suddenly revealed body —*

— but too late.

Over her slip she is wearing the most Rube Goldberg-like thing you ever saw. (It was called the Kepplinger Holdout and was a series of pulleys and cords that hid a remarkable number of cards. The thing worked, believe it or not, by using the knees, and is generally thought of as being the greatest card-cheating device of the past century.)

ANNABELLE
(embarrassed)
I didn't wear it 'til the break —

MAVERICK
— and you never needed to. Here's my gift to you: the truth. You were one of the six best players out there. *(pulling the* HOLDOUT *off her)* Get rid of this.

ANNABELLE
(confused, embarrassed, touched)
Would you believe me if I told you it didn't work? Look—all the cards are
still there—contraption just jammed on me, I couldn't get it to function.
(now, as her arms go around MAVERICK) Let's hope I have better luck with you.
(As they fall on the bed—)

CUT TO

THE KEPPLINGER HOLDOUT. *As suddenly, on its own, it starts working. An ace of spades
rises, blocking our view.* HOLD *on the card, then—*

CUT TO

MAVERICK AND ANNABELLE,

leaving the gangplank together. This is good-bye and neither of them is all that happy.

MAVERICK
Where you headed?

ANNABELLE
(a shrug—she doesn't know)
Someplace else.

MAVERICK
I'm going there too. Want to travel together? I could use the protection.

CUT TO

ANNABELLE. *Long pause. Then—*

ANNABELLE
No. *(She moves to him)* Understand this—I *want* to go with you—it
would be wonderful, we could fight for years. *(beat)* But now, wherever I
end up, whatever name I choose, I'm me. If *we* go, all I'd ever be is Bret
Maverick's girl.

CUT TO

THE TWO OF THEM. *A final embrace. Meaningful. They separate.*

ANNABELLE
(moved)
You take care. *(starts off)*

MAVERICK
Annabelle?
(she turns back)
Here. *(he hands her a wallet he's just taken from her purse)*

ANNABELLE
(*impressed*)

You're good.

MAVERICK

There's hope for me.
(*And this time, as they do separate —*)

CUT TO

THE HALF MILLION IN CASH.

Separated into two piles. The satchel is alongside.

PULL BACK TO REVEAL

COOP, *nervously waiting alone in a rocky place on the edge of nowhere. A small fire is the only illumination. A stream flows by.*

Now, the sound of a horse walking slowly. The horse stops.

COOP *draws his gun, cocks it — it makes a distinct sound —*

— kuh — <u>lick</u> —

— he stares out into the darkness, ready for anything. Then he relaxes, puts the gun back into its holster.

COOP

Where the hell you been?

PULL BACK TO REVEAL

THE COMMODORE. *He moves to the fire.*

THE COMMODORE

I had to say good-bye to a thousand people, at least it seemed like that. And I couldn't risk looking like I was rushing anyplace. (*beat*) You don't seem happy to see me.

COOP
(*angry*)

I thought you and me were in this thing together — you win, I do nothing. Someone else wins, I do what I did. (*beat*) Why the hell didn't you tell me Angel was in it too?

THE COMMODORE

What did Maverick say to the lady? "You never want to give everything away." If he'd won, we'd have gone thirds. Dumb bastard — the real thing I wired him to do, he messed up — keep Maverick from the game — too good.

                                    COOP
I just don't like secrets.

                              THE COMMODORE
Then you probably won't like this one either.

CUT TO

THE COMMODORE as suddenly he draws his gun, cocks it —

— there's that sound again —

— kuh — <u>lick</u> —

— and the gun is aimed at COOP's heart.

                              THE COMMODORE
I've decided against sharing it with you —

                                    COOP
                                  (shocked)
— a deal's a deal.

                              THE COMMODORE
In a perfect world, that's true. *(ready to fire)* I just want you to know I've
never worked with a more honest man in my life.
                                  (Now —)

A familiar sound

— kuh — <u>lick</u> —

                              MAVERICK (over)
*— don't give odds on its being a long one.
                              (As they spin —)*

CUT TO

MAVERICK, moving in fast, gun drawn. With speed and precision he grabs THE COM-
MODORE's pistol, rips COOP's from its holster. They raise their hands as he gestures for
them to stand close together. He shoves the money in the satchel.

                                  MAVERICK
                    (during this — to THE COMMODORE)
I almost fell asleep with boredom following you — you and that idiot
speech about my wisdom — how could you expect me to fall for that? *(to*
COOP) But you...you fooled me. And not many can. But you saved me,
so I won't kill him or you. *(beat)* Just remember, the whole world knows
what you are. All your life's work, all the good you did, you wiped it away.

COOP

You're young, so you don't know that much about mistakes, but you're making one now. *(beat)* You can't leave me alive.

CUT TO

COOP. CLOSE UP. And we've never seen him like this — out of control.

COOP

What you said, every word, that's right — I changed every decent thing for that money — *(building)* — and you better believe I'm coming for it! *(bigger)* I don't care where you go, one night you'll relax — and guess who'll be there waiting?

CUT TO

MAVERICK. Puts the satchel full of money down.

MAVERICK

You couldn't sneak up on a corpse, Coop; not anymore. You're just another decrepit has-been.

CUT TO

THE COMMODORE, scared, as MAVERICK studies his pistol.

THE COMMODORE

What're you gonna do?

MAVERICK

It's a problem — if I don't kill you, what *do* I do?

CUT TO

MAVERICK, quickly taking the bullets from THE COMMODORE's gun, heaving the gun and the bullets into the stream.

CUT TO

COOP, watching, the fury still there.

CUT TO

MAVERICK taking the bullets from COOP's pistol —

— all the bullets but <u>one</u>. He tosses them into the stream. Then he puts the lone bullet back into the gun.

MAVERICK

Maybe the fairest thing would be to just let one of you kill the other —
(And with that —)

CUT TO

THE GUN, *as he heaves it high,* <u>*high*</u> *into the air and*

CUT TO

COOP *and* THE COMMODORE, *staring up after it and*

CUT TO

MAVERICK, *watching them, satchel in hand, gun drawn, backing away and*

CUT TO

THE GUN, *spinning in the night and*

CUT TO

COOP, *still staring up, beginning to guess where it might land and*

CUT TO

THE COMMODORE, *watching* COOP *and*

CUT TO

MAVERICK. *The shadows have him and he's gone and*

CUT TO

COOP, *starting to move and*

CUT TO

THE GUN, *beginning its arc down and*

CUT TO

THE COMMODORE, *suddenly sticking a leg out, tripping* COOP *and*

CUT TO

COOP, *beginning to fall and*

CUT TO

THE COMMODORE, *heading for where the gun might fall and*

CUT TO

THE GUN, *dropping fast and*

CUT TO

COOP, *and he gets his balance, quickly goes into a roll, bounces up, breaks into a run and*

CUT TO

THE COMMODORE, *no match for COOP's speed and*

CUT TO

THE GUN, *landing, and*

CUT TO

COOP, *the first one there, grabbing it, whirling and*

CUT TO

THE COMMODORE, *a dead man and he knows it. Panic starts.*

CUT TO

COOP. *Wild. Moving in on the other man.*

> **COOP**
> Give you a choice — I can either wound you bad or put you out of your double-crossing misery.

CUT TO

THE COMMODORE. *A total fold. He's all but starting to cry as we*

CUT TO

COOP. *Aiming. Starts to pull the trigger, stops —*

> **COOP**
> Nah — I never did a cold-blooded murder yet and I won't 'til I find Maverick. *(anger pouring out)* — but if I ever so much as *hear* your name — if I ever find you're in the same town as me so I might see your *face* — if I ever get wind that you've hired any more of your secret "*helpers*" —

> **THE COMMODORE**
> *(terrified)*
> — I won't — please — I swear —

> **COOP**
> *(beat)*
> — I think you've come to a very wise decision.
> *(HOLD ON THEM a moment, then —)*

CUT TO

A LARGE COMMUNAL BATHROOM

in a fancy hotel. A couple of tubs, some sinks, thick towels.

MAVERICK lies happily in one of the tubs. Eyes closed. His clothes are piled nearby. His gun too. Beside it: the satchel.

He is at peace, listening to the sound of the wind music —

Now another sound cuts through —

— kuh — <u>lick</u> —

As MAVERICK whirls —

CUT TO

COOP, standing there, with the drop on MAVERICK. He isn't smiling.

> **COOP**
>
> *Decrepit has-been?*

CUT TO

MAVERICK. Not a sound.

CUT TO

COOP, closing in. Louder.

> **COOP**
>
> *Couldn't sneak up on a corpse?*

> **MAVERICK**
> *(beat)*
>
> Actually, I kind of liked that one.

CUT TO

MAVERICK, watching as COOP holsters his gun.

> **COOP**
>
> Lucky for you I have a forgiving nature. *(Now he starts taking off his coat. Sincerely)* What is as deeply moving a religious experience as cheating a cheater?

> **MAVERICK**
>
> I take it the Commodore will not be a problem.

> **COOP**
>
> Not if I'm any judge of sleezy human behavior.

> **MAVERICK**
>
> Pappy?

> **COOP**
>
> Hmm?

MAVERICK

We ever been rich before? At the same time?

COOP
(thinks, then shakes his head)
I'm sure I would have remembered.
(And on that —)

CUT TO

A DECK OF CARDS.

It is being manipulated dazzlingly with one hand — exactly as MAVERICK *did before in the stagecoach.*

PULL BACK TO REVEAL

We are in exactly the same spot as before only now it is COOP *that is manipulating the cards.*

BOTH MEN lie relaxed, eyes closed, in tubs. There is a sense of peace and harmony until —

— that sound again —

— kuh — lick —

— and as BOTH MEN open their eyes —

CUT TO

ANNABELLE, holding her gun, aiming at them, grabbing up MAVERICK's and COOP's guns. Then the satchel —

— now, as she takes their clothes too —

ANNABELLE

You're a remarkable family.

MAVERICK
(to COOP)
How'd she figure that?

ANNABELLE

Give me *some* credit — you don't own the exclusive on tells — *(rattling it off as* MAVERICK *had done with her)* — you're both the same height, you've got the same build, you've got the same eyes, you both kiss the same way, you both draw your guns the same way — *(a breath)* — and you both sing the same wrong words to "Amazing Grace." *(Now, she studies their naked bodies in the tubs)*

CUT TO

ANNABELLE. CLOSE UP.

ANNABELLE
Oh my yes, there are just a lot of splendid similarities... *(She smiles her dazzling smile, goes to the door, opens it, blows a kiss — impossible to say to which man — and good-bye)*

MAVERICK *and* PAPPY. *They stare at the door a moment. Neither of them seems anxious to get moving or particularly upset.*

PAPPY
Woman with her looks can't hide.

MAVERICK
(nods)
Whenever we decide to catch her — *(snaps his fingers)* — it's done.

PAPPY
(nods too)
The truth? If someone had to rob us, I'm glad it was my little Annie. *(He's never called her that before)*

CUT TO

MAVERICK, *as this registers.*

MAVERICK
Your little *what? (beat)* I'll tell you the *real* truth — every time you got near her, it was... *(squints)* ... I'm looking for the right word — you are, after all, the man who raised me and I hold you in the highest respect... *(beat)* ... It was dis*gus*ting.

CUT TO

PAPPY, *as this registers.*

PAPPY
(chuckles)
My my, green with envy.

CUT TO

THE TWO OF THEM. *Some heat now.*

MAVERICK
You're right. *(beat)* After all, when she's a hundred, you'll only be a hundred and thirty-five.

PAPPY
I would be careful if I were you — just know that splendid creature was almost your stepmother.

> MAVERICK

She was a lot closer to being your daughter-in-law.

> PAPPY

Would have been sheer disaster — you're totally lacking in the maturity needed to satisfy a woman like that.

> MAVERICK

Not what she said.

> PAPPY

I know what she said about *you* — and I would never humiliate you by repeating those terrible words.

> MAVERICK

I don't believe you.

> PAPPY

Neither do I.

Now they both start to laugh, lie back. A pause.

> PAPPY

Bret? Remember that time you cut the ace of spades?

> MAVERICK

When she was dying? Yessir.

> PAPPY

This was even more amazing.

> MAVERICK
> (beat)

She was in my mind the whole way.

> PAPPY
> (nods)

Comes as no surprise.

CAMERA BEGINS TO PULL BACK.

And now MAVERICK begins to hum "Amazing Grace."

PAPPY joins him, doing the harmony.

CAMERA CONTINUES PULLING BACK

MAVERICK starts to sing the song.

PAPPY joins him, doing the harmony.

It's just lovely.

CAMERA PULLS BACK AND BACK.

THE TWO OF THEM sing on. Their voices ring out loud and clear.

They've never sounded better.

Let's leave them there . . .

FINAL FADE OUT.